Constitutional Transition and the Travail of Judges

AF621588

This book looks at the history of the courts in South Korea from 1945 to the contemporary period. It sets forth the evolution of the judicial process and jurisprudence in the context of the nation's political and constitutional transitions. The focus is on constitutional authoritarianism in the 1970s under President Park Chung Hee, when judges faced a positivist crisis as their capacity to protect individual rights and restrain the government was impaired by the language of the new Constitution. Caught between the contending duties of implementing the law and pursuing justice, the judges adhered to formal legal rationality and preserved the fundamental constitutional order, which eventually proved essential in the nation's democratization in the late 1980s. Addressing both democratic and authoritarian rule of law, this volume prompts fresh debate on judicial restraint and engagement in comparative perspectives.

MARIE SEONG-HAK KIM is a legal historian and attorney at law. She specializes in Korean, Japanese, and French law. She is the author of *Michel de L'Hôpital* (1997) and *Law and Custom in Korea* (2012) and is the editor of *The Spirit of Korean Law* (2016). She is the recipient of the National Endowment of Humanities Fellowship and the Fulbright Senior Scholar Grant. She was a fellow at the Collegium de Lyon, the Netherlands Institute for Advanced Study, and the Freiburg Institute for Advanced Studies. As a native of South Korea, she graduated from Ewha Womans University in Seoul and received her PhD and JD from the University of Minnesota. She is a member of the Minnesota Bar since 1995.

Constitutional Transition and the Travail of Judges

The Courts of South Korea

MARIE SEONG-HAK KIM

CAMBRIDGE
UNIVERSITY PRESS

CAMBRIDGE
UNIVERSITY PRESS

University Printing House, Cambridge CB2 8BS, United Kingdom

One Liberty Plaza, 20th Floor, New York, NY 10006, USA

477 Williamstown Road, Port Melbourne, VIC 3207, Australia

314-321, 3rd Floor, Plot 3, Splendor Forum, Jasola District Centre, New Delhi - 110025, India

79 Anson Road, #06-04/06, Singapore 079906

Cambridge University Press is part of the University of Cambridge.

It furthers the University's mission by disseminating knowledge in the pursuit of education, learning and research at the highest international levels of excellence.

www.cambridge.org
Information on this title: www.cambridge.org/9781108465571
DOI: 10.1017/9781108633543

© Marie Seong-Hak Kim 2019

This publication is in copyright. Subject to statutory exception and to the provisions of relevant collective licensing agreements, no reproduction of any part may take place without the written permission of Cambridge University Press.

First published 2019
First paperback edition 2021

A catalogue record for this publication is available from the British Library

Library of Congress Cataloging in Publication data
Names: Kim, Marie Seong-Hak, author.
Title: Constitutional transition and the travail of judges : the courts of South Korea / Marie Seong-Hak Kim, St Cloud State University.
Description: New York, NY : Cambridge University Press, 2019. | Includes index.
Identifiers: LCCN 2018055110 | ISBN 9781108474894
Subjects: LCSH: Courts – Korea (South) – History. | Judges – Korea (South) – History. | Constitutional law – Korea (South) – History.
Classification: LCC KPA1572 .K57 2019 | DDC 347.5195/01–dc23
LC record available at https://lccn.loc.gov/2018055110

ISBN 978-1-108-47489-4 Hardback
ISBN 978-1-108-46557-1 Paperback

Cambridge University Press has no responsibility for the persistence or accuracy of URLs for external or third-party internet websites referred to in this publication, and does not guarantee that any content on such websites is, or will remain, accurate or appropriate.

In memory of my parents

Contents

Figures

Tables

Preface

The writing of this book has taken much longer than I envisioned. Along the way, I came to realize the full extent of the daunting task I had taken on. Attempting to make sense of law and justice in modern Korea has been particularly challenging because much of it covers a period of Korean history I lived *in loco*. I was a high school and then college student in Seoul in the 1970s and spent the early part of the 1980s there before moving to the United States. Watching the unfolding of Korean politics from afar since then, I thought that there was a story to tell about this pivotal era in the contexts of law and the courts and that my perspectives as both an insider and an outsider might be of some use in helping readers understand it better. I was especially interested in the role of judges, as I grew up in the family of a Supreme Court justice. The following pages represent a modest effort on my part to fulfill a historian's duty to be faithful to the facts, in ways that I believe are not very different from a judge's duty to be faithful to the facts and the law. My late parents and my family have shared, in spirit and in person, my long and continuous journey to study different legal traditions of the world. I hope this book brings Christopher, John-Paul, and Joel a deeper understanding of my native country.

The research and writing of the book have been supported by fellowships from the Netherlands Institute for Advanced Study (NIAS) (2013–2014) and from the Freiburg Institute for Advanced Studies (FRIAS) where I was a Marie Curie Fellow of the European Institutes for Advanced Study (EURIAS) (2016–2017). To these and other institutions, and above all the many individuals who graciously offered me inspiration and encouragement, I remain deeply grateful.

1 *Introduction*

This book is a history of the courts in South Korea from 1945 to the contemporary period. It sets forth the evolution of the judicial process and jurisprudence in the context of the nation's constitutional changes and political vicissitudes. Modern Korean history has never had a dull moment. The nation's division following independence from Japanese colonial rule (1910–1945) erupted into the Korean War (1950–1953), and the confrontation between North and South Korea continues to this day, keeping the peninsula on a seemingly perpetual high alert. South Korea's rapid transformation from a war-torn former colony to a global economic powerhouse and, above all, its peaceful evolution from authoritarian rule in the 1970s and early 1980s to a vibrant democracy have brought much adulation from the outside world, as well as confidence and pride for Korean people. Behind all this attention, however, lies a source of profound national self-rumination. As the country evolves into a mature democracy, the challenge of evaluating its not-so-distant, less-than-liberal past has posed serious questions for scholars and the general public alike, often giving rise to deeply divided and ideologically tinged debate. Central to this discussion is the role of the courts in the nation's political transitions.

Since democratization in 1987, the Supreme Court of Korea (Taebŏpwŏn), the highest court from the birth of the Korean republic in 1948, and the ordinary courts it headed have been subject to criticism for their supposedly dismal record in protecting citizens' rights during the authoritarian years. The backlash against the judiciary is in line with the recent trend in historiography to draw a sharp line between the pre- and postdemocratization eras, contrasting the republic's early years under conservative rule with the subsequent years under more progressive rule. This demarcation has yielded a lopsided view of the judicial past, paying scant attention to the courts of the pre-1987 period while highlighting their post-1987 activities.

Historical writings on the judiciary seem reflective of a chasm running deep in Korean politics and society, something that the remarkable achievement of democratization has not blotted out; rather, the advent of liberal democracy may have exacerbated the problems by bringing them to light. The cold-war crisis in the postwar years not only resulted in the north–south divide but also created profound fissures among South Koreans. There exist two contending narratives of modern history, largely predicated on the appraisal of the governments that ruled Korea in its first several decades. Since the beginning of the republic, successive regimes devoted major efforts to fending off threats from the communist North and suppressed or sidelined political opposition that they perceived as a threat to national security. One current of historical discourses sees these early years of the republic as a period of existential struggle, which entailed certain coercive political practices that were dictated by the exigency of the nation's survival. The opposing narrative contends, in contrast, that provocation from North Korea was exaggerated by the regimes to maintain their grip on power. While the first view highlights economic developments in the 1960s continuing into the 1970s and the 1980s, the second view points out that South Korea's industrialization during this period was accompanied by tremendous suffering and sacrifices by workers.

This discursive divide, with acute sociopolitical underpinnings, can also be seen as a generational rift. The older generation expresses frustration at the younger folk's seeming indifference to the struggles it had undergone to ensure the nascent republic's survival and to pave the way for prosperity. In turn, the younger generation shows less tolerance for illiberal rule and beholds the democratization in 1987 as the renewal of the true ideals of the republic that allegedly had long been compromised and distorted by cold-war politics. These competing viewpoints have proved difficult to reconcile, as they sharply split public opinion and shaped rigid political contours of historiography. The history of the judiciary in its first forty years has mostly been written from the second perspective. General consensus among scholars and observers is that the governments before democratization effectively curbed the authority and power of the judiciary, which became a powerless bystander or, worse, a silent abettor of the repressive regimes.

The Supreme Court's record indeed appears a far cry from the remarkable stride made by the Constitutional Court of Korea (Hŏnpŏp Chaep'anso). The Constitutional Court, which opened its doors in 1988, is arguably the most successful and pivotal institution in modern Korea. Free from baggage of the past, the constitutional tribunal has served as the symbol of a break in Korea's judicial as well as political past. The juxtaposition of the new and the old courts then raises a question why the ordinary courts were unable to exercise judicial muscles to protect individual rights as vigorously and effectively as their new constitutional counterpart. The Supreme Court has received little attention in recent scholarship. The disparity between the fecund and ever-increasing amount of literature on the Constitutional Court and the paucity of serious works on the Supreme Court attests to the general scholarly disenchantment with the latter. Scholars have so far tended to focus on the political ramifications of judicial activities, without adequate attention to their legal meanings. They often shied away from studying the courts under authoritarian rule in depth, apparently on the assumption that such an effort would amount to legitimizing the illiberal governments. But glossing over the period as a sort of lost era and writing off the courts as inevitable occurrences of autocratic rule contribute little to the understanding of the nation's modern history. This book undertakes an empirical study of the role of the ordinary courts in South Korea (hereinafter referred to simply as Korea) under particular legal orders with emphasis on judicial decision-making, considered in the broader theoretical contexts of the rule of law and judicial independence.

A brief outline of Korea's constitutional evolution is in order. The country's record of constitutional revision has often been contrasted with Japan's. Both countries adopted a liberal constitution after World War II under US aegis. While the Japanese Constitution, promulgated in 1946, has never been amended, the Korean Constitution of 1948, the first constitution following independence, has undergone as many as nine revisions.[1] The founding Constitution of the republic created an independent and professional judiciary under the solid principle of the separation of powers. The strong executive power under President Rhee Syngman (Yi Sŭng-Man) (1875–1965) during the First Republic (1948–1960) often dwarfed the judiciary, and the government undertook constitutional revisions in 1952 and 1954 to push through its political agenda, but the courts largely

[1] The Constitution of the Republic of Korea [Taehanminguk Hŏnpŏp] (July 17, 1948). The transliteration of Korean characters follows the McCune–Reischauer system.

maintained their autonomy.[2] The Rhee regime came to an abrupt end in April 1960 after democratic protests forced the president to step down. The Second Republic (1960–1962) adopted a parliamentary government system and envisioned progressive reforms such as the election of judges.[3] Within a year, however, the government was toppled in May 1961 by a military coup waged by General Park Chung Hee (Pak Chŏng-Hi) (1917–1979). A new constitution was issued in December 1962, marking the beginning of the Third Republic (1962–1972), and Park took office as president in October 1963.[4] Under this democratic Constitution, the Supreme Court exercised unencumbered judicial review power.

The political climate quickly changed in 1969 when President Park led the constitutional amendment to allow him a third presidential term.[5] In 1972, Park spearheaded the promulgation of a new constitution, ushering in the Fourth Republic (1972–1980).[6] This document, commonly known as the Yusin (revitalization) Constitution, concentrated power in the president's hands. Political opposition was suppressed by laws backed by the constitutional provisions that explicitly limited civil liberty and human rights. After seven years of heavy-handed rule, Park was assassinated in October 1979. The ensuing military coups brought General Chun Doo Hwan (Chŏn Tu-Hwan) to power, and the Fifth Republic (1980–1987) began.[7] Authoritarian rule continued until 1987, when it gave way to popular demands for democracy. The new liberal democratic Constitution that was promulgated in October of that year remains in force today.[8] The Sixth Republic has witnessed peaceful changes of power since (one president was removed by impeachment in 2017).

These checkered political trajectories, with all-too-frequent constitutional revisions in tow, have had serious repercussions on the judiciary. Of particular poignancy was the 1972 Constitution, under which provisions guaranteeing fundamental rights stood side by side with provisions stipulating the limitation of the same rights. The Constitution allowed for broad emergency powers, and President Park ruled with a series of

[2] Constitution (July 7, 1952); Constitution (November 29, 1954).
[3] Constitution (June 15, 1960); Constitution (November 29, 1960).
[4] Constitution (December 26, 1962).
[5] Constitution (October 21, 1969).
[6] Constitution (December 27, 1972).
[7] Constitution (October 27, 1980).
[8] Constitution (October 29, 1987).

draconian emergency decrees (*kingŭp choch'i*) that were placed outside judicial review power.[9] In comparison, the Constitution of 1980 was overall a democratic document, other than the method of electing the president by an electoral body, a holdover from the previous era. The legal orders during the Fourth and the Fifth Republics were thus qualitatively dissimilar, although authoritarian politics continued. The clashing narratives of modern Korean history center on the Fourth Republic. The following chapters focus mainly on the 1972 Constitution and the thorny problems it posed to the courts.

The State of Questions

The Yusin Constitution ushered in constitutional authoritarianism, in which government abuses were committed with constitutional authority. The problem with authoritarian legalism is obvious: an independent judiciary is a condition necessary for the operation of the rule of law, but a judiciary bound by an illiberal constitution and laws can impede the very ideal of the rule of law, which could effectively pit judges against justice. The courts and judges in authoritarian regimes have of late become a subject of increasing attention.[10] This development coincides with the recent tendency among legal theorists to take a more critical look at the coherency of the notion of the rule of law.[11] Traditional scholarship has equated the rule of law with political liberalism in a democratic regime, different from rule by law under which law is used by the government only to legitimize its illiberal policies. But studies have shown that the rule of law exists in

[9] Constitution (1972), Art. 53(4). For the Park presidency, see Byung-Kook Kim and Ezra F. Vogel (eds.), *The Park Chung Hee Era: The Transformation of South Korea* (Cambridge, MA: Harvard University Press, 2011); Hyung-A Kim and Clark W. Sorensen (eds.), *Reassessing the Park Chung Hee Era, 1961–1979: Development, Political Thought, Democracy, and Cultural Influence* (Seattle: The Center for Korean Studies, University of Washington Press, 2011).

[10] See, among others, Hans Petter Graver, *Judges against Justice: On Judges When the Rule of Law Is under Attack* (Heidelberg: Springer-Verlag, 2015).

[11] Joseph Raz, "The Rule of Law and Its Virtue," *The Authority of Law: Essays on Law and Morality*, 2nd ed. (Oxford: Oxford University Press, 2009, 1979), 210–229; Martin Loughlin, *Sword and Scales: An Examination of the Relationship between Law and Politics* (Oxford: Hart Publishing, 2000).

authoritarianism.[12] In an authoritarian rule of law, the regime in power resorts to an instrumental use of laws as it tries to engender a stable legal and economic environment. This insight is important because it provides a new frame of reference from which one can examine the role of courts and judges in relation to political power.

There is scholarly agreement that rational institutions of law facilitate and sustain economic growth. Max Weber wrote that formal rationality, with the presence of general and transparent laws, leads to a fair and predictable administration of justice.[13] According to Douglass C. North, protection of property rights and consistency in contract enforcement are critical for economic progress.[14] Authoritarian regimes thus have reason to adhere to legal procedures and comply with judicial decisions. They profess commitment to legality and allow judicial autonomy.[15] Yusin Korea was a paradigmatic example of this authoritarian rule of law, under which dictatorial and liberal elements were fused in law and the constitution. Court judgments, once rendered, were not resisted by the government.

When illiberal regimes observe strict legal procedures, however, judicial quandary can compound. If the basic rights of citizens are

[12] Jens Meierhenrich, *The Remnants of the Rechtsstaat: An Ethnography of Nazi Law* (Oxford: Oxford University Press, 2018); Tom Ginsburg and Tamir Moustafa (eds.), *Rule by Law: The Politics of Courts in Authoritarian Regimes* (Cambridge: Cambridge University Press, 2008); Jothie Rajah, *Authoritarian Rule of Law: Legislation, Discourse and Legitimacy in Singapore* (Cambridge: Cambridge University Press, 2012). The notion of "*Rechtsstaat*" in the civil law tradition has a narrower scope than the notion of "rule of law" in the common law tradition: the *Rechtsstaat* equates to the formal or procedural conception of the rule of law.

[13] Max Weber, "Sociological Categories of Economic Action," in Guenther Roth and Claus Wittich (eds.), *Max Weber, Economy and Society: An Outline of Interpretive Sociology*, vol. 1 (Berkeley: University of California Press, 1978), 85–86. A formal approach to justice exists "where the legally relevant characteristics of the facts are disclosed through the logical analysis of meaning and where, accordingly, definitely fixed legal concepts in the form of highly abstract rules are formulated and applied." Weber, "Economy and Law (The Sociology of Law)," ibid., vol. 2, 657.

[14] Douglass C. North, *Structure and Change in Economic History* (New York: Norton, 1981); Douglass C. North, *Institutions, Institutional Change, and Economic Performance* (Cambridge: Cambridge University Press, 1990); Douglass C. North and Barry R. Weingast, "Constitutions and Commitment: The Evolution of Institutions Governing Public Choice in Seventeenth-Century England," *Journal of Economic History* 49 (1989), 803–832.

[15] Empowering the judiciary and boosting trust and confidence in the justice system are important for regimes to make up for their questionable legitimacy, or "legitimacy deficit." Ginsburg and Moustafa, "Introduction," in *Rule by Law*, 6.

endangered under a constitution and statutes, should judges refuse to implement them? Here arises a dilemma of unjust laws, an enduring question in legal philosophy. Judges face a dilemma when they are obligated to enforce a law they believe is wrong or repressive. Since judicial duty is to implement the law, rather than to create or modify it, they cannot refuse to apply the unjust law on the grounds of their disagreement. Yet, when they act in accordance with the judicial oath, they compromise their conscience, and injustice may result. Law – officially promulgated rules backed by the state authority – and justice – the principle of rendering to each person what he or she deserves – should ideally be one and the same thing, but in reality they can come into serious contention.

The complexity of judicial choice has long captivated legal theorists and philosophers. Historical examples abound. The intellectual anguish of judges in the antebellum United States, torn between judicial duty and personal conscience over slavery, was perceptively discussed by Robert Cover.[16] According to Cover, most abolitionist judges in the North enforced the notorious Fugitive Slave Act of 1850, not because they agreed with it but because they decided they had an obligation to uphold the existing law. In the twentieth century, a similar issue dramatically emerged when judicial complicity with oppressive power in Nazi Germany and occupied Europe during World War II gave rise to debates over the clash between legal positivism and natural law theories.[17] Legal positivism distinguishes the validity of a legal order from the consideration of morality, whereas natural law theory posits that a law which violates basic demands of morality and justice cannot be qualified as a genuine law. The conflict between the two tenets also reverberated in apartheid South Africa, where the formalistic and positivistic approach embraced by lawyers and judges was blamed for the repressive legal system.[18] In Korea, the government ruled with the supra-constitutional executive decrees and legislative enactments

16 Robert M. Cover, *Justice Accused: Antislavery and the Judicial Process* (New Haven: Yale University Press, 1975).

17 See the classic Hart–Fuller debate: H. L. A. Hart, "Positivism and the Separation of Law and Morals," *Harvard Law Review* 71 (1958), 593–629; Lon L. Fuller, "Positivism and Fidelity to Law – A Reply to Professor Hart," *Harvard Law Review* 71 (1958), 630–672.

18 David Dyzenhaus, *Hard Cases in Wicked Legal Systems: South African Law in the Perspective of Legal Philosophy*, 2nd ed. (Oxford: Oxford University Press, 2010).

railroaded by the ruling party in the National Assembly, and judges encountered a classic moral-legal dilemma.

Here it must be stressed that the Korean legal system, fraught as it was with political persecution and human rights violations, did not, by any stretch, amount to an immoral legal order mired in genocide, slavery, or racial discrimination. Nor did it demonstrate the kind of impunity of a military dictatorship in Latin America waging a so-called dirty war during which a massive number of people disappeared. The scope of state violence was grave but still limited in comparison with contemporary authoritarian countries elsewhere.[19] To point out the relatively low number of convictions and punishments on political charges in Korea is not to play down the egregious reality of illiberal rule. Under the emergency decrees, people were sent to jail for absurd charges that infringed upon their fundamental rights such as freedom of speech. One unjust imprisonment is one too many. Rampant police brutality and human rights violations were well recorded. The images of bleak military courtrooms in which civilians were declared guilty of the crime of criticizing the government forever haunt the national memory. While citizens' rights suffered, however, Korea was not a lawless wilderness.

The regime insisted on holding judicial trials, by military or civilian courts, even when political repression was at its peak. This is precisely what rendered the role of the law and courts all the more important. How many of these trials deserved to be cast aside as show trials and judicial travesty would hinge on the extent of the process we recognize as procedurally due and substantively just. It points to a question when a law can be called a law. This kind of inquiry would be necessary before one attempts sweeping assessment of the judiciary.[20]

[19] Despite Korean military dictatorships' reputation for repressiveness, executions or killings for antiregime activity between 1972 and 1987 were much fewer than those in Taiwan or the Philippines. Sheena Chestnut Greitens, *Dictators and Their Secret Police: Coercive Institutions and State Violence* (Cambridge: Cambridge University Press, 2016), 238–239.

[20] Examples of blanket, often less than accurate, portrayals: "there has not been one full acquittal in a political case since the Yushin Constitution came into effect in 1972," Adrian W. Dewind and John Woodhouse, *Persecution of Defence Lawyers in South Korea: Report of a Mission to South Korea in May 1979* (New Work: International Commission of Jurists, 1979), 36; "Torture, forced disappearances, extra-judicial killings and mass executions occurred with disturbing regularity in Korea from the end of World War II until the election of Kim Young-Sam in 1993," Paul Hanley, "Transitional Justice in

Korea featured a historically depoliticized professional judiciary. The main strength of the traditional East Asian legal order lay in the uniformity and comprehensiveness of law.[21] The deeply seated principle of deference to political authority during Korea's monarchical period was reinforced under colonial rule.[22] After independence, the dominant notion of legislative sovereignty – the general will of the Korean people – fostered judicial restraint. The partition and the ensuing standoff between North and South Korea further resulted in the judicial stance to heed broadly the doctrine of political question. Political leaders regularly tinkered with the constitution and manipulated laws, but judges did not view it as their essential task to impose judicial imprimatur on them. The beliefs that the making or amending of the constitution was a political act better not meddled with by the courts and that judicial duty was to apply the existing laws to particular cases, not making or correcting them, had been deeply entrenched, continuing into the late twentieth century.

Cover's insight – that the dilemma of the judge, caught between formal responsibility and a personal sense of justice, cannot be simply dismissed as a deficiency in moralism – has universal resonance. Whether in the nineteenth-century United States or twentieth-century Korea, the structural limitations of the constitution, the weight of judicial tradition steeped in formalism, and the narrow view of judicial duty together affected the ways in which judges decided the cases that came before them.[23] This of course does not mean judges are always sheltered behind the constitutional provisions. But their adherence to law can be as critical as their commitment to substantive justice and fundamental standards of morality. At issue in authoritarian legality is not so much the will of the judges as the institutional and

South Korea: One Country's Restless Search for Truth and Reconciliation," *University of Pennsylvania East Asia Law Review* 9 (2014), 140.

21 William R. Shaw, *Legal Norms in a Confucian State* (Berkeley: Institute of East Asian Studies, University of California Berkeley, Center for Korean Studies, 1981).

22 Marie Seong-Hak Kim, *Law and Custom in Korea: Comparative Legal History* (Cambridge: Cambridge University Press, 2012).

23 A judicial dilemma is not an alien notion in Korea. In 1952, a judge professed in a series of essays the profound predicaments he faced in performing judicial duties. Yu Pyŏng-Chin, *Chaep'angwan ŭi komin: Yu Pyŏng-Chin pŏmnyul nonjip* [The Dilemmas of a Judge: A Collection of the Legal Writings of Yu Pyŏng-Chin], ed. Sin Tong-Un (Seoul: Pŏmmunsa, 2008). For Judge Yu, see Chapter 2, note 92.

constitutional frameworks in which they perform their duties. Scholars have pointed out that judicial disinclination to oppose emergency powers in many jurisdictions in the world evinced less the judges' desertion of duties than their disposition to exercise independent judgment in compliance with their professional ideals that required competent practice.[24] The Korean experience reminds one that the authority of the judiciary has little to do with the democratic or undemocratic nature of governmental institutions. In Korea, the gap between constitutional normalcy and emergency lay outside the realm of judicial resolution.

Some comparisons with other countries may be of help. Singapore has received much attention from scholars for its remarkable economic success and government efficiency. Recently, its political and economic trajectories have been portrayed as a hallmark of authoritarian legalism and an embodiment of Ernst Fraenkel's "dual state" thesis. Fraenkel (1898–1975), a German jurist who fled the Nazis to the United States, argued that two different kinds of states, the prerogative state and the normative state, stood side by side during the years 1933–1938.[25] While the governmental system (the prerogative state) exercised arbitrariness and violence in public law matters, the legal order in private law matters (the normative state) was safeguarded in statutes, court decisions, and administrative agency actions, with the basic principles of capitalism, such as private property and contracts, protected by the judiciary. Fraenkel's dual state has been regarded as the archetype of the modern authoritarian rule of law, and Singapore has been seen in light of the similar coexistence of the parallel and contending legal orders.[26] The government in Singapore has promoted

24 Mark J. Osiel, "Dialogue with Dictators: Judicial Resistance in Argentina and Brazil," *Law and Social Inquiry* 20 (1995), 482. For judicial roles in various constitutional contexts, see Tom Ginsburg and Alberto Simpser (eds.), *Constitutions in Authoritarian Regimes* (Cambridge: Cambridge University Press, 2014); Diana Kapiszewski, Gordon Silverstein, and Robert A. Kagan (eds.), *Consequential Courts: Judicial Roles in Global Perspective* (Cambridge: Cambridge University Press, 2013).

25 Ernst Fraenkel, *The Dual State: A Contribution to the Theory of Dictatorship*, trans. E. A. Shils, Edith Loewenstein, and Klaus Knorr (Oxford: Oxford University Press, 2017, 1941).

26 Kanishka Jayasuriya, "The Exception Becomes the Norm: Law and Regimes of Exception in East Asia," *Asian-Pacific Law & Policy Journal* 2 (2001), 119–123; Rajah, *Authoritarian Rule of Law*, 42–43. The authoritarian government in Singapore attained its political interest by following the rules

economic development by guaranteeing a free and stable business environment while simultaneously maintaining various legal measures limiting civil and political rights. The city-state remains today a polity governed by a single party, the People's Action Party, which has been in power since 1959. Its case seems to show that an authoritarian government can, through careful operation of law, construct and manage a system sufficiently rational to allow economic liberty without allowing political liberty to its fullest sense.

Korea in the 1970s exhibited the basic elements of dual-state legality as well: emergency laws and other constraints in public law matters coexisted with free, constitutionally guaranteed economic activities in private law matters. The courts' ability to perform the equitable and effective administration of justice in civil law was rarely obstructed, even at the height of the state of emergency. Unlike in Singapore, however, in Korea the bifurcated state was not in for the long haul. The regimes could put a limit on political liberties through systematic deployment of legal measures only for a while; they were ultimately unable to prevent legal rationality in the economic sphere from impacting political and civil liberties.

The Korean situation evokes the political thought of another German theorist. It epitomized how Carl Schmitt's (1888–1985) conceptual framework of the state of exception was marshaled into cold-war politics through the high stakes of national security.[27] Since the nation's division after World War II, Korea remains the only country in the world still mired in the cold-war conflict. After the Korean War, the primacy of defending the country from communism loomed over practically every aspect of the national life. It has been argued that the exigencies of national security set Korean conservatism apart from modern Western conservatism, in the sense that the former was above all permeated with the need to ensure domestic political stability to repulse threats from communist agitators from within.[28]

"written in the constitution and enforced in the courts," all without jeopardizing international investors' confidence in the system. Gordon Silverstein, "Singapore: The Exception that Proves Rules Matter," in Ginsburg and Moustafa (eds.), *Rule by Law*, 78.

27 For Carl Schmitt, see Chapter 4.

28 Kang Chŏng-In, *Hanguk hyŏndae chŏngch'i sasang kwa Park Chung Hee* [Contemporary Korean Political Thought and Park Chung Hee] (Seoul: Ak'anet, 2014), 238.

Also, it called for active government intervention in economic policy. For most of Korea's modern history, national security, economic development, and the state's strong directive presence under the classic *dirigisme* were indissolubly tied together. Throughout the 1960s and 1970s, the government repeatedly – and not unreasonably – asserted that all-out effort for industrialization and economic growth would be the most powerful defense against the communist regime in the North. President Park assiduously stressed that the building of a self-reliant economy was a precondition for reunification and democracy.[29] The nation's survival and economic self-sufficiency were leitmotifs throughout his presidency. Under the 1972 Constitution, threats – and perceived threats – to the state's security and sociopolitical and economic orders were conjured to rationalize the government's call for a vast scope of emergency powers.

The need for national security initially caused and legitimized the separation of the normative and prerogative states, but it eventually undermined the line dividing the two. Once South Korea had achieved economic prosperity, leaving North Korea lagging far behind, it became more difficult for the government to continue on its existing track of illiberal policies.[30] Unable to admit that its entire national security program had been a politically motivated stratagem, the regime in the 1980s was compelled to loosen its grip on political control in the face of popular resistance. A defining feature of the authoritarian rule of law is its preference for efficiency to liberty.[31] The Korean case fully corroborated it. Yet, the symbiosis of national defense and the all-out pursuit of economic development in Korea outlined its own distinct institutional design of the dual state. Fraenkel declared in 1941, with remarkable prescience: "The Dual State is the necessary political outgrowth of a transitional period wrought with tension."[32] Korea's authoritarian rule and the judiciary's role in it can be analyzed in a similar evolving framework.

29 Ibid., 243–246, 293–296.

30 A standard modernization theory posits that democracy is more likely in developed countries. Barbara Geddes, "What Do We Know about Democratization after Twenty Years?" *Annual Review of Political Science* 2 (1999), 115–144.

31 "[T]he 'gospel of efficiency' has been substituted for the worship of liberty." Fraenkel, *The Dual State*, 71.

32 Ibid., 208.

Constitutional Authoritarianism

Authoritarian regimes, by definition, would allow a degree of judicial independence only so far as they have little to fear from courts, and the endurance of the courts may thus be seen as evidence of judicial complicity.[33] Yet, governments enhance judicial power in anticipation of the advantages of self-restraint.[34] It is for this reason important for the courts to maintain rational legal frameworks by safeguarding the minimum due process of law and to hold the government to its avowed commitment to constitutionalism. Where the role of the court as the constitutional remedy to political overreach is constitutionally precluded, the remaining option would be to induce the regime to restrain itself in wielding power, with its agents bound by the formal laws it set out. The position of Korean courts can be seen in this light. The main concern of the Supreme Court was to avoid politicizing the judicial process. The judiciary struggled to preserve the rudimentary framework of legality and the *Rechtsstaat*, no matter how diminished and truncated at the time, and it ultimately proved essential to ushering in liberal democracy and the substantive rule of law in the late 1980s.

It has been argued that South Africa overcame apartheid by drawing on its normative and legalistic order which had stood side by side with the prerogative order.[35] Similarly in Korea, democratization took place without serious rupture because the normative order had been preserved from the aggression by the prerogative state. Upholding formal rules and procedure, the courts helped overcome the partitioned legal state and resolve the dichotomy in legality. The fact that decline in public trust in the judiciary in the repressive political realm had coexisted with society's continuing deference to competent judicial practice and adjudicative fairness was critical.

The Korean case thus suggests an alternative model for developmental states for the transition from a formal rule of law to a substantive

33 Gretche Helmke and Frances Rosenbluth, "Regimes and the Rule of Law: Judicial Independence in Comparative Perspective," *Annual Review of Political Science* 12 (2009), 358.

34 Stephen Holmes, "Lineages of the Rule of Law," in José María Maravall and Adam Przeworski (eds.), *Democracy and the Rule of Law* (Cambridge: Cambridge University Press, 2006), 24–25.

35 Jens Meierhenrich, *The Legacies of Law: Long-Run Consequences of Legal Development in South Africa, 1650–2000* (Cambridge: Cambridge University Press, 2008).

rule of law. In the short term, however, there is no denying that the courts implemented thoroughly politicized laws and were unable to meet the expectation of the citizens that they serve as a bulwark against the repressive regime. After democratization, the strong tides of transitional justice surged, and a number of judicial and nonjudicial measures were undertaken with the goal of confronting and rectifying the past of political repression and persecution. The legality of the laws under authoritarian regimes was subjected to scrutiny, and many judicial decisions that had applied those laws were reopened and the judgments overturned. Starting from 2010, both the Supreme Court and the Constitutional Court ruled that the emergency measures issued by President Park were unconstitutional.[36] These decisions seemed to reflect distinct developments of constitutionalism taking place in the global realm. The growing attention to human rights in recent years has led to a tendency to resort to the notions of natural law, and the resulting shift toward judicial activism has given rise to the problem of an unconstitutional constitution.[37] The key question is whether courts, institutions created by a constitution, can declare constitutional

[36] Supreme Court [S. Ct.], 2010To5986 (*en banc*), December 16, 2010 (finding Emergency Decree No. 1 unconstitutional); S. Ct., 2011Ch'ogi689, April 18, 2013 (finding Emergency Decree No. 9 unconstitutional); S. Ct., 2013To2631, May 16, 2013 (finding Emergency Decree No. 4 unconstitutional). Separately, Constitutional Court [Const. Ct.], 2010HŏnPa70, 132 & 170 (consol.), March 21, 2013 (declaring Emergency Decrees Nos. 1, 2, and 9 unconstitutional). For an analysis of these decisions, see Marie Seong-Hak Kim, "Travails of Judges: Courts and Constitutional Authoritarianism in South Korea," *American Journal of Comparative Law* 63 (2015): 601–654; Marie Seong-Hak Kim, "Constitutional Jurisprudence and the Rule of Law: Revisiting the Courts in Yusin Korea (1972–1980)," *The Hague Journal on the Rule of Law* 5 (2013), 178–203. In this book, all Supreme Court cases are cited to the official texts provided by the Supreme Court of Korea in Taehanminguk Pŏpwŏn Chonghap Pŏmnyul Chŏngbo [The Republic of Korea Courts General Law Report], at http://glaw.scourt.go.kr; all Constitutional Court cases are cited to the official texts provided by the Constitutional Court of Korea in Hŏnpŏp Chaep'anso Chŏngbo [Constitutional Court Law Report], at http://search.ccourt.go.kr. The Romanization of Korean characters in the case numbers follows the McCune-Reischauer system.

[37] See Yaniv Roznai, *Unconstitutional Constitutional Amendments: The Limits of Amendment Powers* (Oxford: Oxford University Press, 2017); Yaniv Roznai, "Unconstitutional Constitutional Amendments: The Migration and Success of a Constitutional Idea," *American Journal of Comparative Law* 61 (2013), 657–719.

amendments void on the grounds that they violate the superior norms of that constitution. By conducting judicial review of the emergency decrees, overriding the provision in the 1972 Constitution that prohibited judicial review, the highest courts in the 2010s effectively stated that judges in the 1970s should have refused to apply a positive law sanctioned by the Constitution because it contravened the basic rights and liberties and contradicted fundamental principles of justice. Those decisions resorted at once to the natural law theory and the new direction of judicial conscience at the turn of the twenty-first century. Yet the idea of a more politically attuned judiciary has deepened, rather than alleviated, skepticism about the independence of the judiciary.

The subtlety of these multifaceted considerations has been obscured amid the scholarly propensity to focus, in a reductionist sort of way, on the theme of the dichotomy of judicial resistance and acquiescence to authoritarian rule and also the tendency to equate judicial passivity with political complicity. At a minimum, the oversimplified view that the courts were inoperative, even irrelevant, before democratization needs revision. The following chapters set forth analysis of jurisprudence against the historical, political, and constitutional backdrops, highlighting major judicial decisions. Attention is paid to the dissenting opinions that the governments tried to withhold from public view and even excised from the official court report; they provide concrete examples of how judges tried to navigate through the conflicting duties of their office in specific political situations.

Chapter 2 surveys Korea's legal traditions and examines the making of the legal system in the new republic between 1945 and 1962. The colonial legal legacy is ascertained. Chapter 3 discusses the dominant jurisprudential stances of the Supreme Court between 1962 and 1972, including an analysis of the famous State Tort Claims Act decision of 1971. The subsequent three chapters focus on the period under the 1972 Constitution, dealing respectively with the laws, the courts, and the judges. Chapter 4 explains the changes in legal structure brought about by the Yusin Constitution and the issuance of emergency decrees. Chapter 5 examines the judicial process under the new constitutional order and revisits the infamous People's Revolutionary Party Reconstruction Committee case of 1975. Chapter 6 discusses the Korean judges' dilemmas of unjust law in the comparative and theoretical contexts.[38] Chapter 7 examines the developments between 1980 and 1987, from the collapse of the Yusin system to the delayed recovery of democracy. The Supreme Court opinions of President Park murder trial in 1980, in particular the dissenting opinions, are analyzed in detail. Chapter 8 discusses the evolution of constitutional jurisprudence after democratization in 1987 by focusing on the decisions of the Supreme Court of 2010 and the Constitutional Court of 2013 concerning the emergency decrees. Chapter 9 provides a conclusion.

The difficulties in studying the courts in the authoritarian years must be articulated at the outset. While antislavery judges in the nineteenth-century United States openly discussed the laws they disagreed with and fretted about their plight of having to apply them, Korean judges did not have such a luxury. Whereas there was enough ambiguity in antebellum statutes to allow judges to decide cases in accordance with their personal convictions if they had so chosen, this was not the case in Korea. More critically, when judges were worried about political reprisal for the decisions they made, justice was bound to suffer. The challenge for a legal historian, then, is to infer jurisprudential and juristic belief from the terse language in judicial opinions which were pervaded with mechanical and seemingly callous positivistic reasoning.

The judicial past during the authoritarian period remains in large part a subject of rebuke and regret rather than reasoned reflection. Hindsight informed by "outcome knowledge" risks obscuring an accurate understanding of the past.[39] Calling for an objective, historical analysis of the role of the courts is different from arguing for the exoneration of illegal

[38] Original court documents relating to major human rights cases in the 1970s, including military court decisions, defense appeals motions, and other important materials, are available in facsimile in Hong Sŏng-U and Han In-Sŏp (eds.), *Inkwŏn pyŏllon charyo chip (1970 nyŏn dae)* [Collection of Sources for Defense of Human Rights (The 1970s)] [hereinafter *Inkwŏn pyŏllon charyo chip*], 6 vols. (Seoul: Kyŏngin Munhwasa, 2012). The materials of key cases spanning from the 1960s through the 1980s and the memoirs of the individuals implicated in them are gathered in Han Sŭng-Hŏn Pyŏnhosa Pyŏllon Sakŏn Sillok Kanhaeng Wiwŏnhoe (ed.), *Han Sŭng-Hŏn pyŏnhosa pyŏllon sakŏn sillok* [The Truthful Record of the Defense Cases of Attorney Han Sŭng-Hŏn], 7 vols. (Seoul: Pŏmusa, 2006).

[39] Citing Horst Dreier in *Staatsrecht in Demokratie und Diktatur: Studien zur Weimarer Republik und zum Nationalsozialismus* (2016), Jens Meierhenrich has warned that reliance on outcome knowledge can distort "the contingency of the historical situation"; he has also highlighted the danger of "limits of perception" (*Schranken der Wahrnehmung*) voiced by Michael Stolleis in his *A History of Public Law in Germany 1914–1945*, trans. Thomas Dunlap

repression in the authoritarian past or attempting a defense for the judicial profession. Postulating judicial dilemmas does not mean explaining away the record of the judiciary. To the contrary, it highlights the need for court decisions to be examined in the concrete texts of the constitutional and legal provisions the judges must give allegiance to. If judges believed they were applying unjust laws without being complicit in injustice, it is necessary to explain how they could think so. Likewise, if judges in the posttransitional years believed they should take an active role and even review the validity of a constitutional provision, it is crucial to examine what that meant for the law, constitutionalism, and justice. While one justly celebrates the remarkable achievements under the new constitutional order, one must also be wary of the temptation to set aside the predemocratization years as an inconvenient past to be excised, because otherwise it may lead to the loss of an important opportunity to learn from history.

This book sets forth a historical account of the courts that were entrusted with the dual duties of implementing the laws and promoting justice at a time of particular challenges of constitutional transition. Scholars point to a growing trend in the world of the judicialization of politics and the politicization of law. When courts are increasingly asked to resolve political matters, revisiting the history of the courts that resisted getting entangled with politics may seem counterintuitive. But the Korean judiciary's uphill battle to safeguard even the semblance of the rule of law and due process deserves a candid exposition, untrammeled by perceptions, presumptions, or preconceptions laden with agenda.

Korean politics today, despite its stable and mature democratic system, continues to exhibit a disjointed and deadlocked polity, beset by the burden of its historical past. An open, evolutionary interpretation of the judiciary, cutting through the country's constitutional and political thickets, can illumine the way Korea addresses the relationship between legality and substantive justice. Regrets of the past, unaccompanied by critical historical reflection, can only go so far; one hopes instead to take a constructive step toward breaking free from the ideological confines that have long hounded Korean society. Through a balanced understanding of the record of the Korean courts, this book aims to explore the role of the courts in comparative law and politics.

(Oxford: Oxford University Press, 2004), 251. See Meierhenrich, *The Remnants of the Rechtsstaat*, 9, 19–21.

2 *The Making of the Constitution and the Courts, 1945–1962*

The promulgation of the Constitution of 1948 was the apotheosis of the general will of the Korean people, free from long foreign rule. It was an embodiment of the popular aspirations for liberal democracy, distilled during the three years of the US military occupation following independence from the Japanese colonial domination. The Japanese Constitution of 1946 had just been promulgated, also under the auspices of the occupation forces, but the two countries' founding documents were reflections of each nation's unique historical and political backgrounds.[1] The drafters of the Korean Constitution were mindful of the need to efface the vestiges of the colonial institutions and at the same time to modify and integrate them into the new republic's governing structure.[2] The choices made at this time in defining the scheme of the separation of powers and the authority of the judiciary remained essentially undisturbed in the republic's history.

One can identify three main elements that influenced the nature and direction of the nascent Korean judiciary: legal tradition, colonial memory, and national security. An important facet of Korea's legal culture was faithful adherence to the law texts. During the Chosŏn dynasty (1392–1910), devotion of the magistrates to the law codes had been deeply entrenched, continuing into the colonial period. Much of postcolonial law and the legal system was simultaneously a conscious

1 The Japanese Constitution was issued on November 3, 1946, to take effect May 3, 1947. See Chaihark Hahm and Sung Ho Kim, *Making We the People: Democratic Constitutional Founding in Postwar Japan and South Korea* (Cambridge: Cambridge University Press, 2016).

2 Major controversies of modern Korean history concern how to explain the relationship between the colonial era and the founding years of the republic. For contending viewpoints, see Song Kŏn-Ho et al., *Haebang chŏnhusa ŭi insik* [Understanding the History before and after Liberation], 6 vols. (Seoul: Hangilsa, 1979–1989); Pak Chi-Hyang et al., *Haebang chŏnhusa ŭi chae insik* [Reconsidering the History before and after Liberation], 2 vols. (Seoul: Ch'aeksesang, 2006).

rejection and retention of the colonial legacy. The fact that the post-colonial courts were in many respects successors to the Japanese courts led to a decision by the constitution-makers to limit the courts' power vis-à-vis the legislature, in particular to do away with judicial power to review the legislation of the National Assembly. The truncated jurisdiction of the ordinary courts in constitutional matters skewed the parity in the relationship between the judiciary and the political branches. Subject in principle to the all-powerful legislature, the judiciary in practice submitted to the executive power. The tradition of deference to the written codes and political authority combined with the recognition of legislative supremacy to create distinct features of the judiciary in the burgeoning republic. The division of the country and the exigency of national security also had indelible effects. South Korea's epic struggle against communism and the acute senses of national crisis dating from the Korean War fostered an expansive conception of the political question doctrine, under which the courts restrained themselves from intervening in the administration's policy decisions.

This chapter surveys the evolution of the courts and the making of the constitutional system in the early republic. It has been suggested that a country's historical preference and commitment in legal beliefs and institutions stand steadfast despite extraneous impingement.[3] Legal historians have adopted the path-dependence theory in explaining, for example, the respective postwar institutional development in Western and Eastern Europe.[4] Similar insights can be applied in the Korean case.

The chapter starts with a brief discussion of the characteristics of law and courts in the dynastic era and proceeds to the foreign occupations and the modern Korean state. One can argue that the adoption of the relatively narrow boundaries and functions of judicial power early on in the Korean republic contributed to and at the same time impeded

[3] "The interaction of beliefs, institutions, and organizations in the total artifactual structure makes path dependence a fundamental factor in the continuity of society." Douglass C. North, *Understanding the Process of Economic Change* (Princeton: Princeton University Press, 2005), 52.

[4] Hans Petter Graver, "Why Adolf Hitler Spared the Judges: Judicial Opposition Against the Nazi State," *German Law Journal* 19 (2018): 845–877; Hans Petter Graver, "Judicial Independence under Authoritarian Rule: An Institutional Approach to the Legal Tradition of the West," *The Hague Journal on the Rule of Law* 10 (2018): 317–339.

judicial independence. The successive governments did not hesitate to exploit the limited power of the courts to their advantage. By recognizing its subordinate status in the hierarchy of powers, however, the judiciary carved out a space that allowed it to maintain distance from political upheavals while preserving a high degree of professionalism. Frequent alterations in the constitutional structure left the courts relatively unscathed although, to be sure, there were incidents of egregious violation of their independence. Judges sought autonomy within the bounds imposed by the law; they viewed their role as applying preexisting legislative norms within the power granted by the constitution. How the courts grappled with, and steered through, the various historical and political pressures and interferences illuminates not only the judiciary's but also the republic's early history.

Judicial Tradition, Old and New

The Korean judiciary bears the load of tradition. It is normal that judges' interpretations and decisions in different countries are influenced by the legal culture in which they belong. One of the dominant aspects of Korean legal thought and practices was a formalistic and positivistic approach to law. Legal positivism, among its many definitions, can be summed up as a stance in which laws are interpreted with textualist restraint, avoiding expansive liberal interpretation. To explain old law in terms of modern theories has its limits and pitfalls, yet it can help bring into relief the characteristics of the legal tradition. Legal formalism in Korea has a double provenance: the indigenous legal culture from the dynastic period and the European legal theories imported during the colonial period.

The Supremacy of the Codes

Chosŏn Korea, like the Chinese empires, boasted sophisticated and advanced written legal codes. The *Kyŏngguk taejŏn* (Great Code for Administering the Country), completed in 1471, was the fount of legality, enlarged and supplemented several times during the dynasty's history. The elaborate law codes, predominantly penal, were supposed to provide a comprehensive system of rules and punishments, encompassing all possible cases and circumstances of infraction.[5] Legality was determined in reference to a hierarchy of norms. Legal interpretation and jural postulates embodied judges' internalization of formal propositions about law. The idea that textual exegesis was the only recognized means of implementing the law was well grounded. Chosŏn magistrates were ordered to mete out punishment according to the gravity of offenses, as explicitly and minutely as stipulated in the codes. The state ensured that the judges did just that, without attempting arbitrary decisions. The codes were treated with overwhelming reverence: whenever the existing code was modified, profuse apologies were added to explain why new enactments were necessary.[6]

A frequently cited statement from Chŏng Yag-Yong (1762–1836), arguably the most prominent jurist during the Chosŏn dynasty, illustrates the prevailing concepts of justice and the purposes of judgment. In his handbook for magistrates, *Mongmin simsŏ* (Admonitions on Governing the People), Chŏng advised magistrates to lay down the open code books in front of them while judging a case and to avoid by all means discretionary or fence-sitting decision-making. His dictum highlighted the authority of the written law: "Laws are the commands of the sovereign. To fail to respect them is to be disrespectful of the sovereign's commands. How could a subject dare to do that?"[7]

Emphasis on the law codes made the justice system in Korea, and elsewhere in East Asia, relatively certain and predictable, endowing it with the kinds of positivistic elements that are idealized in modern times as the core elements of the rule of law. An oft-quoted statement of Joseph Raz posits that the law becomes law only when it can guide behavior.[8] The conventional view that East Asian countries lacked the principle of legality has been thoroughly disputed. Scholars have

[5] Kim, *Law and Custom in Korea*, 21–25.

[6] Jérôme Bourgon and Pierre-Emmanuel Roux, "The Chosŏn Law Codes in an East Asian Perspective," in Marie Seong-Hak Kim (ed.), *The Spirit of Korean Law: Korean Legal History in Context* (Leiden: Brill, 2016), 19–54. For China, see, among others, Geoffrey MacCormack, *The Spirit of Traditional Chinese Law* (Athens, GA: University of Georgia Press, 1996).

[7] Chŏng Yag-Yong, *Yŏkchu Mongmin simsŏ*, vol. 4 (*Ch'ŏngsong* section, Part I, in *Hyŏngjŏn*). English translation in *Admonitions on Governing the People: Manual for All Administrators*, trans. Byonghyon Choi (Berkeley: University of California Press, 2010).

[8] "If the law is to be obeyed *it must be capable of guiding the behavior of its subjects*. It must be such that they can find out what it is and act on it" (emphasis original). Raz, "The Rule of Law," 214.

shown that the Chinese (and by extension Chosŏn) codes were instead the epitome of the principle of *nullum crimen, nulla poena, sine lege* (no crime, no punishment, without law), many centuries before that concept took root in Europe.[9] This is an idea that no offense may be punished unless a prior statute has defined it and set out the penalty. In short, the Chinese and Korean penal law limited judges' activities to finding and imposing a prescribed punishment for an offense, no more, no less. By compelling officials to observe the intricate provisions of the code, the emperor and the king aimed to protect the subjects. Conformity to a uniform law, restricting the arbitrary decisions of the judges, was the gist of the Korean – and East Asian – notion of justice. In later periods, government forces' penchant to craft and forge legal provisions for political gains was itself primed with this deep-seated tradition of the sanctity of written law.

William R. Shaw (1945–1993) was one of the finest scholars of Korean legal history. According to Shaw, statist values were solidly embedded in Confucian officials' frame of mind.[10] These officials persisted in perceiving the state as a dogmatic construction, legitimized by a system of norms. Shaw stated, "The most important source of tension in Yi government was not between legal norms and Confucian moral conceptions" but "between central law and no law; between the combination of law and morality together embodied in the codes and local interests; and between the civil morality of the state and the personal moral insight of Confucian scholars and high officials alike."[11] Credence in the moral propriety of the penalty in the code meant a magistrate's personal feelings or emotional reaction had to give way to the formal written law. Even a high minister who was "torn as a Confucian between his strong emotional reaction to th[e] crime and his commitment to the supremacy of law – that is, his confidence in the moral propriety of the penalty in the Code – supported the formal written law in spite of his personal feelings." As Shaw noted, "[t]he magistrate was expected to uphold the laws, both in the performance of

9 Jérôme Bourgon, "The Principle of Legality and Legal Rules in the Chinese Legal Tradition," in Mireille Delmas-Marty and Pierre-Etienne Will (eds.), *China, Democracy, and Law* (Leiden: Brill, 2011), 169–188.

10 William R. Shaw, "Traditional Korean Law and Its Relation to China," in Jerome Alan Cohen, R. Randle Edwards, and Fu-mei Chang Chen (eds.), *Essays on China's Legal Tradition* (Princeton: Princeton University Press, 1980), 302–326.

11 Ibid., 309.

his administrative duties and in the resolution of criminal cases and lawsuits," and he was frequently punished for his failure to do so.[12]

To be sure, there was a deeply grounded expectation in society that magistrates make decisions in a way to achieve fairness in the particular case. Legal disputes often took the form of supplication to the magistrates in which the parties emphasized morality and virtue, denouncing the opponent for his or her lack of human decency. Private disputes were mostly settled based on informal controls and sanctions, which presumably embodied social virtue. While substantive notions of equity based on Confucian morality were an important part of legal culture, however, they did not obscure the essential commitment to law. The Chosŏn magistrate's moral insights, informed with Confucian ideals of human sentiment, ethical considerations, and the importance of harmony and equity in society, did not lead him to forsake legality. Rather, the emphasis on order and proper procedure promoted a formal rational approach to law.

East Asian civic virtue has often been equated with the notion of fundamental law in Europe. Scholars have compared Chosŏn Confucianism to modern constitutionalism, arguing that the Confucian concept of *li* (*ye* in Korean) – ritual propriety – served as an operational instrument analogous to constitutional limits. Chaihark Hahm has persuasively argued that Confucian rituals functioned in premodern East Asia as a public political norm that effectively restrained and disciplined political rulers.[13] Surely the centrality of Confucian rituals did not mean that they amounted to a kind of bridle on the ruler in the form of institutionalized machinery.[14] Absent independent law courts, the written law codes incorporating Confucian

[12] Ibid., 309–310.

[13] Chaihark Hahm, "Law, Culture and the Politics of Confucianism," *Columbia Journal of Asian Law* 16 (2003), 234–301; Chaihark Hahm, "Ritual and Constitutionalism: Disputing the Ruler's Legitimacy in a Confucian Polity," *American Journal of Comparative Law* 57 (2009), 135–203. The political legitimacy of officials, wrote Hahm, "depended on correctly regulating their conduct according to *li*." Chaihark Hahm, "Constitutionalism, Confucian Civil Virtue, and Ritual Propriety," in Daniel A. Bell and Chaibong Hahm (eds.), *Confucianism for the Modern World* (Cambridge: Cambridge University Press, 2003), 45.

[14] Judicial courts in European monarchies claimed that royal power was held in check by the justice embodied by the law courts. According to the sixteenth-century French writer Claude de Seyssel, the three "bridles" that checked royal power were religion, justice, and police (ordinances). Claude de Seyssel,

canons served in East Asia as the exclusive source of normative authority of law and justice. In Chosŏn Korea, legal norms paralleled morally unobjectionable principles, and the legitimacy of the state was grounded on the righteousness and solemnity of its law. The conception that government actors must behave in accordance with the law and prevent the arbitrary exercise of power buttressed the legitimacy of the state. One can find the prototype of the rule of law and latent constitutionalism in premodern Korea as readily in the supremacy of the state codes as in Confucian morality and ethics.

The formalistic approach to law in the Chosŏn legal culture was reinforced under colonial rule. Korean law underwent profound transformation on the models of Japanese law and the legal system, and the traditional ideology of positivistic legality was not only sustained but bolstered by Japanese jurisprudence. Japanese law in the early twentieth century was heavily influenced by legal science in German-speaking countries, in particular the jurisprudence of the Kelsenian school.[15] The Austrian legal theorist Hans Kelsen (1881–1973) posited law as a discipline separate, by and large, from moral or political issues. Kelsen famously summed up his theory of legal positivism in the following terms: "[T]he validity of a positive legal order does not depend on its conformity with some moral system."[16] It was an idea that law had no necessary connection to moral standards and that moral illegitimacy did not entail the invalidity of a given legal order. Kelsen's concept of legal validity focused on the correctness of legal form rather than the correctness of the law's content based on its conformity with ethical standards.[17] His philosophy of positive law found an eager audience among jurists in East Asia where respect for written state codes had long prevailed.

The Monarchy of France, trans. Donald R. Kelley (New Haven: Yale University Press, 1981).

15 For Korean colonial law and jurisprudence, see Kim, *Law and Custom in Korea*. For Japanese law, see John O. Haley, *The Spirit of Japanese Law* (Athens, GA: University of Georgia Press, 1998).

16 Hans Kelsen, *Pure Theory of Law*, 2nd ed., trans. Max Knight (Berkeley: University of California Press, 1967), 67. See also Hans Kelsen, "Law, State and Justice in the Pure Theory of Law," *Yale Law Journal* 57 (1948), 377–390; Hans Kelsen, *Introduction to the Problems of Legal Theory*, 1934, trans. B. L. Paulson and S. L. Paulson (Oxford: Clarendon, 1992).

17 Frank Haldemann, "Gustav Radbruch vs. Hans Kelsen: A Debate on Nazi Law," *Ratio Juris* 18 (2005), 168.

One may argue that in traditional East Asia the code was itself an embodiment of morals and, therefore, to explain it in terms of legal positivism would have little meaning. As Shaw pointed out, "the notion of civil morality effectively subsumed virtually all the possible daily-life activities of the people and a major portion of official administrative performance as well."[18] Yet this does not negate the fact that the text of the law was taken seriously in East Asian legal culture. This formalistic legal tradition was harmonized with the modern legal theory by the Japanese jurists through their work of *Japanisierung* of European law. Generations of Korean jurists were educated during Japanese rule.[19] They came to occupy major judicial and academic posts in the postcolonial period, continuing the positivistic juristic stance from the colonial era.

In sum, legal interpretation in Korea was long governed by the formal propositions of legality. The judge's authority was predicated on the authority of the law; justice and legitimacy derived less from a judge's empathy or compassion than from his impartiality. Whether for a magistrate in Chosŏn, a colonial judge, or a modern Korean judge, impartiality meant abiding by the law. Justice or equity was not a vague, freewheeling notion but a concept tightly interwoven with the law. With the founding of the Constitution in 1948, judges availed themselves of constitutional arguments to express juridical postulates through legal reasoning. But even under the constitutional framework, or rather because of the belief in the written constitution as the highest law, the positivistic jurisprudential tendency predominated. This tradition steered judges to concern themselves with what the law was, rather than what the law ought to be.

Apart from the effects of lingering legal theories, the continuing presence of colonial law had immediate and overwhelming impact in postcolonial Korea. The constitution-makers and jurists struggled to overcome the legal legacy of colonialism.

18 Shaw, "Traditional Korean Law," 310.

19 Odaka Tomō, a professor of law at the Keijō (Seoul) Imperial University from 1928 to 1944, studied under Kelsen sometime between 1928 and 1930. Tomō's Korean students dominated the legal field in postindependence Korea. See Matsuo Keiichi, "Odaka hō tetsugaku no keisei" [The Formation of Odaka's Legal Philosophy], *Kōbe hōgaku zasshi* 15 (1965), 1–47; Kim Ch'ang-Rok, "Odaka Tomoo ŭi pŏp sasang" [Odaka Tomō's Legal Thought], *Pŏpsahak yŏngu* 46 (2012), 433–458.

Overcoming the Colonial Burden

Colonial law did not disappear with liberation. Independence unleashed earnest efforts to expunge the traces of colonialism, but the law and legal institutions built by the Japanese remained largely intact, escaping the blunt of decolonization efforts. The paradox that the intense condemnation of the colonial experience was accompanied by the equally focused replication of the colonizer's legal system to form the foundation of the modern Korean system has been amply pointed out.[20] Conventional historiography has portrayed colonial law as an instrument of imperial domination coercively imposed on the native population. This view, while valid, would have inherent limits if it stopped at merely stressing the destructive effects of colonial law without adequate consideration of its postcolonial effects. Law, a key apparatus for the construction of the state, features one of the most durable effects of colonialism. The fact that there was relatively little effort in newly independent societies to undo the legal institutions bequeathed from colonial rule attests to the importance of colonial legacy. In the early twentieth century, Japan and Korea had to deal with a common set of problems arising from the competing ideas of traditional East Asian and modern Western values and legal principles, and it was natural that Japanese law became an important source and reference point for postcolonial Korea.[21] Throughout the second half of the century, jurisprudence of the Japanese courts served as a framework and benchmark for Korean courts, either to follow or to depart from, depending on specific circumstances. Japanese judicial decisions proved more than persuasive authority in Korea.

The continuing presence of colonial law in Korea was in part a result of evolving political situations. Immediately following liberation, the southern half of the Korean peninsula was placed under US military rule. The United States Army Military Government in Korea (USAMGIK), in occupation from September 1945 through August 1948, was foremost concerned with ensuring political and legal

20 Kim, *Law and Custom in Korea*, 300.

21 See Sŏ Hi-Sŏk, "Hanguk minpŏp e taehan Ilbon minpŏp ŭi yŏnghyang kwa hyanghu ŭi kwangye: pigyo pŏp ŭi yŏngu taesang ŭro sŏŭi Ilbon minpŏp ŭl wihayŏ" [The Influence of Japanese Civil Law on Korean Civil Law and the Future of Their Relationship: Japanese Civil Law as a Subject of Comparative Law], *Minsa pŏphak* 52 (2010), 101–156.

stability.[22] Its cautious stance led to a peculiar state of the sources of law in Korea. The American occupying forces abolished a number of colonial laws of a discriminatory and political nature, such as the notorious Law of Preserving Public Order, but ordered the retention of most colonial laws and the legal structure.[23] The USAMGIK Ordinance issued in November 1945 stated in part:

> Until further ordered, and except as preciously repealed or abolished, all laws which were in force, regulations, orders, notices or other documents issued by any former government of Korea having the force of law on 9 August 1945 will continue in full force and effect until repealed by express order of the Military Korea. All local laws and customs will continue in force until repealed by competent authority.[24]

This measure was deemed necessary to avoid a legal vacuum and to guarantee the smooth operation of the courts before the codification of Korea's own laws.[25]

The general election for the National Assembly in the South took place on May 10, 1948. On July 17, the first Constitution of the independent state of Korea was proclaimed.[26] The Constitution provided for limited but continuing effect of colonial and US occupation forces' laws. Article 100 of the Constitution stated: "the current laws and regulations [*pŏmnyŏng*] continue to have the force of law so long as such laws are not contradictory to this Constitution." There were four sources of law in force at the time of the constitutional promulgation. First, there was Korean customary law. In 1912, the colonial government issued the Ordinance on Civil Matters (Chōsen Minjirei

22 See Mun Chun-Yŏng, *Pŏpwŏn kwa kŏmch'al ŭi t'ansaeng: sabŏp ŭi yŏksa ro ingnŭn Taehanminguk* [The Birth of the Courts and the Prosecutor's Office: The Republic of Korea as Seen in the History of the Judiciary] (Seoul: Yŏksa Pip'yŏngsa, 2010); Hahm and Kim, *Making We the People*, 177–183.

23 USAMGIK Ordinance No. 11 (October 9, 1945). Hanguk Pŏpche Yŏnguhoe (ed.), *Mi kunjŏng pŏmnyŏng ch'ongnam: Yŏngmunp'an* [The Complete Collection of the Laws and Regulations of the US Military Government: English Edition] (Seoul: Hanguk Pŏpche Yŏnguhoe, 1971). Selected texts of the ordinances are available at https://en.wikisource.org/wiki/Category:USAMGIK_Ordinance.

24 USAMGIK Ordinance No. 21, Sec. 1, Retention of Laws (November 2, 1945).

25 Mun Chun-Yŏng, *Pŏpwŏn kwa kŏmch'al*, 610.

26 Yi Hŏn-Hwan, "Chŏngch'i kwajŏng e issŏsŏ ŭi sabŏpkwŏn e taehan yŏngu: Hanguk hŏnjŏngsa rŭl chungsim ŭro" [A Study of Judicial Power in the Political Process: Focusing on Korean Constitutional History] (PhD diss., Seoul National University, 1996), 78–79.

in Japanese; Chosŏn Minsaryŏng in Korean).[27] Under this ordinance, Japan's Civil Code became the governing law in the colony, but it was allowed that a significant part of private law matters among Koreans be regulated by Korean customary rules, which included the laws of the Chosŏn dynasty and the Taehan Empire (proclaimed in 1897). Under articles 10 through 12 of the ordinance, matters of capacity, family and succession, and real property rights were decreed to be governed by Korean customs instead of Japanese laws. Second, there were statutory laws issued by Japanese colonial authorities between 1910 and 1945. Third, there were ordinances issued by the US military government between 1945 and 1948. Finally, there were public laws enacted by the Korean Interim Legislative Assembly, which met for the first time in December 1946. Among these various sources of law, the most important were the laws of the second and the third categories. The effect of Article 100 of the Constitution was that the majority of colonial laws and also the laws issued under US military occupation continued to have legal force in the independent Korean state until they were abolished or replaced by subsequent laws.

There was compelling urgency to draft Korean codes to end this odd situation in which Koreans continued to live under the laws of foreign occupation forces. But the outbreak of the Korean War in 1950 delayed the codification efforts. Japan's criminal and civil laws continued as the laws of the land in postcolonial Korea until the Korean Criminal Code came into force in 1954 (promulgated in 1953) and the Korean Civil Code in 1960 (promulgated in 1958). The rush to create the codes may have been responsible for the legislators' heavy reliance on Japanese laws. In fact, not just the content of the laws but also court organization remained closely based on the Japanese models.

Court Organization

Postcolonial Korea retained almost intact the colonial court structure and organization, which had been modeled after the metropolitan Japanese court system. The main foundation of modern courts which had been laid in 1908 when Korea was under Japan's protectorate rule

[27] Issued on March 18, 1912, as *seirei* No. 7, taking effect on April 1. Kim, *Law and Custom in Korea*, 154–155, 173.

(1905–1910) remained unchanged throughout the twentieth century.[28] On October 11, 1945, the US military government dismissed the entire body of Japanese judges and prosecutors. Changes were less than comprehensive, however, as most Korean personnel of the colonial government were kept.[29] Thirty-nine judges and twenty-three prosecutors who were appointed at this time had served in the colonial court.[30] A court-compiled source lists the names of 539 judges who retired or resigned between August 15, 1948 and September 30, 1975.[31] Among them, fifty-five judges had been appointed during the colonial period (before August 15, 1945) and 131 during US military rule (from September 7, 1945 to August 15, 1948).[32] Many of them had passed judicial exams held in Korea, Japan, or Manchukuo and served as judges or worked in various capacities such as judicial clerks, scriveners, or interpreters. The first Chosŏn Attorney Examination was held in October 1947, continuing in 1948 and 1949, from which new judges and prosecutors were recruited.[33] It was replaced in November 1949 by the Civil Service Examination for Judicial Personnel. Later renamed Judicial Examination, it served as the sole entry to a legal career until recently (a new bar examination started in 2012 in conjunction with the establishment of the law school system). When there was a serious shortage of judges and prosecutors, for

[28] For creation of colonial courts, see Kim, *Law and Custom in Korea*, 156–172. See also Yi Sŭng-Il, *Ch'ongdokpu pŏpche chŏngch'aek: Ilche ŭi singmin t'ongch'i wa Chosŏn Minsaryŏng* [A Study on the Legal Policy of the Chosŏn Government General: Colonial Rule by Imperial Japan and Chosŏn Minsaryŏng] (Seoul: Yŏksa Pip'yŏngsa, 2008).

[29] Hahm and Kim, *Making We the People*, 178. For the number of judges in the colonial courts (1910–1944), see Kim, *Law and Custom in Korea*, 161, Table 5.2.

[30] *Maeil Sinbo*, October 13, 1945, cited in Sabŏpsa P'yŏnch'an Wiwŏnhoe, *Yŏksa sogŭi sabŏppu* [The Judiciary in History] [hereinafter *Yŏksa sogŭi sabŏppu*] (Seoul: Sabŏp Palchŏn Chaedan, 2009), 37–38, 137, 147.

[31] Pŏpwŏn Haengjŏngch'ŏ, *Hanguk pŏpkwansa* [History of Judges in Korea] (Seoul: Yukpŏpsa, 1981), 250–276.

[32] Douglas MacArthur, Commander-in-Chief of the US Army Forces, Pacific, proclaimed the establishment of military control "over Korea south of 38 degrees north latitude and the people thereof" (Proclamation No. 1, September 7, 1945).

[33] A comprehensive list of judicial personnel, from the establishment of modern courts in 1895 (Korea's first Court Organization Act was promulgated that year) through 1995, is provided in Pŏpwŏn Haengjŏngch'ŏ, *Pŏpwŏnsa* [History of the Courts] [hereinafter *Pŏpwŏnsa*], vol. 2, *Charyojip* (Seoul: Pŏpwŏn Haengjŏngch'ŏ, 1995), 584–593.

example in the aftermath of the outbreak of the Korean War, special regulations were issued to allow recruitment outside judicial examination, as happened on December 7, 1950. There was remarkable continuity in the judiciary across the colonial and US occupation era and the Korean republic.

Under Japanese rule, judicial power emanated from the colonial governor. Colonial courts were subordinate to the governor general, who exercised executive, legislative, and judicial powers concurrently. Courts were part of the administration, although judges largely performed their tasks independently. The structure in which the executive served as the guarantor of judicial independence was decisively rejected in Korea's new Constitution. The 1948 Constitution created the Supreme Court (Taebŏpwŏn) and the lower courts.[34] Kim Pyŏng-Ro (1887–1964) took office as the first chief justice in September 1948, and five justices of the Supreme Court were appointed on November 1.[35] The Court Organization Act had been issued on May 4, 1948, as an interim government regulation. It was succeeded by the Court Organization Act (Act No. 51) that took effect on August 15, 1949. The Appeals Courts (Kodŭng Pŏpwŏn) and the District Courts (Chibang Pŏpwŏn), already in existence from the colonial period, were declared to have been established by the new law.[36] The postcolonial courts were born with a colonial handicap. Because many judges who filled the posts had served in the colonial courts, the judiciary was regarded as the continuation of colonial bureaucracy. The general public distrust of the courts was reflected in the limited role of incumbent judges in the constitution-making process, which was dominated by practicing lawyers and scholars.[37] Judges thus had little

34 Constitution (1948), Article 76 (1) and (2). During the colonial period, the highest court was the Chōsen Kōtō Hōin in Seoul, and there were three appellate courts, in Seoul, P'yŏngyang, and Taegu. Kim, *Law and Custom in Korea*, 156–162.

35 Justices Kim Ch'an-Yŏng, No Chin-Sŏl, Kim Ik-Chin, Yang Tae-Kyŏng, and Ch'oe Pyŏng-Chu. The official transfer of judicial power from the USAMGIK to Korea took place on September 13, 1948.

36 Supplemental Act, art. 70, of Court Organization Act, issued on September 26, 1949, taking effect retrospectively on August 15, 1949. There are six appeals courts: Seoul, Taegu, Kwangju (1952), Pusan (1987), Taejŏn (1992), and Suwŏn (2019). There are eighteen district courts.

37 Min Pok-Ki, Na ŭi pŏpkwan sijŏl [My Times as a Judge], *Pŏmnyul Sinmun*, September 28, 1981.

say in the discussion of creating the judicial review system. The retention of colonial judicial personnel was necessary to run the court system, but many balked at the idea of endowing the judiciary with sizable powers, in particular the power to strike down statutes passed by the nation's representative body.

The Constitutional Review System

The Japanese postwar Constitution provided judicial review based on the US prototype, in which ordinary courts exercised power to review both legislative enactments and administrative regulations. In contrast, the 1948 Korean Constitution created a binary system separating legislative enactments from executive orders. Article 81 (1) of the Constitution provided that "the Supreme Court has the power, in accordance with the law, to review as the last resort whether orders, regulations, and administrative measures [*myŏngnyŏng, kyuch'ik*, and *ch'ŏbun*] violated the constitution and the law." Article 81 (2) stated that "when whether the law [*pŏmnyul*] is in violation of the constitution becomes material to adjudication, the court shall refer the question to the Constitutional Committee and adjudicate according to its decision." A new constitutional review organ, the Constitutional Committee (Hŏnpŏp Wiwŏnhoe), was entrusted with the review of statutes issued by the National Assembly, while the ordinary courts, headed by the Supreme Court, were given the power to review administrative decrees and regulations.

The result was a hybrid system that followed the continental European scheme of dualistic constitutional review but did away with separate administrative courts. The Administrative Litigation Act of August 24, 1951, designated the appeals court as the court of first instance for litigation of administrative orders and dispositions. This structure continued until 1998 when an independent administrative court was created in Seoul, which turned administrative litigation into a tripartite review system. In Korea's effervescent history, each constitutional change brought about recalibration of the constitutional review system, but the dual judicial review arrangement has remained a distinctive element of the Korean system to the current 1987 Constitution. The only exception was the 1962 Constitution of the Third Republic, which adopted the US model whereby the regular courts, headed by the Supreme Court, reviewed both statutes and regulations.[38] As will be seen in later chapters, this unique structure continues to have serious repercussions today.

What were the reasons behind the creation of a bifurcated constitutional review system? Some clues could be found in the situation in West Germany. After the war, the German Constitutional Court (Bundesverfassungsgericht) emerged as a powerful new institution with unchallenged authority, while other courts struggled to overcome the stigmas of their immediate past.[39] The Korean founding fathers, including Yu Chin-O (1906–1987), wanted to create a similar constitutional adjudicatory body with pristine, unblemished authority and reputation. There was consensus that the power to review the constitutionality of laws enacted by the National Assembly, a body representing the sovereign will of the independent Korean people, needed to be entrusted with a new, untainted institution, rather than the old courts which lacked "sufficient credibility and authority."[40] Skeptical about the democratic legitimacy of the courts, with their colonial heritage, Yu was perhaps more concerned that conservatism prevalent in the judiciary would impede flexible interpretation of the Constitution.[41] It has been argued that the conservative position of the US Supreme Court during the New Deal era dissuaded Yu from establishing an American-style judicial review system.[42] Yu also believed that most ordinary court judges, while experienced in civil and criminal law, lacked knowledge in public law such as constitutional law.[43] Considering that administrative litigation normally takes place in the form assumed by constitutional litigation, however, it is

38 Constitution (1962), Art. 102; provisions on the judiciary remained unchanged in the constitutional revision of 1969.

39 Peter L. Lindseth, "The Paradox of Parliamentary Supremacy: Delegation, Democracy, and Dictatorship in Germany and France, 1920s–1950s," *Yale Law Journal* 113 (2004), 1349; John Ferejohn and Pasquale Pasquino, "Constitutional Adjudications: Lessons from Europe," *Texas Law Review* 82 (2004), 1675–1676; Donald Kommers, *The Constitutional Jurisprudence of the Federal Republic of Germany*, 2nd ed. (Durham: Duke University Press, 1997).

40 Yu Chin-O, *Hŏnpŏp kich'o hoegorok* [Reminiscences on the Making of Constitutional Law] (Seoul: Ilchogak, 1980), 53.

41 Yi Yŏng-Rok, "Che 1 Konghwaguk Hŏnpŏp Wiwŏnhoe chedo ŭi hyŏngsŏng" [The Formation of the Constitutional Committee System during the First Republic], *Hŏnpŏphak yŏngu* 11 (2005), 310–316.

42 Hahm and Kim, *Making We the People*, 183.

43 Yu Chin-O, *Hŏnpŏp kich'o hoegorok*, 41–43; Yi Yŏng-Rok, "Che 1 Konghwaguk," 319.

likely that the eventual choice of the dual constitutional review system, under which the ordinary courts were entrusted with the review of administrative laws only, was a compromise measure when the mistrust of judges who had served in the colonial courts was prevalent.

The Constitutional Committee opened its doors on February 21, 1950. It was composed of five justices of the Supreme Court and five members of the National Assembly, headed by the vice president.[44] This composition shows that the committee was foremost expected to play the role of coordinating the positions of the legislature and the judiciary. The Constitutional Committee could review the law only when "the full bench of the Court decides that the law was unconstitutional and requests the review of that law's constitutionality."[45] Thus, the Constitutional Committee exercised its power over a challenged law only when the Supreme Court first found it unconstitutional in a sort of preliminary review and requested the final review by the committee. This double-tier, or filtering, system, in which the jurisdiction of the Constitutional Committee hinged upon the decision of the Supreme Court, left in reality significant control in the hands of the ordinary courts. Some contemporary observers have argued that contrary to the conventional view Korea's judicial review system was closer to the US system than to the continental European system.[46] Still, legislative supremacy, closely tied to nationalistic sentiment, denied the Supreme Court the authority to review legislative acts.

The issue of the power of the judiciary vis-à-vis the political branches aside, a practical reason for creating the division of labor between the constitutional adjudicatory body and the ordinary courts can be found in the status of the laws inherited from the colonial period. Under colonial rule, Japanese laws (*hōritsu*) enacted by the Diet, such as the civil and criminal codes, and imperial decrees (*chokurei*) were imposed in Korea through the colonial governor's regulatory power in the form of executive decrees (*seirei*).[47] In 1948 these colonial decrees remained by far the most important sources of law in the Korean republic.

44 Constitution (1948), Art. 81 (3).

45 Constitution (1948), Art. 81 (2); Hŏnpŏp Wiwŏnhoe Pŏp (Constitutional Committee Act) (February 21, 1950), art. 9.

46 Yi Kyŏng-Ho, "Kunjŏng pŏmnyŏng ŭi wihŏn simsakwŏn ŭn pŏpwŏn e itta nŭn p'allye" [The Decision that the Power to Review the Military Government Laws and Regulations Resides with the Courts], *Seoul Taehakkyo pŏphak* 1 (1959), 444.

47 Kim, *Law and Custom in Korea*, 140–154.

The task of deciding whether they had continuing effect under Article 100 of the Constitution was not different in practice from determining their constitutionality under Article 81 (1). Both operations involved deciding whether a legal source conformed with the Constitution when the question became material to adjudication. One can argue that determination of the continuing validity of law is different from constitutional review because, strictly speaking, a regulation that was in breach of the Constitution under Article 100 lost its legal force retroactively from the time of the promulgation of the Constitution, whereas a regulation that was found unconstitutional through constitutional review lost legal force from the time of the court's rendering of that decision.[48] In reality, however, there was little material difference.

More serious was the unusual situation in which foreign laws continued to be the dominant sources of Korean law. Granting the power to review the colonial legal sources, along with the US military government ordinances, to ordinary courts made sense because, under both Article 81 (1) and Article 100, ordinances and regulations remained valid until they were declared by the court otherwise. This way, it was not necessary to create special administrative courts as in the European system.[49] Because the colonial and the USAMGIK decrees were of a provisional nature, there was not much resistance to allowing the regular courts to review their validity. Legislation enacted by the National Assembly was a wholly different matter, however. Conscious effort was made to distinguish between the laws, properly enacted by the nation's republican representative body, and the regulations and decrees of the foreign powers, mere vestiges of occupation. It was imperative not to grant the latter the title and status of "law" (*pŏmnyul*). Nationalistic concerns dovetailed with practical needs to settle on a basic arrangement that remained entrenched in the successive Constitutions, all the way to the current 1987 Constitution.

The problem was that the 1948 Constitution was silent on the definitions of laws and administrative decrees and left the division of

48 Constitutional Committee Act, art. 20. This issue is discussed in detail in Chapter 8.

49 Yu Chin-O, *Hŏnpŏp haeŭi* [Interpretive Exposition of the Constitution] (Seoul: Myŏngsedang, 1949), 171; Chang Yŏng-Su, "Kyubŏm t'ongje ŭi ponjil e pich'uŏ pon Taebŏpwŏn kwa Hŏnpŏp Chaep'anso ŭi yŏkhal" [The Role of the Supreme Court and the Constitutional Court Seen in Terms of Normative Control], *Koryŏ pŏphak* 55 (2009), 59.

authority between the Constitutional Committee and the ordinary courts far from clearly delineated.[50] The jurisdictional uncertainty became a serious issue for the first time in 1960, more than ten years after the birth of the Constitution. In 1959, the Seoul Appeals Court was asked whether colonial laws and the military government ordinances had force significant enough to be deemed equivalent to legislation and should thus be subject to review by the Constitutional Committee. Interestingly, basically the same question arose some fifty years later in a jurisdictional clash between the Supreme Court and the Constitutional Court. In 2010, the issue concerned not the laws of the foreign occupation forces but the emergency decrees declared by the president in the 1970s. But the underlying question was the same – that is, whether executive decrees were equivalent to legislation in importance and subject to constitutional review by the constitutional tribunal instead of the ordinary court.[51]

The next section examines the unfolding of this dispute in 1959. When the Appeals Court decision was appealed to the Supreme Court in 1960, the case became the first administrative law case deliberated *en banc* by the highest court. The *Kyŏnghyang Sinmun* case involved a number of thorny legal questions that would continue to adorn the chronicle of Korean constitutional history.

Kyŏnghyang Sinmun *Case (1959–1960)*

Kyŏnghyang Sinmun was a leading opposition newspaper, vocal in its criticism of the government and the ruling party. Between January and April 1959, the daily newspaper published several articles which the government claimed were false and incendiary. For four days from February 2, it ran installments of an essay under the title "The Principle of Majority Rule and Ethics," discussing the dangers of the tyranny of the majority and plebiscitarian democracy. On February 4, a column, without a byline, suggested that President Rhee Syngman's government was teetering on the verge of dictatorship

[50] The Supreme Court had already conducted a quasi-judicial review in 1947 even before it was granted the power by the Constitution. 1947MinSang88, September 2, 1947 (abolishing art. 14 of the colonial Civil Code). See Kim, *Law and Custom in Korea*, 275–277.

[51] These are the cases regarding the constitutionality of the emergency decrees from the 1970s. See Chapter 8.

and warned that the true democratic will of the people, when suppressed in a rigged ballot, would be forced to break forth in a violent revolution.[52] It was a daring indictment of rampant electoral fraud being committed by the regime. The reaction of the government was swift and decisive. In April, it launched criminal investigations of the newspaper on suspicion of inciting rebellion and violating the National Security Act, and revoked its publication license.[53] The law the government invoked to close down the newspaper was the USAMGIK Ordinance No. 88, issued in May 1946, that allowed the government to cancel or suspend the publication license upon violation of law. In June, the newspaper sought an injunction against the government order at the Seoul Court of Appeals (Seoul Kodŭng Pŏpwŏn). It argued that article 88 of the military ordinance had lost its legal force under Article 100 of the Constitution because it conflicted with guarantees of freedom of the press. Alternatively, claimed the newspaper, the provision, even if it had maintained legal effect, was erroneously applied by the government because the original decree had aimed at preventing Communist Party propaganda, not suppressing the freedom of the press.

In June, the Seoul Court of Appeals granted the injunction, ruling that the government was not allowed to make an administrative disposition merely on suspicion of criminal law violation before the final adjudication by the court.[54] Upon this decision, the government

[52] The segments were a translation of a previously published writing by Ferdinand Aloys Hermens, professor at Notre Dame University. *Kyŏnghyang Sinmun*, February 2–5, 1959. For the background of the case, see Hŏnpŏp Chaep'anso, *Hŏnpŏp Chaep'anso 20 nyŏn sa* [hereinafter *Hŏnpŏp Chaep'anso 20 nyŏn sa*] (Seoul: Hŏnpŏp Chaep'anso, 2008), 77–79; Myŏng Sun-Ku, "Ajikto sara innŭn pŏp, 'Chosŏn Minsaryŏng': Chosŏn Minsaryŏn ŭi sogŭpchŏk p'yeji rŭl chean handa" [The Law That Is Still Alive, 'Chosŏn Minsaryŏng': Calling for the Retroactive Abolition of Chosŏn Minsaryŏng], *Chŏsŭtisŭ* 103 (2008), 226–236; Han Sŭng-Hŏn, *Chaep'an ŭro pon Hanguk hyŏndaesa* [Modern Korean History Seen through the Court Trials] (Seoul: Ch'angbi, 2016), 151–182; *Pŏpwŏnsa*, 278–282; Pŏmnyul Sinmunsa, *Pŏpcho 50 nyŏn yasa* [Unofficial History of the 50 Years of the Judiciary] (Seoul: Pŏmnyul Sinmunsa, 2002), vol. 1, 457–466; *Yŏksa sogŭi sabŏppu*, 60.

[53] National Security Act was enacted on December 1, 1948 (Act No. 10) and has been revised a number of times. Detailed discussion of this law is in Chapter 3.

[54] Seoul Kodŭng Pŏpwŏn [Seoul Court of Appeals] (Seoul Ct. App.), 4292Haeng26, June 26, 1959. The court panel consisted of Judges Hong Il-Wŏn, Kim Chŏng-Kyu, and Ch'oe Po-Hyŏn. To issue an injunction against a government order, the court must find that its challengers are likely to prevail and that irreparable harm would result in the meantime.

retracted its publication license revocation order and issued instead an order suspending the newspaper's publication indefinitely. *Kyŏnghyang Sinmun* filed for a new injunction and requested that the court certify article 88 of the Military Government Ordinance for review by the Constitutional Committee. It argued the ordinance unjustly restrained the freedom of the press and thus conflicted with Article 100 of the Constitution. On August 8, the Court of Appeals rejected the constitutional review certification motion on procedural grounds: the power to review the challenged ordinance belonged to the Supreme Court, not the Constitutional Committee.[55] The Court wrote that the "law" (*pŏmnyul*) as referred to in Article 81 (2) of the Constitution meant laws that were enacted and promulgated by the National Assembly and that the military government ordinances were "decrees and ordinances" in the meaning of Article 81 (1) of the Constitution. Therefore, the power to review whether article 88 (1) and (4) of the Military Government Regulation violated the Constitution resided in the court, and the newspaper's constitutional review request to the Constitutional Committee had to be dismissed. In short, the Appeals Court held that the Constitutional Committee's review power was limited to laws procedurally enacted by the National Assembly, and that administrative decrees were not covered under this definition even if they regulated matters that pertained to legislative issues or had legal effects equivalent to legislation.

Kyŏnghyang Sinmun had argued that article 20 (1) of the Constitutional Committee Act, which provided that the laws or law provisions declared unconstitutional would lose legal force prospectively, was a violation of the Constitution as it did not allow retroactive application of the unconstitutionality decisions. On this issue, the Appeals Court wrote: "Whether article 20 of the Constitutional Committee Act is unconstitutional is not material to the administrative adjudication of this case as long as the above military government decree is not a subject of constitutional review by the Constitutional Committee."

Subsequently, on August 29, the same court dismissed the newspaper's injunction request and also its request to void the publication suspension order.[56] It noted that under the Constitution the freedom of

[55] Seoul Ct. App., 4292Haeng103, August 8, 1959. The court panel consisted of Judges Kim Ch'i-Kŏl, Kim Yun-Haeng, and Ch'oe Yun-Kwŏn. See *Tong-A Ilbo*, August 8, 1959 (evening ed.).

[56] *Tong-A Ilbo*, August 29 (evening ed.), August 30 (morning ed.), 1959.

the press was not an absolute freedom that could not be limited by law and that the provision allowing suspension or closure of newspaper publication did not exceed the limits allowed by the reasonable legislative purpose of maintaining public order and welfare. The newspaper had claimed that the provision in article 88 (4) that the publication permit could be cancelled or suspended when there was a breach of "law" (*pŏmnyul*) was overbroad in violation of the constitutional principles and thus automatically lost its legal force with the promulgation of the Constitution. The Appeals Court rejected this argument as well. It reasoned that the language "law" in article 88 (4) did not point to the USAMGIK ordinance, because in other sections of the same article the ordinance was clearly referred to as "regulation" (*ryŏng*). The "law" in the article instead pointed, explained the Court, to the specific laws governing acts that could jeopardize social order or public welfare in the process of editing, printing, and publishing. Construed this way, it ruled, article 88 (4) was not overbroad and did not violate constitutional principles. Therefore, the ordinance could not be regarded as having lost its effect conclusively under Article 100 of the Constitution.

The Appellate Court's opinion gave rise to heated debate. Commentators were divided over whether *pŏmnyul* in Article 81 (2) of the Constitution meant law in the formal procedural sense – that is, the enactment by the legislature only – or whether it included laws involving legislative matters broadly. One group of scholars argued that the Appeals Court's decision was reasonable because colonial decrees and foreign military government ordinances that were in breach of the Constitution should be seen as having lost their legal force from the time of the promulgation of the Constitution, not from the moment they were found unconstitutional.[57] The court's review of the constitutionality of the military government regulations amounted to not more than confirming their conformity to the Constitution, a determination qualitatively different from the Constitutional Committee's review of a statute which, when found unconstitutional, lost its legal effect prospectively, with the exception of criminal laws which became void retroactively. The foreign occupation forces' regulations were laws imposed on the Korean people against their will and hence could not be regarded as the law at the same level as legislation of

[57] Yi Kyŏng-Ho, "Kunjŏng pŏmnyŏng."

the National Assembly. Article 81 (1) had been created with this specific and unique situation in mind, in which the laws of the foreign occupation powers continued to have force even after the promulgation of Korea's own Constitution. In this view, the constitutional drafters clearly intended to distinguish the laws enacted by the National Assembly from the foreign orders that only had provisional effects. These commentators thus argued that the Appeals Court's position aligned more closely with the spirit of the Constitution.

Those who criticized the Appeals Court decision pointed, on the other hand, to the fact that colonial and USAMGIK decrees regulated de facto legislative matters and had legal force equivalent to statutory laws.[58] They claimed that relegating those decrees to a status inferior to legislation simply because they did not undergo the procedural formality of statutory enactment was neither realistic nor reasonable. More than a few of these "old" decrees had been partially modified by the legislature and subsequently issued as statutes; they were approved through the legislative, not regulatory, process, because they concerned matters grave enough to be governed by legislation. As the laws thus revised were subject to constitutional review by the Constitutional Committee, these scholars contended, other colonial decrees needed to be treated the same.[59]

Legal issues aside, the reception of the court decision was to a large degree predicated on its political implications. Many in the legal circles were in favor of the ruling that the military government decree was not a law to be reviewed by the Constitutional Committee, but they were critical of its conclusion that the decree was constitutional. According to the former chief justice Kim Pyŏng-Ro (he retired in 1957), "petitioning constitutional review of the military government decree to the Constitutional Committee is itself a violation of the law"; the decree "was something that the Americans created by resorting to their legislative technique in order to suppress the communists," so applying it to suspend the publication of *Kyŏnghyang Sinmun* was equally wrong.[60]

58 Ŏm Min-Yŏng, "Ŏllon ch'ulp'an ŭi chayu wa haengjŏng chŏk chaeryang" [Freedom of the Press and Administrative Discretion], *P'allye yŏngu* 1 (1959), 464–494.

59 Yi Ch'ang-Sŏk, "Ku pŏmnyŏng ŭi wihŏn simsakwŏn" [The Power to Review the Constitutionality of the Old Laws and Regulations], *Pŏpche* 2 (November 1959), n.p., available at www.moleg.go.kr.

60 *Tong-A Ilbo*, August 9, 1959 (morning ed.).

The public's expectation that the court would stop the government from punishing the press for political reasons was not met, rendering the decision unpopular.

Kyŏnghyang Sinmun appealed to the Supreme Court. Several months later, in February 1960, the Supreme Court delivered its ruling. In a closely watched judgment, the highest court reversed the Seoul Appeals Court decision and held that the case would be referred to the Constitutional Committee.[61] Its reasoning was that the USAMGIK Ordinance at issue regulated the publication of newspapers and periodicals but did not stipulate the conditions for the cancellation or suspension of the publication permit, raising the question of unconstitutionality.[62] Note that the Supreme Court did not consider whether article 88 of the military ordinance had lost legal effect through the working of Article 100 of the Constitution. By certifying the case for review by the Constitutional Committee, the Court nevertheless recognized that the jurisdiction of the Constitutional Committee extended over not only enactments of the National Assembly but also administrative provisions that "concerned a matter the effect of which was commensurate with the effect of law."[63] The gist of the ruling was that even administrative decrees could be treated as statutes regardless of their procedural provenance.

This decision received sharp criticism. Observers argued that the Court, construing the scope of *pŏmnyul* broadly, ran counter to Article 81 of the Constitution that had created the binary constitutional review system in the first place. They pointed out that emphasis on the formal procedural sense did not mean that an absolute legislative procedural formality was required for the Constitutional Committee to exercise its review power. For example, emergency orders issued by the president, as provided in Article 57 of the Constitution, had legal force equivalent to legislation and their review power squarely belonged to the Constitutional Committee.[64] For these scholars, the Appeals Court's decision to distinguish legal sources strictly based on procedural formality would have solved the problem without lingering uncertainty surrounding Article 81 of the Constitution. By blurring the language regarding the division of jurisdiction in Article 81, they argued, the Supreme Court effectively rendered

61 S. Ct., 4292HaengSang110, February 5, 1960. See *Tong-A Ilbo*, February 6, 1960 (evening ed.).

62 *Hŏnpŏp Chaep'anso 20 nyŏn sa*, 79.

63 S. Ct., 4292HaengSang110.

64 Yi Kyŏng-Ho, "Kunjŏng pŏmnyŏng," 445–446.

Article 100 of the Constitution meaningless.[65] The Court's vague and indecisive position may have been deliberate, though. It chose not to address the Appellate Court's important ruling on separating the request for injunction against the suspension of publication permit (an administrative law matter) from the request to overturn the suspension order (a criminal law matter).[66]

The main controversy surrounding the decision was its impact on media freedom. Because the case involved the government's undisguised effort to silence the opposition newspaper, public attention centered on its political ramifications for the state's restriction of press freedom. Those who had expected the highest court to review the challenged ordinance, strike it down promptly, and restore *Kyŏnghyang Sinmun* were disappointed. Many criticized the judicial courts, in particular the Appellate Court, for focusing unduly on legal technicalities.[67] Political, rather than legal, aspects of the case dominated discussion, obscuring the question of the construction of constitutional and legal language. This may have been partly unavoidable considering the tense political situations at the time. Opposition to President Rhee's government rapidly escalated, prompting in turn the latter's harsh measures to suppress it.

The Supreme Court decided to forward the case to the Constitutional Committee, but the latter was not in a position to take up the matter. Under the Constitution revised in November 1954, the Constitutional Committee was to be composed of five Supreme Court justices, three members of the lower house of the National Assembly, and two members of the upper house of the National Assembly.[68] But the establishment of the upper house had not been undertaken, and the Constitutional Committee could not form its membership. It meant there was no properly functioning constitutional adjudicatory body. The Supreme Court dispatched the case, knowing well that there was no one to receive it. There is reason to believe that the Court tried to buy time as the political climate was turning explosive. Nationwide protests erupted after the massive irregularities accompanying the elections of March 15.[69] Eventually, antigovernment demonstrations

65 Ibid., 448–452.
66 *Tong-A Ilbo*, February 6 (evening ed.), February 7 (evening ed.), 1960.
67 Yi Hŏn-Hwan, "Chŏngch'i kwajŏng," 145–147.
68 Constitution (1954), Art. 81.
69 The chair of the Constitutional Committee, Vice President Chang Myŏn, resigned following the protests.

evolved to broad-based citizen uprisings, culminating in the student revolution of April 19. President Rhee stepped down on April 26. The day when the president announced his resignation, the Supreme Court granted an injunction against the publication suspension order, "due to the fact it is impossible to have the constitutionality of the law reviewed."[70] The Court's rulings in February and April were indicative of its stance to avoid, as much as possible, a resolution of cases on constitutional grounds, especially in volatile political circumstances.

It was not the end of this curious case. In May, an individual filed a criminal complaint against all the sitting Supreme Court justices for failing to perform their duties. The prosecutor refused to press charges, upon which the complainant moved the Appeals Court to compel the prosecutor to act. It seemed likely that the court would indeed let prosecution proceed. In November, six justices filed a petition to recuse three judges at the Appeals Court in the case. The case was assigned to a different panel, which rejected the challenge to the state's decision not to indict.[71]

In hindsight, one sees that the Appeals Court decision of 1959, had it been sustained, could have resolved a number of legal and jurisprudential questions that would resurface in the court. Among the many issues that the *Kyŏnghyang Sinmun* case presaged, one can signal only a few. First, the question of distinguishing the determination of a law's continuing effect from the determination of its constitutionality spawned ongoing confusion. The question of the retroactive effect of the court's finding that a law was not in conformity with the constitution was another. When the Constitution was rewritten numerous times, the effect of constitutional revision on existing laws inevitably raised sticky questions. This issue reemerged in 1985 and most spectacularly in 2010 and 2013 over constitutional review of the emergency decrees. Equally serious were competing jurisdictional claims arising from the distinction between law and regulation. In the 2010s, the Supreme Court and the Constitutional Court were pitted against each other regarding which court had authority over the review of presidential decrees issued under the Yusin Constitution.[72] The Supreme Court in 2010 followed the Appeals Court's reasoning of 1959 that the review of

[70] S. Ct., 4292HaengHang12.

[71] Han Sŭng-Hŏn, *Chaep'an ŭro pon Hanguk hyŏndaesa*, 177–179.

[72] See Chapter 8.

administrative regulations pertained to the ordinary courts, whereas the Constitutional Court in 2013 embraced the Supreme Court's position of 1960 recognizing the jurisdiction of the Constitutional Committee.

Constitutional Decisions

The *Kyŏnghyang Sinmun* case reflected a volatile state of constitutional review in the First Republic. Both the Constitutional Committee and the Supreme Court maintained deference to acts of the legislature and also to discretionary acts of the executive power. In the early years of the republic, the constitution was viewed mainly as a document that laid out the administrative institutional structure of the state, with relatively little ramification for individuals. It represented more an aggregate of fundamental ideals than the source of specific rights in concrete situations.[73] Constitutional adjudication as a means to enforce individual rights against the state was still a new idea, and the boundaries between ordinary disputes and constitutional controversies were not clear-cut. Constitutional jurisprudence shows that the adjudicative bodies were keen on preserving procedural due process but less so on scrutinizing substantive laws.

Between 1948 and 1960, the Constitutional Committee rendered two decisions invalidating the laws. In 1952, it struck down the Agricultural Land Reform Act of 1949. Under this law, revised in March 1950, appeals against government action could be made to the Appeals Court, but not the Supreme Court, as the court of last resort.[74] The committee declared that citizens had the right to have their cases heard by the Supreme Court as the final appellate authority. It cited Article 76 of the Constitution, which stated that "judicial power is vested in the Supreme Court and lower courts," and Article 22, which guaranteed the citizen's right to be tried in conformity with the law by competent judges. The same day, the committee declared unconstitutional

[73] Chaihark Hahm, "Beyond 'Law vs. Politics' in Constitutional Adjudication: Lessons from South Korea," *International Journal of Constitutional Law* 10 (2012), 6–34.

[74] Constitutional Committee [Const. Comm.], 4285HŏnWi1, September 9, 1952. See *Hŏnpŏp Chaep'anso 20 nyŏn sa*, 70–72; Yoon Dae-Kyu, "Judicial Review in the Korean Political Context," *Korean Journal of Comparative Law* 17 (1989), 137–138.

a section of a law that decreed that trials for certain crimes committed during national emergency be conducted by a single-judge court of a district court or its branch court with no appeals allowed except when the defendants were sentenced to death or more than ten years in prison.[75]

Here, a brief discussion of the appeal system is in order. Korea does not have discretionary jurisdiction like the one in the United States, in which the Supreme Court can exercise a *certiorari* power. In Korea, parties can bring a case to the highest court without obtaining prior approval. It has been pointed out that people have a tendency to push their cases all the way to the Supreme Court, regardless of the chances to prevail. The Court of Appeals reviews *de novo* the decisions of the court of first instance, reexamining the facts as well as the laws. Since the appellate court is not bound by any factual or legal conclusion drawn by the lower court, the parties can submit new evidence and make new legal arguments. The Supreme Court's review is in principle limited to legal questions. The grounds of appeal to the Supreme Court include violation of the constitution, laws, ordinances, or regulations, as well as factual errors in cases that resulted in the death penalty or imprisonment for more than ten years.[76]

The absence of discretionary jurisdiction means the Supreme Court has no right to refuse to hear a case. It follows that, when a case had been disposed of on a specific legal ground, other parties may raise the same issue in their cases and the Court ends up rendering the same rulings repeatedly. The number of cases disposed of at the highest court level is phenomenal. Most decisions are rendered in a formal opinion, resulting in a heavy workload for the justices. In January 1981, the Act on Special Cases to Expedite Litigation and Related Matters was enacted. It limited the grounds for appeal to the Supreme Court to violations of the constitution and departures from Supreme Court precedent. Parties who claimed errors in interpretation of law by the

[75] Const. Comm., 4285HŏnWi2, September 9, 1952. The Special Decree regarding the Punishment of the Crimes under the Emergency Situations had been issued as a presidential emergency order on June 25, 1950, the day when North Korea invaded the South. The decree was revised and issued as law on January 30, 1951 (Act No. 175). *Hŏnpŏp Chaep'anso 20 nyŏn sa*, 72–73. See note 92 in this chapter.

[76] Hyŏngsa Sosong Pŏp [Criminal Procedure], art. 383, promulgated on September 23, 1954, and revised on December 13, 1963 (Act No. 1500); this provision remains the same in the law revised in 2017.

lower court could appeal by obtaining permission to appeal through the special process.[77] But the law was abolished in September 1990 on the grounds that it limited the citizen's fundamental rights to trial. A new law came into force in July 1994 to allow the Supreme Court to dismiss nonpenal cases without deliberation where it determined there were no legal grounds for appeal.[78] But the principle of tripartite review remains firmly established as a basic right of citizens.

After much meandering through the *Kyŏnghyang Sinmun* case, article 88 of the Military Occupation Decree was replaced during the Second Republic by a statute, the Law on the Registration of Newspapers and Political Parties.[79] Other colonial and military occupation regulations survived, incorporated into various forms of legal sources. The burden of past foreign rule persisted in constitutional jurisprudence for much of modern Korean history.

The 1948 Constitution provided a separation of powers, but the political branches adopted a heavy-handed approach to place pressure on the judiciary. The main instrument that allowed the executive branch to control judges was the judicial reappointment system.

Judicial Tenure and Independence

The judicial selection system instituted during the colonial period continued into the postcolonial period with little change. Courts were staffed by career judges who were recruited through a strictly merit-based examination.[80] Under the Court Organization Act of 1949, those who passed the highly competitive judicial exam and received training were qualified to be appointed to posts as judges or

77 See Song Sang-Hyŏn, "Taebŏpwŏn ŭi kinŭng kwa sosong ch'okchin dŭng e kwanhan t'ŭngnyepŏp sang ŭi munjechŏm" [Functions of the Supreme Court and Problems regarding the Act on Special Cases to Expedite Litigation and Related Matters], *Sabŏp haengjŏng* 23 (1982), 14–19, 65; Pŏpwŏn Haengjŏngch'ŏ, *Sosong ch'okchin tŭng e kwanhan tŭngnyepŏp sihaeng kyŏlgwa ŭi punsŏk* [Analysis of the Results of the Implementation of the Act on Special Cases to Expedite Litigation and Related Matters] (Seoul: Pŏpwŏn Haengjŏngch'ŏ, 1987).

78 Youngjoon Kwon, "Korea: Bridging the Gap between Korean Substance and Western Form," in E. Ann Black and Gary F. Bell (eds.), *Law and Legal Institutions of Asia: Traditions, Adaptations and Innovations* (Cambridge: Cambridge University Press, 2011), 176; Yi Si-Yun, *Minsa sosong pŏp* (Seoul: Pagyŏnsa, 2003), 34.

79 Enacted on July 30, 1960.

80 Constitution (1948), Art. 76.

prosecutors or to obtain a license to practice law as an attorney. Once installed, judges followed an elaborate promotion scheme emphasizing professional qualifications. This structure ensured substantial autonomy within the judicial hierarchy, but it incurred at the same time the criticism that the chief justice of the Supreme Court and other senior members of the hierarchy exercised excessive power in the court administration. The judicial recruitment system continued with little change into the early 2010s.

Under the 1948 Constitution, the chief justice of the Supreme Court was appointed by the president with the consent of the National Assembly.[81] The appointment of the Supreme Court justices, capped at nine in number, was made by the president on the recommendation of the Judicial Council, consisting of the chief justice and the justices of the Supreme Court and the chief judges of the appellate courts.[82] The number of the justices and also the method of their appointment changed over time.[83] Lower court judges were appointed by the president on the request of the chief justice based on the recommendation of the Supreme Court Justices Council.[84] The Secretariat of Court Administration (today known as the National Court Administration) was established in the Supreme Court.[85] Judges enjoyed security of tenure under the constitutional provision that "no judge is dismissed, suspended, or subjected to reduced pay unless due to impeachment, criminal punishment, or disciplinary actions."[86] They were subject to mandatory retirement. Under the Court Organization Act, the chief justice of the Supreme Court had to retire at seventy years of age and all

81 Constitution (1948), Art. 78.

82 Court Organization Act (1949), art. 5, art. 37. The 1948 Constitution, Art. 72 (11), provided that the appointment of the Supreme Court justices must be approved by the cabinet.

83 Under the 1987 Constitution, the Supreme Court justices are appointed by the president with the consent of the National Assembly on the recommendation of the chief justice (Art. 104).

84 Court Organization Act (1949), art. 38. Currently, judges are appointed by the chief justice of the Supreme Court with the consent of the Supreme Court Judicial Council. Constitution (1987), Art. 104.

85 Court Organization Act (1949), arts. 64–69. See Chŏng Chong-Sŏp, "Hanguk pŏpwŏn chedo ŭi pyŏnch'ŏn kwa kwaje" [The Evolution of the Korean Court System and Its Tasks], *Hŏnpŏphak yŏngu* 4 (1998), 188–219.

86 Constitution (1948), Art. 80.

other judges at sixty-five.[87] In practice, it was rare for judges to stay in court until their legal retirement age, except for those who made it to the Supreme Court or the senior positions at the appellate courts. It was long the norm for a legal professional to start his or her career as a young, inexperienced judge and end it as an old and skillful, and more affluent, attorney in private practice.

Of greater significance than mandatory retirement was the fact that judges were appointed for ten-year terms, requiring periodic renewal. The Constitution stated: "The judge serves for ten years and can be reappointed as determined by law."[88] The constitutionally mandated judicial term supposedly aimed at maintaining the quality and vitality of the court personnel. In the review for reappointment, all relevant elements were to be taken into account, including job performance, competence, personality, and even health, and in many cases there was plenty of room for subjective consideration. As it turned out, the reappointment process served as an instrument for political reprisal. Initially, neither judges nor the public seemed to grasp the full potential impact this system would have on judicial independence. The constitutional provision did not draw much attention until 1958, when the time came for the first cohort of judges who had been appointed in 1948 to go through reappointment.[89] There was no law to regulate the process.

Two conflicting opinions emerged: one was that a judge whose term expired would be automatically renewed to a new term unless there were cause to deny him or her reappointment; the other was that a judge's appointment had to be actively renewed by the president at the end of the existing term. A bill, supported by the Supreme Court, was presented to the National Assembly in June 1958 to revise the Court Organization Act to provide that "the judge is deemed reappointed unless he or she receives a notice of nonreappointment from the president," and that the issuance of such a notice had to be approved by the Judicial Council.

87 The specific age has fluctuated over time: at present, the Supreme Court justices including the chief justice must retire at seventy and all others at sixty-five. In 2002, the Constitutional Court upheld the mandatory retirement provision. 2001HŏnMa557 (finding art. 45 (4) of the Court Organization Act constitutional). See *Pŏmnyul Sinmun*, November 1, 2002.

88 Constitution (1948), Art. 79. Under the 1987 Constitution, the chief justice of the Supreme Court serves for six years, with no possibility of renewal; the Supreme Court justices serve a six-year renewable term; other judges serve a ten-year renewable term (Art. 105).

89 *Pŏpwŏnsa*, 272.

The government submitted its own bill stipulating that a judge's appointment be renewed only upon the submission of his or her application and approval by the president. On October 16, the government bill was passed, and the Judicial Reappointment Act took effect, requiring a positive presidential decision for the continued tenure of judges.[90]

In November and December 1958, the president excluded thirteen judges from reappointment out of fifty-seven whose terms had expired.[91] The following year, in December 1959, he refused to reappoint seven judges out of seventeen. The cases of several judges who failed to be reappointed, despite the chief justice's recommendation, suggested that their exclusion was politically motivated, in relation to the decisions they had written that irked the administration. Among them was Judge Yu Pyŏng-Chin (1914–1966) of the Seoul District Court.

Judge Yu was widely regarded as the voice of judicial conscience who courageously resisted political pressure under President Rhee's government.[92] He was responsible for a series of noteworthy decisions in 1958. That year witnessed the eruption of vehement protests against the president and his actions, including the deployment of police forces in the National Assembly to secure an amendment to the National Security Act. Cho Pong-Am, former minister of agriculture and chair

[90] Yi Hŏn-Hwan, "Chŏngch'i kwajŏng," 120–121. On October 21, the Regulation on the Reappointment of Judges was issued as a Supreme Court regulation.

[91] *Yŏksa sogŭi sabŏppu*, 59; Kukka Chŏngbowŏn, *Kwagŏ wa taehwa, mirae ŭi sŏngch'al* [Dialogue with the Past, Reflection on the Future] [hereinafter *Kwagŏ wa taehwa*], vol. 4 (Judiciary) (Seoul: Kukka Chŏngbowŏn, 2007), 178.

[92] In 1952, Judge Yu candidly discussed his agony over the Special Decree regarding the Punishment of the Crimes under the Emergency Situations, issued at the outbreak of the Korean War in June 1950. See Chapter 1, note 23, and also this chapter, note 75. South Korea recaptured Seoul in September but was forced to retreat from the capital the following January. The decree imposed severe punishments, including the death penalty, on those who had collaborated with the communists while Seoul and other parts of the country were under the enemy occupation. The general public opinion supported harsh measures. Judge Yu pondered: "What is the nation? What should we do when the law ignores reality? Do we always need to follow public opinion?" See Yu Pyŏng-Chin, *Chaep'angwan ŭi komin*, 3. At first, Judge Yu accepted the prosecution's arguments that the defendants deserved heavy sentences due to the serious nature of their crimes during wartime. Later on, however, he rendered several acquittals. He said he realized that he had a duty not just to follow the law and public opinion but also to help lead them to reason. For a short biography of Judge Yu, see Ch'oe Chong-Ko, *Hanguk ŭi pŏmnyulga* [Jurists of Korea] (Seoul: Seoul Taehakkyo Ch'ulp'anbu, 2007), 458–481.

of the Chinbodang (Progressive Party), was President Rhee's main political rival. Cho and his associates were charged in January 1958 with espionage and violation of the National Security Act.[93] Judge Yu found Cho guilty of a single charge of the National Security Act and sentenced him to five years of imprisonment, while acquitting seventeen other defendants. This decision caused uproar among government supporters, and Judge Yu received threats to his personal safety. The state appealed, and Cho was found guilty by the Supreme Court on July 2, 1959, and executed on July 31.[94]

In April 1958 Yu Kŭn-Il, a student at Seoul National University, was charged under the National Security Act. Yu (no relation to the judge) had written an article in the campus newspaper advocating the proletarian movement in Korea.[95] His case was brought to the Seoul District Court. The three-judge panel, presided by Judge Yu, noted that the article was written purely for an academic purpose. Despite the radical tone, the court held, the defendant had merely presented his ideas on socialist democracy, and it could not be seen as violation of the National Security Act.[96] This decision was affirmed by the Seoul Appeals Court, much to the chagrin of the government, and Yu was eventually acquitted.[97] Few doubted that Judge Yu's subsequent nonreappointment was related to these decisions.[98]

93 Yi Hŏn-Hwan, "Chŏngch'i kwajŏng," 138–143.

94 Han Sŭng-Hŏn, *Chaep'an ŭro pon Hanguk hyŏndaesa*, 133–139. In 2011, in retrial, the Supreme Court rendered a posthumous not-guilty verdict. Ibid., 142–144.

95 *Kyŏnghyang Sinmun*, December 21, 1957.

96 Seoul District Court [Seoul Dist. Ct.], 4291HyŏngKong74, April 3, 1958. The court panel consisted of Judges Yu Pyŏng-Chin, Yi Pyŏng-Yong, and Pae Ki-Ho. See Kim Ch'ŏl-Su, "Chayu kwŏn chŏk kibon kwŏn e kwanhan p'allye ŭi kyŏnghyang" [Jurisprudential Tendency regarding the Right to Liberty as a Fundamental Right], *Seoul Taehakkyo pŏphak* 11 (1970), 111; *Kyŏnghyang Sinmun*, April 4, 1958; *Pŏmnyul Sinmun*, July 28, 1958.

97 Seoul App. Ct, 4291HyŏngHang1281, January 7, 1959. The court panel consisted of Judges Kim Hong-Sŏp, Im Hang-Chun, and Kim Yun-Haeng. The court opinion is printed in Han In-Sŏp, "Ryu Kŭn-Il ŭi sunan (1)" [Yu Kŭn-Il's Ordeal (1)], *Minju sahoe rŭl wihan pyŏllon* 85 (2009), 84–93.

98 In June, Yi T'ae-Sun, the vice principal at Yongsan Middle School, was found not guilty of espionage by the court presided over by Judge Yu. *Kwagŏ wa taehwa*, vol. 4, 178. The nonreappointment of another judge, An Yun-Ch'ŏl, was also a political retaliation. Judge An had ordered, against the government's wishes, a suspension of custody in the case of Sŏ Min-Ho, a member of the opposition party in the National Assembly. In each of these cases, the chief justice's recommendation for reappointment was overridden.

The requirement that judges be reappointed at regular intervals was retained in the subsequent Constitutions. Apart from the ten-year cycle, each change of the ruling regime resulted in the revision of the Court Organization Act, triggering reinstallation of all incumbent judges. It was through this process that politically motivated judicial purges took place, in 1961, 1973, and 1981. As will be seen in later chapters, even Supreme Court justices were not spared the fate of punitive nonreappointment.

While it is true that the First Republic was marked by strong presidential power, the courts were not merely submissive to the government. The fact that the judiciary was not a rubber stamp is evidenced by the reactions of none other than President Rhee. In a speech delivered on February 20, 1956, at the National Assembly, Rhee criticized the "troublesome" state of the judiciary – troublesome not because it did not have enough power but because it had too much power.[99] He deplored: "the judges wield an unprecedented amount of power, more than anywhere in the world," freeing suspects at will and arbitrarily ignoring the evidence presented by the police and prosecutors. In his view, this problematic situation was caused because "the Constitution said judges could do whatever they wanted, without worrying about the penalties even when they committed errors in adjudication." Rhee asserted that "it is necessary to place limitations on the power of judges so that laws can be properly implemented." The response from the chief justice, Kim Pyŏng-Ro, was calm but firm: even the Supreme Court could not interfere with the decisions of the lower courts; the judiciary could not, and would not, implement laws in prior discussion with the executive branch.[100]

Chief Justice Kim stepped down on December 15, 1957, after reaching the retirement age of seventy years. The Court Organization Act was revised on December 23 to insert the language that "the chief justice automatically becomes a justice" (art. 15), replacing the language that "the chief justice is selected from the justices." The revised law also provided that the appointment of the chief justice would be made by the president "on the recommendation by the Judicial Council" (art. 37). The previous law had stated that "the assignment of the duties of the chief justice is done by the president on the

[99] *Tong-A Ilbo*, February 21, 1956.
[100] Yi Hŏn-Hwan, "Chŏngch'i kwajŏng," 107–108.

Figure 2.1 Judicial Council, 1958. The Judicial Council, consisting of the Supreme Court justices and the appellate court chief judges, met on January 21, 1958, after President Rhee Syngman rejected the Council's choice for the new chief justice of the highest court. At the center is Acting Chief Justice Kim Tu-Il. *Collection of Kyŏnghyang Sinmun.*

recommendation of the Judicial Council." The Judicial Council submitted the name of Kim Tong-Hyŏn (1892–1962), a former Supreme Court justice, but the government opposed (see Figure 2.1). A bill was presented in the National Assembly on February 21, 1958, to revise the Court Organization Act again on the grounds that the Constitution did not require the recommendation of the Judicial Council for the appointment of the chief justice and that the law restricting the president's constitutional right to appoint the chief justice was unconstitutional. The Constitution (Article 78) only stated that the chief justice of the Supreme Court was appointed by the president with the consent of the National Assembly. President Rhee strenuously refused Kim's appointment; the Judicial Council equally adamantly rejected the president's preferred candidate.[101] After much wrangling, in June 1958, Cho Yong-Sun (1898–1975) was appointed the second chief justice of the Supreme Court.

[101] *Yŏksa sogŭi sabŏppu*, 56–57.

Less than two years later, in April 1960, the democracy movement brought down President Rhee's government and the First Republic. A new constitution was promulgated on June 5, and the Second Republic was inaugurated under President Yun Posun [Yun Po-Sŏn] (1897–1990) and Premier Chang Myŏn (1899–1966). The new government adopted a parliamentary cabinet system.

Political Mutations

The 1960 Constitution provided for the Constitutional Court to replace the Constitutional Committee.[102] The Supreme Court retained, as before, the power to review the constitutionality of inferior norms such as executive orders, regulations, or administrative measures. The Constitutional Court, inspired by the model of West Germany, was expected to become a more effective body than the prior Constitutional Committee and also to free the ordinary courts from political pressures.[103] The Constitution introduced judicial election. Under the new system, the chief justice and the justices of the Supreme Court were to be chosen by an electoral college, and other judges were to be selected by the Council of the Supreme Court Justices and appointed by the chief justice.[104] The president was thus deprived of the power to appoint judges, and the court personnel decision became entirely within the purview of the Supreme Court. On April 26, 1960, a law was enacted to create the Electoral College, consisting of fifty incumbent judges and fifty others qualified for judgeship. Nine candidates for the chief justice position and forty candidates for the Supreme Court justiceship launched fierce campaigns, raising concerns in some legal circles about the politicization of the

[102] Constitution (1960), Art. 81. See *Hŏnpŏp Chaep'anso 20 nyŏn sa*, 76.

[103] The government enacted in 1960 the Act for the Punishment of Those Involved in the Rigged Election and the Act for the Restriction of the Civil Rights of Those Who Committed Counterdemocratic Actions. They allowed retroactive punishment of the politicians and government officials of the First Republic. The trials conducted under these laws met public outcry because many defendants were acquitted for insufficient evidence or were sentenced to relatively light punishment. Dai-Kwon Choi, "Law and Social Change: The Korean Experience" (PhD diss., University of California, Berkeley, 1976), 220–221.

[104] Constitution (1960), Art. 78 (1); Art. 78 (3). See Chŏng Chong-Sŏp, "Hanguk pŏpwŏn chedo," 197–199.

judiciary.[105] The election slated for May 17 never took place, however, due to the military coup on May 16 waged by General Park Chung Hee. The law for the establishment of the Constitutional Court, passed by the legislature on April 17 after much delay, became moot, and the Constitutional Court never opened its doors.

The military coup unleashed a serious political mutation. General Park dissolved the National Assembly and, on May 17, established the Supreme Council for National Reconstruction (Kukka Chaegŏn Ch'oego Hoeŭi) to serve as the supreme state organ. On June 6, the Supreme Council issued the Emergency Measures Act for National Reconstruction. Article 24 of this law declared that the Constitution of the Second Republic would continue its force only to the extent that it was not in conflict with the Emergency Measures Act. This meant the virtual suspension of the Constitution. With the revision of the Court Organization Act on August 12, all judges were made to undergo reappointment. From this time on, judicial reappointment became a regular process each time a new constitution came into effect. It was not until after democratization that the political use of the system was blocked. The 1987 Constitution stipulated that all judges, other than the chief justice and the justices of the Supreme Court, who were in office at the time of the enforcement of the Constitution be considered as having been appointed under the Constitution.[106] In the meantime, in 1961, fifty-two judges, about 18 percent of the judicial corps, left the court (forty-seven judges left in the form of resignation and five in dismissal).[107]

On June 30, Cho Chin-Man (1903–1979) was appointed the third chief justice, and on September 1 eight justices were installed to the Supreme Court. Between 1959 and 1961, the membership of the Supreme Court had been structured on two levels, consisting of not more than nine *taebŏpkwan* (today's Supreme Court justice) and not more than eleven *taebŏpwŏnp'ansa* (at the rank of the district court chief judge) (see

105 Min Pok-Ki, Na ŭi pŏpkwan sijŏl, January 4, 1982; *Yŏksa sogŭi sabŏppu*, 62.

106 Constitution (1987), Supplementary Articles, Art. 4. The exclusion of the chief justice and the justices from the provision was due to the changes in the appointment procedures and the appointing authorities in the new Constitution; in principle the highest court justices were governed by the same rule as other judges.

107 *Yŏksa sogŭi sabŏppu*, 66; *Kwagŏ wa taehwa*, vol. 4, 178. The special Revolutionary Court and the Prosecutor's Office were created on June 21 to punish antistate and antination activities (art. 22 [2]).

Figure 2.2 Courtroom in the Supreme Court, circa 1960. Far left on the bench is *Taebŏpwŏnp'ansa* Kim Hong-Sŏp, known as "Judge Apostle." At the left-hand side is a prosecutor, who is wearing the same judicial robe as the judges, adorned with the Korean national flower of Mugunghwa (the rose of Sharon). *Collection of the Supreme Court Library of Korea.*

Figure 2.2). This bi-level system was now abolished. In July 1962, the Supreme Council created the Committee for Deliberation on the Constitution. The Third Republic (1962–1972) was officially born with the promulgation of the Constitution on December 26. Park Chung Hee was elected president on October 15, 1963, by direct popular vote. The new Constitution took effect on December 17, 1963, coinciding with the opening of the National Assembly.

Under the 1962 Constitution, the chief justice of the Supreme Court was appointed by the president upon the nomination by the Judicial Recommendation Council with the consent of the National Assembly.[108] The Constitution specified that the president was bound by the nomination once it was approved by the legislature. The Judicial Recommendation Council consisted of four judges,

[108] Constitution (1962), Art. 99. The chief justice served a single term of six years, Art. 100 (1).

two practicing lawyers, a law professor designated by the president, the justice minister, and the chief prosecutor. The number of Supreme Court justices was increased to not more than sixteen.[109] The justices were appointed by the president upon the nomination by the chief justice with the consent of the Judicial Recommendation Council.[110] The president was bound by such a nomination. Judges of the lower courts were appointed by the chief justice upon the resolution of the Council of the Supreme Court Justices. The 1962 Constitution provided broader protection of judicial tenure than the previous Constitutions. It stated that "no judge shall be removed from office by impeachment or a sentence of imprisonment or heavier punishment, nor shall he be suspended from office, have his salary reduced or suffer any other unfavorable treatment except by disciplinary action."[111] Thus judges could not be dismissed through disciplinary actions alone. The revised Court Organization Act of 1963 provided that the chief justice of the Supreme Court recommend the renewal of judicial terms, to be granted by the president.[112]

The new Constitution adopted the US-style judicial review. The Supreme Court was given the power to review the constitutionality of all the laws – that is, the acts of the National Assembly as well as executive orders, regulations, or administrative measures. Article 102 (1) of the Constitution provided: "The Supreme Court shall have the power to decide with finality the constitutionality of a law [*pŏmnyul*], when a determination of its compatibility with the Constitution is a prerequisite to the trial of a case." The case and controversy requirement was this way inserted for the first time into the Korean Constitution; abstract review was not allowed as the constitutionality determination had to be a condition precedent for the resolution of a case. It was not immediately clear from the constitutional language whether lower courts, not just the Supreme Court, also had the power to declare statutes unconstitutional, but in November 1966 the Supreme Court held that "all courts have the power to determine the unconstitutionality of a statute regardless of the level of the court."[113]

These constitutional guarantees solidly augmented the authority of the judiciary. Not many anticipated, however, that the Supreme Court

109 Constitution (1962), Art. 97.
110 Constitution (1962), Art. 99.
111 Constitution (1962), Art. 110.
112 *Yŏksa sogŭi sabŏppu*, 66.
113 S. Ct., 66To1456, December 6, 1966.

would vigorously exercise judicial review power against the political branches. This was the opinion shared by the members of the Supreme Court itself. One of the Justices, Yi Yŏng-Sŏp (1919–2000), who participated in the drafting of the Constitution, expressed his skepticism about the prospect for active judicial review.[114] He stated: "Under the circumstances of our country, it is very difficult for the judiciary to fulfill its mission. Considering history and today's geopolitical situations on the international scene, there remain questions about the judges' ability to do their duties."[115] What Yi referred to, above all, was continuing concerns about national security and state interest, which presupposed deference to the legislature and a broad scope of political acts. Justice Yi's reservations notwithstanding, there is no dispute that under the mandates of the 1962 Constitution the courts were granted the authority to exercise dynamic judicial functions. And the courts did, as will be seen in the next chapter.

[114] Yi was chief justice of the Supreme Court from 1979 to 1981.
[115] *Hŏnpŏp Chaep'anso 20 nyŏn sa*, 92.

3 *Jurisprudential Evolution, 1962–1972*

The Constitution of the Third Republic was by all accounts a democratic constitution. It guaranteed fundamental rights of the citizens and provided for substantial judicial power and independence. In a relatively relaxed political climate, the lower courts occasionally took the bold action of declaring statutes unconstitutional. Overall, however, the record of the Supreme Court during this period shows that it maintained judicial restraint in constitutional interpretation. From the First through the Third Republics, constitutional adjudicatory bodies – either the Constitutional Committee or the Supreme Court – were reluctant to declare unconstitutional the actions of the political branches. Instead of readily reading an unconstitutional intent in the laws and regulations, they tried to restrict the legal effects of questionable measures by construing them narrowly.

Viewed against this prevailing tendency, then, the Supreme Court's decision in June 1971 striking down a law that the government emphatically claimed to be pivotal to national interest was nothing less than a thunderbolt. This decision of the State Tort Claims Act case marked the first and the only time before 1987 that the Court declared a statute unconstitutional on substantive grounds and refused to enforce it.[1] The case arose from challenges to the actions of the administrative agency undertaken under color of law. The courts had from early on made it clear that administrative suit was part of civil suit and that administrative agencies should not be given any privileged status.[2] Still, they tended to remain cautious about voiding government actions implementing statutes.[3] The fact that the highest court in 1971 chose to place citizens' rights before state interests made this case one of the most celebrated in Korea's judicial history.

1 S. Ct., 70Ta1010 (*en banc*), June 22, 1971.
2 S. Ct., 4285HaengSang29, June 19, 1952.
3 *Yŏksa sogŭi sabŏppu*, 501.

It is important to stress, however, that the 1971 decision was not a sudden *volte face* of the Supreme Court. A careful look at related cases dealt with by the Court in 1970 and 1971 shows that this judgment came at the end of lengthy and strenuous efforts to restrict the implementation of the challenged law without having to find it outright unconstitutional. After this monumental case, the Supreme Court returned to its traditional position of refraining from rendering a constitutional ruling on sensitive political matters. There was no significant shift afterward in the Court's perception of the scope and boundaries of judicial power; there was no liberal progressive turn. These considerations make the 1971 decision all the more remarkable, deserving examination in the full context of jurisprudential evolution. The case has been the subject of much discussion, but extant studies tend to focus on its political significance without adequately investigating its jurisprudential meanings. There has been little sustained attention from scholars to the activities of the Supreme Court before and after this landmark decision.

This chapter shows that the Supreme Court, operating under the 1962 Constitution, consistently maintained a moderate stance, trying to avoid open confrontation with the government. It attempted to mitigate the objectionable results of laws and regulations by interpreting them tightly and scrutinizing the legislative intent the government imputed to them. This way the judiciary could avert – for a while at least – a constitutional standoff with the political branches.

Legislative Supremacy and the Courts

The 1948 Constitution granted the president the power to declare martial law.[4] Article 13 of the Martial Law Act enacted on November 24, 1949, stated that "special measures may be taken by the commander of the forces enforcing martial law with regard to arrest, detention, search, residence, change of residence, speech, publication, assembly, and collective action within the area under martial law, when deemed necessary for military operation." The government claimed that "special measures" in this provision allowed exception to the judicial warrant clause in Article 9 (2) of the Constitution which said that "arrest, detention, or search requires a judicial warrant."

[4] Constitution (1948), Art. 64.

In 1953, the Constitutional Committee refused to strike down the Martial Law Act provision as a violation of the Constitution but declared that, even under martial law, arrest, detention, or search was not allowed without a judicial warrant.[5] It wrote: "The basic idea of Article 9 of the Constitution is to protect the personal liberties of citizens, and it makes it clear that no person shall be subjected to arrest, detention, search, interrogation, punishment, or involuntary labor except as provided by the law."[6] The committee reasoned that one would need to surmise that the legislature did not intend to enact a law in contravention to the Constitution. Therefore, "it will be not only appropriate to the basic spirit of the Constitution but also consistent with the standard interpretation of the statute that we construe article 13 of the Act to mean that the special measures concern only those matters that are not repugnant to Article 9 (2) of the Constitution." In conclusion, the committee held that "it cannot be argued that article 13 of the Martial Law Act violates Article 9 of the Constitution" but at the same time affirmed that "arrest, detention, or search can be made only upon the presence of a warrant issued by a judge."[7]

The result was that the Constitutional Committee imposed its own interpretation of the statute to find it constitutional. This way it defeated the application of the law as intended by the government without striking it down. It was an approach not very different in substance from the modern constitutional tribunal's "modified decision" (*pyŏnhyŏng kyŏlchŏng*), setting forth limited constitutionality or limited unconstitutionality of a challenged law. The first "limited constitutionality" decision was rendered in 1989.[8] Since then, the Constitutional Court has frequently resorted to this mechanism, holding that the statute at issue is valid but would become invalid if it were interpreted or applied in a way that the Court deemed unconstitutional. One sees that recourse to a conditionally constitutional decision or a decision of inconformity to the constitution was already in place in

[5] Const. Comm., 4286HŏnWi2, October 8, 1953. See *Hŏnpŏp Chaep'anso 20 nyŏn sa*, 74–75; Choi, "Law and Social Change," 255–256. For analysis, see Kim Ch'ŏl-Su, "T'ongch'i kujo e kwanhan hŏnpŏp p'allye ŭi kyŏnghyang" [Jurisprudential Tendency regarding the Constitution as a Governing Structure], *Seoul Taehakkyo pŏphak* 14 (1973), 95–123.

[6] Const. Comm., 4286HŏnWi2, October 8, 1953.

[7] Ibid.

[8] Const. Ct., 89HŏnMa38, July 21, 1989.

the 1950s. The 1953 decision can be compared with one rendered the following year. In 1954, the Constitutional Committee ruled that the president's declaration of martial law, made in accordance with the Martial Law Act, was not subject to judicial intervention. Once legally issued, the constitutive elements of martial law were presumed valid.[9] These two cases show that, during the early years of the republic, the desire to keep the legislative enactments and the executive policy decisions valid remained paramount but that the constitutional adjudicatory bodies still managed to control the implementation of laws.

Cases regarding the laws promulgated in the aftermath of the military coup of 1961 shed important light on the Supreme Court's stance during the Third Republic. As seen in Chapter 2, the Supreme Council for National Reconstruction issued the Emergency Measures Act for National Reconstruction, effectively suspending the Constitution of the Second Republic. The Supreme Court ruled that the Emergency Measures Act had force equivalent to the Constitution.[10] The Court held that the revolutionary council, put in place following the coup, had constituent power, and that the constitutional authority of the Emergency Measures Act could override the existing Constitution.[11] Subsequently, the military government issued a series of emergency laws. On July 1, 1961, the Supreme Council issued the Special Provisional Act regarding the Punishment of Particular Crimes.[12]

In January 1963, the Supreme Court acquitted a defendant charged under the Special Provisional Act. This law had been revised on December 8, 1961, to add the crime of "disseminating falsehood with the purpose of maligning the government."[13] The Court's antipathy to this provision restricting freedom of speech was apparent. It found that the defendant wrote a letter "filled with abusive language unfit for a citizen" but, because that letter had been written on November 24, 1961, he could not be punished under the revised law. The defendant also wrote letters on March 27 and April 21, 1962, "with the contents brimming with profanity and falsity extremely

9 Const. Comm., 4286HŏnWi2, October 8, 1953.
10 S. Ct., 4293Sŏn39, June 15, 1961. Kim Ch'ŏl-Su, *Wihŏn pŏmnyul simsa chedo ron* [A Theory of the Constitutional Review System] (Seoul: Hagyŏnsa, 1983), 452.
11 S. Ct., 4293Sŏn39, June 15, 1961.
12 T'ŭkchŏng Pŏmjoe Ch'ŏbŏl e kwanhan Imsi T'ŭngnye Pŏp (Act No. 640).
13 Act No. 818, art. 3 (3).

slanderous to Chairman Park," but such acts were not covered under the law that aimed to punish slandering the government. The Court wrote: "Punishing the defendant under this law would result in the infringement of the basic human rights guaranteed by Article 9 of the Constitution and violation of its spirit."[14]

In November 1963, the Supreme Court heard a constitutional challenge to the Provisional Measures Act regarding Jurisdictions over the Crimes for the Execution of Revolutionary Tasks. This law provided that certain crimes listed in the law were subject to a trial by the military court. The Court dismissed the suit, largely relying on its 1961 precedent.[15] The Emergency Measures Act was a de facto constitutional document, noted the Court. Its article 3 stipulated the "fundamental rights of the citizens provided in the Constitution are protected as long as they do not conflict with the execution of revolutionary tasks." Because the Provisional Measures Act regarding military jurisdiction was proclaimed under the authority derived from the Emergency Measures Act, its constitutionality could not be contested. The Court pointed out that adjudication of jurisdictional dispute concerned the determination of which court – ordinary or military – had jurisdiction, not the determination of whether granting jurisdiction to one court would be more reasonable than granting it to the other.[16]

Compare that case with the decision rendered in May 1965. The defendant had been convicted in March that year under article 2 of the Special Provisional Act regarding the Punishment of Particular Crimes. The Supreme Court reversed.[17] It said that, now that the National Assembly had opened its doors under the new Constitution promulgated on December 17, 1963, the task of national reconstruction initiated by the military revolution and promoted under the Special Provisional Act should be considered completed. In this situation, the state was not allowed to resort to provisional laws to punish the defendant. The law was not officially abolished until March 1966, but it apparently did not deter the Court.[18] Despite these occasional biting opinions, however, the Supreme Court overall did not veer far from its basic stance of deferring to the political branches in policy matters.

14 S. Ct., 62To266, January 31, 1963.
15 S. Ct., 63Ch'o8, November 7, 1963.
16 Ibid. See Kim Ch'ŏl-Su, *Wihŏn pŏmnyul simsa chedo ron*, 453.
17 S. Ct., 65To276, May 25, 1965.
18 Act No. 1744, March 26, 1966.

Political Questions and Judicial Deference

The spring of 1964 was a season of tense national emotions, as talks for normalization of diplomatic relations between Korea and Japan were in progress. The Korean government negotiated for economic aid and loans from Japan but opponents of the treaty talks claimed that Korea was abandoning decolonization efforts.[19] On June 3, fierce student demonstrations erupted in Seoul, later known as the 6.3 Protest, the first large wave of protests since President Park came to power. The president declared martial law in Seoul.[20] Civilians were arrested and put to court martial on charges of treasonous insurrection (*naeran*).[21] The legality of martial law was promptly contested in court. The defendants put forth several related arguments: first, the government's declaration of martial law was null and void because there was neither a war nor an armed conflict and therefore the requisite elements were not met; second, the defendants were charged with crimes for acts that had been committed before the imposition of martial law; and third, the facts alleged in the charges against them did not constitute the crime of insurrection.

In July 1964, the Supreme Court rejected all three grounds of challenges.[22] It affirmed the jurisdiction of the military court and declined to review the constitutionality of the government's exercise of emergency powers, holding that the president's declaration of martial law could not be declared void insofar as it was not conclusively in conflict with the constitution and the laws and that the case thus lacked judicable controversies. The Court first considered whether the Martial Law Act was presumptively suspect under the Constitution, rendering

19 Victor D. Cha, "Bridging the Gap: The Strategic Context of the 1965 Korea–Japan Normalization Treaty," *Korean Studies* 20 (1996), 123–160.

20 Paul Y. Chang, *Protest Dialectics: State Repression and South Korea's Democracy Movement, 1970–1979* (Stanford: Stanford University Press, 2015), 53.

21 Martial law was replaced by the garrison decree on August 26. Garrison decrees were similar to martial law in that both deployed military troops in cities to maintain domestic peace and order, but under the former (*wisuryŏng*), intended to guard military units, the garrison commander had to consult with the local government and the police before ordering the soldiers' use of arms. See Yi Kwang-Wŏn, "Wisuryŏng ŭi haesŏk kwa ippŏp panghyang" [Interpretation of Garrison Decrees and Legislative Directions], *Pŏphak nonch'ong* 24 (2011), 231–260.

22 S. Ct., 64Ch'o3, July 21, 1964.

the president's decision to declare martial law reviewable by the court. It concluded that whether the imposition of martial law was necessary was a policy question, to be decided by the political branch:

> The imposition of martial law cannot be said conclusively null and void on the grounds that it did not explicitly meet the required elements under Article 75 of the Constitution, article 4 of Martial Law Act, and article 4 of the Martial Law Implementation Act. As to martial law that cannot be seen ipso facto invalid, the question of whether its declaration was justified must be decided by the National Assembly, not by the Court.[23]

The proclamation of martial law was "an act of a political and military nature in the highest degree," and the determination of its legitimacy was vested in a political organ, not in the judiciary. The Court then discussed the jurisdiction of the martial law authorities:

> Under articles 11 and 12 of the Martial Law Act, all administrative and judicial administration in the affected areas becomes, upon the declaration of martial law, subject to the martial law commanders, and the authorities immediately take control and direct all administrative and judicial institutions. . . . Under article 16 of the Martial Law Act, those who committed the crimes listed under article 15 and article 16 in the areas under martial law are subject to court martial. It must be seen as applicable to civilians ... no matter whether they committed crimes before or after the declaration of martial law.[24]

The Court opinion firmly established the political question doctrine in Korea. This theory deriving from US constitutional law, equivalent to French *acte de gouvernement* and German *Regierungsakt*, posits that courts should refuse to hear a case which presents questions requiring a high level of political judgment. Although the Supreme Court did not use the term itself, its position was clear: the substantive validity of the declaration of martial law was a question that remained beyond judicial guidance, control, or interference at any point. Deciding whether society was in extreme danger necessitating the restoration of public order by military power was within the prerogative of the president. It is interesting to note that, while stressing that

[23] Ibid.

[24] Ibid. This decision followed the precedent of the Constitutional Committee, 4286HŏnWi2, October 8, 1953, which ruled that martial law, once issued, was presumed to be valid. For analysis, see Kim Ch'ŏl-Su, "T'ongch'i kujo," 117–118.

the national security determination was beyond its power, the Court still chose to enunciate its own observation of security concerns, writing:

> The current situation of Korea is marked by continued hostility with North Korea under ceasefire. North Korea, concentrating immense military power to the north of the demilitarized zone, is always looking for opportunities to invade the South, and continues to dispatch spies to disrupt and destroy our security, so the modern kind of warfare is in effect in continuation. . . . In the midst of the declining security and rising anxiety as a result of widespread demonstrations that erupted since March 1964 ... the president issued martial law in the area of Seoul.[25]

It was a petty bench case, in which the court normally issues its judgment as a unanimous decision.[26] But this case was notable because it was accompanied by a weighty supplemental opinion by one of the panel members. Here, before continuing with the court opinion, a brief description of the deliberation process would be helpful. A case that reaches the Supreme Court is assigned to one of the petty bench panels, composed of three or four justices, in which one justice is designated the presiding judge and another the rapporteur; the latter examines the case and recommends a disposition to the panel. When all the members of the panel concur in the rapporteur's recommendation, it becomes the opinion of the court. If the panel members fail to reach consensus, the case is sent to a council of all court members to deliberate, known as *en banc*, in which the decision is made by majority vote. Under the Third Republic, *en banc* deliberation was required for cases in which the constitutionality of a statute or an administrative regulation was in issue or when the Supreme Court deemed it necessary to reverse its precedent.[27]

In the 1964 case, Justice Han Sŏng-Su wrote a supplementary opinion regarding the justiciability of martial law declaration. Under Article 75 of the Constitution, the president has the power to declare

25 S. Ct., 64Ch'o3, July 21, 1964.

26 The bench consisted of Justices Pang Sun-Wŏn (presiding), Son Tong-Uk, Han Sŏng-Su, and Na Hang-Yun.

27 Court Organization Act (1963), art. 7, December 12, 1963. See Pak U-Tong, "Taebŏpwŏn chŏnwŏn habŭi ch'e chaep'an e issŏsŏ ŭi ŭigyŏn ŭi p'yosi" [Expression of Opinion in the Supreme Court *En Banc* Decisions], *Sasilsim kwa pŏmnyulsim*, 2nd ed. (Seoul: Hanguk Sapŏp Haengjŏng Hakhoe, 1994, 1982), 680–707.

martial law in accordance with the law and, upon declaration he must notify the National Assembly without delay; the National Assembly can demand its abolition and upon such demand the president must lift it immediately. Article 75 was thus a special provision governing the political act of martial law declaration, observed Justice Han, creating an exception to Article 102 of the same Constitution that required cases or controversies for judicial review. Therefore, he argued, the fact that martial law proclaimed by the president was subject to approval by the National Assembly did not restrict the Supreme Court's power to examine its validity, and whether the president's decision to declare martial law was ipso facto invalid could be decided by the Court as part of the question whether the prerequisite elements for declaring martial law had been met. For Justice Han, the dispositive reasoning of the case should have been based on the separation of powers. He wrote:

> As long as the president's decision to declare martial law cannot be objectively seen as ipso facto invalid (whether it is ipso facto invalid is decided by the court as part of the determination of whether there are prerequisite elements for adjudication), it follows that martial law is valid until it is abolished.

Therefore, he concluded:

> Apart from the question of whether the martial law commander can decide that the trial takes place at the Seoul Criminal District Court within the martial law territory, the present case must be determined in accordance with the procedures that are valid at the time of the trial. Because the declaration of martial law cannot be seen as ipso facto invalid, the ordinary martial law military court under the Capital Security Command has jurisdiction over this case.[28]

Justice Han's opinion can be seen as an important qualifier for the Court's position to refrain from second-guessing the ability of government officials to choose the course of national security policy.

There is much truth in the observation that the Supreme Court during this time was often passive, predisposed to invoke the political question doctrine, especially when it wished to avoid difficult constitutional questions.[29] Equally true, nevertheless, is the fact that there

[28] S. Ct., 64Ch'o4, July 21, 1964.

[29] See Kŭm Hyo-Chŏn, "Hanguk hŏnpŏp II: Kwŏnwi chuŭi hŏnpŏp ŭi sŏngnip kwa punggoe" [The Korean Constitution II: The Making of the Authoritarian Constitution and Its Demise], *Kongpŏp yŏngu* 17 (1989), 91–111.

existed genuine, overwhelming national security issues in Korea. The problem was that, while the Court struggled to construe the constitution and the laws in a way that would strike a balance between the demands of individual rights and the political branch's power to conduct state policy, its tradition of deference enticed the presidents to resort to martial law solutions and also to turn – all too eagerly – to a broad use of security laws.

National Security and the Laws

Throughout the early decades of the Korean republic, the successive governments tended to blur the boundaries of internal and external threats. The distinction between political dissent and national security danger often became murky, as the regimes used security laws to suppress opposition, punishing persons who were antigovernment rather than procommunist.[30] From the 1950s through the 1970s, many Korean people, in particular the generation that lived through the Korean War, accepted the state discourse, warily, mainly because they were fearful of another communist invasion. The war's lasting trauma can be illustrated in a remark by Justice Yi Hoe-Ch'ang, who served as a Supreme Court justice from 1981 to 1986 and from 1988 to 1989.[31] In his memoirs published in 2017, he wrote:

> Those who experienced the Korean War, including myself, continued to live under the constant fear of another invasion from the North. . . . I used to have dreams in which the sky was black covered with fighter jets. I would jump up from a nightmare hearing a scream that the North attacked the South again. This may be something that those who did not experience the Korean War would have difficulty to understand.[32]

30 See Justine Guichard, *Regime Transition and the Judicial Politics of Enmity: Democratic Inclusion and Exclusion in South Korean Constitutional Justice* (New York: Palgrave Macmillan, 2016); James M. West and Edward J. Baker, "The 1987 Constitutional Reforms in South Korea: Electoral Processes and Judicial Independence," in William Shaw (ed.), *Human Rights in Korea: Historical and Policy Perspectives* (Cambridge, MA: The East Asian Legal Studies Program of the Harvard Law School, The Council on East Asian Studies, Harvard University, 1991), 221–223.

31 Justice Yi, born in 1935, started his judicial career in 1960. Famous for authoring many important dissenting opinions, Yi later served as prime minister (1993–1994), and was a presidential candidate in 1997 and 2002.

32 Yi Hoe-Ch'ang, *Yi Hoe-Ch'ang Hoegorok* [Yi Hoe-Ch'ang Memoirs] [hereinafter *Hoegorok*] (Seoul: Kimyŏngsa, 2017), vol. 1, 240–242.

The ordeal of war heightened security concerns, ready to be abused by the regimes.

The two major security laws were the National Security Act (Kukka Poan Pŏp) and the Anticommunist Act (Pangong Pŏp). The National Security Act, enacted on December 1, 1948, by the Constituent Assembly, aimed to punish individuals and groups that sought to overthrow the new state. The law, the issuance of which preceded the promulgation of the Criminal Code in 1953, was comprehensively rewritten on June 10, 1960 (Act No. 549).[33] The revised article 1 provided:

> An individual who organized an association or group for the purpose of claiming the title of the government or changing and disturbing the state (hereinafter called an antistate organization) or any person who supported such a group shall be punished in the following categories: (1) The head of the organization is subject to death or life in prison; (2) The officials or those who participated in leadership roles are subject to death, life in prison, or imprisonment of not less than five years; (3) The others are subject to imprisonment of not more than seven years.

Article 2 incorporated by reference articles 92 through 99 of the Criminal Code. For example, the Criminal Code provided in article 98:

> (1) An individual who committed espionage for an enemy nation or assisted in the commission of espionage is punishable by death, life imprisonment, or imprisonment of not less than seven years; (2) An individual who revealed a military secret to an enemy nation is subject to the same punishment as in the preceding section.

When a member of an antistate organization or a person under the orders of an antistate organization committed espionage as defined in this article, that person was subject to punishment under the Criminal Code.

It is instructive that the short-lived Second Republic – a liberal government – tried to revise the National Security Act to tighten its provisions. Prime Minister Chang Myŏn argued in March 1961 that the changes made to the law in June 1960 weakened its key elements so much that under the current law "one cannot punish the Communists even when they have been caught."[34] Chang warned of threats from the

33 Hyŏngpŏp [Criminal Code] (Act No. 293, September 18, 1953).

34 Yi Hŏn-Hwan, "Chŏngch'i kwajŏng," 134–135.

Communist Party in the North that incited oppositions to the Korea–United States economic treaty and the Korea–Japan talks.[35] The bill to revise the law was abandoned after the military coup in May, but it shows that security concerns were perennial, regardless of the ideological orientation of the government. The National Security Act continued to exist in postdemocratization years, although certain provisions were relaxed.[36]

The Anticommunist Act was promulgated on July 3, 1961 (Act No. 643), by the Supreme Council for National Reconstruction. Designed specifically to block the activities of the communist organizations, the law overlapped with the National Security Act in many respects. The main difference was that, while the National Security Act required the evidence of the intent or purpose to overthrow the government, the Anticommunist Act did not, and the latter's less stringent elements made it more readily resorted to by the government. Its article 1 defined the antistate organization as "the organization the activities of which support communist groups." Articles 4 and 5 were the two provisions most frequently invoked by the state. Article 4 (1) stated:

> An individual who benefited an antistate organization by praising, encouraging, or supporting it or benefited by other means the activities of an antistate organization shall be punished by imprisonment of not more than seven years. The same shall apply to an individual who formed such an organization or was affiliated with it for the purpose of committing such acts.[37]

Article 5 (1) punished "an individual who had contacts with or received money from a member of an antistate organization or an overseas communist group or anyone under its order with the knowledge that such acts would benefit the said organization or group."

These provisions, phrased in broad and vague terms, were prone to abuse. There were persistent criticisms that the government used them to target political dissidents. How effective were the courts in protecting citizens from the government's zealous pursuit of criminal

[35] *Tong-A Ilbo*, February 15, 1961 (evening ed.).

[36] See Guichard, *Regime Transition*.

[37] This provision was revised on March 18, 1968 (Act No. 1997) to include in the prohibited activities benefiting the "components" of an antistate organization and "communist organizations outside the Republic of Korea."

prosecution in the name of national security? In an attempt to ascertain the judicial process surrounding the security laws, one can examine in detail a case, the so-called Research Group for Comparative Study of Nationalism (Minjokjuŭi Pigyo Yŏnguhoe) case. Commonly known as the Minbiyŏn affair, it began in 1965 with the prosecution of several university student protesters but soon became entangled with a massive espionage case called the Tongbaengnim (Korean name for East Berlin) case, an incident that roiled the country and even created a diplomatic relations issue between Korea and West Germany. The unfolding of these two cases presented a legal thicket in a most convoluted sense, full of procedural intricacies. They attested that the courts took security and political crimes laws seriously – not any less than the government and prosecutors did – and paid utmost attention to ensuring due process.

Minbiyŏn and Tongbaengnim Cases (1965–1969)

Violent student demonstrations followed the signing of the Basic Relations between Japan and the Republic of Korea in June 1965. In the fall, the government charged nine students of the Liberal Arts College at Seoul National University with crimes including treasonous insurrection.[38] In March the following year, the Seoul Criminal District Court threw out the insurrection charges.[39] Treasonous insurrection meant an uprising for the purpose of destroying the state order and, noted the court, the small number of defendants, fewer than ten, could in no way lead to such an uprising. Even if the defendants had anticipated other students and citizens would join them in rising up against the government, the state did not prove that the defendants conspired to organize an uprising to destroy the government. The court found only two defendants guilty of making illegal explosives. In July, the Seoul Appeals Court acquitted the defendants of all charges. It upheld the finding that they did not incite citizens to revolt against the government and hence there was no conspiracy for insurrection or instigation of violence. It ruled that the devices the students concocted could inflict no harm to humans and could not be regarded as explosives. The court also held that, although the declaration issued by the defendants cited passages from the publications of the Communist International, it

[38] *Kyŏnghyang Sinmun*, October 12, 1965.
[39] *Tong-A Ilbo*, March 2, 1966.

could not be seen as having benefited the communists or having attempted to help the enemy, and therefore the Anticommunist Act was not applicable. In March 1968, the Supreme Court dismissed the prosecution's appeal.[40]

This was not the end of the affair, however. By July 1967 the government had already filed charges against some of the same individuals along with others under the National Security Act. The prosecutors argued that the study group that they belonged to, Minjokjuŭi Pigyo Yŏnguhoe, was in fact an antistate organization that tried to overthrow the government.[41] While the trial of the second case was in progress, in December that year the prosecution filed a motion to add the alternative charge of violation of the Anticommunist Act, claiming that the organization was an illegal group which was created to praise and encourage acts of the communists. The state made an unusual move of proposing two separate punishments for the defendants in the primary and alternative charges.[42] On December 16, the Seoul Criminal District Court acquitted five defendants of security law charges, ruling that the group was a mere study circle, not an antistate organization. Only two defendants – Professor Hwang Sŏng-Mo of Seoul National University (a sociologist and the faculty advisor of the Minbiyŏn) and one former student – were found guilty and received less than three years of prison term for conspiring to incite illegal student demonstrations. In April 1968, the Seoul Appeals Court affirmed the not-guilty verdicts on the main antistate organization charges, while finding several defendants guilty of conspiring to turn the study club into an illegal association.[43]

While the Minbiyŏn case was unfolding, the country was jolted by the announcement by the Korean Central Intelligence Agency (KCIA, Chungang Chŏngbobu) that it had uncovered a massive espionage ring grounded in East Berlin. In July 1967, as many as 194 individuals, including prominent intellectuals based in West Germany and elsewhere in Europe, were implicated in this alleged underground communist plot to overthrow the government. They were accused of having received directions from the North Korean embassy in East Berlin. Subsequently, the lower courts found thirty-four people guilty of

40 Decision of March 5, 1968. See *Tong-A Ilbo*, March 6, 1968; *Pŏpwŏnsa*, 639.
41 *Tong-A Ilbo*, July 11, 1967; July 25, 1967.
42 *Tong-A Ilbo*, December 7, 1967; *Kyŏnghyang Sinmun*, December 15, 1967.
43 *Kyŏnghyang Sinmun*, April 17, 1968; *Tong-A Ilbo*, April 17, 1968.

violating the National Security Act, Anticommunist Act, and criminal law and sentenced them to punishments ranging from the death penalty to prison terms. The Minbiyŏn and Tongbaengnim cases became entwined because the government claimed that Professor Hwang, who received a doctorate from the University of Münster in 1960, had been won over by North Korean agents in East Berlin and that, upon his return to Korea, he had created the Minbyŏn to foment antistate activities on campus.[44]

On July 30, 1968, the Supreme Court issued decisions on the two cases, affirming in part and remanding in part for each.[45] In the Tongbaengnim case, the Court rejected the defense argument that article 4 (1) of the Anticommunist Act was overbroad and violated the constitutional principle of no punishment without law (see Figure 3.1).[46] While refusing to strike down the Anticommunist Act as unconstitutional, the Court quashed some parts of the Appeals Court decision and sent it back, explaining that its sentences for twelve defendants, including the death penalty, could not be sustained because the Appeals Court had applied the espionage and the infiltration laws without sufficient evidence. In the Minbiyŏn case, the grounds for remand were procedural.[47] At the appellate level, the state had argued that the defendants planned to organize an antistate organization, and the Appeals Court found the defendants guilty of violating article 4 (5) of the Anticommunist Act which punished those who conspired or plotted. The Supreme Court ruled that the lower court erroneously admitted the evidence presented by the prosecution and, further, that the court's grant of its motion to modify the complaint was defective for its failure to observe proper procedures. The Supreme Court dismissed the state's appeal against the not-guilty verdicts rendered to three defendants.

Upon remand of the Minbiyŏn case, the prosecution filed a motion on November 12 to revise the complaint, substituting the charge of article 4 (1) of the Anticommunist Act with that of article 4 (5). After these corrective procedural steps, the Appeals

44 Han Sŭng-Hŏn, *Chaep'an ŭro pon Hanguk hyŏndaesa*, 221–256.
45 *Tong-A Ilbo*, July 30, 1968; *Kyŏnghyang Sinmun*, July 30, 1968.
46 S. Ct., 68To754, July 30, 1968. The panel consisted of Justices Kim Ch'i-Kŏl (presiding), Sa Kwang-Uk, Ch'oe Yun-Mo, and Chu Un-Hwa.
47 S. Ct., 68To739, July 30, 1968. The panel consisted of Justices Son Tong-Uk (presiding), Pang Sun-Wŏn, Na Hang-Yun, and Yi Yŏng-Sŏp.

Figure 3.1 Tongbaengnim (East Berlin) Case Trial, 1968. The Supreme Court delivered the judgment on July 30, 1968. The defendants were absent from the courtroom. On the bench, from left to right: Justices Kim Ch'i-Kŏl, Sa Kwang-Uk, Ch'oe Yun-Mo, and Chu Un-Hwa. *Collection of Kyŏnghyang Sinmun.*

Court rendered the same sentences as those given in the earlier decision.[48] On March 18, 1969, the Supreme Court dismissed appeals from both the defendants and the prosecutors.[49] In the Tongbaengnim case, the Seoul Appeals Court made modifications of its earlier sentences, which the Supreme Court affirmed on March 31, 1969. At last the two cases came to a conclusion. Their labyrinthine and drawn-out proceedings illustrated the high-stakes nature of security law cases. It showed, if nothing else, that the courts did not grant free rein to overzealous prosecutors wielding security laws as political weapons.

Judges often came under various forms of pressure and harassment because of their decisions in political cases. Within days of the Supreme Court's remand of the East Berlin decision in July 1968, broadsheets circulated accusing the four justices who deliberated on the case of communist sympathies. Letters threatening their safety were delivered

[48] *Tong-A Ilbo*, November 26, 1968.
[49] S. Ct., 68To1772, March 18, 1968.

to their residences.[50] In August, Justice Ch'oe Yun-Mo, one of the panel members, submitted his resignation.[51] A year later, Justice Chu Un-Hwa, who was the rapporteur of the case, also stepped down.[52] Both justices denied that their resignations resulted from the Tongbaengnim case, citing instead health and financial reasons. It is true that many Supreme Court justices suffered from low salary and excessive workload, but it is not unreasonable to suspect that their departure was related to the backlash following the court decision.[53]

Justice Ch'oe was well known in the legal circles for his steadfast position that security laws needed to be construed narrowly. In April 1966, he had dissented from a case where the majority of the Supreme Court opted for a loose construction of the National Security Act. The Court held that the intent to usurp the government power and change the nature of the state, the key element in the Act, could be found in an attempt to "create an organization in order to overthrow the government" and that the law did not require the specific intent to "change the foundation of the state by creating a communist regime or a monarchy."[54] The majority of the justices were ready to find an attempt to overthrow the government was punishable under the Act even in the absence of the intent to destroy the republican or democratic system. In his dissent, Justice Ch'oe strenuously argued that the requisite intent in the National Security Act was the specific intent to establish a communist regime or destroy the democratic republican foundation of the state, not a general intent to overthrow the government. He explained that the legislature intended the National Security Act, in separation from criminal laws which also punished the attempt to overthrow the government, "to protect the existence and safety of the Republic of Korea that upholds liberal democracy from the communists and similar groups."[55] His opinion, although a dissent, remained a distinct jurisprudential tenet in the Supreme Court, to be retaken up by justices in later years in the face of government pressure. At any rate, Justice Ch'oe's abrupt resignation illustrated the extent of judicial stress in security cases.

[50] *Pŏpcho 50 nyŏn yasa*, vol. 1, 735–738.
[51] *Chung-Ang Ilbo*, August 15, 1968.
[52] *Chung-Ang Ilbo*, August 21, 1969.
[53] Han Sŭng-Hŏn, *Chaep'an ŭro pon Hanguk hyŏndaesa*, 248.
[54] S. Ct., 66To152, April 21, 1966.
[55] Ibid., Ch'oe Yun-Mo, J (dissenting).

The last few years of the 1960s witnessed increasing belligerence by North Korea. On January 21, 1968, thirty-one North Korean military commandos crossed the demilitarized zone and infiltrated into Seoul. Their goal was to attack the Blue House, the presidential residence. They roamed around the northern part of the country and were loose in Seoul for several days, advancing within one kilometer of the Blue House. All were eventually killed by the police and one captured, but South Koreans were deeply shaken. In October, another North Korean incursion into the southeastern villages of Uljin and Samchŏk occurred. North Korean antics also targeted the United States. On January 23, 1968, the USS *Pueblo*, a United States Navy intelligence ship, was seized and its crew members detained by the North Korean navy. The eighty-two surviving hostages were not released until December that year. In April 1969, North Korea shot down a US reconnaissance plane over the East Sea. In December, a Korean Airlines plane was hijacked by the North. All these incidents touched a nerve with the public, elevating the level of urgency on security measures. It is fair to conjecture that judicial interpretation of security laws was not entirely insulated from these developments.

Before long, Korean politics entered into a period of serious domestic tension. President Park had first been elected to the presidency in October 1963. As his second four-year term drew to a close, he led the amendment of the Constitution in 1969 in order to rule for a third. The new Constitution went into effect on October 21. The presidential election took place on April 27, 1971, and Park defeated his opponent, Kim Dae Jung (Kim Tae-Chung) (1924–2009) by a narrow margin.[56] It was in these volatile situations that, on June 22, the Supreme Court declared the State Tort Claims Act unconstitutional. When the Court dropped the bombshell, Park was about to be sworn in to his office. Park may have had reason to view the Court's action as an obstruction to his national policy and, simply, a personal snub. In hindsight, these developments signaled the advent of a new constitutional order some sixteen months later, which would wrest judicial review power away from the courts. First it is necessary to examine this monumental case in detail.

[56] Hak-Kyu Sohn, *Authoritarianism and Opposition in South Korea* (London: Routledge, 1989), 31–32. Kim later became the president of Korea from 1998 to 2003.

The Court in Action

The Korean Constitution provides for the state tort liability. Article 27 of the 1948 Constitution stated, in part:

> A person who has sustained damage by unlawful acts committed by public officials in the course of their official duties may claim compensation from the state or a public agency. But this does not relinquish civil or criminal liabilities of the public officials concerned.[57]

This provision was retained almost intact in Article 26 of the 1962 Constitution, by simply replacing "person" with "citizen" and deleting the words "civil or criminal."

In 1951, in the midst of the Korean War, the State Tort Claims Act was enacted to deal with state liability claims arising from actions incidental to military service. Its article 2 repeated the constitutional requirement of state compensation. A major change came when a revised State Tort Claims Act took effect on March 3, 1967.[58] The new article 2 read:

> (1) Where a public official in the course of his or her official duties inflicted damage to another by intention or negligence, the state or local governments shall provide compensation. But where an active military serviceman or an employee of the military forces suffered death in battle, death on duty, or injury during combat action, drill, or performance of other official duties, or sustained the said damage in a military camp, barrack, war vessel, ship, aircraft, or other transport apparatus used for military purposes, and where that person or the bereaved family is entitled to disaster compensation or bereavement allowance or pension by means of other law provisions, no damage claim can be filed under this law and the articles of the Civil Code.
> (2) In cases falling under the main provision of the preceding section, the state or local governments may demand reimbursement to the relevant public official who caused such damage by intention or gross negligence.

This revision effectively denied the ability of members of the armed forces and civilian employees of the military who died or were injured by unlawful acts of public officials in their official duties to seek damages under civil law torts claims as long as they were entitled to state compensation.

57 Constitution (1948), Art. 27.
58 Act No. 1899.

The proviso in article 2 (1) was added with the specific purpose of reducing the burden on the national treasury.[59] It was a desperate effort by the state to stem soaring liability payments. Korea began dispatching troops to the Vietnam War in 1964, and at its peak there were fifty thousand Korean soldiers in active combat duty there. From 1964 to 1973, some three hundred thousand Korean soldiers fought in the war.[60] With this massive war effort, the number of accidents during combat and training rapidly rose, in addition to casualties sustained in action. Indemnity suits against the state increased, because the amount of compensation paid by the state was much smaller than the amount that could be granted in a civil liability suit. The proviso of article 2 (1) was promptly challenged as a violation of the Constitution.

Before article 2 (1) drew national attention, however, it was article 3 of the same law that received constitutional scrutiny. Article 3, titled "Compensation Amounts and Other Matters on Injuries and Deaths," required that specified formulas be used to calculate the amount of compensation and prescribed the maximum amount of damage payment allowed to an individual and the bereaved family. Challenges arose that capping the compensation amounts violated Article 26 of the Constitution that protected the citizens' right to demand just compensation from the state. In July 1967, the family of a young boy who was killed by a military truck sued the state. The plaintiff prevailed in both the Pusan District Court and the Taegu Appellate Court. These courts ruled that article 3 of the State Tort Claims Act that set a ceiling on payment using a predetermined formula based on the physical conditions, gender, and age of the victim was unconstitutional; they granted damages to the family disregarding the standards provided in the law.[61] The state appealed to the Supreme Court.

59 See Yi Sang-Ch'ŏl, "Kukka Paesangpŏp che 2 cho 1 hang tansŏ ŭi wihŏnsŏng" [The Unconstitutionality of Article 2 (1) Proviso of the State Tort Claims Act], *Anam pŏphak* 1 (1993), 259–280; Kang Pyŏng-Yong, "Kukka paesang chedo e kwanhan yŏngu: Kukka Paesang Pŏp che 2 cho rŭl chungsim ŭro" [A Study on the State Liability Compensation System: Focusing on Article 2 of the State Tort Claims Act] (master's thesis, Yonsei University, 2002); Dae-Kyu Yoon, *Law and Political Authority in South Korea* (Boulder and Seoul: Westview and Kyungnam University Press, 1990), 184–188.

60 Bruce Cumings, *Korea's Place in the Sun: A Modern History* (New York: W. W. Norton & Company, 1997), 321; Chang, *Protest Dialectics*, 8.

61 Pusan District Court, February 24, 1968; Taegu Appeals Court, June 10, 1969. See *Tong-A Ilbo*, January 29, 1970.

By the time the Supreme Court started deliberation on this particular case, there had been contradicting rulings at the lower court level concerning various provisions of the State Tort Claims Act. Article 9 of the Act was also the target of constitutional contest. This provision stated that parties seeking damage payment could not file lawsuits before the state's compensation review committee had decided on the payment amount. In November 1967, the Seoul Civil District Court held that article 9, requiring a prior decision by the administrative agency before the filing of a lawsuit, was unconstitutional, but its ruling was reversed in June of the following year by the appellate division of the same court.[62] As for article 3, the courts differed in the interpretation of the law's language: some courts ruled that standards imposing upper limits on compensation unlawfully interfered with the court's determination of damages; other courts treated the formulas and standards as mere criteria with no binding force and thus said the provision was not unconstitutional. In January 1968, the Seoul Civil District Court declared that article 3 of the Act was in violation of Article 32 of the Constitution which stipulated that even a law necessitated by national security or public order could not infringe "the essential substances of liberties and rights" of citizens.[63] In short, there was widespread jurisprudential confusion over the interpretation of the Act. It was estimated that about two thousand cases relating to different provisions of the law were pending at the lower courts, waiting for the Supreme Court to rule.[64]

On January 29, 1970, the Supreme Court rendered a decision narrowly addressed to article 3.[65] A newspaper headline summed up the court holding: the Act was "not unconstitutional but [there was] no absolute need to follow it."[66] The Court ruled that article 3 did not violate Article 26 of the Constitution, because the standards laid down in the law did not set the maximum limits of the indemnity amount but merely provided agency guidelines for the compensation review committee. Therefore, the lower courts' grant of damages exceeding the guidelines was not in error.[67] The opinion of the Court read:

62 *Tong-A Ilbo*, January 29, 1970; Choi, "Law and Social Change," 256.
63 Constitution (1962), Art. 32 (2).
64 *Tong-A Ilbo*, January 29, 1970.
65 S. Ct. 69Ta1203, January 29, 1970.
66 *Tong-A Ilbo*, January 29, 1970.
67 Ibid.; *Pŏmnyul Sinmun*, February 9, 1970. See Kim Ch'ŏl-Su, "Ch'ŏnggu kwŏn chŏk kibon kwŏn e kwanhan p'allye ŭi kyŏnghyang" [Jurisprudential Tendency

The provisions in article 3 (1) and (3), listing the standards for the assessment of compensation, merely provide guidelines for the compensation review committee and they cannot be seen as setting a limit on any amount of indemnity. When calculating the indemnity amount under the State Tort Claims Act, the court is not bound by article 3 of that law, and therefore the said law cannot be seen as a violation of Article 26 of the Constitution that protects the rights to demand damage compensation from the state and other public agencies. It follows from this that, while the lower court erroneously decided that article 3 of the State Tort Claims Act was a violation of Article 26 of the Constitution, the court's calculation of the indemnity amount departing from the standards in article 3 of that law was not illegal and the court's error had no effect on its decision.[68]

The Supreme Court thus held that the lower court was mistaken in finding the law unconstitutional but its ruling of the case was nonetheless valid. In short, article 3 was not unconstitutional but the courts did not need to abide by it. Under this ruling, the courts were allowed to continue granting damages irrespective of the standards listed in that law. Recall that in 1953 the Constitutional Committee sustained the Martial Law Act by setting forth a similar conditional interpretation of its provision.[69] In 1970 the Supreme Court resorted to basically the same method. Instead of striking down the law, the Court showed how it must be interpreted so that it could be implemented in a way that was constitutional. Article 3 remained constitutional but lost its status as a special law that limited the rights provided in the Civil Code; it was now relegated to a level of internal regulation binding the administrative agency only. The law was upheld by the Court only because it was held to be not binding on the courts.

Barely a month later, the Supreme Court, in a similar approach, practically abrogated article 9 of the same Act. It ruled, on March 10, that the victim who suffered grave injury when he was overrun by a military truck did not need to wait for the decision of the compensation review committee before filing a suit with the court.[70] The Appellate Court had rejected the suit on the grounds that the party had not met the requirements under article 9, but the Supreme

regarding the Right to Make a Claim as a Fundamental Right], *Seoul Taehakkyo pŏphak* 12 (1972), 121–124; Kim Ch'ŏl-Su, "T'ongch'i kujo," 96.

68 S. Ct. 69Ta1203, January 29, 1970.

69 Const. Comm., 4286HŏnWi2, October 8, 1953. See note 5 in this chapter.

70 S. Ct., 69Ta1772, March 10, 1970.

Court remanded the case, holding that the plaintiff could not be seen as having failed to exhaust the available administrative remedies. The Court again stopped short of declaring the provision unconstitutional but effectively voided it and ruled in favor of the plaintiff against the state.

The state managed to keep the law, but its gain was hollow. As seen at the beginning of the chapter, this approach, tracing back to the Constitutional Committee in the 1950s, is of a nature substantially similar to that of the limited constitutionality decisions by the modern Constitutional Court. In 1970, as is today, there was no statutory basis for the courts to render modified decisions of unconstitutionality. The courts, then and now, refer basically to the same mechanism in order to avoid striking down challenged statutes. Today the Constitutional Court's authority to do so is regularly accepted with little question; the Supreme Court's authority to do so fifty years earlier was controversial. But one sees a continuing pattern of jurisprudence.

Contemporary observers did not fail to notice the real reason behind the Supreme Court's seemingly convoluted approaches: the Court wished to avoid a showdown with the National Assembly and the administration.[71] Its basic goal was to avert, or delay, the formal constitutional examination of the laws as much as possible. Simply put, the highest court did not want to collide openly with the political branches and create a potential constitutional crisis when it needed to protect the victims' rights to obtain just compensation as guaranteed in the Constitution.[72] Judicial maneuvering was a sign of judicial strain, and not all shared this guarded position. Four justices filed a joint concurring opinion.[73] They agreed with the majority's decision to dismiss the state's appeal but disagreed with its interpretations that article 3 merely provided guidelines for the government agency and that the court was not bound by them. For these justices, the law was flatly unconstitutional, illegally restricting the citizens' right to compensation, and should have been so declared. Public opinions were divided likewise: for some, the Court's circumspect position compromised its principles and

71 *Tong-A Ilbo*, January 30, 1970; *Maeil Kyŏngje*, March 10, 1970.

72 The Supreme Court rendered a series of rulings relying on the same reasoning: S. Ct., 19Ta1729, February 10, 1970; 69Ta1069, February 24, 1970.

73 Justices Kim Ch'i-Kŏl, Pang Sun-Wŏn, Na Hang-Yun, and Yu Chae-Pang.

Figure 3.2 Conference of Chief Judges, 1970. Photo taken after the annual conference of the court leaders. The Supreme Court justices are seated in the front row, from left to right: Kim Pyŏng-Hwa (chief court administrator), Justices Min Mun-Ki, Kim Yŏng-Se, Hong Nam-P'yo, Yi Yŏng-Sŏp, Pang Sun-Wŏn, Sa Kwang-Uk, Son Tong-Uk, Min Pok-Ki (chief justice), Kim Ch'i-Kŏl, Yang Hoe-Kyŏng, Na Hang-Yun, Chu Chae-Hwang, Yu Chae-Pang, Han Pong-Se, and Yang Pyŏng-Ho. *Collection of the Supreme Court Library of Korea.*

integrity; for others, its pragmatic approach was justified as it spared the judiciary damaging clashes with the political branches (see Figure 3.2).[74]

Eventually it was article 2 (1) of the State Tort Claims Act that tipped the point. The issue was whether the proviso added in 1967, prohibiting solders and military personnel from filing a civil indemnity suit against the state, discriminated against them in violation of the Constitution. Already in September 1970, the Supreme Court had ruled that payments made to victims' families in accordance with the Civil Service Pension Act did not preclude the state's obligation to pay indemnity.[75] It held that stipends or sustenance payments to the bereaved family, made in recognition of the victim's services, were

[74] Choi, "Law and Social Change," 257.
[75] S. Ct., 69Ta289, September 30, 1970.

different in nature from tort damages. The Court thus ordered the state to pay the surviving family members compensation regardless of article 2 (1) and stipulated that such benefits not be deducted from the damage amount. Even before this ruling, several lower courts had simply chosen to ignore the proviso and apply civil law, treating the cases as ordinary damage suits. Others declared the proviso in violation of the Constitution.[76] Encouraged by these decisions, the victims and their families continued filing lawsuits. In 1971, the Supreme Court finally decided to take up the question.

State Tort Claims Act Case (1971)

The cases before the Supreme Court involved the family of a military serviceman who had been injured in an accidental explosion of a hand grenade mishandled by another serviceman, and also the wife of a soldier who was killed when the military truck he was riding in lost a wheel and fell off a cliff.[77] On June 22, the Supreme Court shook the legal and political world by striking down article 2 (1) of the State Tort Liability Act. In a sharply divided decision, nine to seven, the Court declared that denying civil law compensation to military personnel was unconstitutional. Before this momentous decision can be discussed, it is first necessary to examine an important procedural issue. On June 22, the Supreme Court in fact invalidated two separate laws. Prior to deliberating on the State Tort Claims Act, the justices first dealt with a provision in the Court Organization Act that would have otherwise procedurally blocked the Court from striking the tort claims law down.

The law in question concerned a supermajority voting rule. Under the Court Organization Act of 1963, *en banc* judgments at the Supreme Court were decided by a majority, barring different provisions in the Constitution or other laws; since the 1962 Constitution did not mention whether a majority or a supermajority was required in judicial review, a simple majority of the justices in presence was needed to nullify a law as unconstitutional.[78] The change came in 1970. The new Court Organization Act read:

76 For instance, the decision of the Taegu Appeals Court, 69Na446, December 2, 1969.

77 S. Ct., 70Ta1010 (*en banc*), June 22, 1971.

78 Court Organization Act (1963), art. 59.

Decisions by the entire bench require a majority, unless there are provisions in the Constitution and the laws otherwise. But where the Supreme Court renders a decision in reference to article 7 (1) (1), attendance of two-thirds or more of all the justices of the Supreme Court and concurrence of two-thirds or more of the justices present is required.[79]

Article 7 (1) (1) concerned "where [the Supreme Court] declares a statute, a decree, or a regulation to be unconstitutional." Under these two provisions, normal decisions by the full court required a simple majority but a higher threshold was set up to require a supermajority before a law could be declared unconstitutional. It was no secret that the legislature, dominated by the ruling party, revised the Court Organization Act with the explicit goal of preventing the prospect that the State Tort Claims Act be found unconstitutional. The administration had tried hard to convince the Supreme Court that the new State Tort Claims Act was necessary for national interest. Some justices later reminisced that they were taken aback by the government's frenzied efforts to make them understand why the state was compelled to limit the aggregate liability payments and why the justices should not strike down the law.[80] When neither persuasion nor pleading seemed to work, the government turned to a heavy-handed legislative measure.

The opposition party had decried the patently political nature of the law.[81] Some observers expressed frustration about the initial silence of the Supreme Court over what they regarded as an open affront to judicial independence.[82] When the Supreme Court was ready to take the tort compensation law into its hands, it thus first had to decide whether the supermajority requirement unduly restricted the Court's exercise of its constitutionally mandated power.

Among the sixteen justices, eleven justices joined the majority to find the Court Organization Act unconstitutional; five dissented.[83] Justices who joined the majority were Son Tong-Uk, Kim Ch'i-Kŏl, Sa Kwang-Uk, Hong Sun-Yŏp, Pang Sun-Wŏn, Na Hang-Yun, Hong Nam-P'yo, Kim Yŏng-Se, Han Pong-Se, Min Mun-Ki, and Yang Pyŏng-Ho.

[79] Court Organization Act (Act No. 2222, August 7, 1970), art. 59 (1).

[80] Pang Sun-Wŏn, *Na ŭi kil, na ŭi sŏnt'aek, pŏpcho panbaengnyŏn* [My Way, My Choice, a Half-Century in the Judiciary] (Seoul: Hanguk Sabŏp Haengjŏng Hakhoe, 1994), 189.

[81] *Tong-A Ilbo*, July 15 and July 16, 1970.

[82] Ibid.

[83] S. Ct., 70Ta1010, June 22, 1971.

Justices who dissented were Min Pok-Ki, Yang Hoe-Kyŏng, Yi Yŏng-Sŏp, Chu Chae-Hwang, and Yu Chae-Pang. The majority ruled that the supermajority rule violated the Constitution which granted the Court the right to review the laws without any constraint. The majority stated:

> The provision placed restrictions on the Supreme Court's judicial review function in violation of Article 102 of the Constitution, under which the Court has the power to review legislation by a general rule (that is, a simple majority) without constraint. It has created a situation in which no decision can be made by the majority opinion of the justices, which is contrary to the basic nature of judicial trial.

A statute, an inferior legal norm, could not violate a constitutional norm that provided judicial review power. The Court continued:

> When the Constitution granted the Supreme Court the authority to review the constitutionality of legislation, it did not require a specific fixed number of votes necessary for a law to be found unconstitutional. If the judicial review power of the Supreme Court mandated by the Constitution could be limited by legislation, it would violate the principle of the separation of powers and result in an infringement on the judicial review power without any constitutional basis, in conflict with the purpose of the judicial review system.

The Supreme Court thus nullified article 59 (1) of the Court Organization Act within a year of its revision. It was a notable juncture in court history that the judiciary's tradition of deference to the legislature was explicitly pushed aside.

Having disposed of the supermajority requirement, the Court proceeded to deliberate on the constitutionality of the State Tort Claims Act. It found the provision unconstitutional by a vote of nine to seven. If the Court had not struck down the Court Organization Act, constitutional challenge to the State Tort Claims Act would have failed, two votes short of the eleven votes required under the demised law. Justices who formed the majority were Son Tong-Uk, Kim Ch'i-Kŏl, Sa Kwang-Uk, Yang Hoe-Kyŏng, Pang Sun-Wŏn, Na Hang-Yun, Hong Nam-P'yo, Yu Chae-Pang, and Han Pong-Se. Justices who dissented were Min Pok-Ki, Hong Sun-Yŏp, Yi Yŏng-Sŏp, Chu Chae-Hwang, Kim Yŏng-Se, Min Mun-Ki, and Yang Pyŏng-Ho.

The opinions of both the majority and the dissenting justices in this historic decision deserve close attention. First, we examine the majority opinion. It started by declaring that "denying or limiting the rights of servicemen and civilian employees of the armed forces to seek redress for injury inflicted as a result of an illegal act of a public official violates their rights as provided for in Article 26 of the Constitution."[84] The Court allowed that, under Article 32 (2) of the Constitution, the rights of citizens could be limited, should it become necessary for the preservation of public order and welfare. The central question, then, was whether the challenged law violated the fundamental rights of equal protection of the parties and, if so, whether the state failed to show the necessity sufficient to surmount the highest level of scrutiny. The majority answered both questions in the positive. The Court stated:

> Under Article 9 of the Constitution, every citizen is equal before the law. A statute must not violate the provision that no one can be discriminated against in any aspect of political, economic, social, and cultural life due to gender, religion, or social status. In addition, Article 8 provides that every citizen deserves respect and must be treated with respect, and that the state has the obligation to protect the citizen's fundamental human rights to the highest degree. From this follows, first, that any attempt to limit the rights to demand indemnity from the state as guaranteed under the Constitution must show that the law is necessary for the maintenance of order or public welfare. Second, encroachment on the rights must be as limited as possible, to be allowed only to the extent essential for the maintenance of order or public welfare, and must not infringe upon the basic substance of the rights to demand indemnity. Third, the limitation of the rights must be evenly applied to all affected citizens in accordance with the principle of equality. If the rights of a selected group of citizens, in particular those of the military forces or those employed by the military, are restricted, that restriction must have a valid reason and must be allowed only to the extent that it does not violate the principle of equality as guaranteed in Article 9 of the Constitution. A denial of their rights to demand indemnity beyond these boundaries amounts to the deprivation of the very fundamental rights protected by the Constitution, and must not be allowed for any reason under the Constitution.[85]

The majority next referred to the Supreme Court's earlier decisions that annuity payments available to members of the armed forces and civilian employees were intended to be a mere recognition of their services and sacrifices during their time in the military. Because they were of a nature entirely different from that of tort damages for losses sustained as a result of an unlawful act by the state, they could not bar civil claims. The Court noted that, under the current law, other

[84] Ibid.
[85] Ibid.

public officials including police officers were not barred from seeking damages. The majority acknowledged that article 2 (1) was enacted in response to concerns about the increasing strain on the national treasury. Unlimited tort liability was feared to bring colossal financial consequences to the state. Nevertheless, concluded the majority, the policy goal of reducing government's fiscal burden could not be a reason for denying the people's rights to seek just compensation in violation of equal protection.

The divide between the majority and the dissenters hinged upon what kind of rights were at stake. The majority viewed article 2 (1) as a violation of citizen's equality rights protected by Article 32 of the Constitution, whereas the dissenting justices viewed it as a limitation on the property rights provided in Article 20 of the Constitution. This was an important difference. Article 32 (2) stipulated that "all liberties and rights of citizens" were guaranteed and that "the essential substances of liberties and rights cannot be limited by a law even if that law is enacted for the reason of national security or public order."[86] In contrast, Article 20 provided that, while "the right to property of all citizens is guaranteed," their "contents and limitations shall be determined by law" and further that "the exercise of property rights shall conform to public welfare."[87] The seven dissenting justices viewed the issue as a question of property rights and argued that, while the right to request compensation was a constitutionally protected right, it could still be limited by statutory law. The test to apply when deciding the law's constitutionality was a lower level of scrutiny – that is, whether the legislative restrictions were reasonable. The dissenters wrote:

> The proviso in article 2 (1) of the State Tort Claims Act places limits on the right to demand damages resulting from the reasons as provided. In principle, property right is a right reserved in law and can be limited as necessary for the legitimate purpose of defining the special relationship involving the military forces and military personnel. Therefore it is not possible to find that the law is in violation of the provisions in the Constitution that guarantee the basic rights of the citizens.[88]

[86] Constitution (1962; 1969), Art. 32 (2).
[87] Constitution (1962; 1969), Art. 20 (1) and (2). See note 94 in this chapter.
[88] Dissenting opinion, S. Ct., 70Ta1010, June 22, 1971.

The gap between the two positions was clear. In the dissenters' opinion, the right at stake, a property right, could be limited by the showing of a reasonable state interest.[89] For the majority, in contrast, the law denied citizens' basic equality right that could only be limited by the showing of a compelling state interest. The majority justices concluded that the people's rights to just compensation as allowed in civil law damages amounted to their liberty interest and that the state should not be allowed to subject them to an absurdly low compensation scheme; the legislative purpose in the law, regardless of its potential legitimacy, could not be justified if it led to an unreasonably callous treatment of victims who had suffered the loss of life or limbs.

Public opinion was divided just as sharply. Some observers, critical of the majority opinion, pointed out that the invalidity of the law would bring a result in which those who suffered injury were entitled to higher compensation than those who died in battle. Those in opposition countered that the two situations were not analogous because, while the second group met an honorable death in battle, the first group suffered death or injury due to someone else's negligence. Most injuries resulted from safety accidents, such as military vehicle accidents or mishandling of firearms, and these were not the kind of risks that soldiers or military personnel were expected to have assumed in performing their duties.[90] Contemporary news coverage showed that both sides were concerned about the staggering amount of damage payments the state was liable for.[91] Many years later, Justice Pang Sun-Wŏn, one of the majority, recalled that his colleagues agonized over whether they should put individual rights before state interest.[92] He said that they felt deep pity for the young soldier victims.[93] Justice Pang candidly admitted that, at that time, neither he nor his fellow justices were fully cognizant of the magnitude of their decision to strike down the law. They were convinced of the soundness of their reasoning

89 See the recollection of one of the dissenters: Yang Pyŏng-Ho, *Pŏpcho pan paengnyŏn e irŭn na ŭi sosin* [My Beliefs during a Half-Century in the Judiciary] (Seoul: Kyŏngch'ŏn Aein, 1995), 169–174.

90 See the public debate between two prominent jurists, Kim Kap-Su and Kim Ch'ŏl-Su, in *Kyŏnghyang Sinmun*, July 15, 1971.

91 *Kyŏnghyang Sinmun*, July 13, 1971; *Tong-A Ilbo*, July 13, 1971.

92 Pang Sun-Wŏn, *Na ŭi kil*, 187–192.

93 *Maeil Kyŏngje*, October 4, 1993.

but did not envision that their decision would chart a new course for the judiciary. Both the majority and dissenters remained of the belief that the judiciary should avoid getting involved in political matters. The fact that there was no drastic change in the Court's position after June 1971 was illustrated in its dealings with the state requisition cases.

State Requisition Act Cases (1970–1971)

After the Korean War, compensation for the property requisitioned by the military remained a serious issue. The Constitution guaranteed the rights to just compensation:

1. The right to property of all citizens shall be guaranteed.
2. The exercise of property rights shall conform to the public welfare.
3. Expropriation and use or restriction of private property for public purpose shall be governed by law, but just compensation thereof shall be paid.[94]

The Requisition Act was first enacted on May 1, 1963 (Act No. 1336). The courts consistently ruled that the individual whose property had been expropriated by the state was entitled to adequate civil compensation. In 1967 and again in 1969, the Supreme Court unanimously held that the executive order that limited compensations for the state use of the property to the extent of the government budget was unconstitutional.[95] On January 1, 1970, the National Assembly passed the Special Act for Requisitioned Property Disposition (Act No. 2172). Its article 3 (3) stipulated that the value of the expropriated property would be assessed on the basis of the price at the time of requisition, adjusted by the amount calculated using the standards announced by the head of the tax administration authority.[96]

In March 1970, the Supreme Court ruled that the compensation standards listed in the Requisition Act were merely an internal guideline created by the requisition compensation committee in the Defense Ministry and that as such they had no binding force over the courts'

[94] Constitution (1962), Art. 20.

[95] S. Ct., 67Ta1334, November 2, 1967; S. Ct. 67Ta797, December 30, 1969.

[96] Yoon, *Law and Political Authority*, 189–193. See Yi Su-Hwa, "Kukka anbo wa chingbal ch'ŏbun" [National Security and Requisition Measures], *Pŏmnyul Sinmun*, January 2, 1970.

determination of the compensation amount.[97] The Court confirmed that demanding compensation for requisitioned property was a civil suit, not an administrative suit. After this decision, litigation against the state shot up. On December 31, 1970, the government revised the Special Act for Requisitioned Property Disposition (Act No. 2264) to add the stipulation (article 8[3]) that no compensation be paid beyond the standards provided in Article 21 of the Requisition Act.[98] The revision had the same legislative purpose as the State Tort Claims Act – to ease burdens on the treasury by placing the gamut of limitations on compensation eligibility and scope. Both were claimed to be crucial for national interests.

The situation brought something of a feeling of déjà vu. In February 1971, the Seoul Civil District Court declared that article 21 of the revised Special Act for Requisitioned Property Disposition violated Article 20 (3) of the Constitution.[99] The court ordered that the state pay the compensation based on the current market value as calculated by the court. On March 17, the same court ruled that the government must pay the compensation in cash, not in government bonds to be repaid in installments over ten years.[100] This was a serious matter. A contemporary estimate had it that the court-determined compensation amounts owed by the government during the twenty years beginning in 1950 would be ten times larger than the amounts paid under the government standards.[101]

Tong-A Ilbo reported in October 1971 that, during the twenty-month period from January 1970, the state lost 205 cases involving requisitioned property at the lower court level. All of them were appealed to the Supreme Court.[102] The article's headline, "Procrastination Strategy for

97 S. Ct., 69Ta1561, March 24, 1970.

98 Article 21 of the Requisition Act tied the compensation amount for the state use of the property to that year's tax rates and other compensations to the tax rates at the time of the property's release from requisition. The revised article 8 (2) of the Special Act provided that no lawsuit could be filed for compensation before the state's notification of payment decision, unless a year had passed from the application for compensation. The Requisition Act (Act No. 2263), revised on the same day as the Special Act, further stipulated that no lawsuit be filed before a review of the state's decision, unless sixty days had passed from the application for review (article 24 [2]).

99 S. Ct., 70Ka14816. See *Maeil Kyŏngje*, February 26, 1971.

100 *Tong-A Ilbo*, March 17, 1971; *Maeil Kyŏngje*, March 18, 1971.

101 *Yŏksa sogŭi sabŏppu*, 319.

102 *Tong-A Ilbo*, October 23, 1971.

Appealed Cases," rather accurately depicted the tight spot the Supreme Court found itself in. According to the newspaper, the Court had been explicitly asked by the government to delay its decisions.[103] It was open knowledge that the state did not have the budget from which to pay out once the cases were finalized.[104] The Supreme Court's inaction seemed to contrast with its decisive action in the State Tort Claims Act cases. Following the 1971 unconstitutionality decision, the Court swiftly disposed of ninety-two cases that had been sitting on the docket, and the state lost all of them. The difference between requisition and tort liability cases was that in the former the constitutional interest in issue was property rights, triggering a lower level of scrutiny. The dire situation for the citizens whose property had been taken by the state was grave, but this time the Court could only drag its feet.[105] It is possible that the Supreme Court, having dealt a blow to the government in the state tort liability claims, did not wish to cause more confrontation. The justices seemed to believe that further provocation of the administration would push the president to take drastic action. In hindsight, their premonition was accurate. Barely a year later, the president did precisely what the justices and the public had feared – he set out to rewrite the Constitution.

The resulting legal and political maelstroms and the advent of the 1972 Yusin Constitution are discussed in Chapter 4. It would suffice here to note how the government, through constitutional revision, was able to undo all the courts' work. It turned the unconstitutional State Tort Claims Act constitutional by inserting its key provisions into the new Constitution. Similarly, it prevented judicial scrutiny of the Requisition Act by modifying the constitutional language. In a flash, these laws became judge-proof. Article 26 of the new Constitution promulgated in December 1972 read:

1. A citizen who has sustained damage by unlawful acts committed by public officials in the course of their official duties may claim compensation from the state or a public agency. But this does not relinquish the liabilities of the public officials concerned.
2. A person on active military service, an employee of the military forces, a police official, or others as defined by legislation, who sustains damage in connection with the performance of official duties such as combat action,

[103] Ibid.
[104] Ibid.
[105] *Tong-A Ilbo*, July 6, 1972.

drill and so forth, may not claim damages against the state or a public agency on the grounds of unlawful acts of public officials as committed in the course of official duties beyond the compensation as prescribed by law.

This way, the proviso in article 2 (1) the State Tort Claims Act, once declared unconstitutional, was restored with full constitutional force. Likewise, Article 20 (3) of the 1972 Constitution read:

3. Expropriation and use or restriction of private property for public purpose, and the standard and method of compensation thereof, shall be determined by law.

Compare it with the provision in the 1962 (and 1969) Constitution: "3. Expropriation and use or restriction of private property for public purpose shall be governed by law, but just compensation thereof shall be paid." The long-standing constitutional guarantee of just compensation regardless of public interest simply disappeared. With this change in constitutional language, jurisprudential work during the previous years became moot overnight. This was a political solution, reached in a purely political realm.

Not surprisingly, the rule requiring the supermajority for unconstitutionality decisions, struck down by the Supreme Court in 1971, was also revived in the 1972 Constitution. Article 111 stated that an unconstitutionality decision of a statute required "the approval of more than six members" of the Constitutional Committee, which now had the power to review legislative enactments. The supermajority rule, which had figured in the 1948 Constitution, was resurrected and has remained intact in Korea since. The 1987 Constitution declares: "When the Constitutional Court makes a decision of the unconstitutionality of a law, a decision of impeachment, a decision of dissolution of a political party or an affirmative decision regarding the constitutional complaint, the concurrence of six justices or more shall be required."[106] The presence of the

[106] Constitution (1987), Art. 113 (1). The absence of a supermajority rule for judicial review in the 1962 Constitution appeared intended because it required concurrence of three-fifths of the justices for the dissolution of a party (Art. 103). Here, one may mention briefly its contemporary ramifications. Note that Article 113 of the 1987 Constitution requires an absolute number – six – instead of an absolute percentage – two-thirds – of supermajority. An unconstitutionality decision thus requires concurrence of six justices, no matter how many justices are seated at the court at a given time or how many actually participate in the deliberation of a case. The problem of this rule has

supermajority rule in the successive Constitutions seems to affirm the ideal of legislative and administrative supremacy that continued from the republic's birth. The same can be said of state tort compensation. The language of Article 26 of the 1972 Constitution was preserved verbatim in the 1980 and 1987 Constitutions.[107] Does this mean that the reasoning of the Supreme Court in 1971 came to be viewed as less reasonable or desirable? It is a mind-boggling question, especially considering that those justices who struck down the law had to pay, as will be seen in Chapter 4, a dear price for their action.

The political atmosphere rapidly turned rigid. The relationship between the judiciary and the government had already been on a rocky course. In the early summer of 1971, the courts handed out a number of acquittals in politically sensitive cases. On June 29, two days before President Park's inauguration, the Seoul Criminal District Court freed ten students of Seoul National University who had staged a rally inside the opposition New Democratic Party building, urging a boycott of the May 25 National Assembly general election.[108] The government had reportedly asked the court to delay its decision until after the president's inauguration ceremony. The president was not amused. Chief Justice of the Supreme Court Min Pok-Ki (1913–2007) later recalled that he received an angry phone call from him.[109] On July 16, the same district court acquitted three defendants who had been charged with the Anticommunist Act violation for writing and publishing an article in the magazine *Tari*.[110] On July 30, the court rendered a suspended sentence to the Korea University students arrested for participating in an antigovernment demonstration. The Supreme Court heard on July 6 a case involving the magazine *Ssial ŭi sori*, published by the prominent dissident Quaker leader Ham Sŏk-Hŏn. The minister of culture and communication had rescinded the publication registration of

been amply pointed out, which scholars regard as a specimen of poor drafting. See Jongcheol Kim, "Some Problems with the Korean Constitutional Adjudication System," *Journal of Korean Law* 1 (2001), 17–36.

107 Constitution (1980), Art. 28; Constitution (1987), Art. 29.

108 *Tong-A Ilbo*, June 29, 1971.

109 *Tong-A Ilbo*, February 26, 1982. See also Min Pok-Ki, Na ŭi pŏpkwan sijŏl, February 22 and March 1, 1982.

110 *Tong-A Ilbo*, July 16, 1971.

Ham's monthly journal on the grounds that a particular issue had been printed at a facility different from the one indicated in the registration. The Seoul Appeals Court ruled in favor of the journal, and the Supreme Court dismissed the government's appeal.[111] These decisions were sufficient to fuel the tension already brewing between judges and prosecutors.

Judges versus Prosecutors

It was no secret: judges did not like prosecutors and prosecutors did not like judges. This may sound curious because they formed the two elite pillars of Korea's legal system. They passed the same judicial examination and received training together at the judicial school. Despite the shared backgrounds and social status, however, judges and prosecutors were nurtured respectively in a very different institutional culture and hierarchy through their career paths.

As in typical civil law jurisdictions, the Prosecutor's Office in Korea is not part of the judiciary but part of the government bureaucracy.[112] In general, political patronage was more pronounced with prosecutors than judges, which meant the former group could be more vulnerable to outside influence. Conventional wisdom had it that a prosecutor was expected to follow instructions of his superior against his professional judgment, especially in a politically sensitive situation. The culture of hierarchical command may have been a reflection of narrower career opportunities outside office. As seen in the previous chapters, a common career pattern among judges and prosecutors was to serve in office for several years to accumulate experience and then resign from the post to go into more lucrative private practices. The availability of this option was one of the reasons that some judges, particularly lower court judges, were often able to exhibit defiant spirit against government intervention and pressure. The prospects for a prosperous law business after leaving office were more limited for prosecutors than judges, mainly due to the public perception that they lacked expertise in civil law and had fewer connections.

[111] S. Ct., 71Nu62, July 6, 1971. See *Hŏnpŏp Chaep'anso 20 nyŏn sa*, 97; Yi Hŏn-Hwan, "Chŏngch'i kwajŏng," 156–160; Choi, "Law and Social Change," 231–232.

[112] Choi, "Law and Social Change," 564–567.

While in office, however, prosecutors exercised formidable authority, wielding the power to investigate and decide what charges to bring and whether to pursue the case at all. An arrest or a search and seizure by the police was conducted under the direction of the prosecutor. As the government took an increasingly coercive approach in criminal matters, especially in political cases, judges had much to complain about regarding the prosecutors' interference with the judicial process, which they decried as bordering on impudence.[113] The unprecedented drama of a massive strike by judges in 1971 (known as *sabŏp p'adong*) unfolded in this background of complex and seemingly perennial animosity between judges and prosecutors.

Judicial Strike

On July 28, 1971, barely a month after the Supreme Court rendered the monumental decision, the media flashed breaking news that prosecutors had requested arrest warrants for sitting judges on corruption charges. The prosecutors claimed that two judges of the Seoul Criminal District Court, Yi Pŏmnyŏl and Ch'oe Kong-Ung, took bribes from the defense counsel during a trip to Cheju Island to conduct witness examination in a National Security Act case. They were accused of receiving free transportation, lodging, and entertainment. It was a long-accepted practice that attorneys requesting an on-site witness examination paid some or all of the travel expenses of the judges, because the courts did not have sufficient budget for job-related travels and business allowances. The prosecutors' action was thus anything but ordinary. Soon it surfaced that they had assigned secret investigators to follow the judges to build evidence. The press was fed with supposedly scandalous and salacious details of their sojourn on the island.[114] The prosecutors also tried to sway public opinion by stressing that bribery occurred in a case involving a security law violation.

Many in legal circles viewed the incident as a personal vendetta by the prosecutors, bent on destroying the careers of the two judges. Some saw an attempt by the government to intimidate all judges. The two

113 Sohn, *Authoritarianism and Opposition*, 36.

114 Choi, "Law and Social Change," 229; Yoon, *Law and Political Authority*, 218–223.

targeted judges sat in a collegiate panel that had recently handed out numerous acquittals in Anticommunist Act cases. This particular bench rendered nineteen not-guilty verdicts in political cases during the previous six months alone.[115] It turned out that the prosecutor who filed for the judges' arrest warrants was the one in charge of a case on which the same two judges were scheduled to deliver a ruling the following day. To be sure, prosecutors had their own list of gripes. They claimed that judges turned down arrest warrant requests too frequently and were overly lenient to the accused, acquitting them on unreasonable grounds. If the prosecution's aim was to humiliate the hapless judges and tarnish the court's image with bribery charges, however, it backfired, as public opinion turned in favor of the judges.

This incident quickly escalated into a major political crisis. On July 29, judges of the Seoul Criminal District Court submitted their resignations en masse in protest.[116] The next day, forty-four judges at the Seoul Civil District Court tendered resignations, followed by those at the Seoul Family Court, the Taegu Civil and Criminal District Courts, and the Ch'ŏngju District Court.[117] Thirteen judges at the Seoul Appeals Court handed in resignations as well. Altogether, over one hundred judges walked out. This created a spectacle of judges on strike, the first of its kind in Korean history. The judges viewed the prosecutors' actions as nothing less than a declaration of war against them. If they gave in this time, judges told themselves, they would never be able to stop prosecutorial bullying and judicial independence would be lost forever.

Statistics on arrest warrants may shed some light on the tension percolating between judges and prosecutors in these years. Table 3.1 shows the arrest warrants data between 1965 and 1994. The warrant issuance rate showed a gradual decline from 1967 before it went up from 1975. This dip may have frustrated the prosecutors. Yet, close-up numbers for the months leading to the showdown in 1971 show that the issuance rate was actually high: between January and August, the prosecution requested arrest warrants for 71,231 persons, of which warrants were issued for 65,769 persons (92.3 percent).[118] Of those, 46,638 persons (70.9 percent) were prosecuted. The relatively low prosecution rate – that is, high numbers of the

[115] *Tong-A Ilbo*, July 29, 1971.
[116] Ibid.
[117] *Tong-A Ilbo*, July 31, 1971.
[118] *Tong-A Ilbo*, November 9, 1971.

Table 3.1 ***Arrest Warrants, 1965–1994***

	Arrest Warrants Applied	Arrest Warrants Issued	Issuance Rate	Prosecuted	Prosecution Rate
1965	103,780	97,943	94.4%	53,887	55.0%
1966	94,261	88,536	93.9%	52,219	59.0%
1967	100,666	86,711	86.1%	52,934	61.0%
1968	116,580	99,898	85.7%	60,791	60.9%
1969	125,450	106,733	85.1%	67,066	62.8%
1970	123,917	105,068	84.8%	68,442	65.1%
1971	123,250	104,986	85.2%	75,247	71.7%
1972	142,982	122,398	85.6%	92,501	75.6%
1973	142,172	112,225	78.9%	86,654	77.2%
1974	147,918	109,678	74.1%	84,679	77.2%
1975	139,767	130,432	93.3%	99,843	76.5%
1976	143,325	131,811	92.0%	97,070	73.6%
1977	126,239	114,616	90.8%	82,643	72.1%
1978	114,222	103,141	90.3%	73,065	70.8%
1979	114,102	103,010	90.3%	74,454	72.3%
1980	128,765	116,637	90.6%	82,304	70.6%
1981	125,051	115,600	92.4%	81,373	70.4%
1982	131,819	121,476	92.2%	82,808	68.2%
1983	124,774	115,660	92.7%	82,023	70.9%
1984	122,013	113,921	93.4%	81,527	71.6%
1985	119,569	112,039	93.7%	82,569	73.7%
1986	125,196	116,763	93.3%	86,631	74.2%
1987	121,716	113,075	92.9%	86,245	76.3%
1988	128,097	118,516	92.5%	91,362	77.1%
1989	135,584	124,150	91.6%	96,032	77.4%
1990	146,458	134,553	91.9%	103,810	77.2%
1991	142,971	132,448	92.6%	103,582	78.2%
1992	138,223	129,396	93.6%	101,902	78.8%
1993	158,109	148,647	94.0%	118,695	79.9%
1994	145,899	135,723	93.0%	104,083	76.7%

Sources: *T'onggye yŏnbo* (1974), 60; *Sabŏp yŏngam* (1976), 170; *Sabŏp yŏngam* (1985), 381; *Sabŏp yŏngam* (1990), 509; *Sabŏp yŏngam* (1995), 626.

prosecution's decision not to indict those who had been detained – could be viewed as evidence that the state held the accused's rights in low regard.

Under the 1962 Constitution, the accused had the right to request review of the legality of confinement before a judge.[119] The criminal procedure provided instruments analogous to a common law writ of *habeas corpus* proceedings.[120] During the eight-month period from January 1971, 7,801 persons in custody asked for release from detention; among them, 3,101 persons (43 percent) were released by the court order.[121] Acquittals after court trials of the first and second instance during that period numbered 487 cases.[122] The number of acquittals had been consistently on the rise, from 267 in 1968 to 698 in 1969 and 903 in 1970.[123] Most acquittals were due to insufficient evidence and misinterpretation of law.[124] The courts often threw out confessions produced by the prosecution on the grounds that they were extracted illegally by force.

Overall, these numbers were not good news for the prosecutors. In January 1970, a high-ranking official in the Supreme Prosecutor's Office sent out instructions to the police and prosecutors that they take caution before requesting arrest warrants and initiating prosecution.[125] For individual prosecutors, the high acquittal rate could jeopardize their promotion prospects. It was known that the prosecutor's office maintained and posted an internal list on which were recorded the names of those who suffered more than six acquittals the previous year.[126] Judges complained that desperate prosecutors alternated solicitation and intimidation tactics. The standoff between judges and prosecutors in late July was a blowup of a deep-seated, simmering distrust between them.

On July 30, judges at the Seoul Criminal and Civil District Courts issued a manifesto, in which they outlined the patterns of prosecutorial behaviors infringing judicial autonomy.[127] This document, titled "Recommendations for the Protection of Judges' Rights," enumerated

[119] Constitution (1962), Art. 10 (5).
[120] Criminal Procedure, art. 201 (4) to (6).
[121] *Tong-A Ilbo*, November 9, 1971.
[122] Ibid.
[123] *Tong-A Ilbo*, July 29, 1971.
[124] *Tong-A Ilbo*, November 9, 1971.
[125] *Tong-A Ilbo*, January 13, 1970; *Kyŏnghyang Sinmun*, January 13, 1970.
[126] Choi, "Law and Social Change," 683.
[127] Yi Hŏn-Hwan, "Chŏngch'i kwajŏng," 163.

several pointed complaints: (1) when judges rejected prosecutors' requests for warrants or issued rulings unfavorable to the government, especially in cases relating to the Anticommunist Act or the National Security Act, the prosecutors insinuated that the judges were communist sympathizers; (2) prosecutors often inflicted psychological pressure on judges stating that the executive branch had much interest in the outcome of the cases and saying that their own life or death depended on the judges' decisions; they often asked judges to inform them in advance how they would rule; some prosecutors even put a wiretap in the judicial conference room; (3) prosecutors publicly criticized judges for acquitting defendants in criminal cases, claiming that the trials were not properly conducted; some judges suffered serious privacy violations, with government detectives investigating their personal backgrounds, bank accounts, and other private matters, in an apparent effort to turn up dirt on them; (4) some judges had their telephones bugged and were subjected to surveillance in a scheme to entrap them; (5) prosecutors frequently dropped by a judge's chambers to demand arrest warrants in person, causing undue pressure; and (6) prosecutors treated judges as if they were the accused, without hesitating to insult and intimidate them. These were wide-ranging allegations and hefty grievances by the judges, to say the least.[128] The Korean Bar Association (Taehan Pyŏnhosa Hyŏphoe) issued a statement in support of the judges, calling the alleged corruption case a "well-planned sting operation by the prosecution to destroy judicial independence."[129]

On August 1, the justice minister informed the chief justice of the Supreme Court that he had been instructed by President Park to drop the case against the two judges. The minister asked the judges to go back to work but he still rejected the demand that the prosecutors who started all this be disciplined. After frantic behind-the-scenes negotiations by the court and government leaders, the judges eventually withdrew their resignations and returned to work. It was an anticlimactic denouement. The general consensus was that the strike was a fiasco with no gains for the judiciary. Having risen up for the cause of judicial independence, judges achieved little. Chief Justice Min Pok-Ki, who headed the Supreme Court from 1968 through 1978, was criticized for his overly accommodating posture to the administration, but in all

[128] The full text is in *Tong-A Ilbo*, July 31, 1971.
[129] *Pŏpcho 50 nyŏn yasa*, 15–16.

fairness his options were limited. He later recalled that his repeated requests for a meeting with the president were rebuffed, likely due to obstructions by the Justice Ministry.[130]

After the ill-fated strike, the judiciary was visibly shaken. Judges seemed more disillusioned than ever. In August 1971, when the walkout was going on, a newspaper printed an article under the headline "The Judiciary Is Tired." It summed up the atmosphere of pervasive defeatism in the courts. Exhausting and demeaning altercations with prosecutors resulted in low spirits of judges and a dim view of their profession.[131] The press ran articles that Korean judges endured the highest workload in the world in dismal work conditions. Excessive work, exacerbated by low salary, resulted in a constant judicial personnel shortage.[132] It was reported that at the end of July 1971 there were fifty-six judgeships vacant out of 471 posts.[133] Tables 3.2 and 3.3 provide a breakdown of an individual judge's workload at different court levels during the twenty-year period from 1965 to 1984 and from 1985 to 2004. Compared with the rapid increase in litigation cases, the expansion of judicial posts was minimal, especially during the first two decades.[134]

The shortage of judges was in part the judiciary's own choosing. Legal professionals as a whole resisted raising the number of slots for successful applicants of the judicial examination in order to maintain the high quality of judicial personnel and also the prestige of the profession. The scarcity of judges may have achieved those goals in part but it did not help judicial administration as the number of vacancies grew.[135] As noted, judges tended to leave office to practice as private attorneys. Some stepped down when they were passed over in promotion or transferred to an undesirable location against their wishes. In many cases they left for financial reasons. Judicial salaries were never high enough to keep them in office for long when they had the option of private law practice which tended

130 *Tong-A Ilbo*, February 26, 1982.

131 *Kyŏnghyang Sinmun*, August 27, 1971. The Seoul Criminal District Court judges bemoaned: "None of our demands was accepted; we are deeply disappointed with the result." Ibid.

132 *Kyŏnghyang Sinmun*, August 6, 1971.

133 Ibid.; *Chosŏn Ilbo*, August 26, 1971. For judicial vacancies between 1975 and 1979, see Table 6.1 on p. 224.

134 For the increase in civil litigation, see Table 5.4 on p. 193.

135 *Chosŏn Ilbo*, November 29, 1979 (editorial).

Table 3.2 *Judicial Workload, 1965–1984*

Supreme Court			Trials			Nontrial Cases		
Year	Number of Judges	Case Load per Judge	Civil and Family	Admin.*	Criminal	Civil	Family	Misc.**
1965	13	448.2	211.9	16.7	113.0	97.7	1.5	7.3
1966	12	543.7	231.2	17.6	169.9	111.7	1.2	12.2
1967	12	582.3	254.1	40.2	158.8	118.4	0.8	10.2
1968	13	557.7	205.5	22.4	181.9	136.8	1.5	9.6
1969	15	487.4	167.0	12.7	205.3	95.3	1.4	5.6
1970	15	530.4	214.6	16.5	216.9	67.4	1.1	13.8
1971	15	523.1	202.0	21.6	200.3	86.4	1.5	11.3
1972	15	567.9	185.7	20.3	230.1	117.8	3.0	10.9
1973	13	633.8	161.8	26.7	329.4	92.5	1.6	21.8
1974	13	656.4	179.6	23.4	378.2	52.4	1.7	21.2
1975	16	493.6	150.9	18.7	270.8	38.4	1.5	13.2
1976	16	608.0	195.9	22.9	328.1	41.3	2.4	17.4
1977	16	540.2	162.1	24.1	301.9	35.9	3.1	13.1
1978	16	479.2	164.0	32.7	243.6	26.9	2.7	9.3
1979	15	500.3	163.1	38.2	255.7	32.3	2.0	9.0
1980	13	713.5	264.5	57.6	318.0	60.0	4.2	9.3
1981	12	698.1	127.5	43.7	343.7	167.4	4.6	11.3
1982	13	737.2	79.9	50.4	354.2	236.8	4.8	11.2
1983	13	769.0	74.1	65.7	355.0	258.5	5.1	10.6
1984	13	768.9	74.7	72.0	319.3	284.9	5.5	12.4

Appeals Court			Trials			Nontrial Cases		
Year	Number of Judges	Case Load per Judge	Civil and Family	Admin.*	Criminal	Civil	Family	Misc.**
1965	42	190.4	105.0	12.6	28.0	12.3	4.5	28.0
1966	53	171.5	101.9	9.2	23.4	9.8	4.7	22.9
1967	54	429.5	82.7	18.2	30.9	264.0	4.5	29.2
1968	56	287.0	75.0	12.2	38.1	133.1	5.2	23.4
1969	55	675.3	91.7	8.5	50.0	487.2	4.1	31.7
1970	66	325.3	74.7	10.1	48.9	100.8	21.0	20.9
1971	60	201.6	78.1	12.1	64.7	11.8	9.6	25.3
1972	64	499.3	109.4	13.5	80.5	286.7	18.5	29.0
1973	60	314.7	73.0	10.4	76.3	124.7	20.3	10.0
1974	60	354.6	80.3	9.1	65.9	173.9	20.6	4.9
1975	65	346.7	78.9	10.0	68.3	165.1	20.9	4.5
1976	68	428.8	82.9	174.4	97.6	186.1	37.1	8.4
1977	75	329.8	64.4	12.5	80.9	134.1	32.7	4.3
1978	75	285.1	71.6	12.9	61.2	103.2	32.2	4.1

Table 3.2 (*cont.*)

Appeals Court			Trials			Nontrial Cases		
Year	Number of Judges	Case Load per Judge	Civil and Family	Admin.*	Criminal	Civil	Family	Misc.**
1979	74	323.8	84.1	14.8	67.0	115.5	38.0	4.5
1980	78	394.2	93.6	15.6	78.7	164.6	37.8	3.9
1981	84	405.8	85.6	13.4	122.9	135.9	40.8	7.3
1982	96	376.3	82.2	16.5	114.6	110.9	39.0	13.1
1983	101	332.6	81.2	17.4	97.2	88.1	36.6	12.1
1984	111	303.6	68.0	17.0	88.8	80.7	37.2	11.9

District Court			Trials			Nontrial Cases		
Year	Number of Judges	Case Load per Judge	Civil and Family	Admin.*	Criminal	Civil	Family	Misc.**
1965	301	5,676.2	228.5		250.2	967.2		4,229.9
1966	306	5,064.1	208.2		249.9	973.7		3,632.8
1967	305	5,297.2	204.3		258.3	1,402.9		3,431.5
1968	311	6,322.5	203.9		301.7	1,314.0		4,342.3
1969	305	6,910.1	206.5		351.6	1,683.6		4,746.5
1970	309	5,935.4	208.6		365.0	1,075.5		4,286.5
1971	311	5,335.5	222.9		365.3	1,098.4		3,648.9
1972	335	6,892.2	217.7		364.9	1,152.1		5,157.5
1973	365	5,648.0	250.1		391.0	1,097.4	36.5	3,873.0
1974	387	3,815.3	255.0		330.6	953.2	40.1	2,236.4
1975	396	4,210.3	261.6		372.7	865.8	49.4	2,660.3
1976	398	5,081.3	291.0		401.3	846.3	57.9	3,484.8
1977	405	4,124.4	278.1		320.5	803.5	48.5	2,673.8
1978	413	3,995.1	215.1		283.4	738.5	48.8	2,439.0
1979	413	4,194.0	234.0		290.1	817.5	49.1	2,803.3
1980	445	4,788.0	317.0		297.8	1,093.9	59.2	3,020.1
1981	442	5,111.4	472.6		296.9	1,472.6	77.4	2,767.5
1982	463	5,186.7	489.7		284.7	1,585.5	70.8	2,756.0
1983	500	4,773.5	475.2		259.9	1,643.4	77.7	2,330.4
1984	510	4,961.8	580.7		259.5	1,968.8	77.0	2,072.2

Notes: Case load numbers are rounded.
* Administrative; includes patent and election cases.
** Includes juvenile protection, family mediation, summary order, summary trial, warrant, and other miscellaneous criminal matters.
Sources: *T'onggye yŏnbo* (1974), 7; *Sabŏp yŏngam* (1985), 397.

Table 3.3 *Judicial Workload, 1985–2004*

Supreme Court			Trials			Nontrial Cases		
Year	Number of Judges	Case Load per Judge	Civil and Family	Admin.*	Criminal	Civil	Family	Misc.**
1985	12	846.3	83.5	96.1	316.4	335.8	3.2	11.2
1986	13	827.4	92.8	85.8	283.5	347.5	5.9	12.0
1987	13	884.8	130.0	107.1	258.2	375.4	3.2	10.9
1988	13	891.0	128.3	109.6	249.8	386.2	3.5	13.6
1989	13	816.5	98.9	83.0	243.9	370.7	4.3	15.7
1990	13	978.1	229.8	101.9	308.3	318.4	4.9	14.9
1991	13	932.8	375.9	121.8	339.4	71.4	7.1	17.2
1992	13	1,086.3	450.2	176.7	326.0	107.3	10.6	15.8
1993	13	1,264.2	497.8	206.9	352.3	173.5	12.8	20.9
1994	13	1,219.3	496.1	145.6	327.8	217.1	11.9	20.8
1995	13	1,102.3	453.9	164.2	303.8	147.9	11.2	21.2
1996	13	1,209.7	452.8	177.1	323.0	213.2	14.8	28.8
1997	13	1,283.5	469.7	196.1	314.0	262.0	14.0	27.1
1998	13	1,503.5	516.3	180.5	425.8	332.8	13.9	34.2
1999	13	1,985.0	588.9	122.2	532.7	664.9	14.4	61.9
2000	13	2,003.7	586.3	116.5	568.0	650.0	14.1	68.9
2001	13	1,459.6	679.8	116.2	662.5	569.7	14.8	78.6
2002	13	1,908.1	602.2	126.1	702.6	381.9	19.8	75.4
2003	13	1,755.9	571.9	144.1	768.7	172.5	14.6	84.3
2004	13	1,802.9	585.8	146.0	839.8	123.0	18.9	89.5

Appeals Court			Trials			Nontrial Cases		
Year	Number of Judges	Case Load per Judge	Civil and Family	Admin.*	Criminal	Civil	Family	Misc.**
1985	118	314.6	65.3	16.2	83.7	93.3	47.0	9.1
1986	124	307.3	65.3	17.1	80.0	89.7	44.7	10.5
1987	138	319.5	65.9	15.3	72.3	115.4	38.5	12.1
1988	143	310.3	56.8	12.1	64.5	128.4	37.2	11.3
1989	148	296.8	57.1	16.0	70.9	90.0	47.0	15.8
1990	151	342.7	63.6	20.6	79.2	114.9	50.2	14.2
1991	151	395.9	74.0	26.2	90.1	122.5	61.9	21.2
1992	164	408.9	72.6	30.6	76.8	134.9	74.4	19.5
1993	163	399.4	57.3	33.4	85.7	134.8	68.4	19.6
1994	166	190.4	51.4	38.2	71.4	9.8	14.2	5.5
1995	172	185.6	54.7	38.6	58.0	10.5	18.3	5.5
1996	174	203.1	56.7	48.2	51.5	15.8	25.4	5.5
1997	183	220.0	60.9	52.7	52.1	21.7	28.7	4.1
1998	180	184.2	65.1	19.7	58.6	23.5	10.9	6.3

Table 3.3 (*cont.*)

Appeals Court			Trials			Nontrial Cases		
Year	Number of Judges	Case Load per Judge	Civil and Family	Admin.*	Criminal	Civil	Family	Misc.**
1999	162	203.6	69.0	23.1	68.4	25.8	7.3	9.9
2000	162	191.4	68.2	22.4	64.9	22.2	4.2	8.5
2001	172	159.6	76.0	23.8	56.0	16.7	3.9	9.1
2002	189	169.6	67.8	22.8	53.9	14.7	3.4	7.1
2003	196	166.7	72.8	21.7	47.9	15.4	3.3	5.6
2004	199	175.7	77.4	24.6	47.5	16.0	3.7	6.4

District Court			Trials			Nontrial Cases		
Year	Number of Judges	Case Load per Judge	Civil and Family	Admin*	Criminal	Civil	Family	Misc.**
1985	583	4,459.6	582.2		226.9	1,900.0	76.1	1,673.9
1986	643	4,312.2	564.1		221.4	1,906.1	75.6	1,544.9
1987	655	4,035.9	577.6		213.5	1,808.5	76.1	1,360.2
1988	701	3,670.6	475.7		205.3	1,523.3	69.9	1,396.4
1989	748	3,674.8	420.7		207.7	1,304.3	65.7	1,676.4
1990	782	3,819.0	412.4		217.7	1,290.0	63.7	1,835.3
1991	802	4,222.5	439.9		220.3	1,399.7	58.7	2,103.9
1992	832	4,059.5	492.9		210.6	1,476.2	60.2	1,819.6
1993	840	4,576.8	528.7		234.7	1,519.3	67.1	2,227.1
1994	885	4,459.0	549.5		199.3	1,317.3	36.6	2,356.3
1995	921	4,672.7	594.2		214.7	1,634.9	33.8	2,150.8
1996	985	4,437.6	630.0		211.3	1,659.4	37.2	1,891.2
1997	1,047	5,071.9	675.9		203.7	1,888.4	40.2	2,254.1
1998	1,038	6,680.8	944.1	7.2	256.3	3,071.5	50.1	2,340.6
1999	1,043	5,725.6	878.5	8.5	235.4	2,462.4	47.4	2,082.8
2000	1,091	4,563.1	736.4	8.5	219.4	1,790.9	43.3	1,756.5
2001	1,148	3,108.3	804.5	10.3	218.9	1,625.8	49.1	2,099.5
2002	1,229	4,613.5	885.6	9.1	211.9	1,747.5	47.8	1,708.3
2003	1,340	4,775.6	912.3	8.5	197.7	2,484.9	47.3	1,122.7
2004	1,449	4,291.1	867.8	8.5	201.2	2,003.6	43.1	1,165.7

Notes: Case load numbers are rounded.
* Administrative; includes patent and election cases.
** Includes juvenile protection, family mediation, summary order, summary trial, warrant, and other miscellaneous criminal matters.
Sources: *Sabŏp yŏngam* (1995), 642; *Sabŏp yŏngam* (2005), 685.

to be much more rewarding financially. A common saying was that judges took buses to work while attorneys rode in chauffeured sedans. Incentives for midcareer judges to remain in office were scant, exacerbating the situation for those who remained. Former Chief Justice Yi Yŏng-Sŏp once explained why he opposed increasing the number of those who passed the judicial examination: "The most important quality required of a judge is courage. If judges are worried about livelihood after retirement, they would not be able to render courageous decisions." In other words, the guarantee of secure postretirement private practice, with less competition, was viewed as essential to promoting integrity among judges and keeping them insulated from political and social pressures.[136]

The workload of the Supreme Court justices was notorious. The Court had introduced in 1965 the judicial researcher system, akin to the law clerk system in the United States. In Korea judicial researchers were incumbent judges, serving in that capacity for one or two years; from 1975 each justice was allowed two of them, selected from appeals court judges.[137] This system alleviated the work of the Supreme Court justices a little but in turn had the effect of aggravating the shortage of judges in the courtroom.

An interesting yet disturbing episode evidenced dismal judicial remuneration. In 1970, a couple of US soldiers stationed in Korea were charged with murder. The soldiers claimed that they could not expect impartial adjudication because Korean judges, receiving such meager wages, were likely tempted by bribery and corruption.[138] The Korean Justice Ministry was aghast at this "insult," but those Americans at least had a point about the reality of judges' salaries; they were certainly less accurate about judicial professionalism though, as corruption and malfeasance were virtually known in Korean courts.

[136] Yi Yŏng-Sŏp, "Sabŏp sihŏm chedo ŭi kaesŏn," *Kosigye*, 1987, cited in Ch'oe Chong-Ko, *Hanguk ŭi pŏmnyulga*, 543. Judges tried to keep their distance from the public. Most Supreme Court justices packed their lunches at home and ate in their offices instead of the court cafeteria or restaurants, in order to avoid encountering the parties of the cases they presided over. Ibid., 538.

[137] The revised Court Organization Act (1979). See *Yŏksa sogŭi sabŏppu*, 155–157.

[138] *Tong-A Ilbo*, November 5, 1970.

There is general consensus that judges in the first few decades of the republic bore a heavy burden but maintained professional competency and integrity and, overall, were held in high esteem.[139] Many bright young students aspired to a judicial career. The favorable reputation of judges – in contrast to politicians – can be ascribed to the fact that they strictly refrained from political activity and most kept their ideological beliefs private. Yet, judges' independence was fragile (and so remains today) when faced with politically-motivated assaults from prosecutors and the administration.

What was the president's role in the development surrounding the judicial strike? Many suspected that the prosecutors could not have been so brazen unless they had counted on backing from above. President Park had apparently been displeased with the judiciary, especially after the Supreme Court's constitutional decision in early summer. Signs were everywhere that the president was losing patience for what he saw as judicial recalcitrance. There is no evidence to link the president directly to the prosecutors' actions, but it is not difficult to speculate that they knew he would not stand by the judges in the showdown. During the strike, a rumor circulated that the president was ready to declare martial law if the judges refused to return to work. "Judging from President Park's personality," Chief Justice Min later recalled, "he could have easily declared martial law."[140] All in all, the Supreme Court did not want to aggravate the executive branch further without knowing what the president's reaction would be. The Court stuck to the course of abiding to the law. It can be seen as either a tactical or a cowering stance, depending on the viewer's perspective.

139 Low judicial salaries were legendary. In his retirement speech in 1957, the first Chief Justice Kim Pyŏng-Ro famously stated: "My greatest regret is that I demanded too much from judicial personnel. . . . I told them to carry on when they could not possibly make a living with their salaries. I told them that starving to death would be an honorable thing." Hong Sŏng-U, *Inkwŏn pyŏllon han sidae: Hong Sŏng-U pyŏnhosa ŭi chŭngŏn* [An Era of Human Rights Defense: Testimony of Attorney Hong Sŏng-U], ed. Han In-Sŏp (Seoul: Kyŏngin Munhwasa, 2011), 49. This anecdote captures the immense emphasis on judicial integrity and financial sacrifices demanded of judges. Meager salaries forced many judges to step down and open private practices. Hong said he did just that. Ibid., 48.

140 Min Pok-Ki, Na ŭi pŏpkwan sijŏl, March 8, 1982.

Return to Restraint

On January 18, 1972, the Supreme Court heard a challenge to a statute that it was not properly enacted in accordance with the National Assembly Act.[141] The law, National Referendum Act, had been passed surreptitiously by the ruling party in the wee hours of September 14, 1969, in the annex building of the National Assembly in the absence of opposition party members.[142] The plaintiffs claimed that the irregular legislative process violated the Constitution as well as the National Assembly Act. The Court rejected the argument, holding that the legislative process pertained to the National Assembly's prerogative of self-regulation and autonomy.[143] Whether the process was defective had to be decided by the legislature alone. As long as a law was passed, published, and put into effect by the National Assembly, the Court would not intervene to examine its procedural validity. For some scholars, this was a specimen of excessive judicial self-restraint; for them serious irregularity in the process of enactment of law should naturally become the subject of judicial review.[144]

Few doubted that this decision, officially grounded on the principle of the separation of powers, was aimed at preventing a potential constitutional melee. Political stakes were high. Constitutional challenge to the National Referendum Act was in reality a challenge to the validity of the constitutional amendment of 1969, rammed through the National Assembly the same morning, immediately before the passing of the Act. This was the amendment that allowed President Park to run for the third time. The 1969 Constitution was eventually approved by referendum on October 17, taking place in accordance with the National Referendum Act. If the Supreme Court had agreed to scrutinize the legislative process of the National Referendum Act, it would have opened the floodgate for contests to the constitutional amendment of 1969, forcing the judiciary to review the constitutionality of

141 S. Ct., 71To1845, January 18, 1972. See *Tong-A Ilbo*, January 18, 1972; *Kyŏnghyang Sinmun*, January 19, 1971; *Pŏmnyul Sinmun*, January 31, 1972.

142 *Kyŏnghyang Sinmun*, September 15, 1969.

143 S. Ct., 71To1845, January 18, 1972.

144 Kim Ch'ŏl-Su, "Hanguk ippŏp e taehan t'ongje" [Control of Legislation in Korea], *Seoul Taehakkyo pophak* 25 (1984), 146; Kim Ch'ŏl-Su, "T'ongch'i kujo," 113–117.

the Constitution that was currently in force.[145] Striking down the Act would have cast doubt on the legitimacy of the Constitution and, ultimately, the sitting government of President Park. Faced with these colossal implications, the Supreme Court refused to get entangled in politics. Was this an about-face of the Court, having courageously withstood the government six months earlier? The preceding pages in this chapter have suggested that there was no dramatic turnabout, no fundamental change in direction in jurisprudence.

This does not mean downplaying the significance of the unconstitutionality decision in 1971. A contemporary newspaper applauded the State Tort Claims Act decision as "The Judiciary's Self-Help Declaration of Independence."[146] Yet, as the constitutional scholar Kim Ch'ŏl-Su observed, "after the decision the Court returned to judicial restraint."[147] The highest court continued to view its tasks in terms of applying predetermined norms to the facts and guaranteeing legal stability. Its deference to the legislature remained largely unchanged.[148] The presumption of the constitutionality of the law, deeply entrenched in Korean jurisprudential tradition, persisted: a statute should be interpreted, as much as possible, so as not to be in conflict with the constitution, and an unconstitutional legislative intention should not be imputed to a statute unless there was clear evidence. The Court believed that striking down questionable laws of high political implications was not always an optimal solution and that it would be better to sidestep a constitutional crisis if the laws could be interpreted in ways to avoid compromising individual rights guaranteed in the Constitution. Declining to declare a statute's unconstitutionality did not necessary point to supporting them or allowing the government to have its way.

One cannot deny, however, that the judiciary, by adhering to a position of obviating serious formal engagement with constitutional issues, sidelined itself, in particular when the executive branch pushed

[145] The question of the court conducting review of a constitutional amendment is discussed in Chapter 8.

[146] *Tong-A Ilbo*, June 23, 1971.

[147] Kim Ch'ŏl-Su, "Hanguk ippŏp e taehan t'ongje," 146.

[148] Kim Ch'ŏl-Su, *Hŏnpŏphak kaeron* [An Introduction to the study of the Constitution] (Seoul: Pŏmmunsa, 1973), 653–655; Kim Ch'ŏl-Su, *Hanguk hŏnpŏp sa* [Korean Constitutional History] (Seoul: Seoul Taehakkyo Ch'ulp'anbu, 1988), 120–125.

through illiberal policies cloaked with constitutional legitimacy. Soon, institutional limits placed by political regimes caused unprecedented predicaments for judges. The judicial strategy of mitigating objectionable results of the laws through a narrow, strict statutory interpretation seemed no longer a viable option. The next chapter turns to the advent of the 1972 Constitution.

4 *The Yusin Era, 1972–1980 (1): The Laws*

The constitutional revision in 1969 brought few changes to the existing Constitution (amended in 1962) other than allowing a third presidential term. The resulting presidential election in April 1971 was conducted in a reasonably honest manner. Yet Park Chung Hee's new term encountered massive protests almost from the beginning. The political atmosphere quickly degenerated. In December, President Park declared a state of national emergency, citing rising tensions between North and South Korea. This granted the president wide-ranging powers in domestic, diplomatic, and defense matters. It turned out to be a prelude to the political upheaval that unfolded the following year. In October 1972, martial law was proclaimed and the National Assembly dissolved. A new constitution was hastily drafted and approved in a national referendum on November 21. This "Yusin" Constitution, which took effect on December 27, upended Korea's political order – it practically dismantled checks and balances. The legislature was packed by members of the ruling party, and the judiciary lost constitutional review power. The president held complete control over state affairs.

Normally, questions of constitutionality arise when rights promised in a constitution are abridged in the law or when institutions set up by a constitution fail to operate within its constraints. In most cases, the problem is not the constitutional rules themselves but the lack of compliance with them. Most authoritarian regimes feature a facade, or sham, constitution, replete with provisions guaranteeing the protection of human rights, only to be ignored by public officials.[1] The state's violation of fundamental rights usually occurs illegally and summarily,

[1] David S. Law and Mila Versteeg, "Constitutional Variation among Strains of Authoritarianism," in Ginsburg and Simpser (eds.), *Constitutions in Authoritarian Regimes*, 165–195.

departing from the constitutional language. For example, freedom of assembly and freedom of speech are regularly guaranteed, but citizens are punished and imprisoned when they transgress unwritten limits.[2] In constitutional authoritarianism, in contrast, a constitution serves as a practical working principle of government power monopolized by the regime rather than as a restatement of the rights of the citizens, and, further, it features explicit provisions which were inserted for specific political reasons of limiting fundamental rights and sanctioning illiberal laws and measures. In this case, the constitution, not its violation, becomes the heart of the problem.

With the Yusin Constitution, it was the text itself that was troublesome. It was a genuine constitutional document into which elaborate limitations of basic rights were written. Some comparisons with contemporary states and their leaders in Asia may be helpful. It has been argued that President Park and President Ferdinand Marcos (1917–1989) of the Philippines took cues from each other. Marcos, whose final term was to end in 1973, imposed martial law in September 1972.[3] Prime Minister Lee Kuan Yew (1923–2015), who ruled Singapore for more than three decades, also provides an interesting reference point.[4] Each of these politicians apparently believed that he was indispensable – or infallible – in his nation. Still, there may be certain differences. For one, Park was much more reticent in rationalizing the innate virtue of the Yusin system. While he was convinced of the urgency of his policies, Park did not, unlike his Southeast Asian counterparts, tout the merit of paternalistic authoritarianism, even a constitutional one. Park never denied the ideal of Western liberal democracy and was not oblivious of the fact that the 1972 Constitution compromised the core democratic values so prominently enshrined in the 1962 Constitution under which his rule had begun.

2 Giovanni Sartori, "Constitutionalism: A Preliminary Discussions," *American Political Science Review* 56 (1962), 861.
3 Ferdinand Marcos, president of the Philippines from 1965 to 1986, styled his regime "constitutional authoritarianism." Ferdinand E. Marcos, *Notes on the New Society of the Philippines* (Manila: National Media Production Center, 1973). See Carolina G. Hernandez, "Constitutional Authoritarianism and the Prospects of Democracy in the Philippines," *Journal of International Affairs* 38 (1985), 243–258.
4 Lee paid a state visit to Korea in October 1979, a few days before Park's assassination.

To be sure, there were plenty of legitimizing talks of the new system. But Park's exhortation of "Korean-style democracy" had a ring of apologia. Without questioning the goal of liberal democracy, he tried to tell the citizens that the less-than-liberal measures he was enforcing were regrettable but necessary to overcome the obstacles and threats on the way. This may be a testimony to the Korean populace's latent democratic vitality, which even a would-be autocrat could not ignore outright. Park's version of constitutional authoritarianism, foremost in pursuit of economic prosperity, was suffused with hues of excuse rather than unabashed vindication of power. In the process, nonetheless, the president exercised unfettered power and steamrolled opponents.

This chapter examines the constitutional and legal changes brought on under the Yusin system and their impact on the judiciary. One of the most conspicuous and controversial features of the new Constitution was that the president could suspend individual rights by decree. Article 53 of the Constitution granted the president power to issue emergency measures, and between 1974 and 1979 President Park imposed a total of nine such decrees. These executive orders, constitutionally excluded from judicial review, served as the main instrument for the government in suppressing political opposition and sidelining the judiciary. Various other constitutional maneuvers legitimized the president's draconian policies and bolstered his powers. The fact that the politically motivated laws were endowed with constitutional mandates and placed beyond the reach of judicial scrutiny threatened fundamental rights of citizens.

The 1972 Constitution

Park Chung Hee's win in his bid for a third presidential term and his success in overhauling the Constitution were in no small part helped by deep uneasiness among the people over the rapidly evolving situations surrounding the Korean peninsula. A series of international affairs sent shock waves. US President Richard Nixon's Guam Doctrine in 1969 presaged a reduced presence of the United States in Asia, and the prospect of the cutback of the US military in the peninsula created a genuine sense of crisis among Korean people. The withdrawal of some 20,000 military personnel of the US Seventh Division had been completed by March 1971.[5] The United States–China rapprochement from 1971 deepened doubt about American commitment to defending Korea. Park had agreed to deploy Korean troops to Vietnam in part to persuade the United States to maintain its pledge to protect Korea. A panic over possible isolation on the world stage set in across the country.

Park's policies revolved around two central goals: national security and economic prosperity. Declaring martial law in October 1972, Park emphasized the urgency of national self-sufficiency. It often happened, he observed, that under the name of détente "the interests of the Third World and of smaller countries were sacrificed to reduce tension among the major powers."[6] At this specific juncture, he was obliged to "undertake a reform that is best suited to our reality through extraordinary measures, rather than ordinary measures, so that we can actively pursue the dialogue between the South and the North and meet the rapidly changing geopolitical situations." In the same announcement, Park reiterated his commitment to economy. He promised that under martial law "the freedom of economic activities will be guaranteed" and that "in particular foreign investments will be further encouraged and protected."[7] This was when his economic policy, carried out following the two five-year plans for economic development (1962–1966; 1967–1971), was showing signs of success. Economic development, tied with national security, was the single most powerful driving force of Park's regime. On numerous occasions, Park affirmed that economy was his top priority. At the beginning of his military rule, he declared that "the most important task we are facing is industrial development to achieve economic reconstruction."[8] "Poverty opens the path for communism to infiltrate"; industrial advancement meant "winning the economic war" against the North. Ever pragmatic, he stressed that economic success was a precondition for democracy: "poverty, famine, and low income pose the most dangerous challenge

[5] Sohn, *Authoritarianism and Opposition*, 24–28.

[6] The President's Special Announcement, October 17, 1972, in *Park Chung Hee Taet'ongnyŏng yŏnsŏlmun chip* [Collection of Speeches by President Park Chung Hee] (Seoul: Taet'ongnyŏng Pisŏsil, 1973), vol. 4, 297–299.

[7] Ibid., 300–301.

[8] Park's New Year's Letter to Citizens, 1962, cited in Kang Chŏng-In, *Hanguk hyŏndae chŏngch'i sasang*, 245.

to the modern liberal democracy that our nation pursues."[9] He expressed his hope that "our economy, our freedom, and our democracy overflow to the North."[10]

The government policy directions were based on the familiar East Asian axiom of *puguk kangbyŏng* (enrich the economy, strengthen the military), harking back to Meiji Japan (*fukoku kyōhei*) and the last days of the Qing empire (*fùguó qiángbīng*). Japan served in many aspects as a model for President Park's vision for Korea. In the mid-1960s, declining economic aid from the United States convinced him to "reset" the relationship with Japan.[11] Tokyo agreed to provide Seoul with $300 million in grants and $200 million in loans in economic aid, a form of compensation (although not designated as such) for its occupation of Korea decades earlier. The bulk of the money went to construction projects such as building the Seoul–Pusan highway and Pohang Steel Company. Korea did not hesitate to seek technical imports from its former colonizer for industrial works like creating hydropower facilities. The Vietnam War was a boon for Korean economy. Just as the Korean War had stimulated development in postwar Japan, the Vietnam War brought a long-term economic benefit to Korea.[12] Park's national programs were far from irrational or unreasonable; the problem was, rather, that he seemed to believe that he alone, no one else, could carry them out and thus he needed to remain in power at all costs, against all opposition.

Park's third presidential term precipitated the country into a whirl of political turmoil. Student protests exploded. Park invoked the garrison decree on October 15, 1971. Soldiers were deployed at ten major university campuses across the country. The military subsequently arrested 1,889 students, jailing 119 and conscripting 177 into the army.[13] Korea had – still has – a universal conscription system, and whisking dissident students away to military service was not an uncommon government practice in the past.

On December 6, a state of national emergency (*Kukka pisang sat'ae*) was declared. On December 27, the National Assembly, at a session boycotted by opposition members, passed the Special Measures Act for

[9] Ibid., 293.
[10] The president's address, January 17, 1967, cited in ibid., 299.
[11] Chang, *Protest Dialectics*, 18–20.
[12] Charles K. Armstrong, "America's Korea, Korea's Vietnam," *Critical Asian Studies* 33 (2001), 527–539.
[13] Chang, *Protest Dialectics*, 64.

the State Preservation.[14] Its article 2 granted the president, retrospectively, power to declare a state of national emergency. The president was authorized, when necessary to cope with emergency conditions, to impose restrictions on the economy, curtail the freedom of the press, mobilize national human and material resources, prohibit outdoor assemblies and demonstrations, and restrict collective bargaining of workers. In normal times these powers could be exercised only under martial law. The enactment of the Special Measures Act aimed to grant a legal basis to the emergency issued earlier that month; its supplementary article specifically stated that "'the declaration of national emergency' issued on December 6, 1971, is regarded as having been issued by this law."[15] This was but one example of the Park government's scrupulous attention to legality.

The president was ready to turn the emergency into a permanency. On October 17, 1972, martial law was imposed and the National Assembly dissolved. The constitution was suspended. Three weeks earlier, President Marcos had declared martial law in the Philippines, and the fact that Washington did nothing may have emboldened Park. US observers reportedly viewed Park's moves as unjustifiable, but no actions were forthcoming.[16] Things unfolded rapidly. The Emergency State Council announced a draft constitution on October 27. Ten days earlier, the president had acknowledged the extraordinary nature of his actions and promised that the emergency would "suspend the force of some provisions of the Constitution for about two months."[17] As it turned out, the extraordinary and emergency measures would become the foundation of his rule for the next seven years. On November 21, the new constitution was approved in the national referendum by 91.5 percent of voters, with a 91.9 percent turnout. The referendum took place without glaring fraud or coercion, but one could still see the dangers of popular constitution-making through referendum in these numbers. There had been little discussion or campaigning, and public opinion was rarely elicited before the referendum.

[14] Kukka Powi e kwanhan T'ŭkpyŏl Ch'och'i Pŏp (Act No. 2312).
[15] Supplementary Provisions, art. 2.
[16] Don Oberdorfer and Robert Carlin, *The Two Koreas: A Contemporary History*, 3rd ed. (New York: Basic Books, 2014), 31–32.
[17] The President's Special Announcement, October 17, 1972.

Starting with the 1962 Constitution, each constitutional amendment had to be ratified by national referendum. The requirement of a plebiscite for constitutional change affirmed the idea that any limitation on the constitution needed the consent of the people, but this mechanism could be used to consolidate the populist president's power in the extreme. In the early twentieth century, Max Weber (1864–1920) denoted the rising tendency toward a plebiscitarian democracy featuring a powerful executive and a weakened legislature. Weber warned of a dictatorship in which rulers would claim authority through acclamation by the people, only to rule subsequently in disregard of the democratic process.[18] In the late twentieth century, experiences in the post-Soviet countries of changing the constitutional order through referendum seemed to attest to the perils in which charismatic politicians pushed through constitutions that concentrated power in their own hands.[19] The Korean case can be seen in this context.

Some telling examples are as follows. Article 1 of the 1972 Constitution read:

1. The Republic of Korea is a democratic republic.
2. The sovereignty of the Republic of Korea resides in the people, and the people exercise their sovereignty through their representatives or through referendum.

Compare that with the same Article in the Constitution of 1962 (and of 1969):

1. The Republic of Korea is a democratic republic.
2. The sovereignty of the Republic of Korea resides in the people, and all powers come from the people.

The clause "all powers come from the people" was Article 2 of the founding Constitution of 1948, merged into Article 1 in 1962. The change of the language in 1972 was a quintessential specimen of an attempt to devise the institutional framework of a populist democracy. The words "all powers come from the people" were restored in the 1980 and the 1987 Constitution. The latter's preamble

18 Max Weber, "Parliament and Government in a Reconstructed Germany" (1917), in *Max Weber, Economy and Society: An Outline of Interpretive Sociology*, vol. 2, 1451–1459.

19 William Partlett, "The Dangers of Constitution-Making," *Brooklyn Journal of International Law* 38 (2012), 193–238.

declared that the amendment had taken place "through national referendum following a resolution by the National Assembly."

In the Philippines, President Marcos argued that his constitutional "revolution" was legitimate because he governed in accordance with the spirit and letters of the constitutional text ratified by the sovereign will which embodied constituent power. When the validity of the 1973 Constitution was challenged, the Philippine Supreme Court ruled that, while its ratification process was not in substantial compliance with the 1935 Constitution, the new constitutional document was still valid and could remain in force. This decision, *Javellana* v. *The Executive Secretary*, gave an official blessing to Marcos' new political order.[20] No similar suit was brought in Korea challenging the Yusin Constitution's ratification process. This may have been because the Constitution preemptively prohibited any challenge to the actions taken by the government leading to its promulgation. The Supplementary Articles of the Constitution stipulated, in Article 7:

> Laws and regulations passed by the Emergency State Council, along with judicial decisions, budgets, and other measures rendered in accordance with them, shall retain their force, and they are not subject to legal challenge or objection by reason of this Constitution or other causes.

Article 9 further stated that "the special declaration by the president and the emergency measures undertaken upon the said declaration between October 17, 1972, and the date this Constitution came into

[20] Supreme Court of the Philippines, March 31, 1973. See Hernandez, "Constitutional Authoritarianism"; David A. Rosenberg (ed.), *Marcos and Martial Law in the Philippines* (Ithaca: Cornell University Press, 1979); C. Neal Tate and Stacia L. Haynie, "Authoritarianism and the Functions of Courts: A Time Series Analysis of the Philippine Supreme Court, 1961–1987," *Law & Society Review* 27 (1993), 707–740. Marcos stated: "Certainly no dictator would submit himself to the judgment of a higher body like the Supreme Court on the question of the constitutionality or validity of his actions. At the same time, I wanted to emphasize that the revolution which I was leading was a constitutional revolution. It was constitutional because it did not depart from the strictures and limitations of the old and new Constitutions." Marcos, *Notes on the New Society of the Philippines*, 214. See Raul C. Pangalangan, "Human Rights Discourse in Post-Marcos Philippines," in Thomas W. D. Davis and Brian Galligan (eds.), *Human Rights in Asia* (Cheltenham: Edward Elgar Publishing, 2011), 56–69.

effect are not subject to legal challenges." Thus, no legal action or objection to the process of the constitutional amendment was allowed. The Constitution itself comprehensively precluded any contest to the process leading to its promulgation.

The Yusin Constitution provided that the president be elected by the newly created National Conference for Unification (*T'ongil Chuch'e Kungmin Hoeŭi*).[21] Its 2,359 members, chosen by direct popular vote, were sworn in on December 5. Martial law had been lifted only two days earlier. On December 23, Park Chung Hee was elected the eighth president and was inaugurated four days later. Park was the only candidate, gaining 99.9 percent of the total vote. The presidential term was six years, but there was no restriction on the number of times he could serve. This meant that in practice the president was allowed to remain in power for the rest of his life. With the Constitution taking effect on the same day, the Fourth Republic was born. Six years later, in 1978, Park was reelected without opposition. The indirect electoral system continued after Park's death in October 1979, until the constitutional revision in 1987. The presidential elections held on December 6, 1979, and on August 27, 1980, each had a single candidate, electing Choi Kyu Hah (Ch'oe Kyu-Ha) (1919–2006) and Chun Doo Hwan respectively.

From the beginning of the Yusin era, Korean people were bombarded by the government's massive propaganda campaigns. "Korean-style democracy" (*Hanguk chŏk minju juŭi*) was the moniker of the new order. The government claimed that the new Constitution embodied "the democratic system adapted to the realities and ideals of the nation" and that the basic rights of the people were guaranteed to the "fullest extent possible."[22] President Park stressed that the cultivation of "democratic capacity" was a pressing goal; in the meantime, some compromises on Western democratic principles were necessary. He mused that "the free democratic system is superior to any other system known to us, but this remarkable system becomes incomparably vulnerable to defects when it is incapable of upholding itself."[23] He drove home his message: achieving economic growth, democracy, and reunification was one inseparable goal. He stressed that "the healthy development of democracy, the construction of the welfare state, and the

21 Constitution (1972), Art. 39.

22 *Tong-A Ilbo*, October 27, 1972.

23 The President's Special Announcement, October 17, 1972.

cultivation of state power to achieve the nation's reunification by defeating the communists all ultimately depend on the success or failure of economic growth."[24] When the South secured its absolute superiority to the North in economic power and in democracy, reunification of the country would follow.[25]

It is an inescapable irony that Park, by lumping together national security and economic self-sufficiency, ended up letting his achievements in economic development undermine his authoritarian rule. By the time it became clear that the South had far surpassed the North in industrial might, it happened that the urgency of zeal among the people for national reunification had subsided, and so had the concerns for national security, at least in relative terms. It meant in the 1980s the government's coercive policy, which had been predicated on national defense and prosperity, lost its core persuasion.

The tiring slogan of Korean-style democracy was much derided, with reason. During his presidency, nevertheless, Park's pursuit of economic progress and attack on government corruption and inefficiency struck a chord with more than a few Korean people. He made no secret of his disdain for partisan bickering, susceptible to fomenting factional strife and discord. Park's down-to-earth personality and straightforward style were often contrasted with those of President Rhee Syngman, who allegedly rarely revealed his mind and constantly let others speculate on his intentions.[26] Behind the efflorescence of Park's reforming ideals, however, lay the stark political reality: the new Constitution solidly concentrated power in his hands. The Yusin system was a carefully crafted apparatus that left little room for dissension.[27] As Park increasingly turned autocratic, the government's political effectiveness deteriorated. A scholar argued that, in comparative political terms, the Korean

[24] Park's address in 1964, cited in Kang Chŏng-In, *Hanguk hyŏndae chŏngch'i sasang*, 296.

[25] Ibid., 299.

[26] Min Pok-Ki, Na ŭi pŏpkwan sijŏl, January 25, 1982.

[27] See Yang Kŏn, "Hanguk hŏnpŏp III: Che 4 Konghwaguk mit che 5 Konghwaguk hŏnpŏpsa ŭi kaegwan (1972–1988)" [The Constitutional Law of Korea III: A Survey of the Constitutional History of the Fourth and the Fifth Republic], *Kongpŏp yŏngu* 17 (1989): 113–141.

government in the 1960s resembled Brazil but in the 1970s became as inept as the Argentinian and Chilean authoritarian regimes.[28]

A Troubled Legal System

Many articles in the new Constitution were accompanied by the proviso that the rights guaranteed in the document could be modified or limited by law. For example, Article 10 (1) of the 1972 Constitution stated: "All citizens shall enjoy personal liberty. No person shall be arrested, detained, seized, searched, interrogated, punished, subjected to involuntary labor, or placed under probationary supervision except as provided by law." Freedoms of speech, press, assembly, and association were similarly guaranteed "except as provided by law."[29] Workers' right to association, to collective bargaining, and to collective action were protected "within the scope defined by law."[30] The right to unionize in state-run enterprises, public utility businesses, and other enterprises that had a serious influence on the national economy was denied.[31] Most tellingly, Article 32 (2) of the Constitution provided that laws restricting the freedom and rights of the citizens could be enacted "when necessary for the maintenance of national security, order, or public welfare." Note that this article omitted the language in the equivalent provision in the earlier constitutions that even a law necessitated by national security or public order would be unconstitutional if it infringed "the essential substances of liberties and rights."[32] The new Constitution thus expanded the scope of the constitutionally permissible limitation of basic rights through laws. Where the National Assembly was dominated by the ruling party, the aforementioned constitutional language provided ample grounds for legislative abuse.

The president had the power to nominate one-third of the members of the National Assembly.[33] The National Conference for Unification voted to approve or disapprove the entire slate of nominees for a three-year term.[34] In the Ninth National Assembly (1973), seventy-three of

[28] Jorge I. Dominguez, "The Perfect Dictatorship? Comparing Authoritarian Rule in South Korea and in Argentina, Brazil, Chile, and Mexico," in Kim and Vogel (eds.), *The Park Chung Hee Era*, 600–601.

[29] Constitution (1972), Art. 18.

[30] Constitution (1972), Art. 29.

[31] Kim Ch'ŏl-Su, *Hŏnpŏphak kaeron*, 160–161.

[32] Constitution (1962), Art. 32 (2). See Chapter 3, notes 63 and 86.

[33] Constitution (1972), Art. 40 (2).

[34] Constitution (1972), Art. 40 (1).

the 219 members of the National Assembly were chosen by the president through this system. The remaining two-thirds of the seats were assigned to seventy-three constituencies that elected two members, a scheme that enabled the runner-up candidate to gain a seat. This system assured the government party an absolute majority in the legislature. The door was now wide open for a legislative manipulation. The president also had power to dissolve the National Assembly.[35]

The new Constitution can be called an emblem of so-called aversive constitutionalism, in which the builders of a new constitutional order try not to repeat past mistakes and to avoid institutions and principles that went awry.[36] The drafters took to task preemption of all potential challenges to controversial laws. They achieved this either by incorporating the languages of the laws directly into the constitutional articles or by attaching general provisos to the rights guaranteed in the Constitution that they could be limited by law. The State Tort Claims Act and the Special Act for Requisitioned Property Disposition were the classic examples of the first method: statutes passed by the legislature could bar challenges by resorting to explicit constitutional authority which made them unassailable.[37] The phrases "except as provided by law" or "as determined by law" were ubiquitous in the Constitution, throughout the sections guaranteeing fundamental rights. Chief Justice Min Pok-Ki quipped that the Yusin Constitution bordered on being "a childish law," as the government fiddled with its language, excising or inserting specific words and phrases, intent on preventing constitutional objections.[38]

The previous constitutions had required a judicial warrant for arrest. The Constitution of 1962 provided in Article 10 (3): "Warrant issued by a judge upon request of a prosecutor shall be presented in case of arrest, detention, search or seizure." Emergency arrest of a suspect was allowed only "where the criminal has been apprehended at the scene of the crime or where there is a danger that the one who committed

35 Constitution (1972), Art. 59.

36 Kim Lane Scheppele, "Aspirational and Aversive Constitutionalism: The Case for Studying Cross-Constitutional Influence Through Negative Models," *International Journal of Constitutional Law* 1 (2003), 299–300.

37 Constitution (1972), Art. 26 (2) and Art. 20 (3). Kukka Paesang Pŏp (Act No. 2459, February 5, 1973).

38 *Maeil Kyŏngje*, July 17, 1990.

a crime punishable by imprisonment of three years or more might escape or destroy evidence," in which case "the prosecutor can request an ex post facto warrant."[39] The 1972 Constitution maintained the language of warrant requirement but substantially relaxed the requirements for warrantless arrest by deleting the three-year condition. It simply stated:

> Warrant issued by a judge upon request of a prosecutor shall be presented in case of arrest, detention, search or seizure. However, where the criminal has been apprehended at the scene of the crime or where there is a danger that the one who committed a crime might escape or destroy evidence, the prosecutor can request an ex post facto warrant.[40]

The Criminal Procedure revised in January 1973 allowed the police to arrest a suspect without warrant "when there is a probable cause that the suspect committed a crime subject to imprisonment without labor."[41] This provision created uproar among legal professionals, and the revision of the Criminal Procedure on December 20, 1973, reverted to the pre-1973 language of limiting emergency arrest to "when there is a probable cause that the suspect committed a crime punishable by death, life in prison, or imprisonment with or without labor for three years or more."[42] This was an example of how a seemingly casual but surreptitious change of words in the constitution or law could create serious consequences.

Another important change was the abolition of the rights of the accused to request a review of the legality of detention before a judge. This procedure, preserved in all pre-1972 Constitutions, was conspicuously omitted from the Yusin Constitution.[43] The government's proffered reason for denying this crucial right of the accused was that it was redundant with the judicial warrant system, but a closer look at the numbers shows otherwise. During the twelve years from 1961 to 1972, 110,317 *habeas corpus* cases were filed, and 53,224 persons who had been arrested with

[39] Constitution (1962), Art. 10 (3).

[40] Constitution (1972), Art. 10 (3). The deletion from the previous Constitution of the three-year condition ("a crime punishable by imprisonment of three years or more") would have a serious implication for the emergency decrees, which allowed violators of the decrees to be arrested without warrants.

[41] Hyŏngsa Sosong Pŏp [Criminal Procedure] (revised January 15, 1973), art. 206.

[42] Criminal Procedure (revised December 20, 1973), art. 206. See *Pŏpwŏnsa*, 763.

[43] Constitution (1962), Art. 10 (5); Constitution (1972), Art. 10. See Chapter 3, note 119 and accompanying text.

warrant were freed (48.2 percent) by the courts of first instance.[44] In 1967, 9,248 persons requested the review, and 4,776 (50.7 percent) were released. In 1969, as many as 14,167 individuals requested the review, and 6,681 (47 percent) were freed.[45] In 1970, the numbers were 12,273 and 5,607 (45.7 percent). In 1972, the last year before the system was abolished, 13,669 requested the review, and 6,041 (44.2 percent) were released. These numbers bespoke the importance of the detention review proceedings, which served a critical function separate from the warrant requirement. The warrant issuance rates dropped in 1973 and 1974 as the courts were more cautious after the abolition of review proceedings.[46] Needless to say, the outright denial of detention review under the Yusin Constitution was a serious blow to civil liberties. The proceedings were revived in the 1980 Constitution, although the Criminal Procedure excluded from review treasonous insurrection, crime of foreign aggression, security law violation, and crimes subject to death, life imprisonment, or five years or more in prison.[47] After the proceedings were reinstated, the release rate was 41.1 percent in 1981, 47.2 percent in 1982, 46.6 percent in 1983, and 50.8 percent in 1984.[48]

The Yusin Constitution broadened the evidentiary force of confessions. The 1962 Constitution had provided that "when the confession of the accused is the sole evidence against that person, it cannot be used as evidence of guilt or the ground for punishment."[49] That provision simply disappeared from the 1972 Constitution, along with the provision on detention review.[50] Now the accused was deprived of constitutional protection against involuntary confession and could in theory be found guilty on confession alone without corroborating evidence, if the legislature so intended. The provisions in the Criminal Procedure disallowing confessions obtained by duress were still preserved after 1973. Article 309 provided: "When there is reasonable suspicion that a defendant's confession had been made not voluntarily but extracted by torture, violence, or threat or obtained after an illegal extension of

44 *Kyŏnghyang Sinmun*, February 1, 1973. *Yŏksa sogŭi sabŏppu*, 397.

45 Pŏpwŏn Haengjŏngch'ŏ, *T'onggye yŏnbo* 1969 (published in February 1971), 286.

46 See Table 3.1 on p. 95. See the analysis in Pŏpwŏn Haengjŏngch'ŏ, *Sabŏp yŏngam* 1976 (for year 1975), 108.

47 Constitution (1980), Art. 11 (5); Criminal Procedure (revised December 18, 1980), art. 214 (2).

48 *Sabŏp yŏngam* 1985 (for year 1984), 286.

49 Constitution (1962), Art. 10 (6).

50 Constitution (1972), Art. 10.

physical detention or other means, it shall not be admitted as evidence of guilt." Article 310 provided: "When the confession of a criminal defendant is the only evidence against the defendant, that confession shall not be admitted as evidence of guilt." These articles were of diminished assurance, though, where constitutional protections had been scrapped.

Once the Constitution was promulgated, a flurry of new laws followed. In the absence of the National Assembly, which had been dissolved in October 1972, the Emergency State Council – the cabinet – acted as the legislative branch. The emergency legislative council churned out laws with gusto. In January 1973, the Criminal Procedure, Court Organization Act, Prosecutors Office Act, Attorneys Act, and Judicial Disciplinary Act were issued, taking effect on February 1.

The new Criminal Procedure, revised on January 15, substantially reduced the rights of the accused.[51] Under the old version, an individual, once freed from custody, could not be arrested again for the same criminal fact (double jeopardy); the revised article made it possible to arrest the suspect again "when new important evidence emerged" (article 208 [1]). The old law stated that an arrest warrant by a judge was issued at the "request" (*sinch'ong*) of the prosecutor; the new provision read that an arrest warrant by a judge was issued at the "demand" (*yogu*) of the prosecutor (art. 201).[52] Under earlier law, the judge could reject an arrest warrant request without cause; now the judge was required to provide to the prosecutor detailed reasons for rejection in writing with signature (art. 201 [3]). Previously the judge was free to allow bail except where the crimes were subject to imprisonment of three years or more; now the judge had to "obtain the opinion" of the prosecutor (art. 97 [1]). Bail was not allowed when the crimes were punishable by death, life in prison, or "imprisonment with or without labor for more than one year." It became another provision that drew so much opposition that the government backtracked: the language was changed in December to the cases of crimes punishable by death, life in prison, or "imprisonment with or

[51] Article-by-article comparisons of the old and new Criminal Procedure are provided in *Tong-A Ilbo*, January 20, 1973.

[52] This change in terminology was not inadvertent: the word "request" in the 1962 Constitution had been replaced by "demand" in the 1972 Constitution (Art. 10).

Table 4.1 *Pretrial Release, 1970–1984*

	Total Prosecuted	Bail Requested	Bail Granted	Bail Request Rate	Bail Grant Rate	Rate of Release on Bail
1970	69,118	5,909	2,474	8.5%	41.9%	3.6%
1971	75,247	5,787	2,438	7.7%	42.1%	3.2%
1972	92,513	6,782	2,708	7.3%	39.9%	2.9%
1973	86,654	4,052	1,576	4.7%	38.9%	1.8%
1974	84,695	3,692	1,601	4.4%	43.4%	1.9%
1975	99,848	5,600	2,596	5.6%	46.4%	2.6%
1976	97,070	5,808	2,466	6.0%	42.5%	2.5%
1977	82,643	5,018	2,201	6.1%	43.9%	2.7%
1978	73,065	5,024	2,470	6.9%	49.2%	3.4%
1979	74,454	6,102	2,918	8.2%	47.8%	3.9%
1980	82,304	6,876	3,123	8.4%	45.4%	3.8%
1981	81,373	6,769	2,886	8.3%	42.6%	3.5%
1982	82,808	7,982	3,636	9.6%	45.6%	4.4%
1983	82,023	8,627	3,828	10.5%	44.4%	4.7%
1984	81,541	8,666	3,929	10.6%	45.3%	4.8%

Sources: *Sabŏp yŏngam* (1980), 328; *Sabŏp yŏngam* (1985), 383.

without labor for more than ten years" (art. 95 [1]).[53] The prosecutor could appeal instantly the judge's orders of bail, detention cancellation, and stay of execution of detention (art. 97 [3]; art. 101 [3]). Table 4.1 lists the numbers of the defendants released prior to trials between 1970 and 1984. The years 1973 and 1974 showed a sharp decline in the bail applications as a result of the new law. Overall, the pretrial release rate remained below 5 percent.

These changes significantly diminished the judge's discretionary power in legal proceedings. But it was not that the courts simply rolled over. The very first deliberation by the Supreme Court on the prosecutor's instant appeal against the judge's bail order took place on February 16, 1973. The accused, arrested for running a prostitution ring, was sentenced to one year in prison. When his tuberculosis worsened, the court allowed bail on medical grounds, but the prosecutor filed an appeal to prevent his release. The Supreme Court ruled that "the

[53] Criminal Procedure (revised January 15, 1973), art. 95 (1); Criminal Procedure (revised December 20, 1973), art. 95 (1).

prosecution's instant appeal is allowed only for cases involving the error of law; an immediate appeal grounded on the factual error of illness cannot be allowed."[54] After this decision, the chief prosecutor sent a bulletin to prosecutors instructing that they restrain themselves from filing instant appeal requests. He specifically added a comment that, after the Supreme Court's ruling, the public seemed to believe that prosecutors cared little about citizens' rights.[55] The courts tried to safeguard the minimum due process. Article 282 of Criminal Procedure required the defendant be represented by a legal counsel in cases punishable by death, life imprisonment, or imprisonment of three years or more. In September 1973, the Supreme Court ruled that a statement made by a defendant while not represented by a lawyer was inadmissible.[56] In 1975, the Court affirmed its earlier decision that, if the defendant could not afford to hire a lawyer, the court should have appointed a public defender.[57]

In general, nevertheless, one has to conclude that during the Yusin years the initiatives in the criminal process were transferred away from the court to the prosecutor's office.[58] As if these constitutional and legislative changes were not sufficient to tie the hands of judges, the government tried to maintain a firm grip on the judicial and legal personnel by controlling judicial appointments and lawyers' right to practice. As before, judicial reappointment served as a means to intimidate and punish judges. The Fourth Republic began with a dramatic judicial purge, which forced out several Supreme Court justices. It was a delayed political reprisal for the unconstitutionality decision in 1971, for which the Court now paid a dire price.

Beleaguered Judiciary

The 1972 Constitution abolished the Judicial Recommendation Council, a body that previously nominated the chief justice and associate justices

54 *Kyŏnghyang Sinmun*, February 17, 1973.
55 *Tong-A Ilbo*, February 22, 1973.
56 *Tong-A Ilbo*, September 27, 1973.
57 *Tong-A Ilbo*, November 28, 1975; *Kyŏnghyang Sinmun*, November 28, 1975.
58 Han In-Sŏp, "Hŏnpŏp kwa hyŏngsapŏp: kwŏllyŏk chŏngch'i, chiptan kaltŭng kwa pŏp ŭi chibae" [The Constitution and Criminal Law: Politics of Power, Group Conflicts and Rule by Law], *Seoul Taehakkyo pŏphak* 39 (1999), 144; Sin Tong-Un, "Hanguk kŏmch'al chedo ŭi hyŏnhwang kwa kaesŏn ch'aek" [The Current State and the Reform Measures of the Prosecution System in Korea], *Seoul Taehakkyo pŏphak* 29 (1988), 44.

of the Supreme Court. Now the chief justice was appointed by the president with the consent of the National Assembly.[59] The president held the power to appoint all other judges on the recommendation of the chief justice.[60] As to the appointment of Supreme Court justices, the 1962 (and 1969) Constitution had included explicit language that the president was bound by the request of the chief justice made with the approval of the Judicial Recommendation Council ("Upon the recommendation the president shall appoint").[61] The language "shall appoint" was deleted in the 1972 Constitution, which led to the interpretation that the chief justice's request was no longer binding. The term of the chief justice was six years; the previous prohibition on renewal was removed.[62] The number of Supreme Court justices was kept at not more than sixteen. The term of all judges including the Supreme Court justices other than the chief justice was ten years, renewable as determined by law.[63] Previously, the mandatory retirement age at sixty-five years for justices had been stipulated in the Constitution, but the new Constitution simply stated that the retirement age was to be decided by law. The Court Organization Act that came into effect in January 1973 set the retirement age for both the chief justice and justices of the Supreme Court at sixty-five. For the chief justice of the appeals court, it was sixty-three; for others, sixty (art. 39 [5]).

Tucked into the supplementary articles at the end of the Court Organization Act's main text was a provision that stipulated:

> The incumbent judges at the time of the promulgation of this Act must be newly appointed before April 30, 1973, in accordance with this Act. Those who are not appointed by that date are relieved from office on April 30, 1973. But in case a successor is appointed in accordance with this Act, the incumbent can be relieved before this date.[64]

Under this provision, all incumbent judges had to be newly appointed within three months. Reappointment required by this law went directly against the constitutional guarantee of judicial tenure. Under the Constitution, judges could not be dismissed except through impeachment, criminal punishment, or disciplinary actions ("No judge is

[59] Constitution (1972), Art. 103 (1); Court Organization Act (1973), art. 37.
[60] Constitution (1972), Art. 103 (2).
[61] Constitution (1962), Art. 99 (2).
[62] Constitution (1972), Art. 103 (3).
[63] Constitution (1972), Art. 103 (4) and (5).
[64] Act No. 2448, Supplementary Regulations, art. 2.

dismissed, suspended, or subject to reduced pay unless through impeachment, criminal punishment, or disciplinary actions").[65] The judges could be placed in early retirement as determined by law only when they could not carry out official duties due to physical and mental illnesses.[66] The new reappointment measure overrode them all; it was nothing other than a blatant political move, a judicial purge.

On March 31, nine justices of the Supreme Court were relieved of their office, failing to receive reappointment. They were Justices Son Tong-Uk, Kim Ch'i-Kŏl, Sa Kwang-Uk, Yang Hoe-Kyŏng, Pang Sun-Wŏn, Na Hang-Yun, Hong Nam-Pyo, Yu Chae-Pang, and Han Pong-Se. These were the nine justices who had found the State Tort Claims Act unconstitutional. The seven who dissented from that decision were reappointed. Political retaliation could not have been more overt; there was no effort to disguise it. The regime wanted to get its message across to the judiciary. On April 2, the president reappointed 356 judges and appointed twenty-five new judges.[67] Six new justices, Yi Pyŏng-Ho, Han Hwan-Chin, Im Hang-Chun, An Pyŏng-Su, Kim Yun-Haeng, and Yi Il-Kyu, were installed at the Supreme Court. Altogether, fifty-seven judges, including the nine justices above, left the court. This number included those who quit in the form of voluntary resignation, and it is difficult to know precisely how many among them had been compelled to resign in order to avoid nonreappointment.[68] At least three judges who had refused to submit their resignations failed to be reappointed.[69] Few doubted that they were singled out for political reasons. The atmosphere of intimidation hung heavy over the courts.

65 Constitution (1972), Art. 104 (1).

66 Constitution (1972), Art. 104 (2).

67 *Kyŏnghyang Sinmun*, March 27, 1973; *Maeil Kyŏngje*, March 28, 1973.

68 *Pŏpwŏnsa*, 690–691. A source indicates that thirty-eight judges submitted voluntary resignation. *Yŏksa sogŭi sabŏppu*, 86; *Pŏmnyul Sinmun*, April 2, 1973.

69 Among those who left the court was Yang Hŏn, the judge who rendered a not-guilty verdict to Seoul National University students in 1971, and Mok Yo-Sang, the judge who acquitted the publisher of the *Tari* magazine. See Chapter 5, note 84. One of the judges who involuntarily left the court was Kang In-Ae. Kang was the younger brother of Kang Kŭn-Ho, a National Assemblyman of the opposition New Democratic Party. The KCIA reportedly maintained a file on Judge Kang, marking him as an "antigovernment judge and the model of a bad judge." Han Hong-Ku, Han Hong-Ku kyosu ka ssŭnŭn sabŏppu – hoehan kwa oyok ŭi yŏksa [The History of the Judiciary Written by Professor Han Hong-Ku: The History Filled with Regrets and Shame] [hereinafter Sabŏppu], *Hangyŏrye Sinmun*, July 20, 2009.

Attorneys Act

In relation to the tightening political grip on the judiciary, new provisions in the Attorneys Act merit discussion. The law, revised in January 1973, gave the justice minister extensive power to regulate law practices. An important change concerned restricting private practices by retired judicial personnel. As seen in previous chapters, it was a norm that judges and prosecutors left their office in mid-career to launch private practice. Now they came to face a serious hurdle in starting law business. The new law stated:

> Judges, prosecutors, and judge advocates and law enforcement officials who would otherwise be eligible to practice law as an attorney may not open a law office for a period of three years in the same judicial district they had served in during the two-year period immediately preceding resignation, with the exception for those who had completed at least fifteen years of service in their official capacity. Those who left the office by mandatory retirement and the chief justice and justices of the Supreme Court are exempt from this provision.[70]

Thus, judges and prosecutors who left office before completing fifteen years of service were not allowed to practice law at a place where they used to work and likely resided. It meant they would have to open practices away from their home bases, obviously with greater difficulties in soliciting clients. This was a law that directly went against the long-established tradition. Previously judges and prosecutors who left office, either voluntarily or involuntarily, were able to set up offices immediately, without restriction.

The rationale behind the new measure was to prevent former judges and prosecutors from exerting undue influence in judicial cases they now represented as counsel. It was true that incumbent judges treated these attorneys with respect, mainly out of courtesy to their former senior colleagues, a customary practice that some suspected had sway on the results of the cases. But the sudden reform measure was perceived in legal circles to have more to do with punishing judges who left the court for political reasons. The fact that they always had the option of opening private practice had emboldened some younger judges to resist government pressure, but now the new law had the potential to hold back those who otherwise would choose resignation rather than succumbing to the

[70] Pyŏnhosa Pŏp [Attorneys Act] (Act No. 2452, January 25, 1973), art. 8 (5).

strain.[71] The arbitrary nature of the measure was apparent when one considered the size of the judicial district of Seoul. About half of all judges were based in the capital; forbidding them from practicing in the Seoul metropolitan area was simply unrealistic.

Under article 40 (1) of the revised law, the justice minister could suspend attorneys who were charged with a criminal offense even before they were convicted and subjected to disciplinary actions.[72] It is well documented that this provision was used by the regime to persecute human rights lawyers. Attorney Yi Pyŏng-Rin (1911–1986), a former president of the Korea Bar Association and head of the Korea branch of Amnesty International, spent much of his career in resistance against the regime, ended up being accused of adultery, and was disbarred.[73] The charges against Yi were eventually dropped, but damage to this respected human rights advocate had been done, and he had to leave Seoul and go into self-exile. The restrictive provisions of the law were rescinded only after democratization. In 1989, the Constitutional Court struck down article 8 (5) (as incorporated in the Act revised in 1982) as an excessive encroachment on the freedom to work and an unreasonable discrimination against those wishing to open a legal practice.[74] Article 40 (1) was declared unconstitutional in 1991.[75]

Throughout the 1970s, the political branches continued concerted efforts to control the judiciary. Consider the following episode. In December 1972, the government assigned military officers to the courts for surveillance. One of these personnel, a major, stationed at the Seoul Criminal District Court, dispatched a memo to a senior judge of the court, titled "Request for an Advance Notification of Acquittal Decisions." The officer called the judge's attention to a recent acquittal. He officially requested that henceforth the court notify him before rendering a not-guilty verdict so that he could "ask the prosecutor to reinforce evidence or take other necessary measures."[76] Simply baffling, this kind of incidents had a dampening effect on judicial morale. In the New Year's address of 1973, Chief Justice Min Pok-Ki took

71 *Kwagŏ wa taehwa*, vol. 4, 193.
72 Attorneys Act, art. 40 (1).
73 Han Hong-Ku, Sabŏppu, May 21, 2010.
74 Const. Ct., 89HŏnKa102, November 20, 1989. See Han In-Sŏp, "Hŏnpŏp kwa hyŏngsapŏp," 161.
75 Const. Ct., 90HŏnKa48, November 19, 1990.
76 *Pŏpcho 50 nyŏn yasa*, vol. 2, 34.

pains to assure judicial personnel that the constitutional changes "have nothing to do with the reputation of the judiciary" and that the authority of the judiciary would not diminish.[77] But he could not do much other than repeating the government's line that the changes were "necessary to meet the challenges of the times."[78] The chief justice's exhortation did little to lift the spirits of the judges.

Ironically, President Park often publicly professed his respect for judicial independence. He liked to tell judges that he took pride in the fact that he did not interfere with the courts even during the military rule after the coup in 1961.[79] Park avowed in January 1973 that "interference with the independence of the judiciary is not allowed." But he also chided the judges, saying that they "have sometimes rendered suspended sentences in political cases or delayed trials in the name of judicial independence, which lacks common sense."[80] Chief Justice Min later reminisced that the president's displeasure with the judiciary dated back to 1964 when he thought the courts were less than cooperative in quelling demonstrations against the Korea–Japan normalization talks. According to Min, the president fretted about judges' lack of support for crucial national policies.[81] In December 1975, in a meeting with court leaders, Park emphasized that "it is necessary to protect innocent citizens by severely punishing antisocial and unethical crimes."[82] The sweeping changes in Criminal Procedure were necessary to contain what he viewed as judicial obstruction.

President Park envisioned a constitutional order as an expression of sovereign will that was legislative, executive, and judicial, all at once. He said that "in an effort to establish national discipline there can be no distinction between the executive branch and the judiciary."[83] "In the past, each of the three branches attempted to exercise one hundred percent of its constitutional power," but in his opinion "one should not try to exercise all the powers simply because they are provided in the constitution," as it "renders cooperation among the three branches difficult."[84] Park viewed judicial review as a superfluous mechanism that

77 *Pŏpwŏnsa*, 688.
78 Ibid.
79 Min Pok-Ki, Na ŭi pŏpkwan sijŏl, April 26, 1982.
80 *Pŏpwŏnsa*, 689.
81 Min Pok-Ki, Na ŭi pŏpkwan sijŏl, March 22, 1982.
82 *Maeil Kyŏngje*, December 4, 1975.
83 Ibid.
84 *Kyŏnghyang Sinmun*, April 2, 1973; *Tong-A Ilbo*, April 2, 1973.

would merely derail smooth collaboration among government institutions. He opined, "It is my unchanging belief that those in power must act with humility when exercising the power at their disposal."[85] Apparently, it did not occur to him that the ideal of the humble exercise of power should apply to presidential prerogatives as well.

Judicial Review Redefined

The power to conduct judicial review of statutes was wrested away from the ordinary courts and given to the Constitutional Committee.[86] Article 109 (1) of the Constitution provided, in part: "The Constitutional Committee shall judge the following matters: 1. The constitutionality of statutes upon the request of the court; 2. Impeachment; 3. Dissolution of a political party." As in the founding Constitution of 1948, the ordinary courts retained the power to review inferior sources of law such as administrative decrees, regulations, and dispositions, when their constitutionality was a prerequisite to a trial. When the constitutionality of a statute was at issue, the presiding judge or the party could request a constitutional review. The case was then forwarded to the Supreme Court which decided, *en banc*, whether to certify the law to be reviewed by the Constitutional Committee. The Supreme Court thus performed a preliminary review of law; it was to send the case to the Constitutional Committee only when it determined that the law violated the constitution, attaching its own opinion on the issue. Such certification required votes by two-thirds of all the justices. One notes that the requirement of the supermajority votes for an unconstitutionality decision, struck down by the Supreme Court in 1971, had been resurrected and included in the new Court Organization Act.[87]

The Constitutional Committee Act was issued on February 16, 1973. The Committee, which opened its doors on March 19, was called "one of the more mysterious state organs inhabiting the annals of Korean history."[88] Of its nine members, three were nominated by the president, three by the National Assembly, and three by the chief

85 *Kyŏnghyang Sinmun*, April 2, 1973.
86 Constitution (1972), Art. 105 (1).
87 Court Organization Act (1973), art. 7.
88 Jerome Alan Cohen and Edward J. Baker, "U.S. Foreign Policy," in William Shaw (ed.), *Human Rights in Korea: Historical and Policy Perspectives*, 242.

justice.[89] The chairman of the Constitutional Committee was appointed by the president. The members, serving terms of six years, could not be removed except by impeachment or criminal conviction; they could neither join a political party nor participate in political activities. A contemporary commentator wrote that "the legal nature of the Constitutional Committee's power, function, and status is still behind a mystical screen, hindering a better grasp of it."[90] This was a generous assessment; not many doubted that the sole purpose of the committee was to serve as a safety measure for the government. Apparently President Park never got over the Supreme Court's action in 1971 of striking down the law he desperately needed. The 1972 Constitution made sure to prevent a repeat of that debacle. The fact that many repressive laws were endowed with explicit mandates under the new Constitution diminished the chances for constitutional review, but the government did not want to be caught by surprise again. Park feared that any constitutional challenge of the laws might spill into demands for constitutional amendment. The government even wanted to be prepared for the unlikely situation that the Constitutional Committee would actually invalidate a law: the committee was legally required to seek the opinion of the justice minister before rendering an unconstitutionality decision.[91]

Between December 1972 and October 1980, not even once did the Supreme Court certify a case to be heard by the Constitutional Committee. Accordingly, the Constitutional Committee never convened to rule on constitutional matters; technically, there was no constitutional adjudication of legislation during the eight years of Yusin rule. The Supreme Court was mostly blamed for this moribund constitutionalism. Reflecting on the Yusin years, one scholar observed that "the Court apparently was reluctant, or did not bother, to turn to the Constitution Committee with a request to do its job. If any agency was to blame for inaction, it was the Supreme Court. The Supreme Court was not the final reviewing authority and so could easily have referred

89 Constitution (1972), Art. 110.

90 Kim Un-Yong, "Hanguk Hŏnpŏp Wiwŏnhoe ŭi sabŏp chŏk sŏngkyŏk" [The Judicial Nature of the Constitutional Committee of Korea], *Pŏmnyul haengjŏng nonjip* 19 (1978), 44.

91 Constitutional Committee Act, art. 48.

matters of constitutionality to the Committee."[92] This statement is not entirely inaccurate, but it requires elaboration. When the Supreme Court decided there was no issue of unconstitutionality in a case – in other words, the challenged statute was not constitutionally defective – it naturally did not refer that case to the Constitutional Committee. The Court had little incentive to turn to the committee anyway, unless it purported to create a constitutional crisis and wash its hands of responsibility.

The most egregious violation of fundamental rights under the Yusin regime took place through the president's exercise of emergency powers. Such powers had been prescribed in the constitutions since 1948, but their scope was now significantly expanded.[93] President Park's recourse to them contradicted his Yusin rhetoric of democracy, whether Korean-style or any other kind. Intended to suppress and cut short constitutional discussion, they were unequivocally illiberal and undemocratic measures.

Emergency Decrees

Article 53 of the Yusin Constitution granted the president the power to issue emergency decrees. This power was separate from the president's authority to impose martial law which could be declared "in time of war, armed conflict, or similar national emergency, when there is a military necessity or a necessity to maintain public safety and order by mobilization of the military forces."[94] Between 1974 and 1979, President Park imposed nine emergency measures. Previously, the president had to meet stringent requirements before invoking emergency power. For example, emergency orders could be issued only to respond to, not to prevent, a major crisis in order to restore and maintain the security of the state. The president had to report his actions and orders promptly to the National Assembly and obtain approval; if no approval was obtained, such actions and orders lost effect.[95] Under

[92] Yoon, "Judicial Review in the Korean Political Context," *Korean Journal of Comparative Law* 17 (1989), 148.

[93] For the history of presidential emergency powers in Korea, see Young C. Kim, "Politics of Emergency Powers: The Case of Korea," in Shao-Chuan Leng (ed.), *Coping with Crises: How Governments Deal with Crises* (The Miller Center Series on Asian Political Leadership, vol. 2) (Lanham: University Press of America, 1990), 129–172.

[94] Constitution (1972), Art. 54 (1).

[95] Constitution (1962), Art. 73.

the 1972 Constitution, the president now could take emergency measures when he deemed that national security or public safety and order "is seriously threatened" or when he "anticipated" such threats. Article 53 read in full:

1. The president can, when speedy measures are deemed necessary due to natural calamity or grave financial and economic crisis, and when the state's security or public safety and order is seriously threatened or is anticipated to be threatened, take emergency measures concerning the matters of state governance such as domestic affairs, foreign relations, national defense, economic or financial affairs, and judicial affairs.
2. When deemed necessary in the cases under Paragraph 1, the president can suspend temporarily the freedom and rights of the people as defined in this Constitution and take emergency measures with regard to the rights and powers of the Executive and the Judiciary.
3. Upon taking emergency measures as provided in Paragraphs 1 and 2, the president shall notify the National Assembly without delay.
4. Emergency measures taken under Paragraphs 1 and 2 shall not be subject to judicial deliberations thereon.
5. When the causes for the emergency measures cease to exist, the president shall lift the measures without delay.
6. The National Assembly, with the vote of a majority of its members, can recommend to the president that the emergency measures be lifted, and the president shall comply unless there is a special reason to do otherwise.

Article 53 was modeled after Article 48 of the Weimar Constitution of Germany, which granted extraordinary power to the federal president.[96] It is well known that Carl Schmitt's theory of the state of exception carried significant weight among Korean constitutional scholars and that the drafters of the 1972 Constitution heavily relied on

96 Verfassung des Deutschen Reiches [Constitution of the German Reich], August 11, 1919, Art. 48. It read in part: "In the event that the public order and security are seriously disturbed or endangered, the Reich President may take the measures necessary for their restoration, intervening, if necessary, with the aid of the armed forces. For this purpose he may temporarily abrogate, wholly or in part, the fundamental principles laid down in Articles 114, 115, 117, 118, 123, 124, and 153."

it.[97] Of late, scholarship has seen a sort of renaissance of the concept of emergency powers, as authors debated Schmitt with renewed fascination.[98] Many countries after World War II inserted formal provisions of emergency powers in their constitutions. Schmitt drew a conceptual distinction between original constituent power (*le pouvoir constituant*) and constituted power (*le pouvoir constitué*). For him, a sovereign's constitution-making power, from which the constituted powers were derived, was a higher norm than individual constitutional laws. The preconstitutional will of the people was the source of democratic legitimacy, and the president, as the sole custodian of democratic legitimacy, had the exclusive authority to declare a state of exception.[99] Schmitt memorably stated that the "Sovereign is he who decides on the exception."[100] The emergency powers mandated in Article 48 of the Weimar Constitution were an exercise of the *pouvoir constituant*, he argued, and were therefore justifiably placed outside judicial power.

A central issue in the state of exception is the extent to which civil liberties and individual rights can be limited for the sake of national

97 Schmitt's major work, *Verfassunglehre* [Constitutional Theory] (1928), was translated into Korean in 1976 during the Yusin period, more than forty years before the appearance of its English translation, as Kaal Shumittŭ [Carl Schmitt], *Hŏnpŏp iron* [Constitutional Theory], trans. Kim Ki-bŏm (Seoul: Kyŏngmunsa, 1976).

98 Carl Schmitt, *Constitutional Theory*, 1928, trans. Jeffrey Seitzer (Durham: Duke University Press, 2008); Carl Schmitt, *Political Theology: Four Chapters on the Concept of Sovereignty*, 1922, trans. George Schwab (Chicago: University of Chicago Press, 2005). For the recent literature on Schmitt, see, among others, Ellen Kennedy, *Constitutional Failure: Carl Schmitt in Weimar* (Durham: Duke University Press, 2004); David Dyzenhaus (ed.), *Law as Politics: Carl Schmitt's Critique of Liberalism* (Durham: Duke University Press, 1998); David Dyzenhaus, *Legality and Legitimacy: Carl Schmitt, Hans Kelsen, and Hermann Heller in Weimar* (Oxford: Oxford University Press, 1997); William E. Scheuerman, *Carl Schmitt: The End of Law* (Lanham: Rowman & Littlefield, 1999); Peter C. Caldwell, *Popular Sovereignty and the Crisis of German Constitutional Law* (Durham: Duke University Press, 1997); John P. McCormick, "The Dilemmas of Dictatorship: Carl Schmitt and Constitutional Emergency Powers," *Canadian Journal of Law & Jurisprudence* 10 (1997), 163–176.

99 Chaihark Hahm and Sung Ho Kim, "'Stranger in a Strange Land': Carl Schmitt's Politics of Exception in South Korea," in Henry Frendo (ed.), *The European Mind: Narrative and Identity* (Msida: Malta University Press, 2010), 405–411.

100 Schmitt, *Political Theory*, 5.

interest.[101] Compared with Article 48 of the Weimar Constitution, Article 53 of the Yusin Constitution was broader in its scope because, while the German provision listed specific constitutional articles the operation of which could be suspended, the Korean provision left open which particular set of rights could be limited. In this sense, it was closer to Article 16 of the Constitution of the French Fifth Republic.[102] The Korean president's emergency power was yet more extensive than the French equivalent because the former could refuse the National Assembly's request to lift the emergency measures.[103] Under the previous constitutions, emergency orders that did not obtain the legislature's approval immediately lost their force; under the 1972 Constitution the president did not need to obtain the National Assembly's approval and the emergency decrees continued their legal force regardless of its recommendation.

The National Assembly, filled with the members of the ruling party, did not ever request the president to lift the decrees. It was only after Park's death on October 26, 1979, that the legislature asked the new president to abolish Emergency Decree No. 9, which was done on December 8 that year.

Article 53 (4) of the Constitution explicitly stated that emergency measures taken under Articles 53 (1) and 53 (2) were not subject to judicial review. This meant neither the courts nor the Constitutional Committee could rule on their constitutionality. As such, emergency decrees stood beyond any outside scrutiny, either by the legislative

[101] Kim Lane Scheppele, "Law in a Time of Emergency: States of Exception and the Temptations of 9/11," *University of Pennsylvania Journal of Constitutional Law* 6 (2004), 1001–1084.

[102] Constitution de la République française [Constitution of the Republic of France], October 3, 1958, Art. 16. It read in part: "Where the institutions of the Republic, the independence of the Nation, the integrity of its territory or the fulfillment of its international commitments are under serious and immediate threat, and where the proper functioning of the constitutional public authorities is interrupted, the President of the Republic shall take measures required by these circumstances, after formally consulting the Prime Minister, the Presidents of the Houses of Parliament and the Constitutional Council. . . . After thirty days of the exercise of such emergency powers, the matter may be referred to the Constitutional Council by the President of the National Assembly, the President of the Senate, sixty members of the National Assembly or sixty senators, so as to decide if the conditions laid down in paragraph one still apply. It shall make its decision by public announcement as soon as possible."

[103] See André Hauriou, *Droit constitutionnel et institutions politiques* (Paris: Montchrestien, 1983).

branch or by the judiciary; the president was the sole authority in determining the legality of the measures he had undertaken. A prominent constitutional scholar predicted in 1973 that it was unlikely that any procedural irregularity of the decrees' issuance would become subject to constitutional review, because the Supreme Court would adhere to its precedents that whether a law was passed in the National Assembly in a procedurally correct manner was not within the realm of judicial decision.[104]

Considering the initial jolt of the advent of the Yusin order, organized opposition to the system took time to emerge.[105] In the fall of 1973, student demonstrations surged.[106] On December 24, thirty individuals including Chang Chun-Ha, a well-known dissident intellectual, launched the "one-million signature" drive to call for constitutional revision.[107] The campaign quickly grew into a massive grassroots movement, and the government became nervous. A group of the leading members of society mailed an open letter to the Blue House, in which they demanded the protection of the basic rights of the citizens, the restoration of the separation of powers, and a peaceful regime change through open and fair elections. They wrote they were petitioning the president directly because "under the current constitutional provisions and in our country's situation, these necessary changes can become possible by your decision alone."[108] The response was not quite something they had in mind: the President resorted to his constitutionally mandated emergency powers.

Emergency Decrees Nos. 1 and 2

On January 8, 1974, Emergency Decree No. 1 was declared. It prohibited "all activities amounting to denial, opposition, distortion, or criticism of

[104] Kim Ch'ŏl-Su, "Kingŭp choch'i kwŏn" [Emergency Decree Power], *Kosigye* (October 1973), 22.

[105] Yi Sang-U, "Kingŭp choch'i: kŭ paltong kwa tojŏn" [Emergency Decrees: Issuance and Challenge], in Ch'ŏnjugyo Inkwŏn Wiwŏnhoe [Catholic Human Rights Commission] (ed.), *Sabŏp sarin: 1975 nyŏn sawŏl ŭi haksal* [Judicial Murder: The Massacre of April 1975] (Seoul: Ch'ŏnjugyo Inkwŏn Wiwŏnhoe, 2001), 45.

[106] The list of student demonstrations, over twenty incidents in the fall of 1973, is provided in ibid., 46–48.

[107] Ibid., 49–50; Chang, *Protest Dialectics*, 36.

[108] Yi Sang-U, "Kingŭp choch'i," 53–55.

the Constitution" and banned suggesting or instigating a revision or repeal of the Constitution.[109] Citizens were forbidden to deny, oppose, misrepresent, or defame the Constitution of the Republic of Korea (art. 1); to assert, introduce, propose, or petition for its revision or repeal (art. 2); to fabricate or disseminate false rumors (art. 3); to advocate, instigate, or propagate any act or acts prohibited under articles 1, 2, and 3 or to communicate such acts through broadcasting or by any other means (art. 4). Any person who violated or criticized this decree was "subject to arrest, detention, search or seizure, without judicial warrant, and subject to punishment by imprisonment for up to fifteen years" (art. 5). Offenders were to be "tried and sentenced by the emergency courts martial" (art. 6).

Emergency Decree No. 2, issued the same day, established the emergency military courts with jurisdiction over civilian violators of the decree.[110] The emergency ordinary court martial and the emergency high court martial would be presided over by an active-duty general (art. 4 and art. 5); the presiding judge was to be appointed by the president with the consultation of the minister of defense and the minister of justice (art. 9); the director of the Korean Central Intelligence Agency (KCIA) would coordinate and supervise the prosecution of cases under the emergency courts' jurisdiction, in the areas of the information gathering, investigation, and security measures (art. 10); the procedural protections of the accused's rights, as laid out in articles 132, 238, 239, and 241 of the Military Court Act, were not applicable, and there was no limit on the detention period (art. 11); for cases under the jurisdiction of the emergency court martial, the prosecutor could issue a warrant when it was needed for arrest, detention, seizure, or search (art. 12).

Articles 132, 238, 239, and 241 of the Military Court Act dealt with limitations on the detention of suspects by the military police and prosecutors. The exclusion of these articles meant civilian violators of the emergency decree were deprived of even the minimal protections allowed an accused under the military court law. No one doubted that military jurisdiction was merely an extension of the executive branch. The result was an unprecedented restriction of the rights of

109 Presidential Emergency Decree (Taet'ongnyŏng Kinkŭp Choch'i) No. 1, January 8, 1974.

110 Emergency Decree No. 2, January 8, 1974.

citizens. The 1972 Constitution provided that "all citizens have the right to be tried by the judges determined by the constitution and the law" and further that civilians "were not subject to court martial."[111] This much was the same as in the past in that the president could authorize court martial of a civilian only when martial law had been invoked by reason of foreign invasion or insurrection and the civilian courts could not carry on their functions. But the Yusin Constitution conspicuously included the language that these provisions were applicable "except when the president limited the jurisdiction of the ordinary court through emergency decrees."[112] The drafters of the 1972 Constitution had been well prepared; such was the example of foolproof constitution-making.

Violators of the decrees could be arrested without judicial warrant. Note that the 1972 Constitution included the provision that "a warrant issued by a judge upon the request of the prosecutor must be present in the case of arrest, detention, seizure, and search."[113] Was Emergency Decree No. 2 then not a breach of the Constitution? It was, no doubt, except that it was authorized by Article 53, which contradicted the rest of the Constitution. Challenges arose immediately that Emergency Decree No. 1 impinged on the constitutional rights of the citizens, such as freedoms of speech, press, assembly, and association. But that decree had been mandated by a constitutional provision and, further, it was not subject to judicial review. Article 53 (4) overruled prospectively judicial interpretation of all emergency orders, foreclosing any interference from the courts. The explicit constitutional language barring judicial scrutiny led the Supreme Court to reject challenges to the decrees for lack of jurisdiction. This Kafkaesque situation laid bare the nature of the Yusin constitutional order. The emergency decrees existed in a supra-constitutional realm, not reachable by any power other than the president who issued them.

Allowing civilians to be arrested without warrant and subjecting them to military jurisdiction during peacetime dealt a blow, to say the least, to the integrity of the judicial system. The use of court martial for violators showed that the regime was still wary of the civilian courts, no matter how enfeebled they had become. On January 15, the government made the first arrests under Emergency Decree No. 1. Two

[111] Constitution (1972), Art. 24 (1) and (2).
[112] Constitution (1972), Art. 24 (2).
[113] Constitution (1972), Art. 10.

dissidents were swiftly tried and sentenced to fifteen years in prison, the maximum penalty prescribed under the decree. Their appeals were dismissed by the appellate court martial and by the Supreme Court in August 1974.[114]

Among all emergency measures issued by President Park, Emergency Decree No. 3 of January 14 was the only nonpolitical measure, aimed at achieving economic stabilization.[115] The government reduced income and residence tax rates for those in the lower income brackets and instituted graduated taxes for high-income earners. Special low-interest loans were made available to small and medium industries, and employers were ordered to pay wages before any other expenses. Aggravated punishment was imposed on those illegally exploiting workers. For farmers, the government set a higher purchase price for the harvest grains. Finally, the budget was slashed on the expenditures in 1974. These economic measures were highly popular among the citizens, broadly welcomed as a much-needed break for the poor and small businesses. The emergency decree that followed was a completely different story.

Emergency Decree No. 4

On April 3, 1974, Emergency Decree No. 4 was declared.[116] This measure was the regime's hurried response to student demonstrations that were spreading nationwide like wildfire, in particular activities of the National Federation of Democratic Youth and Students (Chŏnguk Minju Ch'ŏngnyŏn Haksaeng Ch'ong Yŏnmaeng, commonly known as Minch'ŏng Hangnyŏn).[117] It outlawed the National Federation and prohibited organizing or joining, praising, encouraging, or sympathizing with it; making contact or communicating with its members; providing them with any assistance; and being involved directly or indirectly in the organization (article 1). Publication, production, possession, dissemination, exhibit, or sale of documents, books, photographic records, or any other measures or expression concerning the activities of the said organization or its members was prohibited

114 S. Ct., 74To1123.

115 Emergency Decree No. 3, January 14, 1974, providing economic stabilization measures. This decree was repealed by Emergency Decree No. 6 on December 31, 1974.

116 Emergency Decree No. 4, April 3, 1974.

117 *Kwagŏ wa taehwa*, vol. 4, 196–197; Chang, *Protest Dialectics*, 70–73.

(article 2). Acts of encouraging, inciting, or advertising the activities prohibited in the first two articles were proscribed (article 3). The decree granted an amnesty period for violators: those who committed the acts prohibited in the first three articles were required to report themselves and their activities to an investigation and information agency before April 8, 1974, in which case they would not be punished (article 4).

The fact that this decree was specifically geared to suppress student activist movements was shown in the article that students who missed classes without excuse or refused to sit their exams, or who participated in individual or collective activities inside and outside school, such as assemblies, demonstrations, protests, or rallies other than legitimate classes and research activities supervised by school authorities, with the exception of regular and nonpolitical activities, were guilty of violating the decree (article 5). Acts of encouraging, inciting, or advertising activities prohibited by the decree and acts of informing others through broadcast, press, publication, or other methods were prohibited (article 6). The education minister was vested with the authority to close universities and schools where the students who violated this decree were enrolled (article 7). Violators of the decree or those who criticized the decree were punishable by death, life imprisonment, or imprisonment for not less than five years, with possible fifteen years of suspension of civil rights; those who attempted the prohibited acts or planned or conspired to attempt them were subject to the same penalties (article 8). Violators were subject to arrest, detention, seizure, and search without warrant and were tried by the emergency military court (article 9). Emergency military court prosecutors could order the confiscation of the seized documents and goods of the violators even when they were not prosecuted (article 10). Finally, local military commanders were required to comply with the request for the deployment of the military forces when such was put forward by the mayors of the cities of Seoul and Pusan or the governors of the provinces for the purpose of maintaining public order (article 11). This last article was inserted to facilitate the use of the troops in suppressing demonstrations and occupying university campuses.

Emergency Decree No. 4 was, in all aspects, a measure intended by President Park to discipline student activists. In theory, students who dared to skip classes to participate in antigovernment protests could be put to death. Throughout modern Korean history, students represented a formidable antigovernment force, in particular since the April Uprising that instigated the fall of President Rhee Syngman in 1960. Only a small percentage of students were politically active, but they were extremely rigid and radical.[118] Park's difficult relations with student protesters started early on, when his policy to normalize diplomatic relations with Japan met vehement resistance in the early 1960s. In the 1970s, they took the brunt of the emergency decrees.[119] It was a familiar sight in the streets of Seoul, especially in the springtime, that students confronted and fought the riot police in a blanket of tear gas.

It was hard to miss the irony in those scenes that the young students were clashing against and crashing into policemen who were just about their age. In the early 1970s, not many went to university, and wearing a tiny university badge on their shirt was a distinct privilege enjoyed by a relative small number of young men and women. All South Korean males, then and now, serve in the military for a period. One could defer conscription while attending school. When college students protested on campus, their less-privileged cohort often sat day and night in drab army buses stationed at the university gates, under the order to stop the demonstrators from spilling out of campus. Perhaps not a few among them longed to be on the other side of those gates. The embattled students, on their part, felt qualms of the guilty conscience of the elite, mixed with a sense of moral indignation against the illiberal regime; it was these complex sentiments that galvanized them in their struggles against the government that they believed was perpetuating injustice and inequity. For the president, on the other hand, those headstrong and impetuous youth needed to be stopped, through intimidation and harsh punishment if necessary.

Within a month of the declaration of Emergency Decree No. 4, the government took into custody 1,024 students; 253 of them were referred to the prosecutor's office.[120] Thirty-two were formally charged on May 27, some also with security laws. As will be seen in Chapter 5, the Minch'ŏng Hangnyŏn case became intertwined with the

118 Oberdorfer and Carlin, *The Two Koreas*, 41.
119 Along with intellectuals, students were the most vocal antigovernment groups during the authoritarian period. Namhee Lee, *The Making of Minjung: Democracy and the Politics of Representation in South Korea* (Ithaca: Cornell University Press, 2009), 18–19.
120 Chang, *Protest Dialectics*, 72.

Inmin Hyŏngmyŏngdang Chaegŏn Wiwŏnhoe case. Minch'ŏng Hangnyŏn defendants stood trial on July 13 and received sentences ranging from the death penalty to fifteen years in prison.[121] Many of those sentences were later commuted, but it was clear that the president was determined to teach a lesson to the student activists.

On August 23, 1974, President Park announced, by way of Emergency Decree No. 5, the abolition of Emergency Decrees Nos. 1 and 4.[122] Eight days earlier on August 15, during the ceremony commemorating Korea's liberation from Japan, Park's wife, First Lady Yuk Yŏng-Su, had been shot and killed by a bullet meant for the president. A Korean resident of Japan who belonged to a pro-North group was arrested at the scene. In the wake of this tragic incident, the president issued a statement that the outpouring of sympathy from the citizens for the death of the First Lady convinced him that "national solidarity has been strengthened to meet any threat from North Korea" and that he wanted to lift the emergency measures.[123] While the two emergency decrees were revoked, however, it was made clear that their rescission had no effect either on the cases that were pending in judicial proceedings or on those individuals who were already serving sentences upon conviction under the decrees. This way the defendants charged in the Minch'ŏng Hangnyŏn case and found guilty were kept in prison. On October 11, the last emergency court martial proceedings took place for defendants charged with Emergency Decrees Nos. 1 and 4.[124]

In Korean law, military court decisions can be appealed to the Supreme Court on the limited grounds allowed in the law.[125] Those convicted at the emergency military courts could in principle bring their cases to the highest court, claiming violation of the constitution, laws, decrees, or regulations by the lower court. In reality, however, the system was stacked against them because the military court procedures required much more stringent rules than those governing civilian courts. The Criminal Procedure Act of 1973 provided that appeals

121 For the texts of the military court's decisions and the defense appeals motions, see *Inkwŏn pyŏllon charyo chip*, vol. 1, 289–581.

122 Emergency Decree No. 5, August 23, 1974.

123 *Tong-A Ilbo*, August 23, 1974.

124 *Kyŏnghyang Sinmun*, October 11, 1974; *Tong-A Ilbo*, October 11, 1974.

125 Kunpŏp Hoeŭi Pŏp [Military Court Act] (revised in 1965), art. 432. This law was comprehensively revised and renamed Kunsa Pŏpwŏn Pŏp in 1987.

could be heard by the Supreme Court "in those cases where the death penalty, life imprisonment, or imprisonment of ten years or more with or without labor has been imposed and the sentence had been the result of a serious mistake of facts or there is a clear reason to believe that the sentence was unjustly excessive."[126] In contrast, the Military Court Act did not have a similar provision, and factual errors or excessive punishments were not allowed as grounds for appeal.[127] This practically shut the door for appeals from civilian defendants convicted under the emergency decrees, forcing the Supreme Court to dismiss them as long as it decided there was no error by the court martial in applying the law. The result was that the military courts' decisions were invariably affirmed by the highest court. The Supreme Court ruled that the argument that the defendants were not guilty because their actions were not harmful or, alternatively, because they acted out of patriotism could not be a valid reason for appeal.

The bizarre and dismal reality of the Yusin-era legal system was in full view. The emergency decrees prohibited discussion relating to revising the Constitution, and, since the Constitution sanctioned the presidential power to issue emergency measures, any challenge to the decrees would have amounted to a demand for constitutional amendment; meanwhile, constitutional scrutiny of these orders was constitutionally barred. This bewildering situation beset the courts. The emergency decrees were simply baffling laws, lacking any modicum of reasonableness, aimed at suppressing political opposition. Many dissidents, students, religious leaders, journalists, and ordinary citizens were harassed and subjected to physical abuse. An anecdote illustrates the widespread resentment among citizens toward the military judges, who often treated civilian defendants with an imperious attitude. In an early case of violation of the emergency decree in January 1974, Christian pastors stood as defendants before the military court. The judge snidely asked the defendants, "How did you, you pastors, get involved in political activities instead of spreading gospel in these emergency times?" To this, a defendant retorted: "What are you doing here, you soldiers, passing judgment on civilians instead of defending the country in these emergency times?"[128] A sentiment of age-old prejudice

[126] Criminal Procedure (1973), art. 383 (4).
[127] Military Court Act, art. 432. See Chapter 7, note 18.
[128] *Pŏpcho 50 nyŏn yasa*, vol. 2, 35–36.

against the military, something that could be traced to the Confucian Chosŏn culture, likely aggravated antagonism against what many people viewed as the despotism of a military regime.

During the nine-month period between January 8, when the first emergency decree was issued, and October 11, when the last trials under Emergency Decrees Nos. 1 and 4 were held, the Ordinary Court Martial tried 203 defendants under one or both decrees; not a single person was acquitted.[129] Among them, 141 were students and two were Japanese nationals. Table 4.2 shows the sentences rendered by the emergency appellate court martial. Many defendants were simultaneously charged with security laws, and the sentences in the table reflect punishments on all charges. The Criminal Code stipulated, under the principle of conceptual concurrence of crimes: "When a single act constituted multiple crimes, the punishment provided for the most severe crime shall be imposed."[130] In most cases, security law charges carried heavier punishments. In the emergency ordinary court martial, fourteen persons received the death penalty, sixteen were sentenced to life imprisonment, and the remaining 173 defendants received sentences ranging from twenty years in prison to a suspended sentence. 190 people appealed. The appellate court martial dismissed seventy appeals and reduced the sentences of 120 defendants.[131] Two-thirds of the defendants were sentenced to more than ten years in prison; those who received sentences of over five years in prison numbered 179, or 88.2 percent.[132]

Among those convicted were Yun Posun, the former president; Roman Catholic Church Bishop Chi Hak-Sun; Reverend Pak Hyŏng-Kyu of the Presbyterian Church; and Professors Kim Tong-Kil, a historian, and Kim Ch'an-Kuk, a theologian, both from Yonsei University. They had been arrested in July 1974 for assisting Minch'ŏng Hangnyŏn students. Kim Tong-Kil famously told the military judge in the courtroom not to bother to show him leniency, because if he were freed he would resume what he had been doing and

129 *Yŏksa sogŭi sabŏppu*, 427–428.

130 Criminal Code, art. 40. The Code provides, under art. 50, "(2) In case of punishments of the same kind, the punishment with a longer maximum term [of imprisonment] and a larger maximum amount [of fine] shall be deemed more severe, and when the maximum term or amount is equal, the punishment with a longer minimum term or a larger minimum amount shall be deemed more severe."

131 *Tong-A Ilbo*, October 11, 1974. The full list of defendants and their military court sentences is provided in *Tong-A Ilbo*, February 15, 1975.

132 *Yŏksa sogŭi sabŏppu*, 429.

Table 4.2 *Sentences Rendered by the Emergency Appellate Military Court in 1974 (Emergency Decrees No. 1 and No. 4 and Security Laws)*

	Death Penalty	Life in Prison	> 15 yrs	15 yrs	12 yrs	10 yrs	7 yrs	5 yrs	< 5 yrs	Stay of Execution	Total
Number	8	13	19	38	18	36	27	20	7	17	203
Percent	3.9%	6.4%	9.4%	18.7%	8.9%	17.7%	13.3%	9.9%	3.4%	8.4%	100%

Note: Sentences include those imposed for violations of the emergency decrees and concurrent security laws, if applicable.
Source: Sabŏpsa P'yŏnch'an Wiwŏnhoe, *Yŏksa sogŭi sabŏppu*, 429.

would be rearrested and brought back to the courtroom; he would rather stay in prison than go in and out senselessly. Defiance was an important element of the prodemocracy spirit pitted against an absurd system.

A total of 108 defendants appealed to the Supreme Court, whereas eighty-two defendants chose not to appeal, among whom seventy-seven were students.[133] Among those who appealed, ten withdrew the petition.[134] Why did such a high number not pursue appeal? A conventional explanation was that the defendants saw no point in appeals as they had no respect for the judicial system. An editorial in *Tong-A Ilbo* stated that the "distrust of the judiciary" prompted the defendants' decision not to appeal.[135] There was indeed little expectation that the highest court would reverse the convictions. The Supreme Court managed to remand a total of four cases to the appellate court martial on grounds unrelated to the emergency measures. Still, normally few defendants would give up their rights to appeal merely because they did not trust the judiciary. Here, one may seek another reason for the low rates of appeals.

A newspaper reported on December 6, 1974, that the government was considering special clemency for emergency decree violators sometime at the beginning of the new year but only for those whose cases reached conclusion.[136] The news was followed by the report of the withdrawals of appeal by defendants, who hoped to become eligible for release through clemency.[137] A court proceeding is concluded when the defendant fails to appeal within the time limit and the sentence becomes final. According to article 379 of the Criminal Procedure, the process at the Supreme Court does not start until at least thirty days have passed from the notice of the reception of the trial records by the Court.[138] As of December 27, the cases of sixty-nine defendants had been received by the Supreme Court.[139] There was significant pressure on the Court to dispose of those cases as quickly as possible to pave the way for their release through presidential clemency. A newspaper reported that the Supreme Court was trying to complete all

133 *Tong-A Ilbo*, November 28, 1974.
134 Thirteen people abandoned appeal to the appellate court martial. *Tong-A Ilbo*, February 15, 1975.
135 *Tong-A Ilbo*, December 2, 1974.
136 *Tong-A Ilbo*, December 6, 1974.
137 *Tong-A Ilbo*, December 9, 1974.
138 *Kyŏnghyang Sinmun*, December 6, 1974.
139 *Tong-A Ilbo*, December 27, 1974.

the proceedings before the end of January but it was highly unrealistic.[140] The government strategy was clear: it pressed the courts to expedite the trials so that it could repeal the decrees, having achieved the goal of putting the targeted individuals behind bars; it would then selectively free the prisoners.[141] The government dangled the possibility of clemency, and it was sufficient to dissuade defendants from pursuing appeals when there was little chance for reversal anyway.

Cleaning Up after the Government

In January 1975, President Park announced that he would call for a national referendum to ask voters whether they supported the Yusin Constitution. On February 12, 73.1 percent of voters cast the ballot in support, a result which the government claimed to be the popular endorsement of the country's path.[142] Three days later, the president issued a special order to release those who were serving sentences under Emergency Decrees Nos. 1 and 4. Recall these decrees had been abolished in previous August but the violators remained imprisoned. The president declared that "now that the historical legitimacy and national justification of the current constitutional order has been reconfirmed by popular will" he decided to free the violators so that "we consolidate the national consensus all at once by allowing them opportunities to participate in the historic task of national rehabilitation."[143]

On February 15, a total of 148 persons were released, out of 203 violators of the decrees. The governmental largesse was implemented through suspended sentences or suspended trials. According to *Tong-A Ilbo*, the administration had asked the Supreme Court to finalize the list of those to be released by February 15, but the Court could not meet that deadline; as of that date, appeals of forty-one cases had been rejected, with one case remanded, and fifty-six cases remained pending.[144] Two days later, twenty-two individuals in the last group were released.[145] Thirty-four people were excluded from release,

140 *Tong-A Ilbo*, January 6 and January 14, 1975.
141 Bernard Gwertzman, "U.S. Aides Press for Seoul Fund," *The New York Times*, July 31, 1974.
142 *Pŏpwŏnsa*, 818.
143 *Tong-A Ilbo*, February 15, 1975.
144 Ibid.
145 *Kyŏnghyang Sinmun*, February 17, 1975.

including the twenty-one persons implicated with the Inmin Hyŏngmyŏngdang Chaegŏn Wiwŏnhoe case, eleven persons charged with the violation of the Anticommunist Act or the National Security Act, and two others.[146] The fact that the violators were freed through suspended sentences or trials, instead of commuted sentences, meant they could be placed back in jail through the cancellation of court orders. Justice Minister Hwang San-Tŏk warned that if the released violators behaved recklessly, "forgetting" the intention of the president to grant them opportunities to participate in the renewal of the nation, their acts would negate the reasons of the release and the government would be compelled to place the defendants back in custody and execute the sentences.[147]

There is no doubt that these developments amounted to a serious compromise of judicial independence. Evidently the trial schedules were dictated by the prosecution and the Justice Ministry.[148] The Supreme Court seemed to act on the cue of the government, obliquely following the direction of the president. An opposition National Assembly member lamented that "the judiciary has become a mere administrative agency and judicial independence no longer exists."[149] Chief Court Administrator Kim Pyŏng-Hwa, appearing before the Assembly, did not deny that the Supreme Court rushed the trials to comply with the government demand. He could only state, in a roundabout way: "We hope that the current system improves so that judicial independence is guaranteed without any restraint in the administration of justice, but the judges are doing their best under the current system in order to preserve their integrity and responsibility as officers of law."[150]

While the executive branch's gestures of leniency were eagerly greeted by the public, the Supreme Court was not celebrating. The government's move essentially meant justices had been obligated to enforce absurd decrees and affirm the verdicts handed down by military courts and then saw their decisions cast aside by the government, which now took the credit from the public for its lenity. The release of prisoners generated a mood of jubilation, and opposition

146 *Maeil Kyŏngje*, February 15, 1975.
147 *Kyŏnghyang Sinmun*, February 18, 1975.
148 *Tong-A Ilbo*, March 27, 1975; *Maeil Kyŏngje*, February 18, 1975.
149 *Tong-A Ilbo*, March 15, 1975.
150 Ibid.

groups proclaimed a victory for democratic struggle.[151] President Park complained that the released prisoners "shouted in triumph claiming that they were innocent, as if they were victorious generals returning from battle, and some newspapers chimed in with them, carrying large photographs of them."[152] While the president griped about the alleged ingratitude, the judges groaned. A judge later recalled that he and his colleagues felt utterly humiliated.[153] Bruised judicial egos notwithstanding, it is a fair assessment that the whole saga of the emergency decrees deeply undermined public trust in the judiciary.

As *Tong-A Ilbo* summed it up, "the issuance of the emergency decrees, imposition of severe sentences, and inevitable subsequent release left a bad taste in the mouth of the jurists who valued the authority of law and legal stability."[154] To put it more bluntly, the judges became fall guys in the unfolding emergency decree drama. The disproportionately harsh punishments, followed by grandiose gestures of clemency, offer a glimpse of the president's frame of mind. It seems that Park wanted above all to scare off his opponents. Twelve people implicated in Minchŏng Hangnyŏn were freed on February 18, 1975, and were placed back in custody after the Supreme Court dismissed their appeals on April 8, only to be released again with a stay of execution.[155] Their hardship through all this should not be downplayed. The Supreme Court continued the trials of Emergency Decrees Nos. 1 and 4 well into the summer of 1975, grudgingly cleaning up the mess the government had made.

In the meantime, yet another emergency decree had already been issued. This one worsened the judges' plight because it entrusted ordinary court judges with the task of trying its violators at first instance.

Emergency Decree No. 9

The spring of 1975 was marked by fierce student protests. On April 8, the president imposed Emergency Decree No. 7 and ordered the temporary

151 Sohn, *Authoritarianism and Opposition,* 79.
152 *Tong-A Ilbo*, February 21, 1975.
153 Pak U-Tong, *P'ansa sil esŏ pŏpchŏng kkaji* [From Judicial Chamber to Courtroom], 2nd ed. (Seoul: Hanguk Sabŏp Haengjŏng Hakhoe, 2000).
154 *Tong-A Ilbo*, February 18, 1975.
155 *Tong-A Ilbo*, April 11, 1975.

closure of Korea University, a hotbed of student demonstrations, and the stationing of troops on campus.[156] Violators would be arrested without warrant and subject to between three and ten years of imprisonment. It was a tense time. Overseas, Saigon fell to the communists on April 30. The country was in panic mode. Would Seoul be next?[157] Emergency Decree No. 7 was repealed on May 13 by Emergency Decree No. 8, and was succeeded the same day by Emergency Decree No. 9. This decree, the last emergency decree issued by President Park and the longest in force (until December 1979), was also the most extreme.[158]

Titled "Emergency Measures for Safeguarding National Security and Public Order," the new decree comprehensively reintroduced the contents of Emergency Decrees Nos. 1 and 4 and restricted even more tightly the rights of citizens to participate in the political process. Its article 1 banned the following activities:

> (1) fabricating and spreading false rumors or making false representation of facts and disseminating them; (2) denying, opposing, distorting, or defaming the Constitution of the Republic of Korea, or asserting, petitioning, instigating, or advertising its revision or repeal by means of assembly or demonstration, through the use of public mass media such as newspapers, broadcasts, or news wires, or by the creation of documents, pictures, records, or other materials; (3) student meetings and demonstrations or political gatherings that did not obtain the school head's prior approval, other than regular classes or research activities taking place under school authorities' control and supervision or irregular non-political activities; (4) any act of willfully criticizing this Decree.

It thus outlawed, in one fell swoop, all public discussion of the Yusin Constitution and the decree itself, and prohibited any kind of unauthorized political activity. One sees how jittery the government

[156] Emergency Decree No. 7, April 8, 1975. This decree aimed to preempt protests expected upon the issuance of the Supreme Court judgment the same day on the Inhyŏktang and Minch'ŏng Hangnyŏn cases. See Chapter 5.

[157] Some commentators noted that two of the lesser-known casualties of the Vietnam War for Korea were democracy and human rights. Cohen and Baker, "U.S. Foreign Policy," 176. Regardless of the regime's attempt to take advantage of the situation for political use, however, the deep sentiment of crisis and dismay Korean people felt watching Vietnam's fate was real.

[158] Presidential Emergency Decree for National Security and Public Order (Kukka Anjŏn kwa Konggong Chilsŏ ŭi Suho rŭl wihan Taet'ongnyŏng Kinkŭp Choch'i), May 13, 1975 (commonly known as Emergency Decree No. 9).

had become over the citizens' continuing demand for constitutional revision. Any media coverage of antigovernment activity was forbidden. Article 2 of the decree prohibited "any act of willfully diffusing the coverage of activities prohibited in article 1 by means of broadcasting, reporting, or other means, and any creation, dissemination, sale, possession, or exhibition of materials containing the expression of those contents."

Article 3 prohibited "the transfer of properties belonging to the Republic of Korea or its citizens abroad for the purpose of hiding them, and the acts of hiding or disposing of the properties overseas that were otherwise to be brought into the country." Article 4 prohibited "obtaining permission to relocate abroad through fraudulently representing facts in the relevant documents or through other unlawful methods, or fleeing abroad."

Article 5 dealt with the punishment of the violators of the decree, specifically aiming at those in universities and media outlets. It stated:

> The relevant cabinet members can issue orders or take measures against universities, organizations, or businesses, or the heads or chief officers thereof, to which the violators of the decree belonged at the time of the crime, including the following: (1) to dismiss or expel staff members, school personnel, or students through the orders of the heads or chief officers; (2) to dismiss or expel the heads or chief officers, staff members, school personnel, or students; (3) to prohibit the acts of broadcasting, reporting, publishing, selling, or disseminating; (4) to close temporarily the businesses or schools, to cease publication temporarily or permanently, to dissolve or close [the organizations and businesses]; and (5) to revoke the approval, registration, permit, leave, or license.

Thus, universities, schools, newspapers, broadcasting companies, or other organizations and businesses could be shut down by the government if anyone affiliated with them were found to have violated a provision of the decree. This was a highly effective method to muzzle the media, because the owners and editors of the media now had to control the actions of their own employees and staff in order to avoid the forced closure of their companies. University authorities and professors found themselves burdened with the duty of surveying their students, basically assuming responsibilities normally borne by the security police of the state apparatus.[159]

[159] Sohn, *Authoritarianism and Opposition*, 85.

Article 6 was geared to suppress media coverage of the activities of the opposition lawmakers. It stated: "The statements of National Assembly members made as part of their legislative duty in the National Assembly are not punished even if they violate this decree. But this excludes those who willfully spread those statements by broadcasting, reporting, or other methods." The government did not want citizens to know what was happening in the legislature. Whatever little resistance and struggle being put forward by the opposition parties should not be reported; the regime was in particular mindful of keeping under the public radar the frequent irregular procedural methods resorted to by the ruling party to push the government agenda.

Article 7 listed punishments: "Violators of this decree or other measures undertaken by the cabinet ministers to implement this decree are subject to imprisonment of one year or more, and the suspension of civil rights for not more than ten years. Those who attempted to commit the crimes above or who prepared or plotted them are punishable by the same penalties." The violators "are subject to arrest, detention, and search and seizure without judicial warrant" (article 8). "The crimes of violating this decree are conducted by ordinary courts" (article 10). The minister of defense could comply with the request for the deployment of the military forces when such was put forward by the mayors of the cities of Seoul and Pusan or the governors of the provinces for the purpose of maintaining public order (article 12). Finally, it confirmed that "this decree or the measures undertaken by the cabinet ministers to implement it are not subject to judicial review" (article 13).

A large part of the decree was a repeat of the earlier emergency decrees. A major difference was that now trials were conducted by civilian courts instead of military courts.[160] Why this change? The president may have felt confident that the ordinary courts, sufficiently emaciated, could not pose serious obstruction to the implementation of the new decree. Or perhaps he came to note the strong antagonism demonstrated by citizens against the military courts. Whatever the reason, now all judges, not just the Supreme Court justices, were assigned to the frontline of the Yusin system.[161]

160 Emergency Decree No. 7 (April 8, 1975) granted jurisdiction to ordinary courts.

161 *Kwagŏ wa taehwa*, vol. 4, 206.

The awkwardly crafted provisions of the decree could have been laughed off as bizarre, if only the regime had not been dead serious about enforcing them. Table 4.3 lists the sentences for the violators of Emergency Decree No. 9 at first instance (district court). The numbers were compiled from the *Sabŏp yŏngam* (*Judiciary Yearbook*) published annually by the Supreme Court. The yearbook does not provide data of the trials of first instance for the year 1975. The report of Truth and Reconciliation Commission lists the numbers of the prosecuted individuals each year as 251 (1975), 176 (1976), 167 (1977), 312 (1978), and 68 (1979).[162] It reveals discrepancies with the numbers from the *Judiciary Yearbook*: 191 (1976); 157 (1977); 215 (1978); and 160 (1979). Table 4.4 lists the sentences rendered at the second instance level (appeals court).

Excluding those violators sentenced in 1979, only two defendants at first instance and five on appeal were freed upon a not-guilty verdict. The majority of defendants received prison terms between one and three years. In 1976, out of 221 individuals who were prosecuted, seventy-seven (34.8 percent) were sentenced to between one year and less than three years; thirty-one (14 percent) between three years and less than five years; and thirty-three (14.9 percent) five years or more. No defendant received a sentence over ten years. The minimum sentence prescribed in the decree was one year in prison, but judges had the discretion of reducing the sentences for extenuating circumstances.[163] Thirty-seven (16.7 percent) persons received less than one year, and thirty-five (15.8 percent) a stay of execution (also known as suspended sentence prior to execution). Over the years, the sentences appeared to become heavier. The number of defendants receiving less than one year or a stay of execution at first instance decreased in 1977 and 1978. The appellate courts tended to reduce the sentences. Those who had been sentenced to more than five years at first instance usually received on appeal a reduction to between one and three years.[164]

162 Chinsil-Hwahae Rŭl Wihan Kwagŏsa Chŏngni Wiwŏnhoe, *2006 nyŏn habangi chosa pogosŏ* [Report of the 2nd half of Year 2006] (Seoul: Chinsil-Hwahae Rŭl Wihan Kwagŏsa Chŏngni Wiwŏnhoe, 2007), 296.

163 Criminal Code, art. 51.

164 *Yŏksa sogŭi sabŏppu*, 431–432.

Table 4.3 *Sentences for Emergency Decree No. 9 Violations (First Instance), 1976–1979*

Year	Received Current Year	Disposed	≥ 10 yrs	≥ 5 yrs	≥ 3 yrs	≥ 1 yr	< 1 yr	Stay of Execution	Indeter.*	Suspension of Civil Rights	Suspended Sentence	Not Guilty	Dismissed	Misc.**	Appealed	Pending
1976	191	221	0	33	31	77	37	35	1	4	0	1	2	0	147	17
1977	157	116	0	13	30	48	12	13	0	0	0	0	0	0	74	58
1978	215	189	0	11	36	106	8	17	10	0	0	1	0	0	158	84
1979	160	195	0	2	19	58	9	13	1	17	2	73	0	1	131	49

Notes: Court statistics for 1975 not available.

* Indeterminate sentence.

** Transfer to juvenile section.

Sources: *Sabŏp yŏngam* (1977), 354–377; *Sabŏp yŏngam* (1978), 476–500; *Sabŏp yŏngam* (1979), 494–519; *Sabŏp yŏngam* (1980), 534–559.

Table 4.4 *Sentences for Emergency Decree No. 9 Violations (Second Instance), 1975–1979*

			Reversed or Partially Affirmed												Appeals Dismissed				
Year	Received Current Year	Disposed	≥ 10 yrs	≥ 5 yrs	≥ 3 yrs	≥ 1 yr	< 1 yr*	Stay of Execution	Indeter.**	Suspension of Civil Rights	Suspended Sentence	Not Guilty	Dimissed	Misc.**	With Arguments	Without Arguments	Charges Dropped	Appealed	Pending
1975	20	11	0	0	2	2	0	0	2	0	0	0	0	1	4	0	0	1	9
1976	185	149	1	19	14	11	2	16	2	0	1	5	0	0	61	17	0	47	45
1977	86	86	0	2	18	10	3	19	0	0	0	0	0	0	30	4	0	29	45
1978	153	130	0	0	23	15	2	19	14	1	1	0	0	2	51	2	0	90	68
1979	206	220	0	0	12	55	5	28	7	0	0	1	18	1	87	0	6	80	54

Notes: * Indeterminate sentence.
** Transfer to juvenile section.
Sources: *Sabŏp yŏngam* (1976), 344–355; *Sabŏp yŏngam* (1977), 354–377; *Sabŏp yŏngam* (1978), 476–500; *Sabŏp yŏngam* (1979), 494–519; *Sabŏp yŏngam* (1980), 534–559.

Emergency in Perpetuity

It must be recalled that government repression was not limited to formal indictments and convictions. Student protestors were regularly rounded up and put in custody overnight. A number of professors were summarily fired from their job under government pressure. Suppression of press freedom was thorough and persistent; even university newspapers were rigorously censored. Obviously "emergency" measures were supposed to remain in force for a crisis situation only, for the shortest period possible. But the president apparently wanted to keep the state of purported emergency indefinitely. It was not abolished until after his death.

The government agency that supervised and coordinated the implementation of the emergency decrees was the Korean Central Intelligence Agency (KCIA). The KCIA Act was issued on June 10, 1961, following the military coup in May.[165] The agency "coordinates and oversees the information gathering and investigation activities by the government agencies including the military" (art. 1), and its director "directs and supervises its personnel and also the personnel in other agencies regarding gathering information and investigation activities as provided in article 1" (art. 4). Initially, the KCIA director, branch chiefs, and agents had the right to investigate crimes "not subject to the direction of the prosecutor," but this provision created conflicts with the prosecutors' office and was deleted when the law was revised on December 14, 1963.[166] Article 10 of Emergency Decree No. 2 explicitly provided the director of the KCIA the power to oversee the investigation of cases under the jurisdiction of the emergency court martial.[167] Emergency Decree No. 9 did not include a similar provision, but it was understood that the KCIA continued to play the central role. During the 1960s and 1970s, it exerted practically unlimited power in dealing with security-related intelligence. In 1981, the KCIA was restructured as the Agency for National Security Planning (ANSP, Kukka Anjŏn Kihoekpu). In 1999, it was incorporated into the National Intelligence Service (NIS, Kukka Chŏngbowŏn).

165 Chungang Chŏngbobu Pŏp [Central Intelligence Agency Act] (Act No. 619, June 10, 1961).

166 *Kwagŏ wa taehwa*, vol. 4, 179–189.

167 See in this chapter, note 110 and accompanying text.

During the Yusin era, the KCIA remained a highly dreaded symbol of state violence. The agency was in full action as the government intensified suppression of media freedom. The National Assembly had already passed a law on December 27, 1971, prohibiting publications that "threatened the security of the nation." The revision of the Media Act in 1973 allowed censorship of newspapers and broadcast media. Security agents were assigned to each media firm. Any reporting on antigovernment demonstrations was forbidden. In the fall of 1974, a group of journalists rose up in protest. On October 24, reporters at *Tong-A Ilbo*, the newspaper known for its independent streak, issued the Declaration of Action for the Freedom of Media, publicly denouncing the government's violation of the freedom of the press. Soon, thirty-one newspapers around the country followed suit. The KCIA quickly stepped in. Starting from December, it coerced businesses and companies to cancel their advertising contracts with *Tong-A Ilbo* and its affiliate Tong-A Broadcasting, effectively cutting off their revenue sources.[168] Even smaller companies pulled out advertisements under the threat of tax audits. As a result, *Tong-A Ilbo* was printed for a couple of months with ominous-looking large blank spaces otherwise reserved for advertisements.

The government action soon backfired, however. Spontaneous citizen campaigns popped up to raise money for the besieged newspaper. "Helping Tong-A" became a slogan of grassroots movements. In January and February 1975, the newspaper was filled with hundreds of tiny, one- or two-line classifieds paid for by individual citizens, with typical wordings like "Go, Tong-A!" People lined up outside the newspaper building in downtown Seoul to wait their turn to purchase a space in the paper. Various fundraising activities sprouted among the citizens – for example, college students would work at coffee shops for a day, and the proceeds were donated to the newspaper. The government eventually withdrew its clumsy tactic, but not before the KCIA succeeded in forcing the newspaper between March and May to dismiss forty-nine journalists and to suspend indefinitely another eighty-four. The fired journalists formed the Tong-A Committee for the

168 *Truth and Reconciliation Activities of the Past Three Years* (Seoul: Truth and Reconciliation Commission, 2009), 88–89.

Struggle to Protect a Free Press.[169] *Chosŏn Ilbo*, another major newspaper company, was also forced to dismiss over thirty reporters.[170]

Few citizens in the 1970s accepted the government's assertion that student or journalist protesters were endangering the country. The majority of Korean people at this time were of the opinion that most emergency decree violators held antigovernment, not antistate, views. Regrettably, muddling antistate and antigovernment activities was a perennial feature of South Korean politics from 1948, as successive regimes tried to equate questioning government policy with spreading North Korean propaganda. To be sure, provocations from North Korea were frequent and exacerbated over the years. In 1974 and 1975, underground tunnels through the demilitarized zone (DMZ), dug by the North to infiltrate the South, were discovered. On August 18, 1976, two US army officers were killed by North Korean soldiers in the joint security area in DMZ.[171] These incidents heightened the sense of alarm among citizens. In short, the line separating political dissents and national security threats became increasingly tenuous.

Why was the judiciary unable to scrutinize more aggressively the laws and actions of the government? The preceding pages have suggested partial answers by referring to the institutional and constitutional changes. When the Yusin Constitution reconfigured the separation of powers and set forth the new standards of constitutionality, it reshaped the spheres and confines of judicial function, seriously curtailing the courts' ability to restrain the government. The next chapter turns to an analysis of the judicial process under the Yusin system.

169 Chang, *Protest Dialectics*, 116–127.

170 Ibid., 124; Han Hong-Ku, "Han Hong-Ku ŭi Yusin kwa onŭl" [Han Hong-Ku's Yusin and Today], *Hangyŏrye Sinmun*, November 13, 2012.

171 Oberdorfer and Carlin, *The Two Koreas*, 45–47, 59–66.

5 *The Yusin Era, 1972–1980 (2): The Courts*

The surreal scenes at court martial in which civilians, bound with thick rope, stood before the uniformed military generals, sitting high on the bench, are forever frozen in public memory. In February 1975, Yang Sŏng-U, a high school teacher, read a poem at a small prayer gathering in Kwangju. His verses, titled "The Winter Republic" (Kyŏul Konghwaguk), compared the Fourth Republic under the Yusin Constitution to the midnight darkness in the frozen winter.[1] The imagery of the silenced and shivering citizens raised the question: where were the courts in those desolate times? The fact that the Supreme Court, which in theory had the power to quash the military court decisions in emergency decree cases, failed to do so subjected it to much backlash. Judges had little faith in the integrity of laws like emergency decrees – few informed Koreans did – during the Yusin years, but they more or less persisted in the belief that they were bound by the duty to uphold the constitution and apply the existing laws to the cases brought before them. By doing so, they could not avoid the criticism that they cast the mantle of lawfulness over government abuses. Still, the courts' insistence to give effect to the will of the law, rather than their own, helped preserve the legal order as an antidote to authoritarian rule.

An important insight in recent research on authoritarian regimes is that they ostensibly advocate the rule of law and normally maintain independent courts. It is part of a strategic choice devised to utilize judicial proceedings for the purpose of legitimating their policies and practices. Even autocratic rulers seek judicial approval. Independent courts are also pivotal because of their role in economic development.

[1] See Youngju Ryu, *Writers of the Winter Republic: Literature and Resistance in Park Chung Hee's Korea* (Honolulu: University of Hawai'i Press, 2015). This poem cost Yang his job; he was imprisoned in 1977 for his antigovernment writings.

Legal foundations for private interests, such as the protection of property rights and the enforcement of contracts, provide the appearance of institutional normalcy and stimulate economy.

In his book on the "dual state" in Nazi Germany, Fraenkel showed how the prerogative state in the public law realm could coexist with the normative state in the private law realm.[2] In the Nazi legal order, wrote Fraenkel, "[p]rivate property still enjoys the protection of the courts from official interference, except where political considerations are involved," for example in matters concerning Jews.[3] The courts, "as guardians of the normative state," upheld entrepreneurial liberty, the sanctity of contracts, private property, competition, labor law, and the law of non-tangible property.[4] The prerogative state had reason not to upset economic stability and market confidence and therefore limited its intervention in economic affairs to suppressing labor protests. "In this way the Prerogative State is able to influence the behavior of capitalists and enterprisers although they are nominally not only controlled but also protected by the Normative State."[5]

Fraenkel's dual state theory offers an important insight for the judicial process in Yusin Korea. Even with the reign of emergency military courts, the regular civil and penal justice system continued to function. The judges went about their jobs and conducted trials much as they had done before. The government did not defy court rulings once they were rendered, even in political cases. In this situation, it was critical for the courts to maintain the ordinary business of the law, as long as the regime's concern for legitimacy still committed it to at least a semblance of judicial independence. This chapter examines jurisprudence in both security and nonsecurity cases. The institution of seemingly perpetual emergency demonstrated the fundamental arbitrariness of the prerogative state, but

[2] Fraenkel, *The Dual State*. Frankel fled the Nazis in 1939 to the United States. A little-known fact about Fraenkel is that he later served in Korea as a legal advisor to the US military occupation forces. His stay in Korea, from 1946 to 1950, came to an abrupt end at the outbreak of the Korean War, forcing him to make a harrowing escape before the advancing communists. Fraenkel's writings during his service in Korea are collected in Gerhard Göhler (ed.), *Ernst Fraenkel Gesammelte Schriften*, vol. 3, *Neuaufbau der Demokratie in Deutschland und Korea* (Baden-Baden: Nomos Verlagsgesellschaft, 1999).

[3] Fraenkel, *The Dual State,* 78.

[4] Ibid., 73–82.

[5] Ibid., 187.

its advances unfolded against the backdrop of the legal norms of the normative state.

The first part of the chapter discusses the People's Revolutionary Party Reconstruction Committee (Inmin Hyŏngmyŏngdang Chaegŏn Wiwŏnhoe) case. Commonly known as Inhyŏktang case, it refers to a trial concluded in April 1975 in which the Supreme Court affirmed the emergency military court decision that sentenced eight defendants to death.[6] It has long been regarded as the epitome of the unjust Yusin system. A book published in 2001 called the trial a "judicial murder."[7] Since then, the epithet "judicial murder" has been solidly affixed to this case, and it has become a byword for the travesty of justice during the Yusin years.[8] While the case has long been at the center of national debate, the actual court opinion has not been adequately studied. The extent to which the laws implemented by courts were substantively irrational or to which judicial interpretations of those laws transgressed the boundaries of justice can be best assessed through the empirical analysis of court decisions such as this and also other security law cases. Meanwhile, major decisions in private law, as analyzed in the second part of this chapter, show that citizens' private rights were actively protected by flourishing jurisprudential activities while their political rights were swept away by the wintry wind of emergency decrees and security laws. Together, these cases help outline a more comprehensive portrait of the judiciary under Yusin rule.

The Prerogative State: Security Cases

The defendants of the People's Revolutionary Party Reconstruction Committee trial were convicted for creating an underground organization to overthrow the government through violence.[9] This case is especially notorious – it still provokes raw emotions among the Korean

6 S. Ct., 74To3323 (*en banc*), April 8, 1975.

7 Ch'ŏnjugyo Inkwŏn Wiwŏnhoe (ed.), *Sabŏp sarin.*

8 Kuk Cho, "Transitional Justice in Korea: Legally Coping with Past Wrongs after Democratization," *Pacific Rim Law & Policy Journal* 16 (2007), 592; Hŏ Il-T'ae, "Inhyŏktang Chaegŏnwi sakŏn kwa sapŏp sarin" [The Inhyŏktang Reconstruction Committee Case and Judicial Murder], *Tonga pŏphak* 40 (2007), 105–125; Pak Hong-Kyu, "Inhyŏktang chaegŏn tanch'e sakŏn kwa pŏp" [The Inhyŏktang Reconstruction Committee Case and Law], in Ch'ŏnjugyo Inkwŏn Wiwŏnhoe (ed.), *Sabŏp sarin*, 235–236.

9 *Pŏpwŏnsa*, 696–697; *Yŏksa sogŭi sabŏppu*, 420–422.

people – because the eight individuals were hanged within eighteen hours of the court ruling. The swift and clandestine manner of execution ordered by the government seemed to embody the Yusin regime's disregard of the most basic sense of human rights, and the case was viewed as a specimen of the egregious abuse of state power. This decision brought harshest criticisms to the Supreme Court and the justices who sat on the bench that they were responsible for the fate of the executed.

The explosive nature of this case is evinced by the fact that the government did not allow the publication of the court opinion in the court's official reports (*Taebŏpwŏn p'angyŏlchip*). Newspapers published only the majority opinion, without mentioning the existence of dissenting and supplementary opinions. It was not until 2005 that the Supreme Court released the entire text of the opinion, thirty years after the original decision, by uploading it to the Court's digital reporting system.[10]

People's Revolutionary Party Reconstruction Case (1975)

The Inhyŏktang incidents involved two separate developments. The 1975 case was allegedly a sequel of the People's Revolutionary Party case some ten years earlier. On August 14, 1964, the KCIA declared that it uncovered a large underground organization that had been created in 1962 under the direction of North Korea. Forty-one individuals were arrested and several were placed on the wanted list.[11] Strikingly, the prosecutors initially assigned to this case decided there were no grounds for charging the defendants under the National Security Act because the requisite intent to overthrow the state was absent.[12] The government then went ahead and indicted twenty-six people under the Anticommunist Act.[13] The following year, thirteen people were convicted and received relatively light sentences ranging from one year in prison to probation.[14] Three years later, in 1967, members of the original organization who had fled to the North but returned as spies were captured and convicted under the National Security Act.

10 Chonghap Pŏmnyul Chŏngbo, at www.scourt.go.kr.
11 *Seoul Sinmun*, August 14, 1964.
12 Chang, *Protest Dialectics*, 73–74; *Hankyŏre Sinmun*, April 18, 2010.
13 *Tong-A Ilbo*, October 16, 1964.
14 *Tong-A Ilbo*, September 21, 1965.

In April 1974, the KCIA announced the uncovering of an attempt to revive the People's Revolutionary Party. Twenty-three individuals were arrested, including several people who had been implicated in the first incident. At the time, KCIA was investigating the National Federation of Democratic Youth and Students (Minch'ŏng Hangnyŏn). As seen in Chapter 4, the president had issued Emergency Decree No. 4 earlier that month aimed at that group. KCIA identified the Inhyŏktang Reconstruction Committee as a force behind Minch'ŏng Hangnyŏn and claimed that it "planned to organize a national advisory board as a transitional government organ with the objective of establishing a government of laborers and farmers," in collaboration with the pro–North Korean residents' league in Japan and local leftist revolutionaries.[15] The government prosecuted a total of 180 people on charges of violations ranging from the National Security Act to the insurrection law in the Criminal Code, the Anticommunist Act, and Emergency Decrees Nos. 1 and 4.[16] The defendants were tried in the Emergency Court Martial. On July 11, the military court sentenced seven people to death, eight to life imprisonment, and six others to twenty years in prison and fifteen years of suspension of civil rights.[17] The case was merged at the appellate level with the Minch'ŏng Hangnyŏn case which had been judged at a separate military court on July 13.[18] On September 7, the appellate court martial affirmed the death sentences of all Inhyŏktang defendants and three Minch'ŏng Hangnyŏn defendants.[19] The case was appealed to the Supreme Court.

The sheer magnitude of the consolidated case – the seriousness of the charges, the large number of defendants, and the harsh sentences rendered by the military courts – was staggering. The government had been vacillating between hard-handed and soft-handed policies. It appeared to have concluded that its lenient policy, such as the repeal of the emergency decrees, was backfiring. Protests against the regime became more turbulent than ever. On February 24, 1975, Justice Minister Hwang San-Tŏk warned that those demanding the release of the Inhyŏktang defendants would be arrested for violating the Anticommunist Act.[20] A newspaper editorial

15 *Chosŏn Ilbo*, April 25, 1974.
16 *Pŏpwŏnsa*, 697–698; Chang, *Protest Dialectics*, 73–77.
17 *Inkwŏn pyŏllon charyo chip*, vol. 1, 716–803.
18 Ibid., 289–500.
19 Ibid., 804–836.
20 *Tong-A Ilbo*, February 24, 1975.

urged the people to hold off speculations and "to wait for the court judgment, with confidence in the judiciary that it will render a decision that brings the truth to light."[21]

The government's strident approach to Inhyŏktang and Minch'ŏng Hangnyŏn cases appeared to be a sign of a regime running out of options. It was concerned about the increasingly negative international media attention to its crackdown on dissidents. The National Assembly revised the Criminal Code on March 25 to make it a crime to disparage the state. This was the first time that the Criminal Code, written in 1953, was revised.[22] The new law stipulated, in article 104 (2):

> (1) Any Korean national who endangers or is suspected of endangering the security, interest, and dignity of the Republic of Korea in foreign country, by insulting or slandering the Republic of Korea or any state organ established under the Constitution, by distorting the truth about it or disseminating false description of it or any other way, shall be punished by imprisonment with or without labor for not more than seven years; (2) Any Korean national who commits the acts proscribed in the preceding section through contacts with foreigners or foreign organizations shall be punished in the same way as in the preceding section; (3) In the case of section 2, violators may be subject to additional punishment of suspension of civil rights for ten years or less.

Under this provision, it was illegal for a Korean national to criticize the government while speaking to foreigners. Koreans residing overseas or traveling abroad were also covered by the law. This blanket prohibition made it difficult for foreign journalists to gather information regarding the country's domestic situations.[23]

On April 8, the Supreme Court upheld the verdicts of the emergency appellate court martial for all defendants but two.[24] The following morning, eight individuals (seven Inhyŏktang and one Minchŏng Hangnyŏn defendants) were hanged.[25] Normally the Supreme Court reserved the right to consider a post-trial motion to

[21] *Kyŏnghyang Sinmun*, February 25, 1975.

[22] Criminal Code (Act No. 2745, March 25, 1975).

[23] This provision, abolished on December 31, 1988, was found unconstitutional in 2015. Const. Ct., 2013HŏnKa20, October 21, 2015.

[24] S. Ct., 74To3323 (*en banc*), April 8, 1975.

[25] *Chosŏn Ilbo*, April 11, 1975. Other Minchŏng Hangnyŏn defendants who had also been condemned to death were spared on a stay of execution.

rehear the case, and indeed this was what the defense had hoped for, apparently based on a promise by the justice minister that the government would not object to such a motion and the accused would have an opportunity to exhaust their rights. But the swift execution of the defendants rendered the issue moot.[26]

It is possible that the Inhyŏktang defendants were given short shrift because they were ordinary people who did not fit the portrait of typical dissidents in Korea. None of them – a high school teacher, a language instructor, a bee farm owner, and so on – were publicly known individuals with social gravitas. The government's claim that some among them masterminded the brainy and fiercely independent student groups behind the scene sounded unconvincing from the outset. A group that grew prominent in the democracy movement were members of the Protestant and the Catholic Church. Influential leaders like Cardinal Kim Stephen Su-Hwan and pastors Mun Ik-Hwan and Pak Hyŏng-Kyu spoke out. The increasingly coercive government measures led to the politicization of new Christian social movements.[27] Rifts arose within the Catholic Church in 1974 and 1975 over the church's rightful role in society. On the one hand, the progressive group, which founded the Catholic Priests' Association for Justice (Ch'ŏnjugyo Chŏngŭi Kuhyŏn Sajedan), was critical of the church leadership's silence before repression; the conservative group, on the other hand, opposed the church's involvement in political matters.[28] Regardless of these differences, overt persecution of religious leaders turned the churches against the government.[29] Reverend Chi Hak-Sun, who was arrested in

[26] Cohen and Baker, "U.S. Foreign Policy and Human Rights," 181–182. For analysis of the case, see *Pŏpwŏnsa*, 697–698; Pak Hong-Kyu, "Inhyŏktang chaegŏn tanch'e sakŏn," 232–234.

[27] See Kim Nyŏng, "Yusin sidae Myŏngdong Sŏngdang esŏ ŭi minjuhwa undong" [Democracy Movements at Myŏngdong Cathedral during the Yusin Period], *Kat'olik sahoe kwahak yŏngu* 10 (1999), 57–80; Chang, *Protest Dialectics*, chapter 2.

[28] *Kat'olic Sibo* [Catholic Times], February 16, 1975. The progressive group helped develop a Korea liberation theology called *Minjung* theology. See Sŏ Chung-Sŏk, "Ch'ŏnjugyo Chŏngŭi Kuhyŏn Chŏnguk Sajedan ŭi ch'ulbŏm paegyŏng kwa hwaltong" [The Background of the Rise and the Activities of the Catholic Priests Association for Justice], *Sarim* [*Sŏngdae sarim*] 27 (2007), 223–248.

[29] Chang, *Protest Dialectics*, 79–90.

July 1974 for giving money to students in hiding, wrote his famous "Declaration of Conscience."[30] In part because of the visibility of these religious leaders and other intellectuals, the Yusin government took heat from international human rights groups such as Amnesty International and members of the United States Congress.[31] The involvement of Christian churches in the antigovernment movement had the important effect of neutralizing the regime's attempt to characterize the democracy movement as a procommunist movement.

The Inhyŏktang defendants received no similar attention and sympathy – at least not before their executions – from the international media. Their plight can be contrasted with that of the students implicated in the Minchŏng Hangnyŏn as well. The students were formally convicted and received harsh sentences, but most of them were freed later under stayed sentences. The government may have decided early on to use the Inhyŏktang case for a deterrence reason without raising too much attention from abroad.[32] In order to understand the full scope of the judicial role in this tragic and controversial case, it is necessary to scrutinize the court opinion.

Analysis of the Court Opinion

The defense arguments iterated many issues that had already been raised in earlier emergency decree trials. An immediate question was the legality of the emergency measures the defendants were charged with. As seen in Chapter 4, Emergency Decree No. 5 which abolished Emergency Decrees Nos. 1 and 4 in August 1974 provided that the new decree had no effect on those who had already been convicted or charged under them. The defense argued that this contravened the constitutional provisions prohibiting retroactive punishment. The first article of the Criminal Code said, "When, after the final judgment in trial, the change of law rendered the act not constituting a crime, the execution of the sentence must be

30 *Inkwŏn pyŏllon charyo chip*, vol. 1, 588–589.
31 Yong-Jick Kim, "The Security, Political, and Human Rights Conundrum," in Byung-Kook Kim and Ezra F. Vogel (eds.), *The Park Chung Hee Era*, 457–482.
32 Yi Sang-U, "Kingŭp choch'i," 82–83.

waived."[33] Since Emergency Decree No. 4 had already been abolished by the time of appeal, claimed the defendants, they could not be punished under it. Further, some of the defendants had already been punished in 1965 under the Anticommunist Act, and therefore charging them again with the same law violated the double jeopardy protection. The Supreme Court rejected these arguments. The activities the defendants were indicted for were materially different from those of ten years earlier. Emergency Decree No. 5 was a new decree that specifically limited the scope of its effect so it was not a retroactive law.

Were the presidential decrees constitutional? Concerning this fundamental question, the Supreme Court could only repeat what it had already said – that it did not have power to review their constitutionality. In January, the Court held that there was no basis to decide that Emergency Decree No. 1 was void due to its unconstitutionality. It wrote that "this Court has affirmed many times the guilty verdicts rendered on the premise that the president's emergency decree is not unconstitutional."[34] The response of the Supreme Court in 1975 was the same: "The arguments that the emergency measures are unconstitutional cannot be accepted according to the interpretation of our Constitution." This circumspect language was, in all consideration, a sad but faithful representation of the constitutional limits that bound the Court.

A key defense argument was that the defendants' actions were justified under their right to resist. This was one of the weightiest substantive questions raised during the trial. They claimed that the right to resist must be interpreted in such a way that, conforming to the natural law order, it legitimized certain acts even if they conflicted with the positive law order. The Court disagreed. It stated:

> Even following the theory proposed by a minority of scholars, [the right to resist] is a right residing in the supralegal natural law order; it is asserted to circumvent the positive law order with the purpose to justify actions that

[33] Criminal Code, art. 1 (3).

[34] S. Ct., 74To3492, January 20, 1975; S. Ct., 74To3498, January 28, 1975. This reasoning was followed in S. Ct., 75To3324, May 27, 1975; S. Ct. 74To 3510 (*en banc*), March 22, 1977.

violated the law. The scope of positive law is premised on preserving the existing constitutional order. In this context, the exercise of judicial power has as its mission the maintenance of the legal order of the state within the bounds of positive law.[35]

In short, the Court could not accept the argument justifying the acts in contravention of the existing constitutional and legal order; unlawful acts should not be allowed on the grounds of the extralegal concept of rights. This solemn judicial pronouncement – namely, the idea that positive laws could not be disregarded simply because they were unjust – was a square affirmation of the Court's belief in its role, fully reflective of its long-held position that judicial duty lay in maintaining the state's legal order within the bounds of written law. The dismissal of the theory of the right to resist epitomized the formalistic stance of the courts in Korea, in which judges remained in deference to the will of the legislature, reluctant to interpret the law in light of their own moral convictions.

The 1975 opinion was not free from certain questionable constructions of the laws, especially the National Security Act. The National Security Act, in article 1, punished an individual who created an organization for the purpose of "claiming the title of the government or changing and disturbing the state." The defense argued that the prosecution did not prove that the defendants intended to usurp the title of the government or change the state's founding identity. The Supreme Court acknowledged that there was no proof that the defendants planned to change the nature of the state after overthrowing the existing government or conspired for rebellion, but it still found that the defendants were guilty of creating an antistate organization for the purpose of usurping the power of the government. The majority of the justices followed the precedent of 1966, in which the Court stated that an attempt to create an organization with the purpose to overthrow the government in the meaning of the National Security Act did not need to be construed narrowly to refer to acts to "change the foundation of the state by creating a communist regime or a monarchy."[36] The 1975 Court thus held that the National Security Act merely required the proof of an attempt to overthrow the

35 S. Ct., 74To3323.

36 S. Ct., 66To152, April 21, 1966; S. Ct., 66To617, July 12, 1966. See Chapter 3, note 54 and accompanying text.

government by violence and a concrete plan to establish a new government afterward.

Incidentally, not the entire Court agreed with this broad interpretation of the National Security Act. In a supplementary opinion, two justices, Yang Pyŏng-Ho and Kim Yun-Haeng, raised a question about the definition of an antistate organization. They argued that the meaning of the act of "changing and disturbing the state" under the National Security Act must be construed narrowly: it meant not just any act of overthrowing the government and establishing a new one but the specific act of "rejecting the democratic republican government system of Korea which is the foundation of our nation and attempting to destroy the basic structure of the state grounded on anticommunism and liberal democracy."[37] These justices pointed out that the purpose of the National Security Act was to protect the country from the threat of North Korea and other communist regimes; this was why this draconian law was enacted separate from the Criminal Code, which also prohibited overthrowing the government through violence. Therefore, they argued that the Act must be narrowly applied to an attempt to destroy liberal democracy and create a communist government sympathetic to North Korea.[38] This concurring opinion harked back to the dissent written in 1966 by Justice Ch'oe Yun-Mo.[39] A third member of the Court in 1975, Im Hang-Chun, filed a separate supplementary opinion, arguing that the National Security Act was a special law and that the government could charge defendants with either the National Security Act or the criminal law provision of conspiring for treasonous insurrection but not both.[40]

These little-known concurring opinions show that there was a line of jurisprudential tradition in the Supreme Court, although of a minority, to construe the National Security Act tightly. They attest that at least some members of the Court tried to prevent the National Security Act from being used for political purposes and to protect citizens from the harsh punishments it called for.

The defendants contested a number of irregular procedures followed in the military courts. They argued that their rights to a public trial

37 S. Ct., 74To3323 (Yang Pyŏng-Ho & Kim Yun-Haeng, JJ., concurring).
38 Ibid.
39 See Chapter 3, note 55 and accompanying text.
40 S. Ct., 74To3323 (Im Hang-Chun, J., concurring).

under Article 24 of the Constitution were violated because hearings were conducted behind closed doors, allowing only one member of each defendant's family to attend. They also claimed that the prosecution witnesses testified in the absence of defense lawyers, who were unable to question them. Here one notes that most detrimental for the defendants was the fact that the lower court trials had been conducted at the military courts, under military court procedures. According to the Military Court Act, the admission or rejection of evidence was within the power of the trial judge and could not be challenged on appeal.[41] Article 89 of that law stated: "The authenticity of record of the hearing procedures observed on the hearing date is recognized in itself without further proof." Under article 85 (2) (5) of the same law, whether the trial was conducted openly must be noted in the trial record, and, if it was not, the reasons thereof had to be explained. In the Inhyŏktang case, the trial record said it was an open trial. The Supreme Court thus ruled that the court record, created under the supervision of the presiding judge, must be respected and that its "absolute evidentiary power" must be recognized unless there were truly exceptional situations otherwise.

The Supreme Court found that the decision by the military judge to issue admission tickets and to allow only ticket-holders into the courtroom, for the purpose of maintaining order during the proceedings, could not be seen as violation of the defendants' right to a public trial. Concerning the claims that the examination of witnesses was conducted without proper notice to the defendants and their counsels and that no defense witnesses were allowed to testify, the Court noted that the trial record showed that the parties were given notice of the examination of the witnesses and also that the counsels were given ample opportunities to communicate with the defendants. From these examples, it is not difficult to see how the fact that the defendants were subjected to court martial deprived them of significant procedural protections. It practically sealed their fate.

Public attention centered on the defendants' claim that their confessions had been extracted through torture. The key evidence for

[41] Kunpŏp Hoeŭi Pŏp [Military Court Act] (Act No. 2630, October 10, 1973).

the state was their confessions made before the prosecutors that they created an underground organization with the goal of establishing a communist state. During the trial, the defendants declared that these statements had been forced under torture.[42] On March 15, Justice Minister Hwang San-Tŏk was called to the National Assembly to answer questions about the allegation of torture. Hwang stated that he had summoned the investigators in charge of the case and that he was convinced torture did not take place.[43] He pointed out that five defendants claimed they were tortured whereas others denied they were tortured. Hwang offered a speculation that the five people who claimed torture did so to assuage their guilty conscience over the fact that their cooperation with the state had led to the arrests of other suspects.

In their appeal to the Supreme Court, the defense counsels invoked article 352 of the Military Court Act which provided that, where there were suspicions that the defendant had been forced to make statements through torture, violence, or threat or during illegally extended custody, those statements could not be used as proof of guilt. It was identical to article 309 in the Criminal Procedure.[44] Here, close attention to these laws is necessary. Korean law distinguished between a confession made before a prosecutor and one made before a police officer or other investigation agent. Article 356 of the Military Court Act, equivalent to article 312 of the Criminal Procedure, read:

(1) The record created by the prosecutor documenting the statement of a criminal defendant or a suspect and the record documenting the results of the investigations by the prosecutor or the military law police may both be admitted as evidence when the person who made the statements acknowledges their veracity during the preliminary hearing or during trial. But the record documenting the statements of the suspect can be admitted as evidence despite the defendant's subsequent statements to the contrary in the preliminary hearing or trial as long as the original statements were made under trustworthy circumstances; (2) The interrogation record of a suspect

42 *Kwagŏ wa taehwa*, vol. 4, 203–204.

43 *Tong-A Ilbo*, March 15, 1975.

44 "When there is reasonable suspicion that a defendant's confession had not been made voluntarily and had been either extracted by torture, violence, or threat or obtained after an illegal extension of physical detention or other means, that confession shall not be admitted as evidence of guilt."

created by investigators other than the prosecutor may be admitted as evidence only when the defendant who was the suspect or the defense counsel recognizes the veracity of its contents in the preliminary hearing or trial.[45]

Under this provision, the statements, including confessions, made before the prosecutor could be admitted even when the defendant denied them subsequently in the preliminary hearing or during trial, unless there was reason to believe that the circumstances under which those statements had been made were not trustworthy.

This provision was based on the principle that the authenticity of the record (known as the protocol) created by the prosecutor documenting the statements of a defendant or a suspect should be recognized as long as they had been made under trustworthy circumstances. Legal theories postulated that prosecutors, unlike police investigators, would not resort to illegal means to elicit an incriminating statement or confession. This principle had been well established from the promulgation of the Criminal Procedure in 1954, and the Supreme Court precedents followed it.[46] While interrogation records created by the prosecution were accorded the presumption of veracity with special indicia of reliability, the courts consistently rejected the evidentiary power of the interrogation record created by investigation agents other than prosecutors when the defendant denied its content in pretrial or during the trial.[47] In the Inhyŏktang case, the defendants' confessions had formed part of the record compiled by the prosecutors.

The Supreme Court agreed that the burden to prove the trustworthiness of the circumstances in which the statements had been made lay with prosecutors but that the necessity to prove it existed only when

45 The only difference in the wording is the "military law police" (Military Court Act) as opposed to "the police" (Criminal Procedure).

46 S. Ct. 72To1469, August 22, 1972; S. Ct. 77To629, May 24, 1977.

47 S. Ct., 76To378, April 13, 1976, reported in *Pŏmnyul Sinmun*, May 3, 1976. This decision was followed in 82To385, July 26, 1983 (if the defendant denies during trial the contents of the documents created by investigation agents based on his statements during investigation, those documents cannot be admitted as evidence, regardless of whether they are interrogation reports, statements, or confessions). See also 75To1089, May 27, 1975 (the testimony of the police officer that the suspect confessed the crime at the police station cannot be admitted as evidence if the latter denies it in court).

there was evidence or reason to question the statements' authenticity.[48] Several defendants testified to the truthfulness of the prosecutorial record during the trials at lower courts, and they did not raise the issue of torture and other prosecutorial misconduct until after the conclusion of the trials. There was insufficient reason, thus held the Court, to set aside the lower court decision that admitted as evidence the documents produced by the prosecutors.

The 1975 Court took much fire for this ruling. In subsequent years, the Supreme Court became more reluctant to acknowledge special reliability for the prosecution protocol.[49] In 1981, a suspect made a confession during the police investigation and repeated it before the prosecutor, and later claimed that the confession to the police investigator had been forced under torture. The Supreme Court held that there was reason to question the voluntariness of the confession recorded by the prosecutor because, even if the defendant had not been compelled by the prosecutor to make a statement, his confession to the latter might have been a natural consequence of the torture perpetrated by the police.[50] It was not until December 2004 that the Court overturned the precedents of the presumption of veracity of the prosecutorial records.[51] The Court's rejection of the long-held theory prompted the revision of the Criminal Procedure in August 2007. The revised article 312 (2) of the Criminal Procedure read: "When the defendant denies the veracity of the creation of the [prosecution's] record, it can be admitted only when the fact that the contents in the record were the same as the contents of the defendant's statement can be evidenced by video recording or other objective methods and only when it could be proved that the statements in the record had been made in circumstances that can be undoubtedly believed to be true."[52] New sections were added to the article to distinguish between the

48 This position was maintained in S. Ct., 97To3234, April 10, 1998; 2004To7900, November 23, 2006.

49 S. Ct., 74To2523, June 28, 1977; 80To2579, December 23, 1980; 82To754, June 8, 1982; 84To378, May 29, 1984; 84To748, June 26, 1984; 86To218, March 25, 1986; 92To769, June 23, 1992; 2000To2617, July 28, 2000.

50 S. Ct., 81To2160, October 13, 1981. This reasoning was followed in 81To3324, February 23, 1982; 82To850, June 8, 1982; 83To1953, September 27, 1983; 84To472, May 15, 1984.

51 S. Ct., 2002To537, December 16, 2004; 2006To7342, January 25, 2007.

52 Criminal Procedure (Act No. 8496, June 1, 2007).

statements made by the defendant or nondefendant during investigation, on the one hand, and the record created by the prosecutor or the police from investigation results, on the other hand.[53]

Having set aside in 2004 its precedents, the Supreme Court ruled in 2006 that the judge's belief of the credibility of the evidence must be based on the statements of the witnesses made in the courtroom and that the conclusion reached by the trial court judge who heard in person the testimonies of the witnesses and defendants must be respected by the appellate court.[54] These decisions together promoted trial-centered decision-making, reducing the vast degree of power and discretion prosecutors had enjoyed. Raising fresh questions against the presumed voluntariness of confessions before prosecutors was an important turning point in criminal jurisprudence.[55] Needless to say, these positive jurisprudential developments came too late for the defendants in the 1975 case.

The Supreme Court's reliance on the court martial records and its reluctance to question prosecutorial integrity obscured and possibly skewed the facts. One can say, with the benefit of hindsight, that the Court's adherence to precedents and dominant legal theories was not prudent when the defendants made the explosive accusations of violence and torture during investigations and, further, alleged intentional redaction of the trial record by the state. Yet the regrettable outcome of the case should be distinguished from the question of whether the Court's interpretation of the existing law was erroneous. At the time of the trial, it was virtually impossible in legal practice to retract a confession once it had been made before the prosecutor.[56] In retrospect, the issue of the reliability of the investigation record revealed how powerless the courts were in protecting the rights of the

53 See Yong Chul Park, "Does It Matter Who Wrote It?: The Admissibility of Suspect Interrogation Record Written by Prosecutors in Korea," *Journal of Korean Law* 6 (2007), 180–190.

54 S. Ct., 2006To4994, November 24, 2006.

55 Still, the Supreme Court carefully delineated the limits of the theory's application. In 1984, the Court ruled that, before admitting as evidence of guilt a confession the voluntariness of which was in question, it must be actively proved that there was no causality between the reason for suspecting its lack of voluntariness and the confession itself. S. Ct., 84To135. See *Yŏksa sogŭi sabŏppu*, 441–442.

56 *Yŏksa sogŭi sabŏppu*, 440.

citizens when state agencies were in collusion with repressive forces. The courts were unable to scrutinize prosecutorial misconduct. Evidence was often manufactured by the state but the courts lacked the ability – and legal grounds – to question its truthfulness. These were the problems of the Yusin criminal law system, which could beset any legal system today.

The lone dissenting opinion in the Inhyŏktang case by Justice Yi Il-Kyu was predicated on procedural irregularities. The appellate emergency court martial summarily accepted the facts found by the lower court martial, without giving the defense the opportunity to examine the defendants anew. The proceedings took place even without the prosecutor's statement of charges on the grounds that it had already taken place in the first-instance trial. The court only heard the defense arguments of appeal. In its judgment, the appellate military court reduced the sentences for four defendants from twenty years to fifteen years. Technically, this amounted to overturning the decision. Justice Yi thus argued that such procedural irregularities required the case be remanded.[57] The majority of the Court ruled, however, that those defects were not material to the determination of the case.

Retrial

Some thirty years later, the assertions of prosecutorial misconduct and police brutality led to the reopening of the Inhyŏktang case and ultimately the reversal of the verdict. It was one of the first cases selected by the Presidential Truth Commission on Suspicious Deaths which was set up in October 2000 to probe past wrongs committed by the government's intelligence services.[58] In September 2002, the commission determined that the incriminating evidence had been fabricated by the KCIA and the confessions obtained through torture. In 2005, the National Intelligence Service (NIS), successor of the KCIA, confirmed the commission's findings, acknowledging that the state had

[57] S. Ct., 74To3323 (Yi Il-Kyu, J., dissenting).

[58] Presidential Truth Commission on Suspicious Deaths of the Republic of Korea, *A Hard Journey to Justice: First Term Report* (Seoul: Samin Books, 2004). The commission was succeeded by Committee for Development through Finding the Truth of the Past, in operation from November 2004 through November 2007.

manipulated the evidence.[59] Upon the state's official admission of misconduct, the court declared that the Inhyŏktang defendants had not received a fair trial. A retrial took place in 2007. The conviction was overturned and the victims received a posthumous not-guilty verdict for the charges of violating the Anticommunist Act, the National Security Act, and the criminal law of conspiring for treasonous insurrection. The charges of violating the emergency decrees were dismissed as the decrees had been abolished.[60] In August that year, the court ordered the government to pay restitutions to the victims' families.[61]

In the course of the retrial, human rights activists criticized the justices of the 1975 Supreme Court for having refused to exercise their independent judgment when the criminal justice process was hopelessly compromised in the brutal system. Some authors went so far as to contend that the judges should be held personally accountable for any capital punishment judgment that was later overturned.[62] Concerns about a miscarriage of justice and wrongful execution are fully justified, but equating a judge's failure to rein in police and prosecutorial abuse and misconduct with that judge's wilfull disregard of the defendants' rights is less than persuasive. One of the surviving defendants of the Inhyŏktang case stated in 2007: "I understand what the expression 'judicial murder' means, but it gives the impression that it was not Park Chung Hee but the judiciary – which was no more than his instrument – that took the lead in killing. That was definitely not the case."[63] This statement rather pointedly summed up the problems in this tragic case. The emergency decrees subjected civilians to court

59 The committee report, originally issued in December 2005, was included in *Kwagŏ wa taehwa*, vol. 2, 202–291.

60 Seoul Central Dist. Ct. (Crim. Div.), 2002ChaeKoHap6 & 2003ChaeKoHap5 (consol.), January 23, 2007.

61 Seoul Central Dist. Ct. (Civ. Div.), 2006KaHap92412, August 21, 2007.

62 Yi Tŏk-In, "Sahyŏng p'yeji ŭi chŏngdangsŏng: Sabŏp sarin kwa op'an e ŭihan sahyŏng" [Justification for the Abolition of the Death Penalty: Judicial Murder and the Death Penalty Resulting from Wrongful Conviction]. *Chung-Ang pŏphak* 12 (2010), 110–140; Hŏ Il-T'ae, "Pŏp waegok haengwi wa sabŏp sarin ŭi pangji rŭl wihan ippŏp chŏngch'aek" [Legislative policy for the Prevention of the Distortion of Law and Judicial Murder]. *Hyŏngsa chŏngch'aek yŏngu* 18 (2007), 5–48.

63 *OhmyNews*, March 27, 2007.

martial, in which the defendants were deprived of procedural safeguards that would have otherwise been available to them. The Supreme Court's punctilious observance of its precedents and formalistic procedures compelled it to uphold the sentences rendered by the military courts.[64]

The death penalty meted out was called for by the National Security Act. The alleged abuse of this harsh law was one of the major grievances during the authoritarian period. The next section considers how the courts dealt with national security questions and relevant laws.

National Security and Anticommunist Acts

It is common for autocratic regimes to try to justify their repressive measures by highlighting threats to state security. In apartheid South Africa, the government frequently invoked security issues.[65] The ruling military juntas in Argentina, Brazil, and Chile all claimed that military dictatorship was necessary to protect the country.[66] Similar claims were made at various times in countries in Asia, such as Singapore, Malaysia, India, Pakistan, Indonesia, and Thailand.[67] Developments in Taiwan and the Philippines were in many ways analogous to those in

64 According to the former president Yun Posun, Park later openly admitted in a meeting with government officials that allowing the eight people to be executed was the greatest mistake of his presidency. *Pŏpcho 50 nyŏn yasa*, vol. 1, 668.

65 Dyzenhaus, *Hard Cases in Wicked Legal Systems*; Robert Coniglio, "Methods of Judicial Decision-Making and the Rule of Law: The Case of Apartheid South Africa," *Boston University International Law Journal* 30 (2012), 497–527.

66 See, among others, Robert Barros, *Constitutionalism and Dictatorship: Pinochet, the Junta, and the 1980 Constitution* (Cambridge: Cambridge University Press, 2002); Lisa Hilbink, *Judges Beyond Politics in Democracy and Dictatorship: Lessons from Chile* (Cambridge: Cambridge University Press, 2007); Anthony W. Pereira, *Political (In)Justice: Authoritarianism and the Rule of Law in Brazil, Chile, and Argentina* (Pittsburgh: University of Pittsburgh Press, 2005); Osiel, "Dialogue with Dictators."

67 See Victor V. Ramraj and Arun K. Thiruvengadam (eds.), *Emergency Powers in Asia: Exploring the Limits of Legality*. Elsewhere, one can point to Egypt under Anwar Sadat between 1970 and 1981. Tamir Moustafa, *The Struggle for Constitutional Power: Law, Politics, and Economic Development in Egypt* (Cambridge: Cambridge University Press, 2007).

Korea.[68] It has been said that the issue of national security was a sort of "legal black hole," a zone in which state actions were presumptively legitimized and went unconstrained.[69] The relationship between security legislation and civil rights poses a thorny topic in many established liberal democracies as well. When defining a security threat is part of the executive judgments, the line between rational and irrational goals is inevitably blurred. The task of balancing the competing interests of national security and individual rights normally falls to the judiciary.

What set Korea apart from most countries is its history of national division. South Korea has been in confrontation with communist North Korea from the beginning of its existence as a modern nation. Since the Korean War, the need to repel the threat from the North dictated national policy. In the 1960s and 1970s, the prospect of another North Korean invasion was more than just a vague notion. In 1975, President Park (see Figure 5.1) stated in an interview with *Time* magazine, "Only 25 miles from Seoul, an enemy is bent on destroying us. . . . I am at a loss to understand criticism of us when we are faced with questions of survival."[70]

Korean politics has been called the politics of enmity: the national division has created the dichotomy of national and antinational, the latter being equated with the enemy of the state who threatened national security.[71] This antithetical formulation continued as one of the most durable characteristics of Korean politics and law. Successive regimes enjoined citizens to be on alert to defend the country not just from the communists in the North but also from their sympathizers within the South. In the late 1960s and early 1970s, the government plastered the country with posters with the slogan, "Let's look again – the visitor in the neighbor's house may be a spy." The government prodding citizens to inform on their neighbors is mind-boggling, to say the least, but what one sees as bordering on a collective paranoia captures the fate of a divided country.

68 Greitens, *Dictators and Their Secret Police*.

69 David Dyzenhaus, "Schmitt v. Dicey: Are States of Emergency Inside or Outside the legal Order?," *Cardozo Law Review* 27 (2006), 2032; Anil Kalhan, "'Gray Zone' Constitutionalism and the Dilemma of Judicial Independence in Pakistan," *Vanderbilt Journal of Transnational Law* 46 (2013), 26–27.

70 "Park: Survival Is at Stake," *Time*, June 30, 1975, 49.

71 See Guichard, *Regime Transition*.

Figure 5.1 President Park Chung Hee and the Supreme Court Justices, 1976. From left to right: President Park Chung Hee, Chief Justice Min Pok-Ki, Justice Yi Yŏng-Sŏp (later chief justice). *Collection of the National Archives of Korea.*

Security laws often overlapped in scope, and the government tended to be less than scrupulous in distinguishing them. An important part of the court's task was to separate different elements of each law and prevent the government from charging a suspect indiscriminately. The crime of espionage was one example. The National Security Act incorporated articles from the Criminal Code by reference.[72] Its article 2 stated:

A member of an antistate organization or a person under the orders of an antistate organization who, in order to carry out its purposes, committed acts prescribed in article 92 through article 99 of the Criminal Code shall be punished in accordance with the respective article.

[72] Since its comprehensive rewriting on December 26, 1958 (Act No. 300), the National Security Act was revised on June 10, 1960 (Act No. 549) and again on September 24, 1962 (Act No. 1151).

Article 3 provided, in part:

A member of an antistate organization or a person under the orders of an antistate organization who committed acts to carry out its purpose shall be punished in accordance with the following categories: (1) Detecting, gathering, or revealing state secrets, or performing an act using explosives is punishable by death or life in prison.

Article 98 of the Criminal Code stated:

(1) A person who acts as a spy for an enemy nation, or aids or abets a spy from an enemy nation, shall be punished by death, imprisonment for life, or imprisonment for not less than seven years. (2) The preceding section shall also apply to a person who divulges military secrets to an enemy nation.

Espionage in article 3 of the National Security Act and espionage in the Criminal Code as incorporated in article 2 of the same law were practically redundant, other than the fact that article 2 came with the heading "Carrying out military purposes" and the heading in article 3 was "Carrying out general purposes."

In 1973, the Supreme Court ruled that the crime of espionage under the National Security Act required proof that the defendant was "a member of an antistate organization or one who received orders from it."[73] If the government failed to show that element, the defendant could not be punished under that law. The following year, the Court expounded in an *en banc* decision on the nature of "state secrets" in espionage.[74] The issue was whether a defendant who was charged with spying under article 98 (1) of the Criminal Code could also be charged under article 3 of the National Security Act for the same act of revealing state secrets. The Supreme Court noted that article 3 (1) of the National Security Act mandated a stiffer penalty (death or life imprisonment) than article 98 (death, life imprisonment, or imprisonment not less than seven years). The Court reasoned that state secrets protected under article 3 (1) of the security law had to be of a nature more serious than the state secrets protected under the Criminal Code as incorporated in article 2. Therefore, concluded the Court, the state was required to specify which acts of the defendant constituted violation of article 3 (1), instead of subsuming them under the broad cover of revealing state secrets and charging the suspect with one or more of related provisions. The Court held that "when a person is found

[73] S. Ct., 73To249, May 8, 1973.
[74] S. Ct. (*en banc*), 74To1477, July 26, 1974.

guilty of espionage for gathering and leaking a state secret, that person must be seen as having committed one crime" and could not be concurrently punished under criminal law and the National Security Act.[75] In another decision the same year, the Court explained that "military secrets," which were the object of article 98 (2) of the Criminal Code, meant classified military information obtained in the line of duty.[76] The defendant could not be punished under either the Criminal Code or the National Security Act when there was no evidence that he had obtained the military secret in question through his job.

The Supreme Court also paid attention to distinguishing the Anticommunist Act from the National Security Act. In 1968, the Court ruled that one of the defendants who communicated information of common knowledge to an agent of North Korea, knowing that it would benefit the communist regime, was guilty under article 4 (1) of the Anticommunist Act but not under either the National Security Act or article 98 (2) of the Criminal Code that punished the disclosure of classified military information.[77] In 1975, the Court stated that, where the defendant was charged with meeting with an agent from the North and promoting and encouraging pro-North propaganda, the state was not allowed to add the charge of knowingly failing to inform the authorities.[78]

The Supreme Court routinely qualified the meaning of "benefiting the enemy" in the Anticommunist Act. Its interpretation was not always consistent. In February 1974, the Court held that, since the purpose of the Anticommunist Act was to stop the activities of communist groups that threatened national security, having contact with members of communist groups or providing them with humanitarian aid without engaging in activities to promote the purposes of those groups did not constitute a crime under that law.[79] In the same year, the Court required the intent to benefit an antistate organization for conviction.[80] An act that resulted in North Korea's benefit was not by itself sufficient grounds for conviction because the intent to aid or abet the enemy was an essential element of the crime. These decisions may be contrasted with earlier decisions. In 1968, the Supreme Court had

75 S. Ct., 74To1477. *Kyŏnghyang Sinmun*, July 31, 1974.
76 S. Ct., 74To1479, August 20, 1974.
77 S. Ct., 68To754, July 30, 1968.
78 S. Ct., 74To3753, February 10, 1975.
79 S. Ct., 73To2186, February 12, 1974.
80 S. Ct., 74To2755, November 26, 1974; S. Ct. 74To3488, January 28, 1975.

held that the defendant who received money from a member of an antistate organization was guilty of article 5 (1) of the Anticommunist Act as long as he was aware that such an act benefited the antistate organization.[81] In the following year, the Court ruled that the intent to benefit an antistate organization was not necessary for conviction under the Anticommunist Act and that the knowledge that an act would be beneficial to the organization was sufficient. If some act resulted in North Korea's benefit regardless of whether it was so intended, the justices stated, that act constituted violation of the law.[82] As alluded to in Chapter 3, these specific decisions in 1968 may have been a reflection of the times when provocations from North Korea were sharply felt; the Court's positions were not immune from fluctuating security concerns.

Article 4 (1) of the Anticommunist Act was problematic because it could be interpreted that any discussion of reunification, or just uttering the name North Korea, amounted to a proposal or propaganda for the enemy regime. Even when it was willing to interpret "benefiting the enemy" broadly, the Supreme Court was consistent in ruling that mere criticism of government policy could not be punished under the Anticommunist Act. In 1973, a defendant told a colleague during lunchtime at work that he hated reservist forces drills so much he would rather cross the DMZ and go to the North during a tourist visit to the demilitarized zone. The auxiliary Homeland Reserve Forces had been established in April 1968, consisting of some 2.5 million men; all veterans were required to remain in the reserve units for a set number of years and received regular training. Overturning the conviction, the justices ruled that "these remarks were complaints uttered in spiteful moments and cannot be seen as something benefiting North Korea."[83] In 1974, the Court affirmed the acquittal of a defendant who was charged with the Anticommunist Act for publishing in his magazine, *Tari*, an article titled "The Student Movement Calling for Social Participation."[84] The Court acknowledged that the content of the article was "somewhat critical of the

[81] S. Ct., 68To754, July 30, 1968.

[82] S. Ct., 66To1337, October 23, 1969.

[83] S. Ct., 73To2602, December 11, 1973. *Kyŏnghyang Sinmun*, December 12, 1973; *Tong-A Ilbo*, December 12, 1973.

[84] S. Ct., 73To3423, May 28, 1974. The Seoul Criminal District Court had rendered a not-guilty verdict in 1971, affirmed by the appellate court in 1973. See Chapter 4, note 69.

current government" and discussed the revolutionary student movements in the past but that it "was within the extent protected under the constitutional protection of freedom of speech." The Court noted that "the student movements in our country sought a new path as cultural movements to dissipate the vestiges of the premodern period and establish the ideology of democratic welfare society"; as such, they "cannot be seen as having an intent to praise, promote, or side with the North Korean communist group" as claimed by the prosecutor.[85]

Still, the Anticommunist Act prohibited circulating books containing communist propaganda. In 1977, Yi Yŏng-Hi, a journalist and professor, was charged under the law for his writings. The Supreme Court affirmed the guilty verdict for Yi, reasoning that "where there are phrases or wording that praise, encourage, and sympathize with the activities of the enemy, and where such expressions, phrases, and wording were used with the recognition that the reader who reads them may be influenced by them, the act of writing them constitutes violation of elements of the Anticommunist Act."[86] Even one section of written material, considered separately from the whole, could be evidence of a punishable act.[87] In 1978, the Supreme Court found that a defendant contributed to the communist cause by duplicating and selling a book written in Chinese on acupuncture that contained a number of paragraphs in praise of Chairman Mao Tse-tung of Communist China.[88] The same year, the Supreme Court sentenced poet Kim Chi-Ha to seven years in prison for his poem *Ojŏk* (Five Bandits).[89]

Different fact situations determined the different fates of defendants. A defendant who praised Ho Chi Minh and other communist leaders of Vietnam was found guilty.[90] The conviction of the defendant who collected North Korean stamps, which included slogans praising and promoting the activities of the North Korean regime and the portraits

85 The Supreme Court's dismissal of the government's appeal was welcomed by the contemporaries as it was rendered in the heat of the emergency decrees. See *Kyŏnghyang Sinmun*, May 29, 1974; *Pŏpwŏnsa*, 694 and 805; Han Sŭng-Hŏn, *Chaep'an ŭro pon Hanguk hyŏndaesa*, chapter 8.

86 S. Ct., 78To2706, January 16, 1979.

87 S. Ct., 74To2080, May 10, 1977. See Kyu Ho Youm, "Judicial Interpretation of Press Freedom in South Korea," *Boston College Third World Law Journal* 7 (1987), 133–159.

88 S. Ct, 78To2254, October 31, 1978.

89 S. Ct., 74To2080, May 10, 1977.

90 S. Ct., 78To880, June 27, 1978.

of its leaders, was affirmed.[91] In contrast, praising and supporting antistate activities in one's personal journal was not a violation of the Anticommunist Act if the writer did not show it to anyone, even if its content would have benefited the communists.[92] Citing and distributing an article published in a foreign newspaper could not be seen as an act benefiting an antistate organization.[93] Uttering simple profanity against the head of the state was not a violation of Anticommunist Act.[94] A defendant who praised the North while drunk was found not guilty.[95] Another was acquitted when he had muttered, "Can you do better than Kim Il-Sung? Is there anything that the present government does well?"[96] Stating "You policemen are as bad as Kim Il-Sung"[97] or "Even if the North communists invade, they do not kill everybody; they kill only the most wicked"[98] could not be seen as a violation of the Anticommunist Act. These examples show, for nothing else, how casually prosecutors invoked the Anticommunist Act to punish the most mundane and innocuous acts as well as remarks of citizens.

The Supreme Court's decisions of security law can be contrasted with its rulings under the emergency decrees. In the latter, convictions were routinely upheld. The defendants were sent to prison for criticizing, or just complaining about, the government. This was the whole point of emergency power. Defendants were often charged simultaneously under the security laws and the emergency decrees. In such cases, the Supreme Court considered the security law charges first and, if they deserved quashing, remanded them without ruling on the emergency decree charges. The following example illustrates a rather curious situation. In 1974, the defendant was charged with violating the Anticommunist Act and Emergency Decree No. 4.[99] He had secluded himself in a hundred-day prayer in a mountain cave on the outskirts of Seoul. While there, he allegedly listened to North Korean broadcasting. He also showed the "wanted" flyer of the Minch'ŏng Hangnyŏn suspects to others and said,

91 *Kyŏnghyang Sinmun*, December 19, 1978.
92 S. Ct., 73To3392, December 9, 1975, *Kyŏnghyang Sinmun*, November 24, 1976; S. Ct. 77To1360, July 12, 1977, *Pŏmnyul Sinmun*, August 15, 1977.
93 S. Ct., 74To 2755, November 26, 1974.
94 *Tong-A Ilbo*, January 17, 1977.
95 *Kyŏnghyang Sinmun*, October 13, 1976.
96 S. Ct., 76To3603, December 14, 1976.
97 S. Ct., 76To2671, September 28, 1976.
98 S. Ct., 75To982, November 25, 1975.
99 S. Ct., 74To 3488, January 28, 1975. *Yŏksa sogŭi sabŏppu*, 424–425.

"What did the students do wrong? The government was so bad the students had to rise up." He was found guilty of promoting and praising the activities of the North regime and also of spreading rumors; he was sentenced by the court martial to ten years in prison and suspension of civil rights for ten years. The appellate court martial reduced his sentence to seven years. On appeal, the Supreme Court held that merely listening to North Korean broadcasting could not be seen as an act of praising, promoting, or agreeing with and benefiting North Korea under article 4 (1) of the Anticommunist Act. It remanded the case to the appellate military court without mentioning the emergency decree violation, simply stating that "since the lower court erred on the interpretation of article 4 (1) of the Anticommunist Act and it is clear that this error affected the decision of the court, it must be quashed with no need to rule on other grounds of appeal."

Note that Emergency Decree No. 4, along with Decree No. 1, had been abolished by this time. With the shutdown of the emergency military courts in October 1974, there was no court to retry the remanded case. The defendant was freed on bail in 1975, but his case remained without resolution for thirteen years. It was only in 1988 that the Seoul Appeals Court acquitted him of the Anticommunist Act charge and dismissed the emergency decree charge.[100]

In September 1974, two Yonsei University students, Kim Yŏng-Chun and Song Mu-Ho, were convicted by the Emergency High Military Court for violation of the National Security Act, the crime of conspiring insurrection, and the emergency decrees. In the aforementioned Inhyŏktang and Minch'ŏng Hangnyŏn Supreme Court decision on April 8, they were the only two individuals whose cases were remanded. The Court decided that their convictions under the National Security Act must be quashed. The lower court had found them guilty on multiple charges but punished them, applying the principle of conceptual concurrence of crimes, under the crime of the National Security Act which carried the most severe punishments among them and imposed aggravated sentences.[101] Since the lower court's judgments on the National Security Act were defective, the Supreme Court held, their cases must be sent back, no matter whether its findings on other charges were not erroneous.[102] After the remand,

[100] *Hangyŏre Sinmun*, May 31, 1988.
[101] See Chapter 4, note 130 and accompanying text; see also Chapter 7, note 30.
[102] S. Ct., 74To3323.

in the absence of the emergency military courts, Kim's and Song's cases seemingly disappeared into a legal void.[103] They were subsequently freed through a suspension of custody, but their cases officially remained open until 1988.[104] This meant they did not have their civil rights restored all those years.They effectively became the "Orphans of Yusin" for over a decade.[105] These cases seemed to confirm that the Supreme Court tried to avoid ruling on the emergency decree charges as much as possible.

Individual Liberty and National Security

Security laws entailed harsh penalties. Table 5.1 lists the number of people prosecuted under the security laws between 1965 and 1994. Between 1970 and 1979, 1,229 and 3,077 individuals were charged under the National Security Act and the Anticommunist Act respectively. The Anticommunist Act was abolished on December 31, 1980, and its provisions were incorporated into the National Security Act. Table 5.2 provides the number of death penalties imposed under the National Security Act, the Anticommunist Act, and regular criminal laws between 1974 and 1984. Table 5.3 breaks down the sentences rendered for those convicted under the two security laws at courts of all levels between 1974 and 1979, the peak years of Yusin rule. A fairly small but consistent number of defendants were subjected to the death or life imprisonment penalties. The numbers for the year 1975 include those who were tried and sentenced by the military courts because they had simultaneously been charged with Emergency Decrees No. 1 or No. 4 or both. The Inhyŏktang defendants were such examples. That year, the Supreme Court dismissed all appeals, involving 125 defendants, in the National Security Act cases; it dismissed eighty-three and remanded seven in Anticommunist Act cases.[106]

One of the differences between security laws and emergency decrees concerned the social stigma attached to those convicted. Violation of the emergency decrees – improvised by the Park regime to silence political opponents and discipline students – did not carry serious social reproach or disgrace. Without downplaying the sufferings of

[103] *Tong-A Ilbo*, March 8, 1985.
[104] *Tong-A Ilbo*, May 26, 1988.
[105] *Tong-A Ilbo*, March 24, 1986.
[106] *Sabŏp yŏngam* 1976 (for year 1975), 354.

Table 5.1 ***National Security Act and Anticommunist Act Prosecutions, 1965–1994***

	National Security Act	Anticommunist Act*
1965	86	124
1966	69	**
1967	131	207
1968	270	381
1969	254	627
1970	204	368
1971	217	276
1972	175	507
1973	164	260
1974	152	228
1975	74	328
1976	121	386
1977	35	322
1978	30	208
1979	57	194
1980	23	136
1981	169	65
1982	171	13
1983	153	**
1984	93	3
1985	178	2
1986	323	5
1987	432	
1988	104	
1989	312	
1990	414	
1991	357	
1992	342	
1993	136	
1994	403	

Notes: *The Anticommunist Act was abolished on December 31, 1980, and was merged with National Security Act.

** Court statistics not available.

Sources: *T'onggye yŏnbo* (1974), 53; *Sabŏp yŏngam* (1985), 369; *Sabŏp yŏngam* (1995), 615.

Table 5.2 *Capital Punishments, 1974–1984*

	National Security Act	Anticommunist Act	Others*	Total
1974	7	1	27	35
1975	8	0	25	33
1976	5	0	27	32
1977	1	2	11	14
1978	0	0	17	17
1979	1	2	15	18
1980	2	3	27	32
1981	1	0	32	33
1982	5	0	30	35
1983	4	0	15	19
1984	1	0	17	18

Note: * Includes murder, robbery resulting in death, and crimes subject to aggravated punishments.
Source: *Sabŏp yŏngam* (1985), 359.

the citizens who went to prison under them, one can say that being convicted under the decrees was sort of a badge of honor among some defiant students and dissidents. It was not an uncommon spectacle in emergency decree trials that the defendants drew vociferous cheers from the courtroom audience while the military prosecutors received loud jeers. The National Security Act and the Anticommunist Act were different matters. In the fiercely anticommunist national psyche, being found guilty under these laws had dire consequences for the defendants and their families.This was in part why the courts took extreme caution in construing them.

After democratization in 1987, a well-respected judge reminisced that he tried to console a junior colleague who was distraught over having to convict defendants for violating Emergency Decree No. 9. He told the young judge that the emergency decree was, after all, a political device and that those he pronounced guilty would likely be freed through government leniency, often with their civil rights restored. In contrast, the senior judge stressed, judges ought not to make compromises in National Security Act cases and must try hard not to condemn innocent citizens as communists.[107]

[107] Pak U-Tong, *P'ansa sil esŏ pŏpchŏng kkaji*, 102.

Table 5.3 *Sentences for National Security Act and Anticommunist Act Violations (First Instance), 1974–1979*

Year	Law	Received Current Year	Disposed	Death Penalty	Life in Prison	≥ 10 yrs	≥ 5 yrs	≥ 3 yrs	≥ 1 yr	< 1 yr	Stay of Execution	Indeter.*	Suspension of Civil Rights	Fines	Suspended Sentence	Not Guilty	Dismissed	Misc.**	Appealed	Pending
1974	NS	152	156	7	7	14	13	8	38	10	20	0	0	26	5	2	1	5	97	60
	AC	228	227	1	2	3	3	13	54	58	71	0	4	0	4	6	0	8	103	87
1975	NS	74	89	8	4	5	8	5	17	22	17	1	0	0	1	1	0	0	58	45
	AC	328	339	0	1	2	3	20	99	95	90	4	10	1	5	7	0	2	160	76
1976	NS	121	139	5	3	11	46	34	11	9	17	0	0	0	0	0	0	3	91	27
	AC	386	403	0	0	4	20	34	142	63	92	4	24	6	3	5	3	3	207	59
1977	NS	35	41	1	1	2	5	10	5	2	13	0	0	0	0	1	0	1	21	21
	AC	322	286	2	3	0	9	19	83	79	77	0	8	0	1	1	2	2	155	95
1978	NS	30	33	0	0	1	8	8	8	2	4	0	0	0	0	1	0	1	22	18
	AC	208	232	0	0	7	7	22	101	34	53	4	2	0	0	1	0	1	134	71
1979	NS	57	41	1	2	2	2	5	4	17	4	0	2	0	2	0	0	0	26	34
	AC	194	213	2	3	3	9	19	51	60	54	5	3	0	2	1	0	1	114	52

Notes: NS=National Security Act; AC=Anticommunist Act.

* Indeterminate sentence.

** Transfer to juvenile section.

Sources: *T'onggye yŏngam* (1974), 224–227; *Sabŏp yŏngam* (1976), 344–355; *Sabŏp yŏngam* (1977), 354–377; *Sabŏp yŏngam* (1978), 476–500; *Sabŏp yŏngam* (1979), 494–519; *Sabŏp yŏngam* (1980), 534–559.

In 1975, the government enacted a new security law called the Social Safety Act (Sahoe Anjŏn Pŏp).[108] The Act was passed by the National Assembly in the middle of the night when only the ruling party was present, a not-uncommon legislative ploy by then. Its procedural irregularity aside, the Act was widely criticized for restricting individual rights. The enactment of this law had been precipitated by the impending release of a large number of inmates who had been convicted for pro-North activities at the time of the Korean War. The prisoners had received life imprisonment, but their sentences were subsequently commuted, making them due for release in the mid-1970s.[109] As their prison terms drew to an end, the government hurried to pass the Social Safety Act, designating certain prisoners as "needing re-education" and subjecting them, upon their release, to administrative supervision ranging from police surveillance to preventive detention. They were ordered to report regularly to the police station near their dwelling (article 4); placed in preventive custody at a place assigned by the president or minister of justice (article 5); or forced to enter a re-education center (article 6).

The Supreme Court in 1979 rejected the motion to certify the Act for constitutional review.[110] This was one of the few decisions in which the Court addressed substantive constitutional issues.[111] The Court acknowledged that the law's measures limited the freedom of the person, the right to choose one's abode, and freedom of travel. But it noted that Article 32 (1) of the Constitution allowed enactment of laws restricting a citizen's freedom and rights when it was necessary for national security, order, and public welfare. According to the Court, the Social Safety Act had the legislative purpose of safeguarding the security of the state by preventing a threat that could be caused by the influx into society of a large number of former communist party members and sympathizers of North Korea. The Court decided that the law was a means to achieve a legitimate legislative goal with minimal restriction on citizens' liberties. Since the scope of the law was limited to preventive measures, found the Court, it was not in conflict

108 Act No. 2769, July 16, 1975.

109 Yang Kŏn, "Hanguk hŏnpŏp III," 124.

110 S. Ct., 78To1680, June 26, 1979.

111 See Kim Kang-Un, "Hanguk e issŏsŏ wihŏn pŏmnyul simsa ŭi silch'e: p'allye rŭl chungsim ŭro" [The Substance of Judicial Review in Korea: Focusing on Precedent], *Pŏphak yŏngu* (Wŏnkwang Taehakkyo College of Law) 12 (1992), 363–384.

with the constitutional principles against retroactivity or double punishment.[112] This decision closely reflected the long-held jurisprudential tendency of the Supreme Court to recognize the legislative prerogatives broadly when dealing with state security. As has been noted, the presumption of the constitutionality of laws and regulations prevailed in Korean judicial culture. The possibility that the government might abuse the law in its implementation was not seen as a reason for declaring the law unconstitutional. The Social Safety Act was replaced in 1980 by the Social Protection Act, which allowed the state to place released inmates under surveillance but not in preventive confinement.[113] The Social Protection Act, revised in 1989, was abolished in August 2005.[114]

Overall, the Supreme Court's record shows that the justices maintained a distance from policy decision-making or execution, not eager to insert themselves into political issues including security matters. It inevitably exposed them to the accusation of sidestepping the issue of human rights abuses perpetrated in the name of the state interests. In contrast, the judicial role in nonpolitical cases was anything but reticent or restrained. The courts did not eschew playing an active role in resolving private conflicts and protecting the property rights of the citizen. The authoritarian government had little say on the courts' operation in private law matters. The jurisprudential development in private law deserves attention.

The Normative State: Nonsecurity Cases

The Yusin regime did not oppose court rulings against the government once they were rendered. The president might have been tempted not to enforce them, but he knew better. The regime was aware that compliance with judicial decisions helped to improve how it was perceived by both domestic and international constituencies. It correctly figured that allowing the courts full autonomy in nonpolitical cases was essential especially when Korea was on a critical path to industrialization. As President Park pushed for

112 *Pŏmnyul Sinmun*, August 20, 1979.
113 Sahoe Poho Pŏp [Social Protection Act] (Act No. 3286, December 18, 1980).
114 Act No. 4089, March 25, 1989; Act No. 7656, August 4, 2005.

high-pressure economic policies, his top priority was to convince foreign business firms that Korea was a safe place for investment.

Some observers have argued that the regime's emphasis on legality was purely instrumental, aimed to compensate for its deficiency in legitimacy and to regularize the repressive politics. In this view, Park's *dirigiste* economic policies set up the edifice of rules and procedures mainly to reassure foreign investors. While there is some truth to this opinion, it does not diminish the importance of law and the role of the courts in promoting a market economy and free enterprise. As the Korean economy expanded, the volume of civil litigation ballooned. Table 5.4 shows a steep increase in civil litigation from the 1960s through the 1990s.

Examination of some of the major decisions in private law reveals a genuinely animated Supreme Court, eagerly engaging in jurisprudential activities. This is a picture notably different from that of the Court reluctant to get bogged down in cases in the political realm. It was certainly distant from the Court's anemic record in the emergency decree cases.

Jurisprudential Developments

In relation to Korea's rapid industrialization in the 1970s, environmental law cases first call for attention. In 1973, a plaintiff claimed that gas emission from a neighboring fertilizer factory contaminated his orchard and the trees could not bear fruit. The Supreme Court found that the factory did not have sufficient equipment for reducing exhaust fumes and that the lack of worker training to treat gas emissions properly caused harmful fumes to spread to the plaintiff's orchard.[115] This was the first case in Korea that recognized environmental liability. A few months later, in a separate case involving the same parties, the Court went further and ruled that the factory could be held liable regardless of its negligence if material damages resulted: "even if the defendant factory had established all the equipment available in modern technology necessary to prevent damages in its operation, it cannot be said that the defendant is not liable to the plaintiff" for the harms it caused. In other words, liability could be established in

115 S. Ct., 71Na2016, May 22, 1973. *Pŏpwŏnsa*, 775.

Table 5.4 *Population and Civil Litigation, 1965–1994*

Year	Population	Civil Cases Filed	Population per Case
1965	28,377,000	62,426	454.6
1966	29,193,000	56,886	513.2
1967	29,784,000	55,302	538.6
1968	30,469,000	56,155	542.6
1969	31,139,000	55,395	562.1
1970	31,469,000	58,134	541.3
1971	32,139,000	61,197	525.2
1972	32,676,000	67,393	484.9
1973	32,905,000	81,986	401.3
1974	33,459,000	87,725	381.4
1975	34,681,000	91,723	378.1
1976	35,860,000	101,727	352.5
1977	36,436,000	98,693	369.2
1978	37,019,000	74,312	498.2
1979	37,354,000	79,328	470.9
1980	37,448,000	120,330	311.2
1981	38,309,000	183,634	208.6
1982	39,113,000	197,945	197.6
1983	39,669,000	206,485	192.1
1984	40,430,000	258,036	156.7
1985	40,806,000	297,999	136.9
1986	41,184,000	320,922	128.3
1987	41,575,000	335,263	124.0
1988	41,975,000	290,448	144.5
1989	42,380,000	271,123	156.3
1990	43,869,000	279,948	156.7
1991	43,801,000	308,806	141.8
1992	44,306,000	362,633	122.2
1993	45,011,000	392,057	114.8
1994	45,426,000	431,999	105.2

Sources: *T'onggye yŏnbo* (1974), 3; *Sabŏp yŏngam* (1976), 113; *Sabŏp yŏngam* (1985), 234, 303; *Sabŏp yŏngam* (1995), 476, 546.

separation from negligence.[116] This ruling was regarded as pivotal in the development of contamination cases. A year later, the Court held that the defendant factory was liable if damages occurred and if it was probable that the damages were caused by the operation of the factory.[117]

A series of product liability cases arose. In 1977, a poultry farm owner sued the producer of chicken feed when his chickens lost feathers and egg production sharply declined. He blamed the chicken feed manufactured by the defendant. The Supreme Court found in favor of the plaintiff. The Court ruled that even if it were not clearly proved that certain impurities in the feed caused chemical, biological, or nutritional changes to result in the constriction of the chickens' ovaries and the subsequent decline in egg production, the causality between negligence and the symptoms of the chickens that were fed the product could be inferred as long as the existence of impurities in the feed was demonstrated.[118] In a similar case, where the needle of a toy syringe was accidentally detached and caused injury, the product liability of the producer could be established, found the Court.[119] Even if the causal relationship between the concrete defect of the product and the harm could not be proved, the negligence of the manufacturer could be presumed as a matter of fact, and the burden of the victim to prove the causality was reduced.

In 1975, the Supreme Court ruled that an illness caused or aggravated by excessive workload must be treated as an injury suffered in the course of employment even if the illness was not directly related to the nature of the work.[120] In 1977, the Court found that, even if drawing up employment contracts was the prerogative of employers, unilateral modification of the conditions of labor that placed certain workers in disadvantage required the employees' consent through collective bargaining.[121] In this case, a worker had accepted the

[116] S. Ct., 73Ta1253, October 10, 1973.

[117] S. Ct. 72Ta1774, December 10, 1974. *Chosŏn Ilbo*, December 12, 1974 (editorial).

[118] S. Ct., 75Ta2092, January 25, 1977. *Pŏpwŏnsa*, 777–778.

[119] S. Ct., 79Ta1772. *Yŏksa sogŭi sabŏppu*, 327.

[120] S. Ct. 75Nu148, October 7, 1975; S. Ct., 78Nu255, October 31, 1978.

[121] S. Ct., 77Ta355, July 26, 1977.

employer's changes in methods for calculating retirement benefits. After he left the company, he learned that the changes resulted in a smaller payment and claimed that the modification of the terms of employment without the consent of the majority of the employees or the consent of the labor union was invalid.[122] The Court confirmed that labor conditions must be determined by free negotiation between the employee and the employer on an impartial and equal footing. It reasoned that allowing the modification of the terms of employment to bind one employee who had consented to them and denying the same change's effect to another employee who did not consent would create a situation in which the employer, using its superior bargaining status, could impose on selected workers terms inferior to the existing working arrangements that had been obtained through collective bargaining.

Statutory Interpretation

In general, legal formalism formed the dominant tendency in jurisprudence in Korea. But scholars have also argued that there was a judicial penchant in the normative realm in the 1970s to emphasize substantive reasonableness in resolving legal disputes. The Supreme Court often took into consideration equity between the parties and tried to provide remedies; if it believed the application of law would result in iniquity, the Court was willing to resort to an alternative reasoning in order to redress the rights of the parties or to render a compromise decision to protect at least a portion of the rights.[123]

Dynamic jurisprudential debate frequently took place within the Court. A case of statutory construction in 1978 illustrated the clashes between realist and textualist interpretations of statutes.[124] Article 55 (1) of the Criminal Law listed various methods the court could use in dealing with the statutory amount of fines. One of them stated: "When determining the fine, the judge can reduce the highest amount allowed in law by half." This provision said nothing about reducing the lowest amount, and it was not clear whether the judge had the discretion to cut only the highest fine by half. The majority of justices ruled that the term "the highest amount" in the statute should be interpreted simply as "the

122 *Yŏksa sogŭi sabŏppu*, 328.
123 O Se-Hyŏk, "Hanguk esŏ ŭi pŏmnyŏng haesŏk" [Interpretation of Laws and Regulations in Korea], *Pŏp chŏrak yŏngu* 6 (2003), 124.
124 S. Ct., 78To246, April 25, 1978.

amount," so that the highest as well as the lowest amounts allowed in fines could be reduced to half. It said:

> It is not impossible, and is even necessary, to "interpret" provisions of criminal law in a way to mitigate their arbitrary effects. ... All laws should be interpreted in a reasonable manner, as long as it does not change their nature, with a view to adjust the laws lagging behind the changing social reality and also to demand their revision by the legislature. It is part of the judicial mission. ... It is not a proper attitude of the court to sit back and say that it must follow conventional interpretations and applications of the law provisions, knowing that they would bring unjust results.[125]

Seven justices disagreed. They stated:

> Where there exists an explicit written provision in law and its meaning is clear but that law has been viewed as no longer suitable for the economic or other social reality which advances faster than the law, the judge must wait for its revision by the legislature. The judge should not willingly change the clear meaning of the provision even in an effort to make it more reflective of social reality or to make punishment less severe for the accused. If, in interpreting the provision in question, we replace the word "the highest amount" with "the amount," as suggested by the majority, it means we go beyond our power to interpret the law, and we will not be able to avoid the criticism that we encroach upon the legislative power of the National Assembly.[126]

The dissenters' position adhered tightly to the formalistic ideology: the role of the judge was to find the law, not to make the law, and not even to correct the law. But the majority's more malleable interpretive position prevailed in this case.

Another example of the sharp division of the Court involved the prosecution of adultery. What is the effect of the withdrawal of the filing for divorce on adultery prosecution? Article 229 (2) of Criminal Procedure provided: "If a party remarries or withdraws the divorce proceeding, the complaint for the adultery charge is regarded as rescinded"; article 232 (1) provided: "The complaint can be withdrawn before the judgment of the initial [divorce] proceeding." The majority of the Supreme Court ruled that, even if the divorce judgment petition was dropped after the trial was completed at the court of first instance

125 Ibid.

126 S. Ct., 78To246 (Yi Yŏng-Sŏp, Chu Chae-Hwang, Kim Yun-Haeng, Kang An-Hi; Na Kil-Cho, Kim Yong-Chŏl, and Yu T'ae-Hŭng, JJ, dissenting).

and the sentence for one of the codefendants rendered, the withdrawal of divorce filing caused the loss of requisite elements of the crime of adultery and the case for the accused spouse dissolved retroactively.[127] The Court viewed article 229 (2) as a limitation to the scope of article 232 (1) and held that its ruling applied even when one of the accused had received a guilty verdict and the revocation of the divorce judgment motion would have no effect on that person's conviction.

The dissenting opinions argued that the majority failed to distinguish whether its ruling applied only on the cancellation of the divorce proceeding or whether it applied also on the withdrawal of criminal accusation. The majority, contended the dissenters, basically nullified both article 230 (1), which limited the filing period of criminal accusation to six months, and article 232 (1), which allowed the withdrawal of criminal accusation only prior to the decision by the court of first instance. By this, the majority defeated the intent of the statutes to reduce legal instability that might result from the situation in which the will of the parties controlled judicial administration even in those cases not requiring the party's complaint (*Antragsdelikt*). The dissenting justices were particularly disturbed by the fact that the majority's ruling would result in the punishment of only one of the adulterous codefendants, thereby violating the principle of equality; further, it would conflict with article 233 of the Criminal Procedure that the filing of criminal accusation, or its rescission thereof, against one of the codefendants in an offense subject to complaint extended its effect to the other codefendant.[128] This was a case that displayed the clear jurisprudential divide in the highest court.

In November 1975, the Supreme Court, for the first time in Korea's judicial history, vacated a conviction on the grounds that the defendant's right to make a statement was deprived. Article 303 of the Criminal Procedure and article 345 (2) of the Military Court Act both required that the defendant be given an opportunity to make a final statement. The highest court found that the Navy Appellate Military Court had violated the law when it rendered a judgment

[127] S. Ct., 75To1449, June 24, 1975 (An Pyŏng-Su, Kim Yun-Haeng, and Yi Il-Kyu, JJ., dissenting). *Pŏpwŏnsa*, 796–797.

[128] Adultery is no longer a crime in Korea, after the Constitutional Court struck down the adultery law in the Criminal Code (art. 241). Const. Ct., 2009HŏnPa17, February 26, 2015.

without granting the defendant an opportunity to do so.[129] Procedural due process needed to be strictly guarded, stressed the Court.

Administrative Litigation

These cases, albeit isolated examples, illustrate that the Supreme Court was not a mere bastion of positivistic reductionism safeguarding the state interest. Administrative law cases are particularly notable. It is noted in Chapter 3 that Korean courts maintained the position that administrative litigation was part of civil litigation and that the actions of administrative agencies should not be treated differently from those of other civil parties. At the same time, one recalls that the prevailing approach of Korean courts was – and still is, to an extent – that economic rights contained an implicit public welfare qualification and that the exercise of rights could be limited by legislation undertaken in consideration of the public good. Article 23 of the Constitution highlights the principle of the public welfare: "The exercise of property rights shall conform to the public welfare."[130] In the 1960s and the 1970s, the implementation of state-led economic initiatives relied heavily on the broad discretionary power of government agencies, armed with the concept of public interest. So-called administrative guidance proliferated as agencies treated regulatory guidance as carrying the force of law. In general, the judiciary was reluctant to be in the way of the government's measures for law and development, such as granting subsidies, tax breaks, and other inducement programs for exporting companies. When administrative actions potentially infringed on individuals' fundamental economic rights, however, the courts actively engaged in their role as an impartial adjudicative body.

Administrative litigation mainly concerned tax assessment, eminent domain, dismissal or disciplinary actions against civil servants, and zoning cases. In 1974, a total of 545 administrative cases were filed at the courts of first instance (appeals courts) and 378 cases were appealed to the Supreme Court.[131] The plaintiff prevailed in 28.6 percent of cases

[129] S. Ct., 75To1010, November 11, 1975. *Tong-A Ilbo*, November 14, 1975.
[130] Constitution (1987), Art. 23 (2).
[131] Pŏpwŏn Haengjŏngch'ŏ, *Sabŏp yŏngam* 1975 (for year 1974), 41–42.

at first instance, partially prevailed in 4.5 percent, and lost in 52.3 percent of the cases; 30.8 percent were withdrawn, and about 14.3 percent of the cases were dismissed. In the second instance, 81.1 percent of the cases were dismissed on appeal, and 18.9 percent were quashed and remanded.[132] In the 1970s as a whole, the state frequently appealed the administrative law decisions, but the success rate was conspicuously low.[133] Between 1971 and 1979, the state appealed 1,654 cases; among them, 83 percent, or 1,372 cases, ended in the state's loss. In the year 1979 alone, the state appealed 275 cases, but 241 cases, or 87.6 percent, were dismissed. Most appeals involved tax litigation, for which the state lost in 88.4 percent of cases on average.

While the government tenaciously pursued appeals, it accepted final court judgments, once they were issued, without resistance. President Park exerted his powers to their fullest, but he complied with court decisions contrary to government interest. This fact set Korea apart from most other authoritarian regimes. Mainly the president was keen on fostering the public's economic confidence. Protection of the interests of individuals by ensuring the stability and predictability of the legal system was crucial for inducing them to participate in the frenzied industrialization spearheaded by the government. Korea availed itself of a highly educated labor force, who took part in an all-out effort for economic growth in expectation for a better return on their hard work. Many endured results of less-than-equitable income distribution but, overall, their labor, thrift, and venture brought prosperity. To argue that Korea's postwar success was possible because people were somehow willing to place public and national interest before their own economic interest is at best dubious and could even prove divisive when how to appraise the merit of the growth-driven state policy during this time still lacks consensus.

While facing frequent defeats in administrative law cases as a whole, the government was in a much stronger position in state tort claims and requisition cases. The seemingly uniform rulings in favor of the state under these laws led people to question the judiciary's ability to protect the citizens' interest from the state.[134] The difference between these two laws and other administrative laws was obvious. As shown in Chapter 3, the government crafted the text of the Yusin Constitution with the specific

132 Ibid., 42. See also the graph in *Yŏksa sogŭi sabŏppu*, 489.

133 *Tong-A Ilbo*, January 19, 1980; *Kyŏnghyang Sinmun*, January 19, 1980; *Maeil Kyŏngje*, January 19, 1980.

134 *Tong-A Ilbo*, March 15, 1975.

goal of preempting challenges to the Special Act for Requisitioned Property Disposition and also the State Tort Claims Act. Those changes conclusively favored the government party, but it did not mean disputes stopped arising. The Supreme Court decisions on these cases reveal how the beleaguered judiciary coped with the Constitution.

Coping with the Constitution

Even after the "constitutional fix," some lower courts refused to implement the requisition law as intended by the government, and cases kept coming to the Supreme Court. Having long avoided making decisions, in July 1975 the Court rejected constitutional challenges to the requisitioned property law by quashing the lower court decision that declared the law unconstitutional.[135] The highest court ruled that it was not possible to challenge the law enacted with explicit constitutional authority. The cases of the State Tort Claims Act were similar but more controversial, because the Supreme Court in 1971 actually struck down the specific language of the law, before the government resurrected it in the 1972 Constitution and the law.[136]

How should the court decide where existing precedents, neither flawed in reasoning nor needing adjustment in social reality, came in conflict with the revised constitution? How should the court deal with a law which, having been struck down as unconstitutional, was subsequently incorporated into the new constitution that replaced the old constitution under which the law had been declared void? If the judge refused to overturn the precedent and disregard the law, he or she would be deciding the case against the current constitution; if the judge overturned the precedent and implemented the law, he or she would not avoid the criticism that the court abandoned the precedent with no reasonable grounds. That there was a new constitution in place would unlikely be sufficient to persuade those who had agreed with the reasoning of the original court. This was precisely the quandary the Supreme Court faced under the Yusin Constitution. Its 1977 decision involved a case in which the questions of legal stability, constitutional authority, judicial conscience, and civil liberties were intricately intertwined.

135 S. Ct. 70Ta340 (*en banc*), July 8, 1975. Yoon, *Law and Political Authority*, 191–192; *Pŏpwŏnsa*, 687.

136 S. Ct., 70Ta1010 (*en banc*), June 22, 1971.

State Tort Claims Act Case Redux (1977)

When the government revived the State Tort Claims Act on February 5, 1973, under the authority of the new Constitution, it expanded the category of people for whom double compensation was prohibited.[137] Not only the military forces and military personnel but also government employees and Homeland Reserve Forces were subject to the exclusion proviso. This revision was the regime's response to a case in which the Seoul District Court collegiate bench held that damages suffered by the Homeland Reserve Forces during drills or duty must be treated like damages suffered by the military forces.[138] Under the new law, any suit demanding compensation from the state could be made only after a decision by the compensation review committee, except when three months had passed from the date of the request for review. Even after the constitutional revision, the application of the State Tort Claims Act remained haphazard. On June 20, 1973, the Seoul Appeals Court ruled that the surviving family of a soldier was entitled to an indemnity payment under the law regardless of the acceptance of bereavement allowance. This decision referred to the authority of the Supreme Court's ruling of 1971 that the proviso in the old State Tort Claims Act was unconstitutional. Yet other courts denied tort compensations, citing the new constitutional provision. Jurisprudential uniformity was once again urgently needed. The Supreme Court long delayed rendering a decision before finally taking up the matter in 1977.

The case before the Court involved restitution for a military serviceman who was killed on April 10, 1970.[139] He was riding in a truck that drove off a cliff due to the negligence of another soldier. The family sued the state for compensation. On June 2, 1972, the Appellate Court found for the plaintiff, citing the Supreme Court's decision of the previous year that invalidated the proviso of article 2 (1) of the State Tort Claims Act.[140] The state appealed. While the case was pending at the Supreme Court, the new Constitution came into effect, reviving the prohibition of double compensation.

[137] Kukka Paesang Pŏp (Act No. 2459, February 5, 1973).
[138] *Chung-Ang Ilbo*, May 24, 1969.
[139] S. Ct., 72Ta1359 (*en banc*), June 7, 1977. Yoon, *Law and Political Authority*, 183–188.
[140] Seoul App. Ct, 72Na131, June 2, 1972.

The problem was that the restored State Tort Claims Act did not provide for those cases filed before the promulgation of the 1972 Constitution.

In June 1977, the Supreme Court ruled that the State Tort Claims Act of 1973 was not unconstitutional, more specifically, it could not be seen as invalid under the pre-1972 constitutional order.[141] It was a ruling that seemed to contradict head-on the celebrated 1971 decision that found the same Act unconstitutional. Did the justices in 1977 undo the achievement of their predecessors, which had been hard earned at the expense of the immense sacrifices made by those justices forced out due to their opinions? The gist of the 1977 opinion was that Article 26 (2) of the current Constitution should be made applicable even to cases that had come up to the court before it was proclaimed. The 1977 Court opinion read in its entirety:

> According to the proviso of article 2 (1) of the State Tort Claims Act that was in force at the time of the accident in question in the present case, a person who has sustained damages by unlawful acts committed by public officials in the course of executing their official duties may claim redress against the state or a public agency, but in case a person on active military service or an employee of the military forces, or a police officer or others as defined by legislation, has sustained damages in connection with the performance of official duties such as combat action, drill, and so forth and where he is entitled to restitution including accident compensation or bereavement allowance or pension, he is not entitled to a claim under that law or other civil law. As long as this provision cannot be seen as having no legal force only because it was in violation of Article 26 of the old constitution and other constitutional provisions, the lower court should have decided whether the case concerned the provision of this proviso and, when it decided that it concerned the proviso, it should have refused the demand for damage compensation.[142]

This terse, awkwardly worded opinion prompted a universal outcry. The main criticism was that the Court departed from its 1971 decision without providing any justification.[143] Indeed, the Court did not even

141 S. Ct., 72Ta1359. *Pŏmnyul Sinmun*, June 13 and June 20, 1977; *Pŏpwŏnsa*, 687, 704.

142 S. Ct., 72Ta359 (*en banc*), June 7, 1977.

143 *Tong-A Ilbo*, June 8, 1977; *Chosŏn Ilbo*, June 8, 1977. Yi Sang-Ch'ŏl, "Kukka Paesangpŏp che 2 cho," 273–274; Kang Pyŏng-Yong, "Kukka paesang chedo."

mention the 1971 ruling in its opinion. This omission was not unintentional. In rendering a decision that contradicted the substance of the holding of the 1971 Court, the 1977 Court tried not to make it necessary to refer to the earlier ruling which had been overridden by the new Constitution. One can speculate that the 1977 Court did not refer to the 1971 decision because it did not want to declare its reversal on its own. The main question facing the Supreme Court was whether a judicial precedent that came to contradict the language of the newly revised Constitution should be sustained. It concluded in the negative: double compensation could not be allowed against the clear language of the Constitution currently in force. This case vividly exemplified how the Court was pigeonholed by the writing of the Yusin Constitution.

Did the justices in 1977 hope to avoid the fate of their predecessors who had been summarily dismissed by going against the president's wishes? Many observers suspected just that. Sustaining the 1971 ruling would have forced the regime to react as it had done before, or worse. Defying the president for a second time on precisely the same issue would have had consequences. In fact, this may have been what opponents of the regime hoped to see – that is, to throw into question the validity of the entire constitutional revision. The justices sitting on the bench in 1977 may have decided that it would be a pointless battle, causing the judiciary to lose a great deal more than it would gain by creating a constitutional crisis. The opinion summed up the unenviable position of the Supreme Court, as it tried not to cross overtly the constitutional and legal boundaries. It does not change the fact that Court ended up disposing of the case in conformity with the interest of the government; it could as well be viewed as proof that the Supreme Court had capitulated to the regime. Still, whether the decision was erroneous in law is a different question altogether.

This was not the end of the story. Subsequent Supreme Court decisions regarding the State Tort Claims Act show that the Court, having evaded a showdown with the government in 1977, proceeded to interpret the law and the Constitution narrowly so as to reduce the law's unfavorable impact on victims and their families. In 1979, the family members of a police officer sued the state under the State Tort Claims Act and civil law. The officer had died from carbon monoxide poisoning due to the faulty heating system in the sleeping quarters for night-duty personnel. The Supreme Court found that "the room used for the sleeping quarters for the night-duty personnel cannot be seen as facilities for combat or drill as provided in article 2 (1) of the State Tort Claims Act"; hence the proviso was not applicable and the families of the deceased officer had the right to demand compensation.[144] The Court's traditional position of redressing individuals' interest as much as possible without causing open confrontation with the government seemed to remain little changed. Article 26 (2) of the 1972 Constitution restricting state tort liabilities survived in Article 28 (2) of the 1980 Constitution as well as Article 29 (2) of the 1987 Constitution.

The 1977 decision revealed the predicament of the judges who had to decide cases according to constitutional provisions no matter whether those had been politically motivated. After all, the Supreme Court was not a constitutional body and was unable to ignore the constitution in force. It is certainly possible that the adoption of a mechanical approach to statutory interpretation served as a way to relieve the judge from judicial accountability and ease his conscience. As a scholar has pointed, the judge is not always innocent in connection with an action that is compelled by the law.[145] At least, one can agree on the premise that the judge must take the law seriously.

The constitutional language as rewritten in 1972 broadened the scope of the validity of legislation and executive orders, compelling the judiciary to implement political laws. This thorny situation brings to the fore the question of the judicial dilemma of unjust laws. The next chapter takes up this issue.

[144] S. Ct., 77Ta2389 (*en banc*), January 30, 1979. *Pŏmnyul Sinmun*, February 19, 1979. Some argued that this decision effectively mitigated the proviso of the State Tort Claims Act and also Article 26 (2) of the Constitution which served as its foundation. *Pŏmnyul Sinmun*, July 16, 1979.

[145] Brian Z. Tamanaha, "Good Casuistry and Bad Casuistry: Resolving the Dilemmas Faced by Catholic judges," *University of St. Thomas Law Journal* 4 (2006), 272–273.

6 *The Yusin Era, 1972–1980 (3): The Judges*

President Park invoked all possible positivist cover for his rule, including national referendum. Once the Constitution was in place, rewritten under martial law, the wayward legislature passed a string of politically motivated laws and the president ruled with emergency decrees which stood outside judicial scrutiny. Judges were in a quandary. They were expected to defend rights guaranteed in the Constitution, but the same Constitution allowed the legislative and executive branches to compromise the liberty of individuals. The Constitution manifested the legitimization of the state, the negation of which, even by reason of the substantive moral insight, could result in the repudiation of the legal order. The judicial process that faced the judges during the Yusin years can lend itself to theoretical debates over legal positivism and natural law ideas and also empirical discussion of judicial functions and behaviors.

This chapter first discusses the predicaments of judges in terms of the recurrent problem in legal theory and history of the judicial dilemma of unjust laws. Judges' dilemma arises when they encounter the legitimacy of unjust norms that were enacted in accordance with prevailing rules of lawmaking.[1] One can turn to historical insights. In his book *Justice Accused* (1975), Robert Cover explained that antislavery judges in the 1840s in antebellum America faced a classic intellectual quagmire between judicial duty and morality. The US Constitution explicitly protected slavery, and many northern judges agonized over the dissonance between their private antislavery beliefs and their public duty to enforce the law. The Korean situation was not unlike the American case in that the dispositional issue was less the morality of the law or the conscience of the judge as an individual than it was the command of the

[1] Matthias J. Herdegen, "Unjust Laws, Human Rights, and the German Constitution: Germany's Recent Confrontation with the Past," *Columbia Journal of Transnational Law* 32 (1994–1995), 592.

law that imposed limitations on basic rights in the name of state necessity. Most judges in Korea deplored the emergency decrees but still applied them in the cases that came before them. Bound by their oath to respect the Constitution and the law, they operated within a framework that would have tied the hands of the most activist judges. Judicial dilemmas are not detached from the issue of judicial independence. This chapter examines the extent to which the judicial process was influenced by the judges' concerns about their careers.

The last few years of President Park's rule witnessed rapidly ossifying government policies, which deepened judges' woes. The political roller coaster teetered precipitously before coming to a screeching halt in 1979. This chapter examines how the judges grappled with the Yusin legal system until it came to its sudden demise with the death of the president.

Judges and Unjust Laws

William R. Shaw explained Korea's postwar judicial history in terms of tension between legal positivism and natural law theories.[2] In his view, the formalist values that had once edified Chosŏn magistrates' principle of impartiality and rejection of arbitrariness continued into the colonial period, but they came under the inordinate influence from Japanese legal science dominated by state positivist philosophy. The statism-informed legal positivism carried over into the postcolonial period, predominant among judges, lawyers, and scholars who had been educated under Japanese rule. It became an "informal orthodoxy" of the authoritarian regime, which Shaw defined as "the view that the state and its laws come into existence before rights, and therefore create whatever rights exist."[3] Changes arose in the mid-1970s and the 1980s, argued Shaw, when new generations of students went abroad to pursue legal studies in countries other than Japan and came back fully imbued with natural law theory. This change could be viewed as a shift in juridical dominance from the German/Japanese school (older generation) and to a US school (younger generation), and it started to

[2] Shaw, "Introduction," in Shaw (ed.), *Human Rights in Korea: Historical and Policy Perspectives*, 9.

[3] Ibid., 8.

break the grip of the state positivism orthodoxy. Shaw thus ascribed democratization and the rise of constitutionalism in the late 1980s to the retreat of colonial legal theories and the spread of natural law theories highlighting the fundamental nature of political rights and freedoms.[4]

Shaw's emphasis on the advent of a new judicial culture at the end of authoritarian rule affirms that constitutionalism in the early years of modern Korea functioned foremost as an ideology of building the state, creating institutional structures and guaranteeing public order, rather than defining the relationship between government and individuals. The Constitution protected individuals by establishing political authority and less so by constraining it. Natural law ideas were not absent in the early generations of Korean jurists, but the individual judge's philosophical orientation and predilection were rarely perceived as the antidote to legislative abuse.[5] Asking whether enforcing laws would support the political goals of the government in power was not the primary concern of the professional judiciary. Judges did not entertain the idea that they had discretion to disregard preposterous but valid laws.

The emergency decree cases did not represent "hard cases." Hard cases are those in which lawyers disagree about how the judge should decide because they present contested points of law.[6] They are not the same as cases involving unjust but brutally blunt laws. The decrees were offensive because they were spelled out in such explicit language, overtly limiting individual rights in exact words. The judges did not need to search diligently for legislative intent. The decrees became hard cases only because they posed a dilemma between conscience and constitutional duty.

4 Ibid., 9–11.

5 For the natural law tradition in Korea, see Pak Ŭn-Chŏng, "Hanguk pŏp chŏrak ŭi pansŏng kwa kwaje" [Reflections and the Tasks of Korean Legal Philosophy], *Pŏp kwa sahoe* 10 (1994), 189–223; Kim To-Kyun, "Hanguk pŏp ch'egye esŏ chayŏnpŏp ron ŭi hyŏngsŏng kwa palchŏn" [The Formation and Development of Natural Law Theory in the Korean Legal System], *Pŏp chŏrak yŏngu* 11 (2008), 183–226.

6 Ronald Dworkin, *Taking Rights Seriously* (Cambridge, MA: Harvard University Press, 1977); Ronald Dworkin, "Hard Cases," *Harvard Law Review* 88 (1975), 105–109.

The Dilemma of Judges

Before the Civil War (1861–1865), Article 4 of the US Constitution, Section 2, Clause 3, provided that a slave who flees to another state must be returned to the owner in the state from which he or she escaped: "No person held to service or labour in one state, under the laws thereof, escaping into another, shall, in consequence of any law or regulation therein, be discharged from such service or labour, but shall be delivered up on claim of the party to whom such service or labour may be due." The much-reviled Fugitive Slave Act (1850) obligated judges to order the return of slaves who fled to another state to their masters. Cover argued that most northern judges felt compelled to implement that law because they believed that their duty was to give effect to the will of the legislature.

Cover distinguished four choices available to the judge caught in the conflict between law and morality: first, apply the law against his or her conscience; second, apply conscience and be faithless to the law; third, resign; and fourth, cheat and state that the law is not what he or she believes it to be and thus preserve an appearance (to others) of conformity to the law and morality.[7] But these choices are only typological formulations, and "[o]nce we assume a more realistic model of law and of the judicial process, these four positions become only poles setting limits to a complex field of action and motive."[8] According to Cover, the responses of most northern judges resolving the problem in favor of legal formalism were characteristic and predictable patterns of judicial performance.[9] The dominant trend of jurisprudence fostered a positivist approach; there was a consistent recourse to formalism and a conscious search for mechanical models for decision. Cover stated, "The notion that out beyond lay a higher law to which the judge *qua* judge was responsible was never a part of the mainstream of American jurisprudence."[10] The "juristic competence of the age" converged with the needs of the antislavery judges to "externalize responsibility" for their decisions.[11]

7 Cover, *Justice Accused*, 6. There may be a fifth possibility: the judge may adopt "ameliorist" solutions and "introduce his own sense of what 'ought to be' interstitially, where no hard law yet exists." Ibid. See Joel Feinberg, "Natural Law: The Dilemmas of Judges Who Must Interpret Immoral Laws," *Problems at the Roots of Law: Essays in Legal and Political Theory* (Oxford: Oxford University Press, 2003), 3–35.

8 Cover, *Justice Accused*, 6.

9 Ibid., 257.

10 Ibid., 29.

11 Ibid., 258.

Cover's main argument is that the "multiplicity of ends served by law will more often than not produce a pattern that is not entirely consistent when measured by a single moral variable."[12] The judges whose opinions he examined tried to rationalize the dissonance between their private antislavery beliefs and their perceived public duties by advancing four justifications. The patterns of judicial response involved three related responsibility-mitigation mechanisms: "Elevation of the Formal Stakes (sometimes combined with minimization of the moral stakes)"; "Retreat to a Mechanistic Formalism"; and "Ascription of Responsibility Elsewhere."[13] The judges' arguments could be summarized as follows: "(1) ordered society depended upon adherence to constitutional limits; (2) the separation of powers doctrine lodged control over slavery elsewhere in the government structure; (3) maintenance of the national union was at stake; and (4) their judicial oath bound them to support the Constitution."[14] Disposed "to think in terms of the values underlying legality and ordered processes,"[15] the antislavery judges elevated the formal stakes, namely, the idea that a concession to individual morality might undermine the separation of powers and compromise the goal of maintaining the union.[16] The judges argued that a concession to antislavery morality would undermine the rule of law. In reality, as Cover suggested, they relied on the separation of powers to place the onus of antislavery action on others and the legislature.

Cover's articulation of the mental framework of the American judges who tried to resolve the jurisprudential dilemma of slave laws can serve as a timeless measure against which one can assess the actions of judges, in particular under authoritarian rule. Before *Justice Accused*, the question of the morality of law and judicial role had erupted in a full-scale theoretical discussion in the twentieth century. The past of German law and judges during the Third Reich presented a major test case for the clash between legal positivism and natural law theory.

12 Ibid., 202. Cover stated that his interest in the antebellum judges had been prompted by his opposition to US involvement in the Vietnam War – and judicial complicity in it – and that his study led him to "the complexities of the process of complicity." Ibid., xi.

13 Ibid., 199. These judicial response patterns are elaborated in ibid., 229–238.

14 James W. Ely Jr., "Review of *Justice Accused: Antislavery and the Judicial Process* by Robert M. Cover," *Washington University Law Quarterly* 1975 (1975), 269–270.

15 Cover, *Justice Accused*, 224.

16 Ibid., 229.

The abomination of Hitler's laws dealt a blow to positivism in the postwar years. German judges, having suffered qualms of conscience for their role in enforcing Nazi laws, were eager to jettison positivism and embrace a revival of natural law as a safeguard against legislative injustice. Karl Jaspers (1883–1969) stated that resort to natural law was a way of pursuing the "purification out of the depth of consciousness of guilt," perceived to be vital to the process of coming to terms with the past.[17] Gustav Radbruch (1878–1949) blamed Nazi injustice on the predominance of positivism in prewar German jurisprudence as judges faithfully enforced Hitler's laws. For Radbruch, "Positivism, with its conviction that 'law is law' made the German jurists defenseless against laws of arbitrary and criminal content."[18] He opined that there was no objective criterion of ethical correctness against which the legitimacy of legal order could be judged.[19] Still, he broadly rejected the arguments of the legal positivists that a judge who refused to apply unjust yet procedurally proper enactments violated his judicial function.

Radbruch's famous "Formula" postulates that a "sufficiently unjust" rule loses its status as a valid legal norm; the "unjust law" is invalid if the conflict with justice is so intolerable as to call for its voidness. Two separate elaborations of Radbruch's Formula are as follows:

(1) The positive law, secured by legislation and power, takes precedence even when its content is unjust and fails to benefit the people, unless the conflict between statute and justice reaches such an intolerable degree that the statute, as "flawed law," must yield to justice.
(2) Where there is not even an attempt at justice, where equality, the core of justice, is deliberately betrayed in the issuance of positive law, then the statute is not merely "flawed law," it lacks completely the very nature of law. For law,

[17] Karl Jaspers, "The Question of German Guilt," cited in Frank Haldermann, "Gustav Radbruch vs. Hans Kelsen: A Debate on Nazi Law," *Ratio Juris* 18 (2005), 172–173.

[18] Gustav Radbruch, "Gesetzliches Unrecht und übergesetzliches Recht," *Süddeutsche Juristen-Zeitung* 1 (1946), 107; Radbrich, *Rechtsphilosophie*, 4th ed., ed. Eric Wolf (Stuttgart: Koehler, 1950), 352. See Heinrich Rommen, "Natural Law in Decisions of the Federal Supreme Court and of the Constitutional Courts in Germany," *Natural Law Forum* 4 (1959), 1–25.

[19] Gustav Radbruch, "Legal Philosophy," in Kurt Wilk (ed.), *The Legal Philosophy of Lask, Radbruch, and Dabin*, Vol. 4 (Cambridge, MA: Harvard University Press, 1950).

including positive law, cannot be otherwise defined than as a system and an institution whose very meaning is to serve justice.[20]

The first formulation focuses on the work of the judge, the second that of the legislator.[21] The famous debate between H. L. A. Hart and Lon Fuller in 1958 and subsequent discussions concerned both formulations. For Hart, it was necessary to distinguish the invalidity of law from its immorality; the truly liberal response to unjust law was to acknowledge that "laws may be law but too evil to be obeyed."[22] According to him, it is "in no sense a necessary truth that laws reproduce or satisfy certain demands of morality, though in fact they have often done so."[23] Hart did not deny that there was an intersection of law and morals, but he viewed the injection of morality into law essentially as a legislative act and not a judicial one.[24] On the other hand, Fuller and natural theorists held that there was a necessary connection between "order" (law) and "good order" (morality).[25] For Fuller, Nazi laws should be denied their legality.[26] In expounding Radbruch's views, Robert Alexy has stated that, although unjust laws are still properly classified as law and ought to be applied by courts in cases coming before them, such laws cease to be law when the injustice reaches a gross or radical level and must give way to the demands of justice.[27] Those laws, for John Finnis, are "peripheral" and "watered-down versions" of law.[28] Yet Herdegen has asked whether Radbruch's theoretical exposition is not mired in circularity and subjective taint: what constitutes "manifest and evident violations" of normativity and

20 Brian H. Bix, "Radbruch's Formula and Conceptual Analysis," *American Journal of Jurisprudence* 56 (2011), 46, quoting from Radbruch, "Statutory Lawlessness and Supra-statutory Law" (1946), 7.

21 Ibid., 46–47.

22 Hart, "Positivism," 620.

23 H. L. A. Hart, *The Concept of Law*, 2nd ed. (Oxford Clarendon Press, 1994, 1961), 185–186.

24 Hart read Radbruch as encouraging the courts to treat the evil laws of the Nazi regime as "not law." Hart, "Positivism," 620.

25 Fuller, "Positivism and Fidelity to Law," 645.

26 Ibid., 660.

27 Robert Alexy, *The Argument from Injustice: A Reply to Legal Positivism* (Oxford: Clarendon Press, 2002), 28–35, 40–68.

28 John Finnis, *Natural Law and Natural Rights* (Oxford: Oxford University Press, 2011), 11.

who will decide that normativity is violated?[29] For Meierhenrich, Radbruch mixed two qualitatively different questions, a philosophical one and an empirical one; his philosophical take on the institutions of Nazi Germany was bound to prove deficient to explain the reality of Nazi law.[30]

More recently, scholars have raised questions about the standard explanation that National Socialist legal theorists and judges rejected the separation of law and morality because they were imbued with legal positivism. For them, the problem was that judges embraced too little, rather than too much, positivism. Ingo Müller presented a sharp indictment of the German legal profession during the Nazi era for its role in the perversion of justice.[31] For Müller, the argument that the positivism of German legal thought was to blame was wrong because judges' behaviors went far beyond the faithful execution of the laws. In his opinion, the Nazi era was one of judicial activism, not passivism. Müller was mainly interested in exposing the alleged moral collapse of the judges, the reason for which should not be obscured behind inanimate legal theories or philosophers. The risk of generalization notwithstanding, his account forcefully portrayed the danger of excessive judicial zeal.

The debate boils down to the question whether bad law is still law.[32] The contending arguments provide insight into the principled foundations of law and reveal the uncertainty inherent in the relationship between the validity of law and ethical standards. They confirm that, even in the classic positivist model of the judicial process, the judge is torn between his or her objective role in the legal profession and the cause of justice. The discussion brings to the surface, then, the fact that what is and is not law and what the judge should and should not do with it – in short, the reality of the judicial process – cannot be sufficiently accounted for in terms of philosophical strictures on morality. Moral failure is indeed a powerful answer, but it falls short of explaining how nearly the entire legal establishment could allegedly participate in injustice.

29 Herdegen, "Unjust Laws, Human Rights," 600.

30 Meierhenrich, *The Remnants of the Rechtsstaat*, 3–14. See also Michael Stolleis, *The Law under the Swastika: Studies on Legal History in Nazi Germany*, trans. Thomas Dunlap (Chicago: Univeristy of Chicago Press, 1998).

31 Ingo Müller, *Hitler's Justice: The Courts of the Third Reich*, trans. Deborah Lucas Schneider (Cambridge, MA: Harvard University Press, 1992).

32 Julie Dickson, "Is Bad Law Still Law? Is Bad Law Really Law?" (October 6, 2008), *Oxford Legal Studies Research Paper*, no. 39/2008, 5, available at http://ssrn.com/abstract=1279599.

The judge's fidelity to law may have different meanings in common law and civil law systems. In the common law tradition, judges are given a dual mandate of applying the law and also developing the law to conform to justice. It follows that they have a positive duty to refuse to enforce unjust laws. Some scholars have argued that there is no real conflict between their official duty and their moral responsibility because judges have the authority, even obligation, to refuse to enforce laws they determine are unjust.[33] In this view, judges have "moral reasons – albeit defeasible ones – to deviate from the law whenever it requires them to reach results that are otherwise objectionable on moral or policy grounds."[34]

In the civil law system, in contrast, judicial obligation to enforce written law is much more clear-cut. Courts have a duty to follow duly enacted statutes, and opportunities for judges to follow their moral judgment against the intent of the legislature are limited. In a country like Korea, where the written Constitution and state law are laws and judicial decisions are not, positive law has much more sway than natural law in the judicial process. As John H. Merryman has noted, the civil law judge has a tendency "to recoil from the responsibilities and opportunities of constitutional adjudication."[35] Exercising control over political powers is hardly the ordinary courts' concern.[36] It is rare – almost never the case – that courts use the Radbruch Formula to refuse the enforcement of otherwise valid legal norms enacted by the legislature.[37] David Dyzenhaus has argued that in apartheid South Africa the "plain-fact approach" adopted by judges had particularly pernicious effects because South Africa was a mixed jurisdiction of civil and common law.[38]

33 Douglas E. Edlin, *Judges and Unjust Laws: Common Law Constitutionalism and the Foundations of Judicial Review* (Ann Arbor: University of Michigan Press, 2008).

34 Jeffrey Brand-Ballard, *Limits of Legality: The Ethics of Lawless Judging* (Oxford: Oxford University Press, 2010), 14. Brand-Ballard argues that "judges are sometimes ethically permitted to deviate from the law in order to avoid results that are only moderately unjust." Ibid., 10.

35 John Henry Merryman and Rogelio Pérez-Perdomo, *The Civil Law Tradition: An Introduction to the Legal Systems of Europe and Latin America*, 3rd ed. (Stanford: Stanford University Press, 2007), 140.

36 John Henry Merryman and Vincenzo Vigoriti, "When Courts Collide: Constitution and Cassation in Italy," *American Journal of Comparative Law* 15 (1966), 665–686.

37 Bix, "Radbruch's Formula," 51.

38 See Dyzenhaus, *Hard Cases in Wicked Legal Systems*.

Korean Judges' Dilemmas

The nature of the wrongs that judges must deal with can be qualitatively different in each country's historical situation. Some Korean scholars have invoked lessons from the Third Reich laws, mainly in an effort to highlight the necessity of corrective measures in the post-democratization era.[39] While calls for transitional justice to confront the wrongs of the past are fully justified, it must be emphasized that comparing Yusin laws to Nazi laws and tossing off allusions to Hitler's justice is a fundamentally ill-conceived effort. The rhetoric of equating the injustices in Korea with those under Nazis or apartheid is plainly wrong, even by implication. Tables 5.1, 5.2, and 5.3 in Chapter 5 – the indictment and conviction statistics of the National Security Act and the Anticommunist Act at the height of authoritarian rule – make the point clear. A report prepared for Amnesty International stated in 1974 that Korea held approximately 1,100 prisoners charged with or convicted of "political crimes" as a result of President Park's "desire for total autocratic and totalitarian power."[40] These numbers, while significant, do not warrant the assertion that state violence under Yusin rule was comparable to that in other authoritarian countries, or under Nazi rule for that matter.

Judicial dilemma comes in many different shades. The examples from the United States, Germany, and South Africa dealt with a morass of invidious inequality. In contrast, what Korean judges faced was a dilemma of legality rather than of the inner morality of laws. Here one sees how the Korean judges' plight compounded: they could not take a righteous moral high ground by rejecting the laws because the laws did not involve explicit ethical questions as in other countries' historical examples. This is not to minimize the seriousness of the laws that suppressed freedom of speech and other basic rights. But the Korean legal order was not wicked or unjust in the same sense as the slavery laws or Nazi laws, which deprived a group of people of their freedom because

[39] For example, Kim Sŏn-T'aek, "Wihŏn chŏk hŏnpŏp kaejŏng e taehan wihŏn simsaron: Yusin hŏnpŏp ŭi kyŏngu" [Constitutional Review of an Unconstitutional Constitutional Amendment: The Case of the Yusin Constitution], *Kongpŏphak yŏngu* 12 (2011), 165–200.

[40] Cited in Gwertzman, U.S. Aides Press for Seoul Fund.

of who they were, instead of what they did. In Korea, there were no equivalent competing moral imperatives. In short, there were different planes of injustice.

American antislavery judges and Korean Yusin judges faced their respective constitutional problem. In a constitutional state, the question of the validity of a law is settled by reference to the constitution. When a constitution itself includes explicit provisions authorizing unjust, unfair, and unreasonable laws, judges are put in a difficult situation. The Fugitive Slave Clause in Article 4 in the US Constitution can be compared with Article 53 in the Korean Yusin Constitution. Just as the slave laws were constitutional, the notorious emergency decrees under the Park regime were constitutional under the strict language of the highest law. In the United States, most abolitionist judges were convinced that a judge's duty was to obey the explicit language of a constitution – in this case, one that recognized slavery – even if it was no longer morally justifiable. Likewise, the Korean courts regularly implemented the emergency decrees which evidently lacked reasonableness or legal intelligibility. American judges could not ignore the plain constitutional provision; nor could Korean judges. Intrinsic in all these circumstances was the conflict between the judge's private conscience and public duty.

During both the Yusin years and the US antebellum years, the dominant judicial attitude was one of a retreat to formalism and the ascription of responsibility, to borrow Cover's terms. In Korea, the judiciary did not openly oppose the regime's constitutional and legislative maneuvering. In many cases, the courts seemed to think that it was the task of elective branches to find a solution to political problems. It was grounded on the principle of the separation of powers. When the constitutionality of the emergency decrees was challenged, the Supreme Court reached the one conclusion that was logically required by the reading of the Constitution: the Court was not authorized to decide on their constitutionality. It stated in 1975: "There are no grounds to find that Article 53 of the Constitution or Emergency Decree No. 1 is void as it violates the explicit provision of the Constitution."[41] It stated in 1977: "Since the emergency decree [No. 9] is based on Article 53 of the Constitution and it is not subject

41 S. Ct., 74To3492, January 20, 1975.

to judicial review under the Constitution (Constitution Article 53 [4]) . . . the arguments predicated on the belief that the above emergency decree is constitutionally reviewable have no merit."[42] These were far from thumping endorsements of the constitutionality of the decrees, and the Court likely wanted to leave it at that. It was not altogether implausible for Cover's judges to argue that the laws were not yet settled and to try to steer the cases in accord with their convictions if they chose to. Similar attempts would not have been an option for Korean judges, where judicial activism was largely viewed as an alien feature of the common law tradition.

It is important to pay attention to the language of the Constitution. The current 1987 Korean Constitution declares: "Judges shall rule independently in accordance with their conscience and in conformity with the Constitution and law."[43] The phrase "in accordance with their conscience" was first inserted in the 1962 Constitution, written after Park Chung Hee's military coup in 1961, and has been retained ever since.[44] It is intriguing that the 1962 Constitution specified that "judges shall rule independently in accordance with their conscience and in conformity with *this* Constitution and law."[45] The designation of "this Constitution" had not been present in the earlier constitutions, including the 1948 founding Constitution, which simply stated, "Judges shall rule in conformity with *the* Constitution and law."[46] The word *this* was retained in the 1972 Constitution,[47] to be dropped in the 1980 Constitution. Various speculations have been made about the fact that these new formulations appeared for the first time in the 1962 Constitution, promulgated under President Park's stewardship. On the one hand, emphasis on *this* Constitution has been seen as a reflection of the positivist outlook that was widely shared among Korean jurists at the time. On the other hand, emphasis on *conscience* has a natural law connotation. In this regard, the simultaneous insertion of "this Constitution" and "in accordance with their conscience" into the article appears disconcerting. But these phrases may not need to be seen as contradictory when one considers that positive law and ideal dictates were long conflated in Korean traditional legal culture. Under

42 S. Ct., 77Mo19 (*en banc*), May 13, 1977.
43 Constitution (1987), Art. 103.
44 Constitution (1962), Art. 98; Constitution (1972), Art. 102; Constitution (1980), Art. 104.
45 Constitution (1962), Art. 102 (my italics).
46 Constitution (1948), Art. 77 (my italics).
47 Constitution (1972), Art. 102.

Confucian ideology, the two were often one and the same, and this framework may have been what the drafters of the 1962 Constitution had in mind. When the two diverge, however, judges are placed in a difficult situation. Indeed, the seemingly innocuous designator "this" in the democratic 1962 Constitution came, ten years later, to fetter the judges in an unanticipated way: under the 1972 Constitution, they were obligated to decide cases in accordance with the language of *this* Constitution, supposedly not allowed to invoke other "constitutional" principles outside the text of the Constitution then in force.

Concerning judicial behavior, one approach that has gained scholarly attention is the institutional analysis focusing on how judges' concerns about their career influence their conscience in the courtroom.

Judicial Profession and Career

Institutional analysis of the judiciary posits that judges, worried about their career prospects, often cave in under pressure from political regimes. The career factor – judicial appointment, promotion, remuneration, and discipline – is open to abuse even in established democracies. In typical civil law jurisdictions, judges, having passed the state examination, move up the ranks of the hierarchy based on a combination of merit and seniority. It has been argued that this bureaucratic promotion system fosters the ideologies of apoliticism and conformism. National and cultural variations exist, but an obvious method for an illiberal government of controlling career judges is to manipulate their promotion and transfer prospects, with the objective of prodding them to interpret the law in accordance with its expectations.

A study of judges under General Augusto Pinochet's rule, from 1973 to 1990, has shown how Chile's judicial career system bolstered pervasive apoliticism and how this institutional ideology caused the courts to fail to oppose the government.[48] According to Lisa Hilbink, concerns of Chilean judges about promotion and career forced them to "avoid taking any stands at all against the government" and to become

48 Hilbink, *Judges Beyond Politics*; Lisa Hilbink, "Agents of Anti-Politics: Courts in Pinochet's Chile," in Ginsburg and Moustafa (eds.), *Rule by Law*, 102–131.

faithful agents of the regime; growing judicial apoliticism yielded to conservatism and conformism to such a degree that they "demonstrated little proclivity to enforce – much less develop – constitutional limits on power."[49] Senior judges who had power not only to discipline but also to decide promotion for younger judges formed an imposing presence that induced the latter to follow their superiors' ideological lead. When the Supreme Court justices curried favor from the political regime, argued Hilbink, the integrity of the entire judicial system dissolved.

Hilbink distinguished apoliticism from legal positivism. Both are based on a conservative understanding of the judicial role and beliefs that law and politics are distinct and the goals of judges and legislators are separate, but the former means fidelity to the executive whereas the latter means a devotion to law. Chilean judges were "inward-looking," yet in implementing the regime's decrees they went far beyond a simple plain-fact application of law.[50] While they took "shelter behind positivist defenses, washing their hands of any responsibility for the brutality and longevity of the authoritarian regime," the judges "were often willing and able to ignore or look beyond the letter of law." Therefore, it is "inappropriate – even generous – to attribute judicial behavior in Pinochet's Chile to a professional commitment to legal positivism."[51] The judges seemingly managed to combine the worst cases of judicial activism and passivism: they "displayed little desire or capacity to defend or promote citizens' constitutional rights or constitutionalism in general"[52] and justified the "anti-legal agenda of the military government."[53]

This is a powerful indictment of the judges, presenting generalized lessons about the danger of apoliticism caused by judicial career aspirations. Yet, is judges' engagement with an apolitical ideology always the central reason for judicial passiveness? This is the question Robert Barros raised when he warned that attributing the failure to restrain the regimes in Argentina and Chile to complicit judges would be deficient if the political and institutional contexts are not fully taken into consideration.[54] When

49 Hilbink, *Judges Beyond Politics*, 207; Hilbink, "Agents of Anti-Politics," 104.
50 Hilbink, *Judges Beyond Politics*, 217; Hilbink, "Agents of Anti-Politics," 103.
51 Hilbink, "Agents of Anti-Politics," 119.
52 Hilbink, *Judges Beyond Politics*, 227.
53 Ibid., 2–3.
54 Barros, *Constitutionalism and Dictatorship*; Robert Barros, "Courts out of Context: Authoritarian Sources of Judicial Failure in Chile (1973–1990) and Argentina (1976–1983)," in Ginsurg and Moustafa (eds.), *Rule by Law*, 156–179.

the government undermined the legal and institutional foundation, argued Barros, the difference between apoliticism and legal positivism mattered little. Aimed mainly to expose the harms of a self-serving judiciary under authoritarian rule, Hilbink's study is less interested in discussing the displacement of constitutional framework and its impact on judicial duties. But the career factor that fosters judicial conformism would fall short of capturing the complex reality without consideration of the constitutional system that predetermined the nature of the judicial process. Institutional analysis needs to go deeper than political appointment and internal discipline by senior judges.

Korea shared the civil service model of Chile. To what extent were Korean judges compelled to cater to the institutional ideology of their superiors under the powerful Supreme Court? How detrimental was the hierarchical career system for the autonomy of individual judges? The Korean case diverges from the Chilean one in some important aspects.

For one thing, the career-type judiciary in Korea insulated judges from, rather than exposing them to, political influences. The career determinants – appointment and promotion – were foremost based on the judge's individual ability and accountability. Judicial examination was an optimum example of democratic meritocracy. The judiciary was one of the ultimate elite groups into which anyone, from any sociopolitical background, could enter and advance his or her social status, purely on the basis of merit. New judges were selected immediately from those who had finished training after passing the judicial examination. Judges were organized along vertical lines, subject to spiraling assignment to courts throughout the country, usually for a period of two to three years for each post. This is a system unique to Korea and Japan.[55] The chief justice of the Supreme Court exercised broad authority over promotion and transfer of lower court judges, but

[55] See John Owen Haley, *The Spirit of Japanese Law* (Athens: University of Georgia Press, 1998); John Owen Haley, "Constitutional Adjudication in Japan: Context, Structures, and Values," *Washington University Law Review* 88 (2011), 1467–1491. Haley's assessment of the Japanese judicial hierarchy holds largely true for Korea. For judicial promotion in Korea, see Neil Chisholm, "The Faces of Judicial Independence: Democratic versus Bureaucratic Accountability in Judicial Selection, Training, and Promotion in South Korea and Taiwan," *American Journal of Comparative Law* 62 (2014), 893–949.

there was little proven favoritism or abuse in assignment and promotion, and political cronyism was minimal. In a well-organized judicial bureaucracy like Korea's, the power of senior judges over individual judges was limited. It was far from the truth that the Supreme Court justices could arbitrarily move the judges around or determine which case should be assigned to which judge. Overall, the internal personnel administration system worked equitably, at least more so than in other sectors of the bureaucracy.[56] The judicial hierarchy was pervaded by a professional and competency-based culture, and this was the source of the public's trust in the courts. While a largely self-governing elite bureaucracy, the judiciary had no distinct social or economic class interest to protect and no sociopolitical legitimacy to perpetuate.

For lower-level judges, their preoccupation with obtaining promotion was neither unique nor unusual. They looked to their superiors to avoid having their decisions overturned on appeal, but it was different from the situation in which internal administrative structure was abused to rein in individual judges. For senior judges, there was no proof that they received preferential treatment by handing down judgments in favor of the government. Promotion of high court judges was political by nature, but rarely was there a public perception that they were dependent on the executive power for their careers. Unlike most American judges who have some political involvement in their careers before being appointed to the bench, almost no Korean judge had prior political experience, and naturally appointment based on patronage or partisanship was nonexistent. This was the case for the Supreme Court as well. Justices were subject to political appointment as in the United States, but their professional qualifications and experiences weighed far more than their political and ideological stances. Impulsive judicial purges as in 1973 notwithstanding, the government could not normally disregard the stringent patterns of judicial elevation in the framework of career bureaucracy in an attempt to recompose the Supreme Court to its liking.

The Korean Supreme Court justices rarely came from a class with vested interest; their diverse social backgrounds could not be farther from the socially and politically connected group which formed the

[56] Yoon, *Law and Political Authority*, 118.

Chilean judges.[57] They were far from a monolithic conservative privileged group that reinforced traditional social hierarchy. High court judges under authoritarian regimes around the world were often accused of collusion with the administration, but Korean justices remained free from similar charges. There were no shared interests between the top level of the judiciary and the regime. Retired military generals often headed government ministries and former cabinet members were rewarded with lucrative business opportunities to manage state-owned entities. It was unheard of that retired justices were given financial benefits for their services in office. Some of them, needing to continue to make a living, opened law practices on their own. In short, judges were seldom – almost never – suspected of keeping close ties with the administration.

It may be instructive to compare the judicial hierarchy in Korea with that in Japan. The two countries share a similar system of judicial selection and appointment, and their judges demonstrate general affinities in juristic assumptions and approaches. Scholars have debated whether Japanese judges are prone to succumb to political influence. Some have argued that judges who decided political cases in ways favorable to the ruling party enjoyed better careers.[58] This opinion reckoned that the dismal record of judicial review by the Japanese Supreme Court was evidence of the lack of judicial independence, mainly ascribed to its personnel system. John Owen Haley has discounted the link between judicial review and political accountability, however, and disputed the view that the Japanese judicial career system jeopardized judges' independence. To the contrary, "the intention of the American drafters of the postwar Constitution and system for career judicial appointment" was that "judges be subject, as in the United States, to political appointment."[59] In other words, the underlying principle was

[57] For an analysis of the personal backgrounds and juristic stances of the justices of the Supreme Court, see "Hanguk ŭi taebŏpkwan kŭdŭrŭn" [The Justices of the Supreme Court of Korea: Who are they?], *Hanguk Ilbo*, December 9, 2006, available at http://blog.naver.com/PostView.nhn?blogId=urmean&logNo=10011624673.

[58] J. Mark Ramseyer and Eric B. Rasmusen, *Measuring Judicial Independence: The Political Economy of Judging in Japan* (Chicago: University of Chicago Press, 2003); J. Mark Ramseyer and Frances McCall Rosenbluth, *Japan's Political Marketplace* (Cambridge, MA: Harvard University Press, 1993).

[59] Haley, "Constitutional Adjudication in Japan," 1485; John Owen Haley, "Review of *Measuring Judicial Independence: The Political Economy of Judging in Japan* by Ramseyer and Rasmusen," *Journal of Japanese Studies* 30 (2004), 235–240.

the same although its implementation was different. Likewise, Japan's adoption of the US judicial review scheme did not prevent its notable indigenization.[60] Japanese courts have been reticent about the idea of invalidating parliamentary enactments or executive decrees on constitutional grounds. In Haley's opinion, the absence of active judicial review should be ascribed not so much to its career and personnel structure as to its particular judicial culture and assumptions. This argument largely applies to Korea.

Reasons for the lack of active judicial review in predemocratization Korea may be found in the general tenets of legal formalism and professionalism. The narrow conception of judicial power led judges to internalize positivist ideology. Apoliticism can come in different forms. In the Philippines, the Supreme Court gave President Marcos a constitutional blessing, nine months before he imposed martial law. In *Lansang v. Garcia* (1971), the Court sustained the president's suspension of the writ of *habeas corpus*. This decision cleared the way for Marcos' constitutional remaking.[61] In Korea, in contrast, the president rewrote the constitution because the Supreme Court was in the way. The Court did not abandon the *habeas corpus* procedure voluntarily, nor did it abdicate judicial review power of its own accord. The court, an institution created by the constitution, could not find grounds for objection for the emergency measures issued under the constitutional mandate.[62] Judges were constrained by the laws, even those passed by the aberrant legislature dominated by the ruling party. In short, Korean judges' apoliticism can be explained better by analysis of the formal concerns of judicial obligation than by the accounts of sociological and anthropological elements or administrative factors in power negotiation.

Preceding discussions of judicial career do not imply that judges were secure in their jobs. Punitive action against individual judges was

[60] Christopher Ford, "The Indigenization of Constitutionalism in the Japanese Experience," *Case Western Reserve Journal of International Law* 28 (1996), 3–62.

[61] Rolando V. del Carmen, "Constitutionality and Judicial Politics," in Rosenberg (ed.), *Marcos and Martial Law in the Philippines*, 88; Rolando V. del Carmen, "Constitutionalism and the Supreme Court in a Changing Philippine Polity," *Asian Survey* 13 (1973), 1050–1061.

[62] Pak U-Tong, *Pŏp ŭi sesang* [The World of the Law] (Seoul: Chisik Sanŏpsa, 2006), 165.

sporadic rather than systematic and overall rare, but its unpredictability may have made it all the more dreadful.[63] No judge was thrown into jail by the administration for political reasons, but judicial independence was precarious. At any rate, it is clear that expounding openly on the moral responsibility of a judge confronted with unjust laws, in the way Cover's antislavery judges had indulged themselves, was not an option in the Korean situation.

To Stay or Step Down

A familiar theme in criticisms of the Yusin courts is that the judges should have quit their positions rather than implementing laws that violated human rights. It is based on the belief that judges must take responsibility for their decisions. The explicit provisions in the 1972 Constitution and the laws left judges with two choices: enforce the law or resign. Few chose the latter option. In postdemocratization years, a number of scholars asserted that the conscientious judge ought to have stepped down and that, by staying in office, Yusin judges fostered injustice. But the problem in this line of thought is that it equates working within an unjust system with supporting that system. More serious, it smacks of reasoning by an armchair critic. Claiming that dissidents and innocent students would have avoided persecution if courageous judges had stood up for justice, refusing to implement unjust laws, seems naive at best.

It has been suggested that the personal harms incurred by a judge for resisting the regime would have been much less severe than the suffering of the human rights victims caused by that judge's ruling. But the view that the Yusin judges fostered injustice by staying in office appears as gratuitous as it is misleading because it ignores the fundamental nature of judicial decision-making. Resignation may underscore the ethical principles of the judge but, if "a judge's resignation is motivated entirely by his desire to preserve his own moral purity," then "he makes a poor hero."[64] In the Korean context, resignation would not have garnered

63 "Judicial perceptions of conceivable risks can be as effective as unambiguous threats" in cowering judges. West and Baker, "The 1987 Constitutional Reforms," 246.

64 Feinberg, "Natural Law," 21.

Table 6.1 *Judicial Vacancies, 1975–1979*

Year	1975	1976	1977	1978	1979
Total Posts	533	550	580	610	640
Occupied	517	515	539	546	546
Vacant	16	35	41	64	94
Vacancy Rate	3.0%	6.4%	7.1%	10.5%	14.7%

Source: Pŏpwŏn Haengjŏngch'ŏ, *Pŏpwŏnsa*, 729.

much heroism anyway, because general expectation was that the former judge would go into more financially rewarding private practice. Due in part to this career pattern, Korean courts chronically suffered from a high vacancy rate. Table 6.1 shows the judicial vacancy level between 1975 and 1979. In 1979, almost 15 percent of judicial posts remained unoccupied.

One should never trivialize the considerable courage required of a judge who decided to leave office in protest or make light of the often-agonizing situation leading to such a decision. The hardship encountered by the judges who left the bench under political pressure is well documented.[65] But judges left or stayed in office for a variety of reasons aside from moral considerations. The decision of judges not to quit is not proof of the absence of judicial conscience, not any more than the growing vacancy rate is an indicator of dereliction of judicial duty. In practical terms, resignation motivated by political reasons achieves little to aid citizens or curtail authoritarianism because in most cases it does not result in the change of an unjust law. Calling for judicial resignation can thus even be self-defeating because theoretically it would give the regime opportunities to pack the courts with more pliable judges. No one disputes the importance of judicial accountability, but ill-placed emphasis on the responsibility of judges may itself turn out to be less than responsible.

The judge exercises his or her authority as a public function. This is why the power of the judge can be less effective against authoritarian laws than that of practicing lawyers or scholars.[66] For a private citizen,

[65] One of the justices forced out in 1980 attested that his application to open a law office was rejected twice. Yang Pyŏng-Ho, *Pŏpcho pan paengnyŏn*, 206–207.

[66] Feinberg, "Natural Law," 16–17.

at stake is personal conscience against unjust law. Scholars and theorists can and should condemn the dictatorship that hides behind the subterfuge of legality. A judge, in contrast, has a duty to apply the law as it was written. According to Dyzenhaus, there was a difference in South Africa between academic critics and human rights lawyers on the one hand and liberal judges on the other hand. Liberal judges often could not but allow the injustice of the law to speak through them.[67] Their service in the judiciary necessarily made them complicit in an injustice committed by the repressive regime. It was very much a case of "damned if you do, damned if you don't."[68]

It has been said that there is something essentially public about a judge's duties.[69] As Hans Petter Graver aptly put it, "A judge who occupies an official role and who must decide according to the law is never truly independent in the sense of being a disinterested third party to the conflict."[70] Borrowing Cover's expression, the judge cannot act as an "insurgent."[71] Because the judge has no right to violate the judicial oath on the grounds that it would be unjust to punish the defendant, he or she must apply the law, and injustice may result. The judges in the highest court, in particular, do not have the luxury of rendering a decision and waiting to see whether it is reversed on appeal. They are obligated to say what the law is as opposed to what it ought to be. A judge at the top of the hierarchy is thus not truly free to be candid.[72] Inevitably, the judge becomes a ready target, because grievances against the alleged justice tend to center on the outcome of the case rather than the judicial process and the reasoning leading to that decision.

Criticized for their perceived complicity with apartheid, South African judges reportedly stated:

67 David Dyzenhaus, "'With Benefit of Hindsight': Dilemmas of Legality in the Fact of Injustice," in Emilios Christodoulidis and Scott Veitch (eds.), *Lethe's Law: Justice, Law and Ethics in Reconciliation* (Oxford: Hart Publishing, 2001), 65–89.

68 Ibid., 82.

69 Feinberg, "Natural Law," 33.

70 See Graver, "Judicial Independence under Authoritarian Rule."

71 Cover, *Justice Accused*, 198.

72 "The higher we climb in the court system, the less effective power to breach official duties do we find." Feinberg, "Natural Law," 17.

A judge, whether positioned by personal conviction on the left, center, or right of the political spectrum, who feels free to ignore the oath of office when compliance with it conflicts with his or her own credo, is no hero. Such conduct is bereft of integrity and is a self-indulgent abuse of judicial power.[73]

This somber statement strikes one as more than a self-justification. It contains certain universal truth. Mary Ann Glendon wrote:

The unique political role of the nation's highest court may require its members at times to show the sorts of excellence that are traditionally associated with executives or legislators – energy, leadership, boldness. But, day in and day out, those qualities are no substitute for the ordinary heroism of sticking to one's last, of demonstrating impartiality, interpretive skill, and responsibility toward authoritative sources in the regular administration of justice.[74]

This ordinary heroism includes resisting the desire to resign from office. Justice Yi Hoe-Ch'ang wrote: "I admire courageous judges . . . who can say no [to political powers], but I also believe it is important for judges to fulfill their duties to maintain the minimum justice of law, even by serving in the 'revolutionary court' under the emergency legal order," so that they could protect the dignity of the people. This is "the cross to be borne by the judges," mused this Catholic judge.[75] Caught between the relentless government onslaught and the public's indignation, the judges in Yusin Korea were in an unenviable situation. For them, adhering to a modest conception of the judicial role, preserving a minimum judicial process, was as much a way of fulfilling judicial duties as it was a matter of survival.

Taming Judges, Blaming Judges

Defendants in the Emergency Decree No. 9 cases were given an open trial in civilian court. For the judiciary, ensuring regular judicial procedures became a critical task. Hong Sŏng-U, one of the human rights lawyers who represented dissidents and student activists in the 1970s

[73] Submission to the South African Truth and Reconciliation Commission, in *South African Law Journal* 115 (1998), 45. Cited in Graver, *Judges Against Justice*, 268.

[74] Mary Ann Glendon, "Partial Justice," *Commentary*, August 1, 1994, at www.commentarymagazine.com/article/partial-justice/.

[75] Yi Hoe-Ch'ang, *Hoegorok*, vol. 1, 221.

and early 1980s, recollected that some sympathetic judges, visibly unhappy with the prosecution, made a point of allowing the defense full freedom to present their case, including chances to blast unjust laws publicly as part of their defense arguments.[76] Still, these judges invariably rendered a guilty verdict. According to Attorney Hong, the only meaning of those trials, if there was any, was that the courtroom provided a rare arena in which the accused dissidents could publicly state their beliefs and voice criticisms of the regime.[77]

The poet Kim Chi-Ha's trial in 1976 illustrated this point. Kim was one of the most famous dissidents during the Yusin years. From as early as 1964, he had been in and out of prison because of what he said and wrote. This time he was in prison from March 1975, prosecuted under the Anticommunist Act. An American scholar, Charles Douglas Lummis, left an eyewitness account of his trial that took place in December 1976 in a courtroom at the Seoul Criminal District Court.[78] The hearing started at 10 o'clock in the morning and lasted until 9:50 in the evening. The defendant's five lawyers took turns making closing statements. Lummis wrote:

> During the entire proceeding the chief judge did no more than announce when a recess would take place and occasionally lean over to see that the tape recorder was working properly. The rest of the time he sat motionless staring at the ceiling, his face fixed in an expression of boredom. . . . The second judge stared down at the desk in front of him and occasionally nodded off to sleep. . . . When the chief judge checked the tape recorder, he was making it clear that the case was to be decided at higher levels of government. The judges were like movie extras hired to make the room look like a courtroom. The real ear of the government was the tape recorder.[79]

The poet began his final statement at 6:45 in the evening and continued without break for three hours. He did not argue that he was not a revolutionary; he only said that he was not a Marxist revolutionary. Lummis commented: "I was struck again by the strange quality of this trial, in which the defendant argues that he is innocent of violating the Anti-Communist Act by describing his philosophy of revolution and

76 Hong Sŏng-U, *Inkwŏn pyŏllon han sidae*, 155–158, 194–195.
77 Ibid.
78 Charles Douglas Lummis, "Korea: The Trial of a Revolutionary Prophet," *New York Review of Books*, April 28, 1977.
79 Ibid.

calling for an overthrow of the government." After disputing the charges against him, Kim outlined how citizens could form a popular front to achieve "the overthrow of dictatorial power, exploitive capitalism, and the neocolonialism to which the Park government is subordinated."[80] Throughout the proceeding, the judges made no effort to stop Kim's speech. Indeed what seemed stranger than the trial's "strange quality" that puzzled this American observer was the fact that open trials like this one continued to take place: defendants were faithfully given their day in court, for all the abusive laws and procedures stacked against them.

The so-called Myŏngdong democracy declaration trial was memorable among the emergency decree trials because the authorities clumsily offered the dissidents a full opportunity to broadcast, literally all over the world, the absurd and suffocating nature of the emergency rule.

Myŏngdong Democracy Declaration Case (1976)

In March 1976, some twenty political and religious leaders, including former president Yun Posun and future president Kim Dae Jung, were charged with violating Emergency Decree No. 9.[81] They had read a statement at a joint Catholic–Protestant prayer service held on March 1 in the Myŏngdong Cathedral, demanding the repeal of the Yusin Constitution. The statement stated: "We demand judicial independence. Without judicial independence, citizens cannot be protected from the tyranny of the powerful. The regime that treats the judiciary as a maid must be seen as having no intention to protect citizens."[82] The government could not condone even this kind of innocuous statement. The case quickly became a public relations debacle for the regime, however. Arrests of so many prominent members of society not only antagonized citizens at large but also drew the attention of international media. As many as twenty-six defense lawyers took part in the proceedings, and the courtroom turned into an arena akin to the National Assembly floor where chaotic partisan fights were taking place on a daily basis.[83]

The irrational quality of Emergency Decree No. 9 was on full display. Since the defendants were charged with violating a decree that

80 Ibid. See also Ryu, *Writers of the Winter Republic*, 57.
81 *Tong-A Ilbo*, March 5, 1976.
82 "Minju Kuguk Sŏnŏn," *Inkwŏn pyŏllon charyo chip*, vol. 3, 4.
83 Hong Sŏng-U, *Inkwŏn pyŏllon han sidae*, 172.

prohibited distortion of facts and dissemination of false rumors, the government had to prove and, in practical matter, the defendants had to disprove the falsity of the contents of their statements. The defense attorneys tried to do this by calling "expert witnesses" to show the truthfulness of the defendants' statements, for example, by demonstrating that the remark that the 1972 Constitution gave President Park power to rule in perpetuity and the Constitution was an undemocratic document was not a misrepresentation of fact.[84] Sparring in the open courtroom over whether the endangered democracy in Korea was falsehood or truth had to cause much embarrassment for the government. No wonder prosecutors made utmost effort to prevent the testimony of defense witnesses.[85] By putting prominent dissidents on trial, the government inadvertently allowed them a forum to air their anti-government opinions.

The presiding judge refused to allow some of the testimony and documentary evidence the defense sought to introduce, but overall legal procedures were steadfastly followed. All defendants were convicted as charged. The Seoul Appeals Court sentenced them to imprisonment of between one and five years.[86] In March of the following year, the Supreme Court dismissed the appeal.[87] A US government official commented on this case in a report to Congress:

> While some criticism of court procedures may be valid, due process under Korean law was observed. Nevertheless, the trial and conviction of individuals on these charges brought under the Emergency measure were adverse developments for the freedom of political expression in Korea.[88]

What this foreign official observed bespoke the reality: the law was observed but human rights suffered.

Min Pok-Ki, the chief justice at the time, later recalled that the Myŏngdong incident was "the most difficult case" the Supreme Court faced during the Yusin period. He said that justices agonized but had no choice but to deliver guilty verdicts as long as existing laws

84 Cohen and Baker, "U.S. Foreign Policy," 182.
85 Ibid.; Hong Sŏng-U, *Inkwŏn pyŏllon han sidae*, 274.
86 Seoul App. Ct., 76No1835. See *Yŏksa sogŭi sabŏppu*, 92, 425–426.
87 S. Ct., 77To44, March 22, 1977. See *Pŏpwŏnsa*, 807–808.
88 United States, Department of State, *Country Reports on Human Rights Practices: Report submitted to the Committee on International Relations, U.S. House of Representatives, and Committee on Foreign Relations, U.S. Senate, 95th Congress, 2nd Session* (February 3, 1978), 250.

were violated.[89] The fact that political spectacles took place in the open courtroom and all defense statements were transcribed as part of the court record was a serious blow for the government. After this public relations fiasco, the government avoided court trials for the most part. Instead, security forces stepped up surveillance to prevent students and dissidents from undertaking political activities.

During this time, President Park was thoroughly consumed with the fear that the United States would abandon its commitment to defend Korea. President Jimmy Carter seemed determined to withdraw US troops from the peninsula. His meeting with Park in Seoul on June 29, 1979, is known as one of the most awkward and frosty state summits between the two nations, in which the presidents locked horns over human rights violations and national security.[90] Carter later reminisced that his talks with "General Park Chung-hee" were "probably the most unpleasant discussions I ever had with one of our supposed allies."[91] Carter specifically demanded the abolition of Emergency Decree No. 9, which Park ignored.

Judges in Uphill Battle

In a small number of cases, the Supreme Court overturned conviction of Emergency Decree No. 9 violation. In 1976, a defendant was found guilty of "fabricating and spreading false rumors or making false representation of facts and disseminating them" in violation of article 1 of the decree. He assaulted someone, and the police officer called to the scene demanded his voluntary accompaniment to the police station. The defendant refused and uttered "our president even doesn't stand a chance before President Bongo," a statement which the lower courts

[89] *Tong-A Ilbo*, February 26, 1982. The Myŏngdong case was retried in July 2013, and the defendants were found not guilty.

[90] See Oberdorfer and Carlin, *The Two Koreas*, 67–86.

[91] Jimmy Carter, *A Full Life: Reflections at 90* (New York: Simon & Schuster, 2015), 134. Carter's memoirs also include the following: "When we concluded our official discussions, General Park asked for a private meeting with me"; "he wanted to talk about my Christian faith. He said that his wife and some of his children were believers (not all Christian) and had urged him to talk to me. After I made a brief presentation and answered his questions, he requested that I ask one of my Baptist friends to come to the Blue House to explore how he might become a Christian. I did this before leaving South Korea, and I was later informed that the requested meeting occurred." Ibid.

construed as a violation of article 1.[92] The Supreme Court quashed the verdict. The highest court ruled that "spreading" a distorted fact or falsehood required the act of diffusing and disseminating a false fact actively and broadly in public and that a mere statement made to a police officer could not be viewed as such.[93]

In 1977, the Supreme Court walked a thin line when it overturned a guilty verdict by the appellate court. The defendant, a pastor, stated in his sermon that the government promoted the cult of personality by forcing the people to pay homage to the tomb of the late First Lady. He also claimed that the government was in collusion with the Unification Church of Reverend Moon Sun Myung (Mun Sŏn-Myŏng) under the guise of fighting communism. Those who called for unity, harmony, and reform were in fact living in luxury drinking imported whisky, he contended, and Korea was increasingly isolated among free nations. The Supreme Court ruled that, even though the defendant's remarks were somewhat exaggerated, their contents were public knowledge readily available in newspapers and magazines and therefore could not be seen as distortion of facts.[94] It wrote:

> The statement that group visits are taking place to the gravesite of the late First Lady has a factual basis. That many members of the National Assembly and senior government officials attend ceremonies sponsored by the Unification Church led by Reverend Moon and that they send village leaders to the training centers run by the Unification Church are also facts. Therefore, the defendant's remarks did not distort the facts. The statement about imported whisky was intended to chastise the leaders in society, and the argument that our country remained isolated among free nations was intended to emphasize the importance of proactive foreign policy. They cannot be seen as distortion of facts.[95]

These decisions are notable in that the Supreme Court poked holes in the government's net of the "distortion of facts" cast far and wide to punish the most innocuous speeches. The 1977 opinion was particularly remarkable because the Court refused to convict the defendant who had equated the government's encouragement to pay tribute to the late First Lady with a personality cult. Decisions like these were

[92] President Omar Bongo Ondimba of Gabon had paid a state visit to Korea several months earlier in 1975.

[93] S. Ct. 1976To876, May 11, 1976. This case attracted keen attention from legal circles and was reported in *Pŏmnyul Sinmun*, May 24, 1976.

[94] S.Ct., 76To4056, February 22, 1977.

[95] Ibid. *Yŏksa sogŭi sabŏppu*, 428.

not many, however. Everyone knew that, once charged under the emergency decree, there was little chance for acquittal.[96] The human rights lawyer Hong acknowledged that even a most conscientious judge could not do much else under the emergency decrees.[97]

The courts kept sending citizens to prison, for criticizing the president, the constitution, or anything else, as required by the emergency decree. Indictments often stated that the defendants committed the crime of shouting "Overthrow the ○○○ [blank] regime"; the court judgments then wrote that the defendant was guilty as charged because he shouted "Overthrow the ○○○ [blank] regime." The prosecutors blotted the name of the president in the court record, supposedly out of reverence, and the judges went along.[98] Here was an example of the utter senselessness of the "Emergency Decree Era": a casual criticism of the president constituted a criminal fabrication of a false rumor, but the authorities felt compelled not to spell out what that president's name was.

One particular acquittal decision deserves mentioning. On November 8, 1976, a judge at the Seoul District Court Yŏngdŭngp'o Branch Court found a defendant not guilty of violating Emergency Decree No. 9.[99] The accused, a high school teacher, said in class that "dictatorship survives longer in less developed countries. The dictator pressures citizens arguing that he alone can lead the country. The political regime in our country wants power until the East Sea dries up and Mount Paektu crumbles down." The court rejected the argument that these statements constituted distortion of facts. In a straightforwardly worded opinion, the court said:

> In Korea, one-person rule existed from 1945, as shown under the Liberal Party rule. It has been repeated in history in both developed and underdeveloped countries. In the evolving process of politics, one tries to remain in power or tries to obtain power; this is a historical and empirical fact, which will be replayed in the foreseeable future. Therefore, it cannot be seen as a false assertion or

96 Hong Sŏng-U, *Inkwŏn pyŏllon han sidae*, 213.

97 Ibid., 159, 188, 272.

98 An unrelated but interesting issue deserves noting. In 2002, the Korean courts started redacting the names of the defendants in public court documents in order to protect their privacy. This policy has been widely criticized in legal circles. Pak U-Tong, "Tangsaja wa p'igoin ŭi irŭm ŭl kamch'un p'angyŏl" [Court Opinions in Which the Names of the Parties and the Defendants Are Omitted], *Pŏmnyul Sinmun*, January 21, 2010.

99 Seoul Dist. Ct., 76KoHap186, November 8, 1976 (opinion by Judge Yi Yŏng-Ku).

distortion of facts. The expression "until the East Sea dries up and Mount Paektu crumbles down" is a metaphor for a long period of time, and it has nothing to do with a distortion or false assertion of facts. The statement by the defendant can be seen as a simple and casual expression of discontent or sentiment that can normally occur in the mind of a free citizen who grows tired of political stagnation caused by one person's domination of power. It cannot be seen as a false assertion or distortion of historical facts.

As a lower-court decision, it was a refreshing opinion, to say the least.[100]

After democratization, the National Intelligence Service acknowledged that officers from KCIA, commonly called "coordinators," frequented the courts to "gather information."[101] The "guidelines" from the political branch were communicated to the heads of the courts.[102] KCIA agents regularly made unsolicited visits to the chambers of the judges who rendered decisions against the government.[103] Government pressure on judges took place mostly in the form of prosecutorial interference in judicial autonomy. In a telling episode in 1977, judges and prosecutors butted heads over the interpretation of the Reservist Force Establishment Act Implementation Decree. Article 13 (2) of the decree said that a "summon notice must be delivered to the individual at least seven days in advance." People were charged for failing to show up for the drills even if they had not received the notice seven days in advance as required by the law. The prosecutors argued that the seven-day notice provision was merely informational and that it was sufficient if the notice had been given any time before the drill date. But the courts disagreed and rendered not-guilty verdicts to the defendants. There were several thousand similar cases, and the prosecution doggedly appealed these acquittal decisions. On May 11, 1977, the Supreme Court affirmed the lower court decisions of acquittal. A newspaper declared that "the prosecutors lost the duel."[104]

After democratization, judges denied that their judgments had been swayed by intimidation.[105] Still, it was true that they, in particular young

100 *Pŏpwŏnsa*, 701.
101 *Kwagŏ wa taehwa*, vol. 4, 165.
102 Ibid., 171.
103 Ibid., 172–173.
104 *Kyŏnghyang Sinmun*, May 14, 1977.
105 Judge Yi Yŏng-Ku stressed that "the judges were not rubber-stamps." *Hangyŏre Sinmun*, February 5, 2007.

judges, felt disillusioned and helpless before the oppressive laws and overbearing administration. Many entry-level judges, who were thrown to the front line of dealing with Emergency Decree No. 9, were in their early thirties or even late twenties.

A small group of defense lawyers, "not more than twenty," took on cases involving "political criminals" in the 1970s.[106] Attorney Yi Pyŏng-Rin resolutely resisted the government, which alternated between threats and entreaties, and ended up finding himself charged with adultery and deprived of his license to practice law.[107] Lawyers like Yi Ton-Myŏng, Yu Hyŏn-Sŏk, Hong Sŏng-U, Cho Chun-Hŭi, Hwang In-Ch'ŏl, Im Kwang-Kyu, Kang Sin-Ok, and Han Sŭng-Hŏn represented defendants in the face of government pressures.[108] The courageous statements and actions, inside and outside the courtroom, of feisty and defiant lawyers seemed to contrast with the dour – or cowering, depending on one's perspective – judges sentencing defendants to prison terms in inane cases.

These lawyers deeply lamented rampant convictions, but they did not dispute that the judges were in a no-win situation. After the demise of the Yusin system, a number of judges remarked that enforcing the emergency decrees was by far the most agonizing experience in their judicial careers.[109] Attorney Hong had mixed feelings: "I try to be understanding, but at the same time I cannot help getting mad when I hear [them] say such things as if they were in a confessional."[110] This kind of ambivalence on the part of the contemporary witnesses was not uncommon. Chief Justice Min reminisced: "in our reality, judicial independence has meaning only in the sense that the judiciary can count on the citizens' trust; other than that, judicial independence does not exist. If the powerful administration wants to do away with the judiciary, it can easily do it anytime."[111] This statement by the old

106 Cohen and Baker, "U.S. Foreign Policy," 212.

107 *Hangyŏrye Sinmun*, May 21, 2010. See Chapter 4, note 73 and accompanying text.

108 Chang, *Protest Dialectics*, 129–134.

109 Pak U-Tong, *P'ansa sil esŏ pŏpchŏng kkaji*, 101–102; Pyŏn Chŏng-Su, *Pŏpcho yŏjŏng* [Reminiscences of a Traveler in the Judiciary] (Seoul: Kwanak Sa, 1997), 79–80. Both Pak and Pyŏn were judges during the Yusin regime. Pak later became a Supreme Court justice (1986–1993) and Pyŏn became a Constitutional Court justice (1988–1994).

110 Hong Sŏng-U, *Inkwŏn pyŏllon han sidae*, 416–417.

111 Min Pok-Ki, Na ŭi pŏpkwan sijŏl, March 1, 1982.

chief justice, who led the judiciary for most of the Yusin period, may be viewed by some as an effort to exculpate the courts that had been under his charge, but it appears more than self-serving rhetoric. Min received round criticism for his role in the Park regime. In Yi Hoe-Ch'ang's opinion, however, the chief justice "tried a different tack at different times, alternating between cooperation and defiance, with the goal of protecting judicial independence."[112] If nothing else, Justice Min's remark captured the plight of the judiciary. Public trust was something that could only be gained when the courts were independent, but judicial independence could not be ensured when public trust in the courts was faltering.

Judicial Conscience and Common Sense

What does it mean that the judges must "rule independently in accordance with their conscience" as required by the constitution? Does "conscience" mean the judge's morality as an individual or the judge's duty to be faithful to the law? Most scholarly opinions agree that the conscience of a judge can be different from the conscience of a private person, only to disagree over which conscience the judge must follow when the two conflict. It has been argued that conscience in the Korean Constitution refers not so much to a judge's subjective morality as to "a sense of duty that the Court should feel that it owes to the public to uphold the rule of law, even if there are political pressures to do otherwise."[113] Nevertheless, the notion of the rule of law is far from clear, and the pressures on a judge can come in many different forms.

Justice Yang Hoe-Kyŏng served on the Supreme Court in the Third Republic before he was forced out in 1973. He stated in 1971 that ideal judging could more accurately be seen as the embodiment of *yangsik* (common sense or reasonableness) than as the embodiment of *yangsim* (conscience).[114] Reasonableness or soundness meant a judge's readiness

112 Yi Hoe-Ch'ang, *Hoegorok*, vol. 1, 266–267.

113 Youngjae Lee, "Constitutional Court Justice Resigns: Conscience and Judging," Korean Constitutional Law: (Occasional) Thoughts on Korean Constitutional Law and the Constitutional Court (June 2, 2005), at koreanconlaw.blogspot.ca/2005/06/constitutional-court-justice-resigns.html.

114 *Chosŏn Ilbo*, August 26, 1971.

to render a decision in fairness, reason, and impartiality without prejudice, that is, to judge in accordance with the law; it was different from a judge's personal sensibility or the public's expectation. Justice Yi Hoe-Ch'ang agreed. He opined that the constitutional language would have posed less difficulty if it had said "judges shall rule independently in accordance with the principles of just and universal truth and reasonableness and in conformity with the Constitution and the law."[115]

Speaking of common sense, it would be less than accurate to say that most Korean judges were pure positivists who insisted that law was one thing and morality another. It is worth noting that some justices and senior judges maintained close personal friendships with prominent human rights lawyers, drawn together in part through their Catholic faith.[116] In 1977, the Court was sharply divided over whether to impose the death penalty on a twenty-year-old youth. The defendant was convicted of killing two persons and committing fourteen incidents of robbery over a period of less than a month, and he was sentenced to death by the lower courts. On appeal, the petty bench of the Supreme Court decided to refer this case to the entire court. It was one of the few occasions that the Supreme Court held an *en banc* deliberation because of disagreement on the sentence.[117] The majority of the Supreme Court, twelve justices, affirmed the death penalty, but four justices, Min Mun-Ki, Im Hang-Chun, Kim Yun-Haeng, and Yi Il-Kyu, objected to it as being too severe and argued instead for life in prison. For them, the harshness of the law should be mitigated by force of circumstances. The crimes had been committed when the defendant was barely over eighteen years of age, having grown up in an orphanage and dropped out of school in the fourth grade. The dissenting justices believed that, as long as whether the defendant was irretrievably depraved was in question, mitigating factors such as the signs of his remorse should be taken into account in determining the punishment; allowing him a chance for rehabilitation would better serve justice. Their argument that "the purpose of our criminal system is more than

115 Yi Hoe-Ch'ang, *Hoegorok*, vol. 1, 290.

116 Catholic faith traditionally maintained a conspicuous presence among Korean jurists, possibly because of the early influence of Judge Kim Hong-Sŏp (1915–1965), who was called "Judge Apostle" (see Figure 2.2 on p. 54). See Ch'oe Chong-Ko, *Sado pŏpkwan Kim Hong-Sŏp: Han pŏmnyulga ŭi sasang kwa sinang* [Kim Hong-Sŏp, a Judge Apostle: A Jurist's Thought and Faith] (Seoul: Yukpŏpsa, 1985).

117 S. Ct., 76To4034 (*en banc*), February 22, 1977.

mere retribution" seemed to touch on a natural law theory.[118] This example may be seen as an isolated case, removed from the genuine issue of substantive justice. It reveals, however, that the justices of the Supreme Court were not always of one mind; it is interesting to note that the three dissenters (other than Justice Yi) often shared their opinions in legal reasoning and frequently joined in dissents.

To date, scholars have paid scant attention to the Court's possible internal division. In Korea, judicial opinions of the Supreme Court are institutional products, and their authorship is not a matter of public record beyond the issuance of dissenting and concurring opinions in *en banc* decisions. Petty bench decisions are rendered unanimously.[119] Naturally, interpretive approaches of the justices often diverged. It is true that in the 1970s there were only a few political cases that produced dissenting or concurring opinions. When there were any, those deemed politically unpalatable by the regime were blocked from public view, excised from the official court report and omitted from the public media reports. Such was the fate of the dissenting and concurring opinions in the Inhyŏktang Chaegŏnwi trial in April 1975 and the dissenting opinions in President Park's murder trial in May 1980, as will be seen in Chapter 7. This consideration points to the risk inherent in a wholesale assessment of the judiciary without careful sifting of the opinions. The need for a nuanced approach can also be exemplified by the cases of contemporary jurists.

Hwang San-Tŏk (1917–1989) was one of the most respected jurists in Korea. Historical appraisal of this eminent scholar is divided because of his political role under the Yusin regime. Hwang was minister of justice from September 1974 before becoming minister of education in 1976. As justice minister, he oversaw the Yusin government's hard-line legal policy, a position that seemed to be a reversal of his stance in his earlier career. He wrote in 1964 on the topics of tyranny and rule by law:

In principle, laws of a democratic state are made to restrain the despotic exercise of power. Therefore, the enactment of laws means the advancement of the rights of the people of the state. But the situations are often the

118 *Tong-A Ilbo*, February 25, 1977; *Kyônghyang Sinmun*, February 25, 1977; also recounted in Pak U-Tong, *P'ansa sil esŏ pŏpchŏng kkaji*, 266–67.

119 Under the Court Organization Act revised in December 1987, Supreme Court decisions must record the opinions of all the justices who participated in the deliberation (art. 15). The Constitutional Court Act (art. 36) also requires that the individual justices indicate their views on all decisions.

opposite in nondemocratic states. In those states, the law plays the role of the instrument of despotic power. The more the laws are enacted, the more restrained the rights of the people become, and the political power pursues despotism more easily under the cover of legality.[120]

Before he joined the cabinet under President Park, Hwang had his share of suffering due to his political views. He was fired by the Ministry of Education in September 1965 from his professorship at Seoul National University, along with twelve other professors at various universities, for having encouraged students to protest against the Korea–Japan normalization treaty.[121] Hwang was a bona fide dissident intellectual.[122] Once he became the justice minister, however,

120 Hwang San-Tŏk, "Pŏp e ŭihan tokchae" [Dictatorship by law], *Sin Tong-A*, October 1964. Cited in Mun Hyŏng-Rae, "Pŏp e naejae toen chŏngch'i wa p'ongnyŏk e kwanhan yŏngu: Yusin ch'eje hyŏngsŏng kwa Inhyŏktang Chaegŏnwi sagŏn ŭl chungsim ŭro" [A Study on Control and Violence Embedded in Law: Focusing on the Establishment of the Yusin System and the Inhyŏktang Chaegŏnwi Case] (master's thesis, Sŏnggonghoe University, 2009), 123. For short biographies of Hwang, see Ch'oe Chong-Ko, *Hanguk ŭi pŏphakcha* [Legal Scholars of Korea], 2nd ed. (Seoul: Seoul Taehakkyo Ch'ulp'anbu, 1989), 300–321.

121 Hwang and these professors were among those who issued a declaration in July 1965 opposing the normalization treaty. The government argued that they violated the Government Officials Act that prohibited public officials from participating in political activities and also that Hwang worked as an editorial writer at the Tong-A Ilbo Company in violation of the law that prohibited a public official from holding concurrent employments. *Tong-A Ilbo*, September 25 and October 21, 1965. Hwang filed a suit contesting his dismissal, arguing that disciplinary actions of professors must be decided by the university personnel committee, that a professor holding multiple positions was not against the legislative intent of the Government Officials Act, and that his signature on the declaration opposing the normalization treaty was an exercise of his fundamental rights as a citizen. *Tong-A Ilbo*, March 5, 1966. On August 11, 1966, the Seoul Appeals Court granted injunction against dismissal and ordered that Hwang be reinstated. The Court said that the resolution of Hwang's suit challenging his dismissal was delayed due to the Ministry of Education's motion to reopen defense arguments and that during this delay Hwang would suffer irreparable harm. *Tong-A Ilbo*, August 11, 1966. After this decision in his favor, Hwang submitted a voluntary resignation on August 25. On August 27, the government voided the dismissal retroactively to September 15, 1965, and his resignation was processed thereafter. *Kyŏnghyang Sinmun*, August 27, 1966; *Tong-A Ilbo*, August 29, 1966.

122 For Hwang's legal philosophy, see Sim Hŏn-Sŏp, "Sŏk-U Hwang San-Tŏk paksa e issŏsŏ ŭi chayŏnpŏp ron kwa pŏp silchŭng juŭi" [Natural Law Theory and Positivist Legal Ideology of Dr. Hwang San-Tŏk], *Seoul Taehakkyo pŏphak* 35 (1994), 72–80.

Hwang wholeheartedly defended the Yusin government policy and justified its criminal laws and procedures.[123] Did he not see the unjust, oppressive nature of the Yusin laws? Why did he advocate them? Did he compromise his scholarly conscience and beliefs because of his desire to promote his career? One can only speculate. Hwang was not the only scholar-turned-bureaucrat whose legal philosophy seemingly underwent a turnabout or at least exhibited marked inconsistency. In a way, his career captures clashes between the natural law theory and positivism, between philosophy and practice, and, ultimately, between justice and law. These were the topics that consumed many other Korean intellectuals as well as ordinary citizens. One cannot ignore the possibility that this eminent jurist believed that the flurry of laws in the 1970s, some undoubtedly repressive, were necessary to protect the country, quintessential for national security and economic growth. He may have thought that the exigency of the times compelled him to adopt a perspective and opinion that he had once rejected. Dismissing him as a turncoat and opportunist would perhaps be too easy. The example of Hwang is a reminder that it is necessary to try a comprehensive assessment of those individuals accused of complicity with power – their achievements, failures, contradictions, and all – before rendering a judgment on their actions and their place in history.

One may set forth some general reflections. Judges hold their offices under state law. Positive forms of legal reasoning allow few possibilities for judicial resistance to the regime. When faced with authoritarian law, as Graver has explained, a judge "balanc[es] evils" and imposes "what he thinks to be the lesser evil in the context of the law that he is applying. This is an inherent part of being a judge."[124] Courts, as organs of the state, can "seldom challenge the core interests of the regime."[125] Judges often behave strategically, avoiding open confrontation with the regime. In Korea, this approach became second nature for

[123] It has been argued that intellectuals and university professors, including Hwang, joined and served in the Park government because they supported Park's policy that followed the modernization theory proposed by University of Chicago Professor Edward Shils. See "Kŭndaehwa int'eligench'ia ron kwa chisigin ŭi pyŏnjŏl nonjaeng" [The Modernization Theory of the Intelligentsia and Controversy over the Intellectuals' Defection], *Chugan Tong-A*, October 19, 2015, 64–67, http://weekly.donga.com/Print?cid=151055.

[124] Graver, *Judges against Justice*, 271.

[125] Ibid., 59.

judges. They seemed to believe that defending the legality of the Yusin Constitution was different from supporting dictatorship. Chief Justice Min Pok-Ki summed it up:

> The judge must obey the current law; he or she is bound by law and must be so. As long as the law is not in conflict with the Constitution, the judge must abide by it regardless of his or her own personal preference. This is why the legislature must make laws in a prudent manner. The courts cannot change them.[126]

Could it be that the judges viewed the current legal norms as rules in flux, comforting themselves with the thought that the unjust system, a temporary phenomenon, would be eventually overcome and that in the meantime their most important duties were to preserve legality and maintain the judicial process?

None of this is to suggest that the record of the Yusin judiciary was justified or beyond reproach. It is a fair assessment that during the Yusin period "the independence of the judiciary was undermined and the courts could not give a defendant in a political case a fair trial."[127] In political cases, defense counsel often complained that court decisions rarely offered sufficient reasoning for their dispositions.[128] Reading court judgments of hastily handed-down convictions on emergency decree cases is disheartening, to say the least.[129] The opinions of the Supreme Court were often formulaic and perfunctory. There is a measure of truth in the notion that justices gravitated to the formulations most conducive to a denial of personal responsibility. When they remained reluctant to descend into the political realm, they were not able to restrain the authoritarian government. One wishes that the justices, at least some if not all, had raised their voices more assertively and more frequently during the Yusin years. Yet envisioning retrospectively a sort of showdown between dictatorial power and the judicial forces arrayed against it would be unreasonable and idealistic at best when the courts lacked the institutional capacity to act independently of political actors.

126 *Tong-A Ilbo*, February 26, 1982.

127 Cohen and Baker, "U.S. Foreign Policy," 212. Most judges adapted and "maintained a safe silence," even when such adaptation meant convicting political defendants based on confessions coerced by police brutality. West and Baker, "The 1987 Constitutional Reforms," 246.

128 Hong Sŏng-U, *Inkwŏn pyŏllon han sidae*, 124.

129 Lawyers complained that some lower court judges simply copied the prosecution's indictments and used them as court judgments. Ibid., 155, 199–200.

After all, judges understood that their duty was to give effect to the will of the law and that, in the dismal reality of the Yusin system, it was crucial to maintain legality. They helped sustain the judicial process in which the lawyers could present their challenges to unjust laws in reference to constitutional ideals. They may have felt relieved, just as the American antebellum antislavery judges did, in concluding that it was not the proper role of judges to engage in politics. The plight of the American judges indeed seems uncannily pertinent to Korean judges: "To strike out against the tide raised the specter of futility; to swim with the tide raised that of complicity."[130] There lay the agony of judges who faced the dilemma of the legality of unjust laws.

The Killing of the President

The assassination of President Park on October 26, 1979, brought the Yusin system to an abrupt halt. In hindsight, Park's assassination, unexpected and shocking as it was, came at the vortex of crisis inching toward some sort of blowup. In July 1978, the National Conference for Unification had reelected President Park to serve six more years. In March 1979, the government ordered the arrest of former president Yun Posun, Kim Dae Jung, and other dissidents. On October 4, the ruling party of the National Assembly voted to expel Kim Young Sam [Kim Yŏng-Sam] (1929–2015), the head of the opposition New Democratic Party, from the Assembly. Antigovernment student demonstrations erupted in Pusan, the country's second-largest city, and spread to the nearby city of Masan. The president's death came at a moment when politics in Korea seemed to be hurling headlong to an uncertain yet inevitable crash.

Park was shot by Kim Chae-Kyu, the head of the KCIA, at a dinner table. Kim was quickly arrested and put on trial. The trial of Kim and his subordinates proceeded at an emergency court martial. The case reached the Supreme Court in February 1980. This trial marked one of the most controversial and contentious moments in Korean judicial history. It is to this case and the turbulent political transitions the next chapter turns.

[130] Cover, *Justice Accused*, 202.

7 *Political Transitions and Rule of Law, 1980–1987*

The months that followed President Park's death on October 26, 1979, were marked by a tense mesh of hope and anxiety over looming uncertainty. Prime Minister Choi Kyu Hah acceded to the acting presidency, and martial law was declared. Nationwide grieving for the passing of the president was followed by a surge of anticipation for the return of democracy. On December 6, Choi was elected president by the National Conference for Unification under the existing constitution, and he made it clear that a new election would take place as soon as a new constitution came into being, not later than early 1980. The National Assembly unanimously called for the repeal of Emergency Decree No. 9, which Choi accepted. The decree was lifted on December 8, after four years and seven months of existence. Sixty-eight individuals who had been serving time for its violation were freed that day. On December 27, some five thousand people were released from prison by presidential pardon on the occasion of President Choi's inauguration.

Aspirations for democracy were abruptly dashed, however. While civilian politicians were jockeying for power, the military hijacked the political process. On December 12, Major General Chun Doo Hwan, who was in charge of the Martial Law Defense Security Command, waged a coup and arrested General Chŏng Sŭng-Hwa, martial law commander and the army chief of staff, for alleged collusion with Park's killer, Kim Chae-Kyu. Having seized power, Chun installed a military junta, crippling the civilian government. This political unraveling had serious repercussions for the Supreme Court. The military clique in power had a crucial interest in how the trial of Kim Chae-Kyu would proceed. It needed to characterize the killing of Park and his security guards as a treasonous insurrection so as to justify the military's intervention and usurpation of power. It also wanted a quick conclusion of the trial so that it could consolidate its grip on politics and stifle the nascent democracy movement. Kim and his accomplices were swiftly tried and found guilty by the court martial.

In the spring of 1980, Korea was undergoing one of the most tumultuous periods in its modern history. Demonstrations erupted all over the country and students again filled the streets. On May 17, martial law was imposed nationwide. All political activities were banned, and the National Assembly was suspended indefinitely. On May 18, student and citizen protests in Kwangju escalated into a massive uprising, which assault troops dispatched by the Martial Law Command violently put down over the next nine days.[1] On May 20, the Supreme Court dismissed the appeals of Kim and others in a sharply divided decision of eight to six. It was the last ruling of political import rendered by the Court operating under the Yusin Constitution.

The first part of this chapter examines the court judgment of Park's murder case (commonly known as the 10.26 *sakŏn*). The last several years have witnessed an explosion of investigative reports and analyses of the assassination.[2] Fierce debate continues to this day over whether Kim Chae-Kyu killed President Park as part of his long-held plan to restore democracy or whether he shot Park impulsively and his action collaterally brought about the demise of the Yusin system. Immensely important as they are, political ramifications of the assassination are beyond the scope of this chapter, which limits its discussion to a legal analysis of the case. The following pages focus on how the Supreme Court dealt with the legal consequences of Kim's crime and what its decision meant for the role of the judiciary during this pivotal time in Korean history.

Under mounting military pressure, President Choi unceremoniously stepped down on August 16, 1980. On August 27, Chun was elected president by the National Conference for Unification, and his

[1] See Gi-Wook Shin and Kyung Moon Hwang, *Contentious Kwangju: The May 18 Uprising in Korea's Past and Present* (Lanham: Rowman & Littlefield, 2003).

[2] The reproduction of the court record of the trial, including appeals motions, is available in *Inkwŏn pyŏllon charyo chip*, vol. 6, 611–947. One of Kim Chae-Kyu's defense counsels has provided a reliable description of the background and the process of the trials: An Tong-Il, *10.26 ŭn ajikto sara itta: An Tong-Il pyŏnhosa ka tŭllyŏ chunŭn 10.26 sakŏn, kŭ chinsil kwa kŏjit* [The October 26th Is Still Alive: The October 26th Incident Told by Attorney an Tong-Il, Its Truth and Lies] (Seoul: Raendŏm Hausŭ Chungang, 2005).

inauguration took place on September 1. The new constitution took effect on October 27. In March 1981, Chun, newly chosen by the rubber-stamp electoral body, was sworn in to serve a seven-year term as the president of the Fifth Republic. While the 1980 Constitution kept the indirect presidential election method inherited from the Yusin years, it abolished the provisions of the 1972 Constitution that had given the president virtually unlimited emergency powers.

In 1985, the Supreme Court was compelled to revisit the emergency decrees. By then, the notorious decrees had disappeared from the law books for several years, but the issue arose regarding their residual effect: what is the legal force of already abolished laws after the promulgation of a new constitution? The case, discussed in the second part of this chapter, is of particular interest because a quarter-century later, in 2010, the Supreme Court departed from its 1985 reasoning when it undertook constitutional review of the emergency decrees.[3] The effect of the "old laws" continued to have serious reverberations in jurisprudence in Korea where there was a succession of constitutional revisions. It was an issue that Korea had to deal with all the way from the birth of the republic. This chapter brings its discussion to the eve of the 2010 decision, which will be the subject of Chapter 8.

Unraveling of the Yusin System

President Park's murder trials went like a blitz. Kim Chae-Kyu and seven others were charged on November 26, 1979, with killing Park and his bodyguards for the purpose of treasonous insurrection and attempted insurrection. The investigation had been headed by none other than General Chun. On December 4, the trial started in the military court. The defense disputed the jurisdiction of court martial. Because all the defendants except one were civilians and the alleged crimes took place before martial law was declared, their lawyers argued that the Seoul Criminal District Court, not the military court, had jurisdiction over the case.[4] On December 7, the Supreme Court dismissed the defense motion. Citing its precedent from 1964, the Court held that the court martial had jurisdiction over those who committed crimes listed in the Martial Law Act, regardless of whether they were

[3] S. Ct., 2010To5986 (*en banc*), December 16, 2010.
[4] *Tong-A Ilbo*, December 4, 1979.

military personnel or civilians and whether the crimes were committed before or after the imposition of martial law.[5]

On December 20, the court martial convicted Kim and his subordinates as charged and sentenced six of them, including Kim, to death. The high court martial affirmed the verdicts on January 28, 1980. The case reached the Supreme Court on February 7, 1980. There was tremendous pressure on the Court to dispose of the case swiftly. It was reported that in March the military regime demanded that the Supreme Court conclude the trial "within one month."[6] The case was assigned to a criminal panel composed of four justices: An Pyŏng-Su, the presiding judge, Yang Pyŏng-Ho, Sŏ Yun-Hong, and Yu T'ae-Hŭng. Justice Yu, the reporting judge, argued for the dismissal of appeal, but Justices Yang and Sŏ disagreed.[7] Because the petty bench could not reach consensus, the case was forwarded on April 10 to the collegiate bench consisting of all the court members.

The Supreme Court was under daily harassment from the Martial Law Defense Security Command to cut short deliberations and reach a quick conclusion. On May 20, the Court issued its decision dismissing all the appeals of the defendants.[8] Considering the magnitude of the case, one may find it disconcerting that it took less than seven months from the crimes to the final verdicts. The aftermath was just as rushed. Kim Chae-Kyu was hanged on May 24. Three days later, on May 27, an army division brutally quelled the uprising in Kwangju.

The 1980 decision can be compared with other major decisions of the Supreme Court, most notably the State Tort Claims Act case in 1971 and the Inhyŏktang Chaegŏnwi case in 1975, discussed in Chapter 3 and Chapter 5 respectively.[9] If the State Tort Claims Act case was the prelude to the Yusin period, the Park assassination case was its coda. Both were sharply divided decisions, nine to seven in 1971

5 S. Ct., 79Ch'o70, December 7, 1979. See *Kyŏnghyang Sinmun*, December 7, 1979. For the 1964 decision (S. Ct. 64Ch'o3), see Chapter 3.

6 *Pŏpcho 50 nyŏn yasa*, vol. 1, 940–941.

7 Yang Pyŏng-Ho, *Pŏpcho pan paengnyŏn*, 202–203. Justice Sŏ Yun-Hong later confirmed the division in the panel. See also *Pŏpcho 50 nyŏn yasa*, vol. 1, 106.

8 S. Ct., 80To306, May 20, 1980.

9 Scholars have also compared the 1980 case with the trial of Presidents Chun Doo Hwan and Roh Tae Woo in 1997 (S. Ct., 96To3376, April 17, 1997). See Sin Dong-Un, *P'allye paeksŏn hyŏngpŏp kakron 1* [One Hundred Selected Judicial Decisions in Criminal Law Provisions I] (Seoul: Kyŏngsewŏn, 1999), 15–27.

and eight to six in 1980. The majority in Park's murder trial consisted of Justices Yi Yŏng-Sŏp, Chu Chae-Hwang, Han Hwan-Chin, An Pyŏng-Su, Yi Il-Kyu, Na Kil-Cho, Kim Yong-Ch'ŏl, and Yu T'ae-Hŭng; the dissenting justices were Min Mun-Ki, Yang Pyŏng-Ho, Im Hang-Chun, Kim Yun-Haeng, Chŏng T'ae-Wŏn, and Sŏ Yun-Hong. Both cases resulted in egregious political reprisals: in the former, all the justices who wrote the majority opinion that displeased the government were forced to leave the court; in the latter, all but one who wrote dissenting opinions that irked the military junta met the same fate.

To be precise, the ways the justices were let go were dissimilar, which may bespeak the differences between the Park and the Chun regimes. In 1971 the Park government, ever obsessed with legality, waited until the new Court Organization Act was passed in February 1973 to require the reappointment of all incumbent judges, and it was through this procedure that the justices were expelled, almost two years after they rendered the unconstitutionality decision. In 1980, General Chun did not bother to wait for legal excuses to punish the dissenting justices, who were removed within ten weeks of the judgment. Five justices – Min, Yang, Im, Kim, and Sŏ – left the Court on August 8; the sixth, Chŏng, who did not file an individual opinion but simply noted his partial concurrence with Sŏ's opinion, survived the initial political ax but failed to get reappointed the following year. Chun preferred to let the public know, unequivocally, why they were forced out; he wanted to send a stark message to the judiciary about what would happen if it dared to cross him. This incident, the worst and most blatant judicial persecution in Korean history, left little illusion about what the courts could and could not do in the face of the government that had no intention whatsoever even to pretend its commitment to judicial independence.[10] Judges were forced to think hard about the personal cost at stake in deciding political cases.

The main significance of Park's murder trial judgment resides in the dissenting opinion, not the majority opinion. In many respects, the majority opinion was a rerun of the Inhyŏktang decision five years earlier. Of course the material legal issues were different: murder in

[10] See Yang Sam-Sŭng, "Pŏpcho kaejoron: Pŏpcho samryun ŭi paramjikhan mosŭp kwa irŭl wihan pangan" [A Theory of Judicial Reform: The Ideal Image of the Three Wheels of the Judiciary and Measures for Its Achievement], *Chŏsŭt'isŭ* 118 (2010), 5–56.

1980 and national security violation in 1975. But many arguments presented by the defense and the reasoning set forth by the bench were similar. Differences came in the form of dissenting opinions. In 1975 a single justice dissented on a procedural matter, and there was no disagreement among the justices on substantive dispositional issues; in 1980 there were five separate dissenting opinions on the interpretations of the key provisions of criminal law. The effect of change in the court membership was minimal. Among the thirteen justices who sat on the bench in 1975, three retired and one died in office during the intervening years. Chief Justice Min Pok-Ki stepped down in 1978, having reached the mandatory retirement age; he was succeeded by Justice Yi Yŏng-Sŏp. Nine justices who had participated in the Inhyŏktang Chaegŏnwi case were still on the bench. Four among the six dissenters in 1980 had been part of the majority in 1975 (the other two joined the court in 1976 and 1979 respectively). The justice who had written the lone dissenting opinion in 1975, Yi Il-Kyu, joined the majority in 1980. The division of the Court in the Park murder case thus had little to do with personnel change (see Figure 7.1).

Indeed, the 1980 decision deserves attention because it brought to light the deep fissures among the justices that had been growing for some time. It is important to remember that the Supreme Court was neither a homogeneous nor a monolithic group. Any institutional analysis must pay careful attention to the underlying diversity in the court. The four justices who dissented in 1980 – Min Mun-Ki, Yang Pyong-Ho, Im Hang-Chun, and Kim Yun-Haeng – had been known for frequently disagreeing with the majority during their tenure. According to a newspaper article published in 2006, Justices Im, Min, and Kim were among the top five on the list of the Supreme Court justices who issued the most dissenting opinions in court history.[11]

Several justices seemed to embrace a new jurisprudential position departing from their earlier stance. For example, in 1975 all the justices declined to recognize the right to resist in Korea's constitutional order; in 1980 a couple of justices openly declared the existence of that right as a constitutional principle. This brings up important questions. Did some members of the Court change their opinions on points of law, or, rather, did they finally decide to speak their minds in the new political

[11] *Hanguk Ilbo*, December 9, 2006 ("Hanguk ŭi taebŏpkwan kŭdŭrŭn").

Figure 7.1 The Supreme Court in Session, 1980. The Supreme Court delivers the judgment on May 20, 1980, in the trial of the assassination of President Park Chung Hee. *Collection of the Supreme Court Library of Korea.*

climate? If the latter, did it amount to an admission that the interpretation of law could not be immune from political situations and must reflect the changed times? If indeed there was a major change in judicial position, does it in a way buttress the criticism that the Court had been swayed by political power all along during the Yusin years?

The fact that the trial took place under the Yusin Constitution and Yusin laws was of paramount significance. After all, this was why the military junta hastened the conclusion of the trial before a new constitution came into force. The defense was aware of this perilous situation, but there was little it could do other than pleading that everyone involved in the trial would act with "a clear sense of history and humility, listening to the will of the people, not consumed by political interests."[12] This solemn – and desperate – call for justice revealed the enormous burden thrust on the Supreme Court. What would be the proper path of a judicial court in its mission to conduct an impartial trial and fulfill justice? Would it be a court that stood aloof from political happenings, even turning a blind eye to them, and

[12] *Pŏpcho 50 nyŏn yasa*, vol. 2, 85; *Hangyŏrye Sinmun*, October 26, 1988.

followed the letter of the written law as long as it was on the books, until the moment of its revision? Or, to the contrary, would it be one that was willing to take into consideration that the law was expected to change and therefore let itself diverge from the letter of the existing law in order to achieve substantive justice and facilitate liberal democracy? What would be the correct meaning of the constitutional requirement that judges "rule independently in accordance with their conscience and in conformity with the constitution and law" in this situation?[13] What if a judge could not at the same time be faithful to the law and to his or her own conscience? What would ensure a fair trial for the accused and "justice served" for all? The list of questions could go on.

The dissenting opinions of the 1980 case were not made public for several years. The regime prohibited their publication, and the media only reported the majority opinion. The official Supreme Court Case Reports and the Court Bulletin (*Pŏpwŏn Kongbo*) omitted any mention of the existence of dissenting opinions. The government even refused requests from legal professionals for the complete text of the decision.[14] The dismal realities of the caged judiciary and the muzzled press could not have been better evinced. It was only in 1986 that the entire text was made available to the public for the first time when it was published in the monthly magazine *Wŏlgan Chosŏn*.[15] It took another four years before the dissents were inserted into the official court reports published in 1990.[16]

President Park Murder Case (1980)

The central issue that divided the Supreme Court was whether the defendants were guilty of murders committed for the purpose of treasonous insurrection or whether they were guilty of simple murders. The majority of the Court said their crimes constituted treasonous insurrection, the dissenters said it did not. Before discussing this key legal question, one needs first to examine several procedural and substantive issues in the case, the kind already visited in the Inhyŏktang Chaegŏnwi case. In 1980 the defense lawyers pointed to various procedural violations in the military

13 Constitution (1987), Art. 103.
14 Yang Pyŏng-Ho, *Pŏpcho pan paengnyŏn*, 357.
15 February 1986 issue.
16 *Taebŏpwŏn chŏnwŏn habŭich'e p'allejip* [The Supreme Court En Banc Decisions Report], *Hyŏngsa p'yŏn II (1978–1989)*, August 1990.

court trials: the examination of witnesses took place without proper notice, depriving defendants of the opportunities to question them; several trial sessions took place behind closed doors in breach of the principle of open trial; and the military judges frequently stopped the defendants from answering questions. The Supreme Court's rulings on these issues in 1980 were the same as in 1975: there was no proven violation of the defendants' rights.

The Court acknowledged that there were certain irregularities in the manner the ordinary military court conducted examinations of the defendants but decided that those defects were either immaterial or adequately cured. For instance, the court martial held witness examinations without notifying the defendants, but the defendants and their counsels stated in the subsequent proceedings that they had no objection to the examination records, thereby waiving their right to contest them. The Supreme Court ruled that under the Military Court Act how much freedom the defendants should be given in making statements was within the discretion of the presiding judge, as long as it did not contravene reasonable practices. "The nature of trial procedures that were followed during the lower court trials can only be proved by the trial record, as stipulated in article 89 of the Military Court Act," the Court said, and the trial record showed that it was an open trial and the defendants and their counsels were given sufficient opportunities to make statements and ask questions. There was no reason to dispute the veracity of that record, ruled the Court.

The defendants claimed that the trial was tainted because during the courtroom proceedings the presiding judges received frequent messages delivered to them from outside, giving rise to suspicion of telephone justice, that is, they were acting on political instructions from above. The Supreme Court said that it was impossible to determine whether the delivery of messages, if it had taken place, conclusively impinged on the independence of the judge. The Court thus concluded that the procedural defects did not materially influence the result of the trial.

The defendants argued that the sentences rendered by the military courts were excessive. The military court procedures tightly limited appellate review on the grounds of excessive sentence. This was an issue that had been raised in 1975 as well. The majority in the Supreme Court admitted that the civilian defendants' rights were substantially curtailed when they were tried in the military court, but said it was beyond the Court's control as long as the military court's jurisdiction was not invalid. It wrote:

The military court is a special court operating separately from the ordinary court, with different missions and objectives. The differences in the scope of the rights of the defendants in the military court and the civilian court had been foreseen by the Constitution and the laws. Article 432 of the Military Court Act does not allow excessive sentence as a ground for appeal, and it cannot be seen as an unconstitutional provision in violation of Articles 8 and 9 of the Constitution.[17]

Notably, one justice dissented. Justice Im Hang-Chun argued that, in cases where a civilian, who was neither a soldier nor a military employee, was given by the military courts extreme punishments such as the death penalty, life imprisonment, or imprisonment of ten years or more, it was not reasonable to limit that person's right to appeal, guaranteed otherwise in the ordinary court proceedings.[18] Depriving a civilian of his right, only because that person was tried under the Military Court Act, would contravene Article 9 of the Constitution that guaranteed equality before the law, he wrote. Note this was an argument that had not been put forward in 1975 when the majority rejected the same challenge by the defendants who were also civilians subjected to court martial.

A key defense argument concerned the right to resist. The defendants of the 1975 trial had claimed that the right to resist must be interpreted in such a way that it justified, in conformity with the natural law order, certain acts that were committed in violation of the positive law order. Likewise, the defendants argued in 1980 that the Yusin system was an antidemocratic government apparatus with no means allowed legally to challenge the existing order, either in theory or in practice. In this situation, resorting to acts prohibited in law could be defined as a lawful exercise of the right to resist, constituting self-defense as prescribed in article 20 of the Criminal Code. The defense specifically demanded that the Court set aside its precedent of the Inhyŏktang case

17 S. Ct., 80To306, May 20, 1980.

18 S. Ct., 80To306 (Im Hang-Chun, J., dissenting). The Military Court Act, article 432, was revised in April 1981 (Law 3444) to add the following two provisions as grounds for appeal to the Supreme Court: "(6) When the recognition of the jurisdiction of the High Court Martial was in violation of law; (7) Where the death penalty, life imprisonment, or imprisonment of ten years or more with or without labor has been imposed and the sentence was the result of a serious mistake of fact or there is a clear reason to believe that the sentence was unjustly excessive." Article 432 (7) is verbatim in the Criminal Procedure Act, art. 383 (4).

that denied the right to resist. The majority of the Court rejected this argument. It largely repeated the language in the 1975 opinion, writing,

> Even if we accepted the argument that the so-called right to resist is an established natural law right and must be recognized as a constitutional theory in modern liberal democracy, regardless of whether it is stipulated in the Constitution or other positive laws, the judge could not apply it as a judicial norm as long as it existed in the realm of natural law alone, and not in positive law. Besides, there is no consensus today, even among the scholars who recognize the existence of the right to resist, on its concrete concept, its scope of obligation, or its constituting elements. It remains a vague and abstract concept.[19]

The Court in 1980 added a critical statement, however, which potentially set it apart from its previous position. The majority wrote: "In our current situation where law provisions regarding such a right are absent in either the Constitution or the laws, we cannot but hesitate to apply the theory of the right to resist as a judicial norm." This was a subtle demurrer, something that had been absent in the 1975 opinion. The Court was not oblivious to the political shifts after President Park's death. The oppressive nature of the Yusin Constitution was no secret, and its demise was near. Still, the Court ruled that, as long as the "current" Constitution was still in force, it could not accept the extra-constitutional concept of the right to resist and depart from its precedents.

Again Justice Im dissented. For him, the Supreme Court in the Inhyŏktang case did not deny the existence of the right to resist; it simply denied the existence of that right as an enforceable judicial norm at the time. He explained:

> Where there are serious encroachments by state institutions into the democratic order that proclaims human dignity as the central value and the fundamental principle in politics, and where the majority of citizens decide, from an objective perspective, that the existence of a democratic constitution itself is being denied and that there is no means to correct it through the methods available in the existing positive law, the citizens cannot just sit and watch and continue abiding by that law. In this situation, it is necessary to recognize the right to resist as a kind of natural law right even if it is not

[19] S. Ct., 80To306. See Chapter 5, note 35 and accompanying text.

written in the Constitution. This right justifies the acts of refusing to obey the laws that infringe on the citizens' human rights and breach the basic democratic order.[20]

According to him, the right to resist could be inferred from the Preamble of the Constitution. The Preamble of the 1972 Constitution stated that Korea "upholds the noble spirit of independence of the March First Movement and the principles of the April Nineteenth Uprising against injustice and the May Sixteenth Revolution." Justice Im wrote:

> The Preamble of our Constitution, which is the basic law of our country, is the reason why one cannot deny the existence of the right to resist. It states that the new democratic republic was established . . . succeeding the spirit of the April Nineteenth Uprising. Thus it calls the uprising of the nineteenth of April a just movement even though it took place through acts that openly violated the positive law in force at the time. . . . Our Constitution views the April Nineteenth movement as an exercise of the right to resist, aimed to sustain and protect the democratic order that was in danger of being destroyed. If the right to resist is recognized in our Constitution, one should ask how it can be denied in judicial determination. . . . The majority opinion states that the right to resist cannot be used as a judicial norm because it is not grounded in positive law, but one cannot argue conclusively that rights in natural law cannot be used as judicial norms.[21]

This was a forceful and eloquent argument that had not been voiced in 1975. Scholars have applauded Justice Im's embrace of the right to resist as an important marker in the jurisprudential evolution in the direction of liberal democracy. In the spring of 1980, nevertheless, with the Yusin Constitution still in place, the majority of the Court did not deem it necessary to set aside its precedent.

The major legal issue concerned whether the defendants committed murder for the purpose of treasonous insurrection. Did their acts meet the elements of the crime of treasonous insurrection? Was the assassination of President Park treason or the murder of an ordinary person? The military regime in power in 1980 had a crucial political

[20] S. Ct., 80To306 (Im Hang-Chun, J., dissenting).

[21] Ibid. This focus on the constitutional preamble as the repository of natural law rights seems to have presaged the modern Korean courts' tendency to draw unwritten constitutional rights from the language of the preamble.

interest at stake: if the killing of President Park was a murder of an ordinary citizen, the military coup of December 12 would lose its legitimacy. It was a prospect that the junta wanted to avoid by all and any means.

The government charged the defendants under article 87 of the Criminal Code, treasonous insurrection, as well as article 88, homicide for the purpose of treasonous insurrection (see Figure 7.2). Article 87 punished one "who participated in violent uprising for the purpose of destroying the nation's territory or subverting the nation's constitutional order"; article 88 punished one "who killed a person for the purpose of destroying the nation's territory or subverting the nation's constitutional order." Article 91 of the Criminal Code defined "subverting the nation's constitutional order" as "overthrowing by force government organs established by the Constitution or rendering their operations impossible." The defense argued that these provisions were inapplicable to the case: Kim Chae-Kyu merely killed a person who happened to be the president, for the sole purpose of restoring democracy, and, even when he intended to change the Constitution after killing the president, "there was no intent to subvert the nation's constitutional order." The majority disagreed. Under article 91 of the Criminal Code, allowed the Court, "the purpose of subverting the nation's constitutional order" meant "illegally destroying the basic political structure as established by the current Constitution and the laws, and as such the provision does not apply to murdering an ordinary person occupying an office in the hope that he will be succeeded by someone else." However, the crime of treasonous insurgency "emphatically does not require that the action purport to change the government to a communist, monarchical, or dictatorial order." This was the same position the Court had taken in 1975 when it ruled that the intent to usurp government power and change the nature of the state under the National Security Act could be found in an attempt to "create an organization in order to overthrow the government," not necessarily requiring an attempt to "change the foundation of the state by creating a communist regime or a monarchy."[22]

In order to support its position, the majority needed to reject the defendants' characterization of the Yusin Constitution as an "illegality." It wrote:

22 S. Ct., 74To3323, following S. Ct., 66To152, April 21, 1966; S. Ct., 66To617, July 12, 1966.

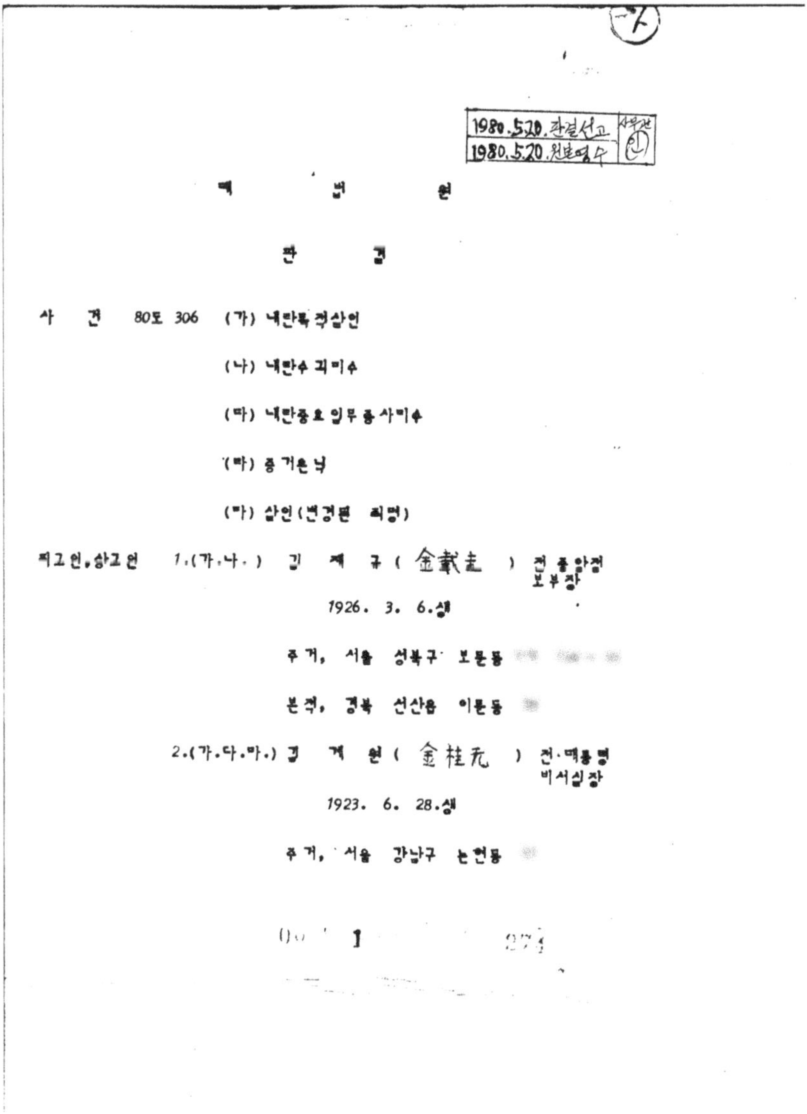

1980.5.20. 판결선고 사무관
1980.5.20. 원본영수 (인)

대 법 원

판 결

사 건 80도 306 (가) 내란목적살인

(나) 내란수괴미수

(다) 내란중요임무종사미수

(라) 증거은닉

(마) 살인(변경된 죄명)

피고인, 상고인 1.(가.나.) 김 재 규 (金載圭) 전 중앙정보부장

1926. 3. 6.생

주거, 서울 성북구 보문동

본적, 경북 선산읍 이문동

2.(가.다.마.) 김 계 원 (金桂元) 전 대통령 비서실장

1923. 6. 28.생

주거, 서울 강남구 논현동

Figure 7.2 The Supreme Court Judgment, 80To306. The cover page of the Supreme Court judgment of the President Park assassination case. The name of the main defendant Kim Chae-Kyu is shown with the charges. *Collection of the Supreme Court Library of Korea.*

It has been acknowledged that the current Constitution includes undemocratic provisions, but the Constitution declares that our country is a democratic republic and sovereignty resides with the people. It stipulates the protection of human rights, guarantees the citizens' basic rights, and provides the separation of powers. It is founded on democracy. Therefore, the arguments that the Yusin Constitution is an illegitimate illegality usurping sovereignty, that it destroyed the basic political structure of a democratic state, and that it itself is insurgency are arbitrary exaggerations and do not deserve serious consideration. The claim that the defendants committed the crimes for "the restoration of democracy" is evidently false.[23]

In other words, in the majority's opinion, the defendants acted with the intent to subvert the current democratic constitutional order. The Court refused to consider the question whether the killing of President Park brought, or would bring, about changes that could result in a more liberal and more democratic constitutional order.

Dissents: Treason That Was Not

Justice Min Mun-Ki, the most senior member among the dissenters, criticized the majority for failing to face the reality of the new political situation. For him, President Park's death changed the entire political dynamic. There was broad consensus among the citizens that the Yusin order must end once and for all. Abrogation of the Yusin Constitution was only a matter of time. As long as the trial was taking place in the midst of national yearning for the restoration of democracy, and as long as efforts to amend the Constitution were fully underway, the Court was obliged to take notice that it was the defendants' acts that unleashed the forces prompting a new democratic order. For this reason, the defendants could not be punished for the crime of treason. Justice Min argued:

An action would constitute treasonous insurrection if it was undertaken with the intent to transform a democratic order into a monarchical order. But if it became clear that somehow there was agreement among citizens to change the constitutional order to a monarchy, that act could no longer be punished as treasonous insurrection. When there was national consensus to abolish the democratic system, the crime of treason would be the act of creating

[23] S. Ct., 80To306.

a democracy, not the act of creating a monarchy. As long as there exists such agreement, insurrection for the purpose of creating a monarchy may still be an insurrection but it cannot be punished as a crime. This is because there has been a change in the nature of the rights that the law must protect; the nation's constitutional order now stands on a different foundation.[24]

In Justice Min's opinion, even though a new constitution was yet to be promulgated and the 1972 Constitution was still the law of the land, in reality Yusin rule had already come to an end. The lower court's decision that the defendants were guilty of treasonous insurrection "might have been correct under the Yusin system" but was no longer so under the current situation. His point was that the Court could not disregard the evolving political reality. Justice Min was optimistic in the sense that his confidence in the collapse of authoritarian rule led him to urge his colleagues to take cognizance of the new reality to avoid going against the flow of history. Of course, whether his impassioned plea correctly perceived the direction of the political wind was a separate question.

Not all dissenting justices agreed with Justice Min that the Court should interpret the law with the changed political situation in mind. Most dissenters took a more restrained approach. Justices Yang, Im, Kim, and Sŏ were of the same opinion as Justice Min that the defendants' acts could not be construed as treasonous insurrection, but they chose to ground their arguments on more legal than political considerations. For them, there was no sufficient evidence that the defendants had tried to destroy by force the office of the president, an institution established by the nation's constitution, or inhibit its function with the intent to usurp political power and illegally overthrow the state's basic governing structure. They argued that, even if the defendants murdered the president and his bodyguards to bring down the Yusin regime, the change of the Yusin system itself did not mean the destruction of the democratic constitutional order, which would otherwise make them guilty of treason under the Criminal Code.

According to the majority, violent acts by a group of people in breach of peace, as well as preparations and aids given for such acts, constituted the crime of insurrection, regardless of whether they achieved the purposes of causing severe destruction of the nation's territory and the rupture of its constitutional order, and the defendants'

[24] S. Ct., 80To306 (Min Mun-Ki, J., dissenting).

acts met those criteria. For the dissenters, however, there simply was no involvement of people numerous enough to wage an uprising in the meaning of insurrection in the Criminal Code. The crime of insurgency required the acts of a group of people who rose up in revolt in order to destroy the state's territory or to breach the nation's constitutional order, but in the present case the defendants were fewer than ten in number, and as such they did not form a group large enough to carry out an insurrection.

Each dissenter presented individual reasoning why there was no treasonous insurrection. Justice Im wrote:

> Insurrection requires the gathering of multiple people, and the meaning of multiple people refers to a minimum number of people that can create a group mentality and mob psychology, to the extent to prompt unreasonable and destructive actions recklessly, overwhelming one's normal thought process and action, and that is sufficient to destroy the peace of a region and to create violence and impose terror.[25]

In the present case there was no such mass psychology in operation. Justice Kim Yun-Haeng agreed, writing:

> The crime of insurrection under article 87 of the Criminal Code is an uprising carried out by a group of people, and uprising in this provision means violence or threat of violence caused by the gathering of a crowd capable of destroying peace in a region.[26]

The acts of the defendants in this case could not be seen as the acts of a large crowd or mob. The two justices' arguments did not come ungrounded. In the Minbiyŏn case examined in Chapter 3, the students, numbering less than ten, had been charged with treasonous insurrection, and the lower courts threw out the charge on the grounds that no one could possibly imagine an insurrection with that small number of people, and the Supreme Court agreed.[27] The defendants in 1980 held onto this precedent with a glimmer of hope, but the two justices' arguments were overruled by the majority.

Was Kim Chae-Kyu's killing of President Park treason? Justice Yang Pyŏng-Ho expounded on the difference between the murder of the president as an ordinary citizen and the destruction of the presidency as a constitutional institution:

[25] S. Ct., 80To306 (Im Hang-Chun, J., dissenting).
[26] S. Ct., 80To306 (Kim Yun-Haeng, J., dissenting).
[27] See Chapter 3, note 39 and accompanying text.

If someone said the killing of the president of a state must necessarily be seen as an act to subvert the state's constitution because the presidency is the highest office in the state hierarchy, that would be an extremely naive and simplistic thinking. The office of the president is an institution of the state government; the president is not the government. . . . The president is one of the civil servants who are accountable to the citizens. The lower court said that the defendant killed the president out of personal grievances but then it turned around and concluded that his act was a murder committed for the purpose of subverting the nation's constitutional order. These arguments contradict each other. The fact that he had personal grievances means he intended to kill a person who happened to be the president.[28]

For Justice Yang, treasonous insurrection, if there had been one, would need to be proved by the development of the events in the aftermath of the death of the president. It had been stipulated that Kim Chae-Kyu, immediately following the killing, called for urgent actions to heighten national security and to restore normality. Those moves could not be seen as a treasonous rebellion.

The dissenters pointed out serious errors in the majority's construction of the insurrection laws. The government charged Kim Chae-Kyu and his subordinates with both article 87 of the Criminal Code, treasonous insurrection, and article 88, murder for the purpose of treasonous insurrection. Justices Kim and Im objected to the majority ruling that the defendants were guilty on both counts. Even if one supposed that the defendants' acts had constituted treason as the majority claimed, the defendants should have been found guilty under one provision, article 87 or article 88, not both. This would have critical consequences for determining their punishments.

Justice Kim carefully explicated the problems of applying these two criminal counts concurrently. Article 87 read in full:

A person who participated in violent uprising for the purpose of destroying the nation's territory or subverting the nation's constitutional order shall be punished according to the following categories: (1) The leader shall be punished by death or life in prison with or without hard labor; (2) A person who participated in or commanded the plot, or engaged in other essential activities shall be punished by death, life in prison, or five years or more in prison, with or without hard labor; the same applies to a person who committed the acts of killing, inflicting injury, or destroying property or

[28] S. Ct., 80To306 (Yang Pyŏng-Ho, J., dissenting).

plundering; (3) A person who simply followed the lead of another or merely participated in a violent uprising shall be punished by five years or less in prison with or without hard labor.

Article 88 read in full:

A person who killed another for the purpose of destroying the nation's territory or subverting the nation's constitutional order shall be punished by death or life in prison with or without hard labor.

According to Justice Kim, those two provisions, seemingly overlapping, were clearly distinguishable. He reasoned that the legislature, by enacting the two independent articles, separated two kinds of acts of killing for the purpose of treasonous insurrection, depending on whether the defendant participated in violent uprising. He wrote: "if the murder took place during violent uprising, that act falls under article 87 and it constitutes the crime of treasonous insurrection, but if the killing took place not during violent uprising, it constitutes the crime of murder committed for the purpose of insurrection under article 88."[29] The two crimes were different and the National Assembly apparently intended to keep them separate.

Justice Kim then explained how the failure to construe the two articles correctly led the prosecutors, and the lower courts, to apply erroneously the law on compound crimes. Under the Criminal Code article providing the principle of conceptual concurrence (*Idealkonkurrenz*), a defendant whose act constitutes more than one crime is subject to the punishment set forth for the most severe crime.[30] Prosecutors routinely sought conviction on multiple charges for a single act and demanded aggravated punishment on the basis of that provision. If article 87 and article 88 punished two different crimes and the defendants could not be found guilty of both crimes, however, the principle of conceptual concurrence would be inapplicable. Justice Kim focused attention on the fact that article 87 distinguished different levels of participation of the actors in treasonous insurrection predicated on the nature of their roles; in other words, the article, subsuming "the crime of violent uprising that conclusively presumed the act of killing and inflicting injury," mandated different punishments depending on whether the killing was committed by the leader of the group or someone who merely followed orders. Article 87 (2) subjected

[29] S. Ct., 80To306 (Kim Yun-Haeng, J., dissenting).
[30] Criminal Code, art. 40. See Chapter 4, note 131.

the one who committed the act of killing, inflicting bodily harm, or destroying property or plundering to the same level of punishment as those who participated in or commanded the plot or played other important role. From this, he reasoned, "If, as the lower court says, the concept of concurrent crimes must always be inferred, there would be no need to single out the ringleader of the crime of insurrection from the rest. The punishment of the ringleader for the crime of insurrection during uprising under article 87 is death or life in prison with or without hard labor, and the punishment for the crime of murder for the purpose of insurrection under article 88 is also death or life in prison without or without hard labor." According to article 87, however,

> In the process of violent uprising for the crime of insurrection, "an individual who committed the act of killing or inflicting bodily harm" belongs . . . to the category of the people who were not the ringleader but participated in or commanded the plot, or engaged in other essential activities, and the punishment for them is death, life in prison, or five years or more in prison, with or without hard labor. So there is a possibility that he is punished only with imprisonment with or without hard labor for five years. If the principle of compound crimes were applied under article 40 of the Criminal Code which imposes the heaviest punishment, however, the defendant would always be subject to death or life in prison with or without hard labor. This gives rise to the problem of proportionality, as it contravenes article 87 (2) that provides the possibility of imprisonment with or without hard labor for not less than five years.[31]

"One may wonder why the punishment for murder committed for the purpose of insurrection under article 88 of the Criminal Code is harsher than the punishment of 'the one who committed killing or infliction of bodily harm' during an uprising under article 87 (2), with seemingly uneven results," wrote Justice Kim. The legislators "may have intended this differentiation with the consideration that in the crime of treasonous insurrection mob psychology tends to push the people to behave recklessly and the degree of reasonable expectation for a lawful behavior is lower than in the crime of murder for the purpose of insurrection," he explained. In other words, someone who was swept into the crowd and killed during an uprising could be seen as deserving less severe punishment than someone who specifically intended and committed the murder in order to instigate and carry out treasonous insurrection.

[31] S. Ct., 80To306 (Kim Yun-Haeng, J., dissenting).

From this, Justice Kim concluded that not only the lower court's decision finding the defendants guilty of treasonous insurrection but also its application of the principle of concurrent crimes were wrong. These legal errors, he pointed out, led to an unconscionable judgment in which the lower court declared Kim Chae-Kyu's subordinates guilty of playing a role in uprising during the crime of insurrection and simultaneously guilty of the crime of murder for the purpose of insurrection and then subsequently sentenced them to death as the punishment for the latter crime. Here, Justice Kim's effort to save the lives of Kim's subordinates seemed evident. This opinion, perhaps the most textualist and technical exposition of the Criminal Code provisions among the opinions presented in the case, rebuked the lower court for its careless and arbitrary application of law that resulted in impermissibly disproportionate punishments for the defendants. More broadly, it chided the courts, including the Supreme Court, for their tendency to allow prosecutors to seek cumulative convictions by piling up charges indiscriminately and to impose aggravated punishments. Unscrupulous application of the principle of conceptual concurrence was an issue that had long been a subject of grievances among defense lawyers. This concern was shared by Justice Sŏ Yun-Hong who disagreed with the majority opinion that some of Kim Chae-Kyu's aides were guilty for treasonous insurrection when they had simply followed the orders of their superiors without any knowledge or recognition that they were participating in allegedly treasonous acts.[32]

These various opinions revealed differences in jurisprudential position among the individual justices, even among the dissenters. Justice Min's opinion was the most hopeful in the sense that it called for the Court to take into account the changed political situation. It amounted to an argument that the Supreme Court could not punish the defendants for treason because the Yusin system all but ended with President Park's death and that, as long as there was national consensus to change the Constitution, the defendants should not be judged under the Yusin laws, including the treason laws. Justice Im's support for the right to resist, departing from his position in 1975, can also be seen as a result of his recognition of the changed times. Justice Yang and Justice Kim, while acknowledging the reality of new circumstances, preferred presenting their reasoning based on the laws and the Constitution currently in force.

[32] S. Ct., 80To306 (Sŏ Yun-Hong, J., dissenting).

Instead of taking a broad politically informed position, Justice Kim interpreted the relevant criminal law provisions narrowly in a way to turn it against the military courts' decision that the defendants were guilty of treason and deserved the death penalty. While he chose to rely strictly on the existing laws and precedents, he drew a conclusion diametrically opposed to the majority opinion.

Here, one may take a step back – digress briefly – to consider the 1980 opinions in the broader context of Korea's jurisprudential history. Some of the arguments proffered by the dissents drew from the Supreme Court precedents and individual opinions. It is interesting to note that the reasoning that defendants could not be punished under the treasonous insurrection law had its roots in the jurisprudence of the colonial court in Korea. Some sixty years earlier, the Chōsen Kōtō Hōin (Chosŏn High Court) under Japanese colonial rule refused to punish Korean protesters under the treasonous insurrection law for practically the same reason.[33] The defendants were prosecuted for their participation in the March First Independence Movement of 1919. The colonial High Court found that the defendants in these nationwide protests against colonial rule interfered with the exercise of the Japanese empire's sovereign power over its territories and violated the state laws, but that their actions, even undertaken with the purpose of disrupting the law and order, did not constitute an insurrection because they lacked the means to execute the purpose. Their peaceful protests "were not the means to accomplish the purpose of subverting the state's basic legal order"; even where the defendants assaulted people who tried to stop them, "such assaults cannot be seen as the means to execute the said purpose."[34] In short, the incidental violent acts that accompanied the protests were not sufficient to render the defendants guilty of treasonous insurrection.

33 *Chōsen Kōtō Hōin* [Choson High Court], judgment of September 18, 1919, *Chōsen Kōtō Hōin Hanketsuroku* [Chosŏn Kodŭng Pŏpwŏn Reports] (Seoul: Kōtō Hōin Shokika, 1908–1943), vol. 6 (Taishō 8), 290–295. For the background of the case, see Kim Sŭng-Il, "3–1 tongnip undong chŏnhu Ssun Wŏn ŭi Hanguk insik yŏngu" [A Study on Sun Yat-sen's Opinion of Korea Before and After the March First Independence Movement], *Hanguk tongnip undongsa yŏngu* 37 (2010), 104–108.

34 *Chōsen Kōtō Hōin Hanketsuroku*, vol. 6, 294–295.

The colonial High Court was under immense political pressure from the government general to convict the protesters as charged. Because the court decision was firmly based on the language of the law, however, the political authorities could not interfere with it, much to their chagrin. That incident is an example of the well-entrenched judicial tradition in Korea, dating to the colonial era, to respond to attempts of political intervention by tightly adhering to the language of the law. This jurisprudential attitude continued into the postcolonial period and into the authoritarian period.

Democracy Delayed

At its core, the 1980 case revealed the difficult task of the Supreme Court to implement the law without becoming its slave. Both the justices of the majority opinion and the dissenters agreed, more or less, that it was impossible to ignore the seemingly seismic shifts in politics that were occurring since President Park's death. The sad truth was that the changes many citizens anticipated failed to come through, as democracy movements were quickly suppressed by the military. It is unlikely that the bold arguments made by the dissenters would have been put forward but for the death of the president and the brief political thaw that followed, but the fact that they dared to express their opinions, under martial law, in defiance of the military regime that was crushing the demonstrators in Kwangju in a most abhorrent way, was nothing short of remarkable.

There is a little-known episode in the aftermath of the trial. Korean law allows defendants to request a new trial. The defense counsels submitted a posttrial motion to the Supreme Court on the same day of the judgment. The hearing was assigned to Justice Kim Yun-Haeng, who immediately issued notices to the parties to submit affidavits regarding the motion. Justice Kim was one of the dissenters, and the defense clung to the hope for a sort of miracle or, more realistically, as one of the lawyers recalled, desperately sought to delay execution.[35] All these efforts became moot, when Kim Chae-Kyu and his subordinates were hanged only four days after the verdict.[36]

[35] An Tong-Il, *10.26 ŭn ajikto sara itta*, 370.

[36] A photo reproduction of the court document signed by Justice Kim on May 22 is available in *Inkwŏn pyŏllon charyo chip*, vol. 6, 946.

The dissenters were soon dismissed from office *en masse*. The military junta was deeply displeased by what it regarded as a challenge to its power. Some in the military reportedly asked: "How can there be dissents in a trial of crimes against the state?" They allegedly blurted out: "we can destroy [the Supreme Court] with one cannonball."[37] The regime demanded that five dissenting justices tender resignation (see Figure 7.3). Their resignations were processed on August 9. Apparently General Chun kept his grudge against them. In September 1980, after he took office as president, Chun complained to Chief Justice Yi Yŏng-Sŏp that the Kwangju uprising would not have occurred if the Supreme Court had dismissed Kim Chae-Kyu's appeal more swiftly. "If the Court had acted expediently, all the troubles would have been avoided," Chun allegedly maintained.[38] In December, Chun reportedly uttered to Chief Justice Yi: "I know where those [dissenting] justices live" – that is, their personal safety was not guaranteed.[39] Kim Chae-Kyu's ill-fated motion for a new trial remained on the Supreme Court's docket for several months, formally dismissed by the Court on September 30.

A new constitution was drafted by the Legislative Council for National Security and was approved in a national referendum on October 22. The Constitution of the Fifth Republic took effect five days later. The Supplementary Rules to the new Constitution exempted the actions taken by the transitional legislative body from any potential legal challenge: Article 6 (3) stipulated that "laws and regulations passed by the State Protection Legislative Committee, along with judicial decisions, budgets, and other measures rendered in accordance with them, shall retain their force, and they are not subject to legal challenge or objection by reason of this Constitution or other causes." With this, any legal contest to the legitimacy of the new regime was precluded.

Martial law was lifted on January 25, 1981. A new round of judicial reappointments unfolded in April. 526 judges were reappointed, and thirty-seven were let go.[40] Among the eight justices who formed the majority in the 1980 trial, only three kept their posts (two had retired), and one of them, Justice Yu T'ae-Hŭng, became the new chief justice

37 *Pŏpcho 50 nyŏn yasa*, vol. 1, 947.
38 Ibid.
39 Ibid., 949–950.
40 *Yŏksa sogŭi sabŏppu*, 99.

Figure 7.3 Justices of the Supreme Court of Korea, 1980. Photo taken in June 1980, shortly before five justices were ousted. From left to right, front row: Justices Chu Chae-Hwang, Yi Yŏng-Sŏp (chief justice), Min Mun-Ki; second row: Kim Yun-Haeng, Im Hang-Chun, Yang Pyŏng-Ho, Han Hwan-Chin, An Pyŏng-Su, Yi Il-Kyu; back row: Kim T'ae-Hyŏn, Chŏng T'ae-Wŏn, Kim Yong-Ch'ŏl, Na Kil-Cho, Yu T'ae-Hŭng, Sŏ Yun-Hong, and Kim Ki-Hong. *Personal collection of the author.*

(1981–1986).[41] The other two ascended to the chief justiceship in succession: Kim Yong-Ch'ŏl (1986–1988) and Yi Il-Kyu (1988–1990) (see Figure 7.4).

The 1980 Constitution retained the constitutional review system of the 1972 Constitution: the Constitutional Committee had the power to review statutes, and the Supreme Court had the power to review executive decrees. As under the Fourth Republic, there was no single occasion that a law was reviewed by the Constitutional Committee during the seven years of the Fifth Republic. The Supreme Court conducted preliminary review of statutes on several occasions but decided that there was no dispute of constitutionality. Overall, the

41 Yu was the rapporteur for Kim Chae-Kyu's appeal at the petty bench level.

Figure 7.4 The Supreme Court Petty Bench, circa 1978. From left to right: Justices Yi Yŏng-Sŏp, Kim Yun-Haeng, Kim Yong-Ch'ŏl, and Yu T'ae-Hŭng. Justice Kim Yun-Haeng stepped down from the Court in 1980 following President Park's murder trial. The other three justices in this photo occupied the chief justiceship in turn between 1979 and 1988. *Personal collection of the author.*

new Constitution restored the protection of basic rights. Article 9 declared that "the state has the duty to affirm and guarantee the fundamental and *inviolable* human rights of individuals."[42] The inadmissibility of confessions obtained by force, a clause missing in the 1972 Constitution, was reinstated in Article 11. Changes like these turned the nature of constitutional legality in the Fifth Republic different from that in the Fourth Republic. The Chun regime was far from a democratic government, though, and grievous human rights violations took place. The judiciary needed to adapt to this new environment.

A case deliberated by the Supreme Court in January 1985 harked back to the Yusin years: it concerned the question of the residual or

42 My italics; this was a revision of Article 8 of the 1972 Constitution that stated "the state has the duty to guarantee to the fullest the fundamental human rights of citizens."

latent legal effect of the emergency decrees after the new Constitution came into force in 1980.

Judicial Ambivalence in the Post-Yusin Era

The 1985 case was a classic relic from the Yusin era.[43] It involved the prosecution of Attorney Kang Sin-Ok, whose court proceedings had remained dormant since 1975. Kang's ordeal started in August 1974 when he was charged with violating the emergency decrees, one day before they were lifted. In order to gauge the scope and nature of this peculiar case, it is necessary to examine the background in detail.

Kang was part of the small but tenacious band of lawyers who took up the defense of emergency decree violators. He was one of the attorneys for the students put on trial for their implications in the National Federation of Democratic Youth and Students.[44] On July 9, 1974, during the court martial at first instance, Kang, frustrated by what he saw as a blatant violation of procedural due process by the bench, blasted the military court comparing it to Nazi German courts. He bristled in his now famous closing argument:

> Whenever I find myself involved in cases like this one, I regret that I studied law. When I was a student, I was warned that law was the servant of power and the handmaiden of politics, yet I refused to believe it. But now I have reached the conclusion that law is indeed the servant of power and the handmaiden of politics. The prosecutors demand the death penalty or life imprisonment for these students because they violated Emergency Decree No. 4; the prosecutors claim that they are communists, when in reality they are only students concerned about our country. . . . [If these students are put

43 S. Ct., 74To3501 (*en banc*), January 29, 1985. For analysis, see Kim Ch'ŏl-Su, "Hŏnpŏp chejŏng kwa ku pŏmnyŏng ŭi hyoryŏk: pyŏnho kwŏn kwa pŏpchŏng moyok" [Constitutional Enactment and the Legal Force of Old Laws and Regulations: The Rights of the Counsel and the Contempt of Court], *Seoul Taehakkyo pŏphak* 29 (1988), 164–192.

44 See Hwang In-Ch'ŏl, "Kang Sin-Ok sakŏn ŭi kyŏnggwa" [The Unfolding of the Kang Sin-Ok Case] (first published in 1988), in Han In-Sŏp (ed.), *Chŏngŭi ŭi pŏp, yangsim ŭi pŏp, inkwŏn ŭi pŏp* [Law as Justice, Law as Conscience, Law as Human Rights] (Seoul: Pagyŏngsa, 2004), 259–272. Hwang was, along with Kang, one of the human rights lawyers.

to death] it would be nothing other than judicial murder. I am a grownup and am standing here as a defense attorney, which is my profession, but I would rather sit there in the defendant seats with the students. Unjust laws do not need to be obeyed; one can resist and fight against unjust laws and illegitimate laws. These students rose up against unjust laws. Imposing them on these patriotic students would irreversibly taint our history in the years to come.[45]

This ardent and daring speech was something that proved too much for the military court. After ignoring repeated warnings and orders from the bench to stop, Kang was slammed with contempt of court and, further, prosecuted for violating Emergency Decrees Nos. 1 and 4, which prohibited criticism of the decrees themselves. It was the first case in Korean history that an attorney was arrested for what he stated in the courtroom as part of a defense. How could defense arguments for those charged with a crime but not yet found guilty be a violation of the very same crime, protested Kang, to no avail. In September, Kang was sentenced to ten years in prison and suspension of civil rights for ten years. By finding him guilty, the military court plainly set aside both article 28 of the Military Court Act, which said "Judges, prosecutors, or defense counsels are not subject to disciplinary actions or any other penalty for acts performed in duty during trials," and article 345 (2), which said "Defendants and their legal counsels can state their opinions and are given the opportunity to make a final argument."

Sitting in prison, Kang, unfazed, penned his own appeals brief. This seventy-page brief was a stinging indictment of the emergency decrees, the legal system, and the entire Yusin order.[46] It was a veritable manifesto of natural law principles and the right to resist. Citing Sophocles' Antigone, St. Thomas Aquinas, Hugo Grotius, and many others, Kang argued that "citizens, who are the source of law," "do not have an obligation to obey unjust laws, and instead they have the right to resist them." According to Kang, Emergency Decrees Nos. 1 and 4 were unjust laws that violated natural law; these laws did not need to be observed because "they are already nonlaws." He even cited Lamoignon de Malesherbes, who defended Louis XVI in his ill-fated

[45] Cited in Kim Ch'ŏl-Su, "Hŏnpŏp chejŏng kwa kŭ pŏmnyŏng," 164–165.

[46] The handwritten text can be accessed at db.kdemocracy.or.kr/isad/view/00480565, Open Archives, Minjuhwa Undong Kinyŏm Saŏphoe (Korea Democracy Foundation). It is printed in Han (ed.), *Chongŭi ŭi pŏp*, 195–258.

trial during the French Revolution, to show that legal counsels had a sacrosanct duty to defend the accused.

Kang's eloquent and learned treatise likely simply aggravated the military judges. The Emergency High Court Martial promptly dismissed his appeal on October 11. Kang appealed to the Supreme Court the following month. The fact that as many as eighty-four attorneys signed their names as Kang's legal counsels in the appeals brief submitted to the Supreme Court showed how aggrieved the legal circles were by his conviction.[47]

An interesting twist of events followed. While his case was still pending at the Supreme Court, Kang was released on February 17, 1975, when President Park decided to free the emergency decree violators as a gesture of national harmony. Kang remained out of jail under the suspension of custody, but his case was still on the docket. This situation continued for ten years until 1985. Why did it take so long for the Supreme Court to act? Evidence shows that it was a deliberate choice by the Court. Kang was not the only one who was stuck in legal limbo for all those years, but his case was also unique.

As seen in Chapter 5, the Yusin system left behind a group of people called the "Orphans of Yusin."[48] When a defendant was charged with both security laws and emergency decrees and when the Supreme Court quashed the security law convictions and remanded the case, the emergency decree charges still remained open even after the decrees were abolished. Attorney Kang's case was different from those cases because he had not been charged with the National Security Act or the Anticommunist Act. This meant the Supreme Court did not have the option of remanding without ruling on the emergency decree charges as it had done in other cases. Kang's case posed a difficult situation for the Court. The only way the Supreme Court could prevent his conviction, which the prosecutors relentlessly sought, was to drag its feet and delay rendering a judgment, and this was precisely what it did. Lawyers familiar with the case later recalled that the justice who had been designated as the rapporteur of the case held off the government pressure long enough, before quietly "filing the case away into the

[47] S. Ct., 74To3501. The facsimile of the appeals brief, submitted on December 21, 1974, is available in *Inkwŏn pyŏllon charyo chip*, vol. 1, 661–697.

[48] See Chapter 5, note 105 and accompanying text.

cabinet."[49] Often the judges in noncustody political cases resorted to this strategy of putting off issuing a decision, hoping that government's attention to the case would fade away.

The government was bent on prohibiting Kang from practicing law. In June 1976, the Justice Ministry referred Kang to the attorney disciplinary committee to have his law license suspended on the grounds that he disgraced the legal profession by causing political scandals. The committee refused to take action, arguing that no disciplinary action could be taken before a final court decision. The Supreme Court was in no hurry. This was how Kang was able to continue practicing law while awaiting the conclusion of his case. It remains anyone's guess how the government would have reacted if the Supreme Court had acquitted Kang. With limited options at hand, the Court sat tight on the case, biding its time. As seen in the previous chapters, this was characteristic of Court behavior. It might not have been an example of the most courageous side of the highest court but was an effective one nonetheless. In Kang's case, it eventually worked.

Kang Sin-Ok Case (1985)

In 1984, long after the dismantling of the Yusin regime and the abolition of the emergency decrees, the Supreme Court decided to open the dusty file cabinet and act on the Kang case. On January 29, 1985, it quashed the verdict of the appellate court martial, holding that the emergency decrees no longer existed and thus his conviction needed to be vacated due to the absence of applicable law.[50] The Court remanded the case to the Seoul Appeals Court because, with the abolition of the decrees, the Emergency High Military Court no longer had jurisdiction over the case.[51] Upon this ruling, the Defense Ministry transferred the case record to the civilian court on February 27.[52] Three years later, the Seoul Appeals Court dismissed the emergency decree charges and

[49] *Pŏpcho 50 nyŏn yasa*, vol. 2, 125; Hong Sŏng-U, *Inkwŏn pyŏllon han sidae*, 96. The rapporteur of the case was Justice Kim Yun-Haeng. Hwang In-Ch'ŏl, "Kang Sin-Ok sakŏn," 271.

[50] S. Ct., 74To3501, January 29, 1985.

[51] *Tong-A Ilbo*, January 29, 1985.

[52] *Tong-A Ilbo*, March 8, 1985; *Tong-A Ilbo*, March 24, 1986.

found Kang not guilty for the contempt of court.[53] Kang had been sentenced under the inference of concurrent crimes, so the court entered a not-guilty verdict so as to bring the most favorable result for the defendant.

The judicial reasoning on the contempt charge deserves attention. The court affirmed that an attorney was not entitled to absolute immunity for conduct during proceedings. For example, engaging in political debate in a courtroom could subject the lawyer to a contempt charge. But in Kang's case the prosecution did not prove that he intended to threaten or obstruct the trial, wrote the court. Kang's invocation of the natural law theory, which arose in the postwar years in reaction to the positive law theory that had served as an instrument of the Nazi regime, was a legitimate exercise of his duties as a defense counsel, and his assertion of the right to resist, grounded on the legal philosophy recognizing universal and permanent justice, did not advocate violence. In short, the court held that Kang's conduct, even if it exceeded the conventional boundaries of the behavior expected of a lawyer, did not constitute the requisite elements of article 138 of the law of contempt of court.

Apart from its tortuous political background, the Kang Sin-Ok case was important because it concerned the question of the residual effect of the abolished laws. The court held that the emergency decree violation charges against Kang deserved dismissal because the law had already been abolished and there was no law to apply. After Kang's saga finally wrapped up, the aforementioned "Orphan" cases that had been left in suspension were resolved the same way. In Korea, the effect of abolished laws continued to be one of the most difficult legal questions because, simply, the laws and the constitutions changed so frequently.[54] Kang became the test case of the controversy that remained at the center of heated debates.[55]

The Supreme Court vacated Kang's conviction in 1985 on the grounds that the constitutional provision that had mandated the emergency decrees was abolished by a new constitution. Article 9 of the Supplementary Rules of the 1980 Constitution stated that "treaties

[53] Seoul App. Ct., 85No503, March 4, 1988. The text of the opinion is available in *Sabŏp haengjŏng* 29 (1988), 84–93. For an analysis, see Kim Ch'ŏl-Su, "Hŏnpŏp chejŏng kwa kŭ pŏmnyŏng," 179–184.

[54] *Tong-A Ilbo*, July 15, 1987.

[55] *Chung-Ang Ilbo*, November 3, 1982.

and laws existing at the time of the promulgation of this Constitution continue their force as long as they do not conflict with this Constitution." A determination of whether the preexisting law had continuing effect under the new constitution should be distinguished from a review of its constitutionality, noted the Court. This was a critical point. If the Court had treated its deliberation as constitutional review of the emergency decrees, it would have had to surmount Article 53 of the 1972 Constitution that placed them outside judicial power. By characterizing the issue as the question of the conflict of old and new laws, the Supreme Court determined it was unnecessary to consider the constitutionality of the emergency decrees. The Court then noted that the presidential power to issue emergency measures as provided in Article 53 was different from its equivalent in Article 51 of the 1980 Constitution. Since these two provisions were in conflict, concluded the Court, the emergency decrees issued under the 1972 Constitution had no continuing or latent force under the 1980 Constitution.

Three justices filed concurring opinions. Among them, Justice Yi Hoe-Ch'ang's opinion is of particular interest. He agreed with the majority that the emergency decrees had no continuing legal force but disagreed with its reasoning. According to Justice Yi, the majority's approach in which it compared Article 53 of the 1972 Constitution with Article 51 of the 1980 Constitution and declared the emergency decrees grounded on the former in violation of the current (1980) Constitution was ill focused and pointless, needlessly muddling the conclusion it had reached. The majority correctly defined the question in terms of the continuing effect of the old law, he argued, but then took the gratuitous step of assessing the emergency decrees from the standpoint of the current constitution. For Justice Yi, Article 51 of the 1980 Constitution had nothing to do with determining the validity of the emergency decrees under the 1972 Constitution. In his opinion, the Supreme Court clearly had the power to decide whether the laws deriving their force from the previous Constitution had continuing legal force. It was well established that an abolished law could be subject to constitutional review if there was sustained encroachment upon the individual's legal interest as a result of that law. However, this was qualitatively different from deciding the validity of the emergency decrees by judging them using the standard of the current Constitution. Yi wrote: "Determining whether the laws lost their effect after the abolition of the constitution is different from determining whether the laws were invalid when seen against the current constitution."

For Justice Yi, whether the emergency decrees conflicted with the 1980 Constitution was irrelevant because they were "constitution-suspending measures that limited the basic rights of the citizens" that were otherwise guaranteed in the same constitution.[56] He cited the Supreme Court's decision of 1978 that the emergency decrees had force equivalent to the Constitution.[57] The legality of the president's emergency powers under the Yusin Constitution was beyond dispute. All the Supreme Court in 1985 had to do, according to Yi, was to affirm the loss of the legal force of the emergency decrees upon the abrogation of the Yusin Constitution. Instead, the majority tried to prove that the decrees were invalid because they conflicted with the Fifth Republic's Constitution and, by doing so, inadvertently turned its deliberation into a de facto constitutional review.[58] This unwarranted approach, implied Yi, approximated judicial presumptiveness and complacency, illustrating the Court's penchant for activism. He stated:

> The basic ideals of a constitutional state require that all state actions and state functions conform to its constitution and laws. Determination of their legality in principle belongs to the judiciary. But it is not desirable for the courts, which do not have political accountability, to conduct a review of highly political acts such as governing, disregarding the political purposiveness or legitimateness, and to let policy decisions be swayed by the court judgments. That can entail serious dangers that the judiciary becomes entangled with political questions and jeopardizes its neutrality and independence by inviting political encroachment upon its own power. This is why the courts must restrain themselves from exercising their power of reviewing those governing acts of a highly political nature and must exclude them from the subjects of review.[59]

Justice Yi warned that the Supreme Court in 1985 risked jeopardizing its independence, first, by failing to affirm that the emergency decrees had been mandated by the Yusin Constitution and, second, by glossing over the fact that under the Yusin Constitution the Supreme Court did not have power to review their constitutionality. By bypassing the

[56] S. Ct., 74To3501 (Yi Hoe-Ch'ang, J., concurring).
[57] S. Ct, 78To813, May 23, 1978.
[58] Kim Ch'ŏl-Su, "Hŏnpŏp chejŏng kwa kŭ pŏmnyŏng," 187.
[59] S. Ct., 74To3501 (Yi Hoe-Ch'ang, J., concurring).

explicit provision of Article 53 (4) – "Emergency measures ... shall not be subject to judicial deliberations thereon" – the majority left the doors open to the misrepresentation of the constitutional and political reality during the Yusin period. The courts naturally had a tendency to stress that they had the right and duty to oppose legislated injustice. Under irregular political situations, however, such ideals could lead them to compromise their own authority and autonomy, argued Justice Yi. His point was unmistakable. By treating the 1972 Constitution as a normal, regular constitution, one inevitably faced problems, because it contained provisions that should not have been part of a normal, regular constitution. Unjust laws such as the emergency decrees should not have been included in the constitution but, unfortunately, they were and, hence, were constitutional. Then it became clear that the emergency decrees lost legal force not because they were unconstitutional but because the Yusin Constitution that had granted the president exceptional powers to issue such decrees was replaced by a new constitution. In order to find the emergency decrees unconstitutional, it would be necessary to find that the Yusin Constitution itself was invalid, but doing so would be outside judicial power. Trying to circumvent this problem, concluded Justice Yi, the Supreme Court might end up politicizing the judicial process.

Three years later, when Attorney Kang's case was tried at the Seoul Appeals Court in 1988, the defense claimed that the emergency decrees were "naturally void" because they "destroyed the democratic republic's fundamental constitutional order." The appellate court rejected this argument and instead embraced the "naturally abolished" theory, heeding the interpretation of the Supreme Court and in particular Justice Yi's argument.[60] Yi's concurring opinion in 1985 was a tour de force, cutting through the jumbled political and legal uncertainties surrounding the Yusin legal order. His insights shed important light on the judicial role in the evolving ideals of the rule of law and judicial independence in Korea.

Rule of Law and Judicial Independence

The basic idea of the rule of law is that law exists as a protection against arbitrary actions of the state. Legal theorists have formulated the

[60] Kim Ch'ŏl-Su, "Hŏnpŏp chejŏng kwa kŭ pŏmnyŏng," 188–189.

notion of the rule of law in two separate categories, a formal version and a substantive version.[61] The formal or procedural conception of the rule of law focuses more on the form of the law and less on the content of the law. It requires that laws comprise rules that are clear, stable, neutral, and generally prospective, that laws be consistently enforced, and that official action match the declared rules. According to Joseph Raz, "conformity to the rule of law is an inherent value of laws,"[62] and "[t]he law to be law must be capable of guiding behaviour."[63] The substantive understanding of the rule of law goes further and views individual human rights and justice as necessary components of the law. The rule of law is construed as a framework in which individual rights are upheld against arbitrary government action. Thomas Carothers has defined the rule of law as "a system in which the laws ... enshrine and uphold the political and civil liberties that have gained status as universal human rights over the last half-century."[64] This definition recognizes intrinsic qualities of law – commitment to promoting justice and equity and protection of human lives – and emphasizes that the government must be subject to those general norms of law.[65] It views the formal conception of the rule of law as inadequate, as its focus on procedural elements may shortchange substantive justice and freedom.

Recently, legal theorists have pointed out that the notion of the rule of law is not always perceived and interpreted in an identical way in various legal traditions and cultural contexts. Some have raised questions about the coherency of the notion of the rule of law itself.[66] A modern state exists to meet a variety of purposes in addition to the promotion of individual liberty, and law is an instrument to achieve those goals. Governmental power, if monopolized, turns to dictatorship, and therefore it is essential to separate powers in a constitution. But since the government serves other purposes as well, there can be additional constitutional values, the efficacy of which becomes just as

[61] Brian Z. Tamanaha, *On the Rule of Law: History, Politics, Theory* (Cambridge: Cambridge University Press, 2004), 91–92.

[62] Raz, "The Rule of Law," 225.

[63] Ibid., 226.

[64] Thomas Carothers, "The Rule of Law Revival," *Foreign Affairs* 77 (1998), 96.

[65] See Lon Fuller, *The Morality of Law*, 2nd rev. ed. (New Haven: Yale University Press, 1969), 157–159.

[66] Martin Loughlin, "The Rule of Law in European Jurisprudence," Study 512/2009, European Commission for Democracy through Law (Venice Commission), CDL-DEM(2009)006, 1–18.

important.[67] Misuse or abuse of constitutional and legislative power is of secondary relevance here as far as a certain constitutional state form had been accepted. Carl Schmitt stated: "[M]isuse of the legislative power and of the law-making process must remain out of consideration in practical terms, because otherwise a differently constituted state form ... would become immediately necessary."[68]

In this perspective, the distinction regularly drawn between rule by law and the rule of law becomes less tenable.[69] One tends to regard the rule of law and constitutionalism as innate ideals, for which the judiciary is the ultimate guardian, while viewing rule by law as equivalent to dominance by repressive laws. But the rule of law, aimed to block an arbitrary government that threatens individual liberty, is not intrinsically different from rule by law in that, as Martin Loughlin has put it, both accept "a concept of law as a system of rules and then to elaborate the institutional conditions that protect the integrity of that rule system."[70] It has been pointed out that the formal rule of law in this sense is not incompatible with dictatorship.[71] Even under an authoritarian rule of law, the regime's commitment to legal stability, transparency, predictability, consistency, and certainty is not less rational or equitable than a democratic government's commitment. Legal norms and institutions can "temper" state agents, "notably the manner in which they wield power," and thus the authoritarian rule of law places "a modicum of institutional limits" on autocratic power."[72]

What separates the formal from the substantive rationality and also the rule of law from rule by law is, then, that the ideas of the ideal rule of law and legality presume that the government should not only be ruled by means of law but also be subject to general norms of conduct – moral qualities – implicit in the idea of law. But this contouring of the rule of law with moral values makes inadequate reference to

67 Raz, "The Rule of Law," 210.

68 Carl Schmitt, *Legality and Legitimacy*, 1932, trans. Jeffrey Seitzer (Durham: Duke University Press, 2004), 14.

69 See Ginsburg and Moustafa (eds.), *Rule by Law*. The essays in this edited volume reject the conventional wisdom that the rule of law exists only in democratic regimes.

70 Loughlin, "The Rule of Law," 14.

71 See Robert Barros, "Dictatorship and the Rule of Law: Rules and Military Power in Pinochet's Chile," in José María Maravall and Adam Przeworski (eds.), *Democracy and the Rule of Law* (Cambridge: Cambridge University Press, 2003), 188–219.

72 Meierhenrich, *The Remnants of the Rechtsstaat*, 231, 248.

more general constitutional values that could derive from democracy.[73] Raz stated it succinctly when he wrote:

> Like other instruments, the law has a specific virtue which is morally neutral in being neutral as to the end to which the instrument is put. It is the virtue of efficiency; the virtue of the instrument as an instrument. For the law this virtue is the rule of law. Thus the rule of law is an inherent virtue of the law, but not a moral virtue as such.[74]

It must be insisted that

> the rule of law is just one of the virtues which a legal system may possess and by which it is to be judged. It is not to be confused with democracy, justice, equality (before the law or otherwise), human rights of any kind or respect for persons or for the dignity of man.[75]

Therefore, warned Raz: "Sacrificing too many social goals on the altar of the rule of law may make the law barren and empty."[76]

Some scholars have argued that constitutionalized emergency laws can be seen – counterintuitively – as positive elements for the rule of law. According to Albert H. Y. Chen, emergency power presupposes the distinction between normalcy and states of exception, and it thus affirms the requirements of liberal constitutional democracy as the norm.[77] Compared with an authoritarian or totalitarian constitution, Chen contends, "a liberal-democratic constitution that contains emergency provisions is still the lesser of two evils" because "the struggle for democracy can be sustained and propelled forward by the idea that it is the struggle for return to normalcy."[78] Indeed, one can argue that legal repression is better than illegal repression, in an absurdly candid kind of way, and that the operation of a constitution with a weakened guarantee of liberty is better than having no constitution or a sham constitution. Repressive law, no matter how reprehensible, follows the rules on the surface. Quoting Raz anew: "It is of the essence of law to guide behaviour through rules and courts in charge of their application."[79] Where the

[73] Loughlin, "The Rule of Law," 14.
[74] Raz, "The Rule of Law," 226.
[75] Ibid., 211.
[76] Ibid., 229.
[77] Albert H. Y. Chen, "Emergency Powers, Constitutionalism and Legal Transplants: The East Asian Experience," in Ramraj and Thiruvengadam (eds.), *Emergency Powers in Asia*, 56.
[78] Ibid., 86, 88.
[79] Raz, "The Rule of Law," 226.

state exercises power in a truly arbitrary manner, there is no need for rules regarding emergency power. Barros, commenting on Chile, has argued that the judiciary's defense of legality under Pinochet "may have prevented a spillover of arbitrary power beyond the realm of emergency punitive control."[80]

These insights can be applied to the role of the courts in Korea. President Park claimed that the new constitutional order aimed to establish a "Korean-style democracy." Whether this notion of Korean democracy was envisioned as a temporary means to achieve a more conventional form of democracy or was crafted merely as an end in itself is open to debate, but one has noted that the Yusin system's emphasis on "this Constitution" appeared almost as a disclaimer or even an apology.[81] All the care the government took to create an "aversive" constitution attested to its ostensible respect for the rule of law.[82] Formal legal rationality and substantive irrationality commingled, and the clash of the formal and the substantive principles of justice – "insoluble conflict," according to Max Weber – diminished.[83] Regardless of how much duplicity was involved in the regime's representation of the threat from the North, the subject of national survival had the effect of blurring the lines between formal and substantive and between rational and irrational. Under the confused state of exception, approved in referendum, it was important for the courts to sustain the impartial legal platform and contain emergency powers within the bounds of the constitution.

A precondition for impartial administration of law is judicial independence. Like the rule of law, judicial independence can be formulated into two different types: one negative and one positive. Negative judicial independence refers to the institutional capacities of courts to act free from external pressures or influences, while positive judicial independence refers to an individual judge's ability to promote justice.[84] A positive conception of judicial independence ultimately involves

80 Barros, "Courts out of Context," 179.

81 See Chapter 6, note 45 and accompanying text.

82 Scheppele, "Aspirational and Aversive Constitutionalism."

83 Weber, "Economy and Law (The Sociology of Law)," in *Max Weber: Economy and Society*, vol. 2, 893.

84 Pamela S. Karlan, "Two Concepts of Judicial Independence," *Southern California Law Review* 72 (1998–1999), 535–558; Karlan, "Judicial Independences," *Georgetown Law Journal* 95 (2007), 1041–1059. Karlan drew from Isaiah Berlin's two concepts of liberty. Berlin, *Two Concepts of Liberty* (1958), reprinted in *Four Essays on Liberty* (1969), 118–172.

subjective judgments, which is why it can come in conflict with the precept of negative judicial independence. The increasing emphasis in contemporary discourses on the former tended to turn the attention away from the danger of the latter and the institutional reality of the courts. The backlash against the judiciary of the 1970s derived in large part from the sentiment that the courts did not fight for independence and instead it was given to them as a result of the struggles by the individuals who were the very victims of the courts. This idea presumed that the judiciary had a foothold from which to check against legislated injustice, but it is worth asking whether there was an institutional or legal framework that would have allowed the judges to launch opposition to arbitrary power. Whether judges are independent, free from pressures or threats, is an empirical question.[85] The rule of law and the independence of judges are mutually reinforcing but also contingent. The state of the judiciary in the post-1987 years highlights this point.

Scholars have identified three sources of threat to judicial independence: from politics, from markets, and from civil society.[86] In Korea, since the late 1980s, threat to the courts from the state has subsided, although not completely. General confidence in the achievement of democratic governance led to emphasis on the positive liberty of judges, with less concern about the external control of the court. The biggest obstacle to judicial independence has been perceived as internal bureaucratic control of judges' careers by their superiors, and various legal reforms have focused on establishing an institutional structure that would ensure the ability of the judges to decide cases in accordance with the law without worrying about their careers.[87] The second kind of threat, from markets, refers to corruption. Judicial corruption that plagued many developing countries has been, at least until recently, rare in Korea. The market factor is relevant to the judge's desire for career advancement. Finally, the rising rhetoric of

[85] Adriaan Bedner, "An Elementary Approach to the Rule of Law," *The Hague Journal on the Rule of Law* 2 (2010), 69. See Peter H. Russell and David O'Brien (eds.), *Judicial Independence in the Age of Democracy: Critical Perspectives from around the World* (Charlottesville: University Press of Virginia, 2001).

[86] Terence C. Halliday, Lucien Karpik, and Malcolm M. Feeley (eds.), "Introduction – The Legal Complex in Struggles for Political Liberalism," in *Fighting for Political Freedom: Comparative Studies of the Legal Complex and Political Liberalism* (Oxford: Hart Publishing, 2007), 1–40.

[87] See Tom Ginsburg, "Korea and the Reform of the Northeast Asian Legal Complex," in Kim (ed.), *The Spirit of Korean Law*, 233–260.

participatory democracy can impose a burden on judges as well. Korean judges have long operated in a relatively cloistered judicial structure, largely free from the pressure to explain their decisions other than in law. But expectations are fast changing. The increasingly assertive public can come at odds with judicial independence in particular because of the tendency in Korea to view the "sentiments of the people" as equivalent to sovereign democratic will. Placing untempered expressions of the popular mood above the legitimate democratic judicial process risks exposing judges not only to volatile whim but also to old threats to their security from a populist government. Ascertaining the proper ideal of judicial role becomes all the more critical in the midst of deepening ideological divides in modern Korean politics.

Judicial Activism and Restraint

Continuing the preceding discussions framed in juxtaposition, one can argue that historically there are two related but distinct ideals of adjudication: the first focuses on the promotion of judicial economy and efficiency, the second on the protection of individual rights. Put simply, these are the separate functions lodged in the ordinary courts and constitutional courts respectively. Merryman and Vigoriti explained that, from the early nineteenth century, ordinary courts in the civil law system in Europe had obligations that were essentially nonconstitutional in nature. The courts of cassation, the highest courts, embraced a politically neutral, conservative position in the area of civil rights.[88] Their primary task was to determine the correct interpretation of statutes. They tended to apply even questionable statutes, expressing doubts but citing their duty to apply the law. Lacking the power to determine the constitutionality of legislation, and charged with broad jurisdictions comprising civil, commercial, and criminal justice, these courts were preoccupied with ensuring the uniform application of the law rather than implementing constitutional objectives and ideals.[89] The courts in Korea before 1987 belonged to this tradition in Europe, imbued with the spirit of judicial restraint. However, the antithetical notions of judicial restraint and activism may prove yet inadequate to

[88] Merryman and Vigoriti, "When Courts Collide," 681.
[89] Ibid.

explain the complex situation of the Korean judiciary. For one thing, the Supreme Court's basic position of maintaining distance from the political process was prompted by as much the spirit of restraint as the needs to weather the frequent and drastic alterations of the constitutions and laws.

One may find it ironic that Justice Yi Hoe-Ch'ang once voiced an eloquent call for judicial activism.[90] In a famous speech given in 1987, Yi, who had just retired from the Supreme Court, stated: "The courts must actively interpret and apply law in order to promote justice ... and exercise the function of creating law through the interpretation of law." He argued that the political question doctrine, the idea that the judiciary ought to defer to the executive branch for matters of a fundamentally policy-making nature – the grounds for judicial restraint – must be narrowly defined. These remarks were widely regarded as a plea from this respected jurist for a more active judicial role. Yet Justice Yi did not advocate a blind activist position that would prod the courts to go beyond what was needed and to enter the terrain of judicial contest for political legitimacy. He opposed judges' submissive passivism or unjustifiable restraints, that is, "closing eyes to justice."[91] Interpreting law in an arbitrary manner or in a way driven by political preferences was not judicial activism. He had already expounded in 1985 that, while the view that the judiciary must always exercise voluntary restraint in policy questions was wrong, "if the judiciary's intervention in political matters is only going to create confusion, instead of fulfilling the purpose of reviewing the legitimacy of law, then restraint is required."[92]

What concerned Justice Yi most was the prospect that the courts' involvement in political decision-making would jeopardize their neutrality and independence. Judicial complicity with injustice can take place in two different ways: judges can quietly enforce unjust laws and take shelter under legal positivism; or they can liberally interpret laws and resort to a teleological method in accord with the regime's political goals. It is part of the ongoing debate over whether too little or too much positivism poses the greater danger. Emphasis on fundamental

[90] Speech of March 28, 1987, published in Yi Hoe-Ch'ang, "Sapŏp ŭi chŏkkŭk chuŭi: t'ŭkhi kibonkwŏn pojang kinŭng kwa kwallŏn hayŏ" [Judicial Activism: Focusing on Its Function of Protecting Fundamental Rights], *Seoul Taehakkyo pŏphak* 28 (1987), 147–161.

[91] Ibid., 148–149.

[92] S. Ct., 74To3501 (Yi Hoe-Ch'ang, J., concurring). See this chapter, note 59.

rights tends to place the subjective criterion of justice over legal certainty; in this framework, legal validity is to be tested by certain minimum standards of justice, presumably by the court. Otherwise, adhering to the standards of substantive justice, while desirable and necessary, can lead to a situation in which judges apply ill-defined, subjective, and potentially arbitrary criteria of justice and the courts exercise undue power. As Justice Yi wrote,

> When the law does not conform to the belief of most citizens and the judge's own sense of justice, the judge can take a conservative stance and try to limit that law's effect by reducing its scope of application. This approach should not be criticized for being passive. As long as the judge does not do it in an arbitrary way, it should be viewed not as judicial restraint but as judicial activism.[93]

He specifically had in mind "the agony of the judges who were faced with the predicament of having to enforce Emergency Decree No. 9 under the Yusin Constitution." He compared it to the dilemma of the antislavery judges who had to enforce the Fugitive Slave Act.[94]

This exhortation came from a judge who spent much of his judicial career under authoritarian rule. It was a sharp indictment of the authoritarian regime and of the feckless and reckless legislature. There is a certain truth – rather an irony – to the observation that the judiciary, the ultimate guardian of the rule of law, is independent only to the extent that it is free from elected officials. Justice Yi's call for measured judicial activism, in reality a call for reasoned restraint, led one to wonder: if the Supreme Court in the 1970s had refused to enforce the laws because they were repressive and were against substantive justice, would it not have undermined the fundamental rationale of legality and the rule of law? Citing Isaiah Berlin, Pamela S. Karlan has warned about "having too unconditional a commitment to the most positive forms of judicial independence," because "these can trench substantially on other important values. Sometimes, factors that look like structural threats to judicial independence from the positive perspective can be equally explicable as structural *protections* for other values that an unqualified embrace of judicial independence undervalues."[95] It would not be too farfetched to argue that the Korean judiciary's reluctance to inject its own will played an important part for sustaining its independence.

93 Yi Hoe-Ch'ang, "Sapŏp ŭi chŏkkŭk chuŭi," 149.
94 Ibid.
95 Karlan, "Judicial Independences," 1043. Emphasis in original.

Democratization and New Judicial Ideals

In 1987, mass demonstrations, known as the June Democracy Movement, compelled the government to make political concessions. Roh Tae Woo (No T'ae-U), Chun's handpicked successor and chair of the ruling Democratic Justice Party, caved in and called for direct presidential election. The entire length of Chun's rule had been marked by torrents of popular protest. The unprecedented violence his regime perpetrated on its own people during the Kwangju uprising irreparably tainted its legitimacy. His so-called social purification campaigns, introduced by the enactment of the Social Protection Law in December 1980, caused serious human rights violations.[96] Still, one must acknowledge that state violence, even at its peak, was not near the level of violence in authoritarian regimes elsewhere in Asia or Latin America.[97] Of course, if Chun became more restrained in using violence after Kwangju and especially toward the end of his regime, it was simply because he had no choice. During the 1980s, the state policies that promoted industrialization and economic prosperity led to the rise of the middle class who, more confident than ever, were no longer willing to put up with the coercive government apparatus.

The edifice maintaining simultaneously the prerogative and normative states became untenable once South Korea had achieved remarkable economic development. The uniquely Korean situation of the intertwinement of national security, economic progress, and state control had upheld the authoritarian system, but economic success and political oppression could go together in Korea only for a while. A liberal democratic constitution was approved in a national referendum on October 27. A free direct presidential election was held on December 16, and Roh was elected president for a nonrenewable five-year term (1988–1993). The Constitution of the Sixth Republic took effect on February 25, 1988. The Constitutional Court opened its doors.

As democracy took root, the time was ripe for the Korean people to reflect on the past and try to come to terms with the injustices committed under the authoritarian regimes.

[96] See *Yŏksa sogŭi sabŏppu*, 437–438; Lee, *The Making of Minjung*, 46–47. A part of the law was found unconstitutional in 1989, and the entire law was abolished in 2005.

[97] According to Greitens, Chun's rule was less violent than has commonly been presumed and became further attenuated later on. Greitens, *Dictators and Their Secret Police*, Chapter 8.

8 Democracy and Travails of Judges, 1987 to the Present

The promulgation of the Constitution in 1987 has been hailed as a defining moment in Korean history, putting to an end the long authoritarian rule and the moribund streak of constitutional justice. Constitutional adjudication became the primary means through which to enforce fundamental norms of individual rights and liberal democracy. The three decades of the activities of the Constitutional Court, operating in tandem with the ordinary courts under the Supreme Court, have been instrumental in dismantling the remnants of illiberal laws and addressing the public demand for transitional justice.[1] A working definition of transitional justice is "a range of approaches that societies undertake to reckon with legacies of widespread or systematic human rights abuse as they move from a period of violent conflict or oppression towards peace, democracy, the rule of law, and respect for individual and collective rights."[2] Civil society lobbied to redress the wrongs perpetrated by the past regimes, and the successive governments responded in earnest.

Corrective justice against the abuse of state power focused, among others, on the judicial record. Investigation was entrusted to government-appointed commissions that exercised quasi-legal power. As individual incidents of human rights violations came to light, judicial conduct in those cases came under scrutiny. Recriminations against the courts, and public bashing against individual judges for the

[1] The Constitutional Court has not struck down the National Security Act but significantly restricted the scope of certain provisions so as to reduce the chilling effect on freedoms of speech and expression. Const. Ct., 89HŏnKa113, April 2, 1990; Const. Ct., 89HŏnMa240, January 16, 1997.

[2] Definition by the International Center for Transitional Justice, at www.ictj.org/about/transitional-justice. See Ruti G. Teitel, *Transitional Justice* (Oxford: Oxford University Press, 2000). For a Korean perspective, see Han In-Sŏp, "Hoehan kwa oyok ŭi kwagŏ rŭl paro chabŭryŏmyŏn: sabŏppu ŭi kwagŏ ch'ŏngsan ŭl wihayŏ" [To Correct the Past Filled with Regrets and Shame: For the Cleansing of the Judiciary's Past], *Seoul Taehakkyo pŏphak* 46 (2005), 84–120.

decisions they had rendered, raised the question of how to balance the calls for judicial accountability with judicial autonomy.

Amid the surge of democratic sensibilities, the courts themselves displayed growing activism with emphasis on a natural law standard of normativity. Previously, the prevailing view in the ordinary courts was that the role of the judge was to apply predetermined norms and ensure legal certainty. From the 1990s, however, heightening aspiration for substantive justice came to overshadow the traditional legal positivism. The shift was witnessed in many retrials. The most notable examples of evolving jurisprudence were cases involving the emergency decrees from the Yusin period. The Supreme Court in the 1970s held that it did not have the power to review the constitutionality of the presidential emergency measures. That was the continued position of the courts in the subsequent decades. In 2010, however, the Supreme Court declared that Emergency Decree No. 1 was unconstitutional. In 2013, the Constitutional Court followed suit, striking down Emergency Decrees Nos. 1, 4, and 9. In 2014, the Supreme Court ruled both Emergency Decrees Nos. 9 and 4 unconstitutional.[3]

These decisions had been much anticipated and were acclaimed by many as pivotal steps for confronting the Yusin government's infringement of the citizens' fundamental rights. At the same time, they were met with concerns by others who saw in the court reasoning signs of the politicization of the judiciary. Divided reactions of the observers aside, it seems safe to suggest that in these decisions each court presented itself as charting a new direction in jurisprudence, with greater attention to judicial conscience and accountability. They also reflected the global trend of the constitutionalization of law, in which the constitutional text became the central instrument applicable in all aspects of adjudication as well as the administration of justice.[4] Statutes are routinely applied and interpreted on the basis of constitutional principles and provisions, in both substance and procedure. In Korea, constitutional law has thoroughly permeated politics, and ensuring the compatibility of law with the higher normative order of the constitution has become a core task for both the Supreme Court and

[3] See Chapter 1, note 36.

[4] Lech Garlicki, "Constitutional Courts versus Supreme Courts," *International Journal of Constitutional Law* 5 (2007), 65.

the Constitutional Court. This chapter examines some thirty years of evolving constitutional justice since 1987.

Transitional Justice and Justice in Transition

The Special Act concerning the May 18 Democratization Movement, enacted in December 1995 under the Kim Young Sam government (1993–1998), had the objective of bringing to justice those who waged military coups in 1979–1980 and committed atrocities during the Kwangju uprising in 1980.[5] Under President Kim Dae Jung's government (1998–2003), the scope of transitional justice extended to the Park Chung Hee era. In January 2000, the Act for Restoring the Honor of Democratization Movement Participants and Providing Compensation defined the "democratization movement" as "activities that contributed to the establishment of the democratic constitutional order and resurrection and enhancement of freedoms and rights of people by resisting authoritarian rule since August 7, 1969, that disturbed the basic liberal democratic order and violated people's fundamental rights guaranteed by the Constitution."[6] The specific date designated in the law was when the bill to revise the 1962 Constitution was passed, paving the way for President Park's third presidential term. The Act explicitly recognized the right to resist authoritarian rule.

Transitional justice measures met procedural challenges. The Special Act of 1995 targeted two former presidents, Chun Doo Hwan and Roh Tae Woo, and their subordinates implicated in the military coups.[7] Since legal proceedings against the alleged offenses by Chun and Roh had been time-barred, the Special Act waived the normal statute of limitations to allow prosecution. The defense contested its legality, arguing that the Act was enacted *ex post facto* to single out and punish a specific group of people in violation of the equal protection clause. After much legal wrangling, the Constitutional Court upheld the law in

5 5.18 Minjuhwa Undong Tŭng e Kwanhan T'ŭkpyŏlpŏp [Act No. 10182].

6 Minjuhwa Undong Kwallŏnja Myŏnghoe Hoebok mit Posang Tŭng e Kwanhan Pŏmnyul [Act No. 6123]. Cho, "Transitional Justice in Korea," 582–584.

7 See Han In-Sŏp, "Kukka pŏngnyŏk e taehan pŏpchŏk ch'aegim mit p'ihae hoebok: 5.18 minjuhwa undong ŭi pŏpchŏk haegyŏl ŭl chungsim ŭro" [Legal Liability and the Recovery of Damages for State Violence: Legal Solutions for the 5.18 Democracy Movement], *Seoul Taehakkyo pŏphak* 43 (2002), 187–237.

February 1996.[8] The tribunal reasoned that under extraordinary circumstances it was obliged to grant exceptions. The public interest in punishing the offenders who committed crimes that were "destructive of the constitutional order" outweighed the necessity of legal stability. A retroactive application of penal laws should be allowed for the purpose of substantive justice, held the Court.[9]

The two former presidents were convicted by the Seoul District Court in August 1996, and the decision was upheld by the Seoul Appeals Court in December.[10] Both courts ruled that the statute of limitations for the crimes against the constitutional order was lawfully suspended and that the prosecution was procedurally free of errors. The sternly worded Appeals Court opinion was a veritable discourse of history, meticulously documenting the regime's illegal usurpation of the state power that entailed the bloody suppression of the Kwangju uprising.[11] The Supreme Court affirmed the following year.[12] A scholar defended retroactive legislation, arguing that deviation from normal legal procedures was necessary in order to satisfy "the popular sense of justice" because "the public was angered by such legal technicalities"[13] and the "government had to consider the people's power."[14] While the result of the court decision was widely welcomed, assertions like the above implying that the legitimate judicial process should comply with the desires and wishes of the people and legal stability should give way to popular mood elicited uneasiness among observers. Both the Constitutional Court and the Supreme Court took pains to stress that their solutions were exceptional – "very limited and special" – for special cases like this one.

During the first decade of the twenty-first century, the focus of transitional justice shifted from punishing political leaders to addressing the plights of individual victims. The government-established

[8] Const. Ct., 96HŏnKa2 and 96HŏnPa7 & 13 (consol.), February 16, 1996.

[9] See Chaihark Hahm and Sung Ho Kim, "Challenge and Change in East Asia: Constitutionalism on Trial in South Korea," *Journal of Democracy* 16 (2005), 32–33.

[10] Seoul Dist. Ct., 95KoHap1228, August 26, 1996; Seoul App. Ct., 96No1892, December 16, 1996.

[11] The court was composed of Judges Kwŏn Sŏng (presiding), Kim Chae-Bok, and Yi Ch'ung-Sang.

[12] S. Ct., 96To3376, April 17, 1997.

[13] Cho, "Transitional Justice in Korea," 586, 588.

[14] Ibid., 585.

commissions scrutinized judicial cases that allegedly involved the illegal exercise of state power and recommended retrials. A number of judicial decisions rendered in the 1970s and 1980s were reopened. In January 2007, the Commission for the Investigation of Past History compiled a list of 589 cases, involving 1,412 individuals who had been prosecuted for violating the emergency decrees. The list was leaked to a progressive newspaper, which published it along with the names of 492 judges who presided over those trials. It created uproar on both sides of the political spectrum. The newspaper justified its decision to publish the list, declaring that "historical judgment is above legal judgment" and that "we cannot grant absolution to those judges" as they failed to fulfill "historical responsibility."[15] Conservative media, on the other hand, expressed fear that the publication of the judges' names, not accompanied by the facts of the cases or court opinions, presupposed judicial wrongdoing, thereby subjecting them to a "trial by public opinion."[16]

It is hardly an exaggeration that the courts were saddled with the burden of the past. There is reason to believe that the Supreme Court felt the need to break from its reputation as a relic of illiberal rule. Its decision in 2010 that found the emergency decree unconstitutional, along with the Constitutional Court's decision three years later, resonated with a sense of justice but also engendered serious questions about constitutionalism, legality, and judicial duty.

Judicial Turnabout: Revisiting Emergency Decrees

Since the enactment of the Democracy Act in 2000, a series of security law cases were reopened. Retrial of emergency decree cases followed. The case that reached the Supreme Court in 2010 involved a Mr. O Chong-Sang. Mr. O had been convicted of violating Emergency Decree No. 1 and the Anticommunist Act. He allegedly uttered in May 1974: "Our country is corrupt; how can it be called a democratic system? Under the Yusin Constitution, democracy cannot develop. It would be better if we sold our country to Japan or if our country collapsed and became part of North Korea. Then at least we would have enough to eat."[17] This remark was found to amount to

[15] *Hangyŏrye Sinmun*, January 30, 2007.

[16] *Tong-A Ilbo*, January 31, 2007; *Chosŏn Ilbo*, January 31, 2007.

[17] S. Ct., 2010To5986.

supporting the North Korean regime and unlawfully criticizing the Constitution. The Emergency Court Martial sentenced him to three years of imprisonment, affirmed by the Emergency High Court Martial. The Supreme Court dismissed the appeal in 1975.[18] Mr. O was not among the prisoners released in February 1975 because he had also been convicted under the Anticommunist Act. Some thirty years later, in October 2007, the Truth and Reconciliation Commission reported that Mr. O had been subjected to police brutality while in custody. The following February, he moved for retrial.

In Korean law, retrial is granted "where, in regard to a person pronounced guilty, clear evidence has come to light that would require a judgment of not guilty or dismissal of the charges, or, in regard to a person sentenced to punishment, clear evidence has come to light that would result in the vacation of punishment or prove an offense less severe than the one in the original sentence."[19] The courts grant retrial in the cases in which the fabrication of evidence, prosecutorial misconduct, or police brutality was suspected. In Mr. O's retrial, the lower court dismissed the emergency decree violation charge on the grounds that Emergency Decree No. 1 no longer existed. This judgment was affirmed by the Seoul Appeals Court.[20] Mr. O appealed to the Supreme Court, arguing that he should have received a not-guilty verdict for the emergency decree charge instead of dismissal. Under the Criminal Procedure, a judgment of not guilty is entered where "the facts against the defendant do not constitute a crime or when there is not enough evidence of the criminal act";[21] a judgment of dismissal is entered where "(1) a final judgment has already been rendered; (2) amnesty has been proclaimed; (3) the prescription period has been completed; or (4) the punishment has been abolished or the applicable acts and subordinate statutes have been repealed subsequent to the commission of the offense."[22] Dismissal means the defendant cannot be held accountable for the charges due to procedural reasons.

While his case was pending, Mr. O filed in March 2010 a constitutional complaint with the Constitutional Court. The constitutional complaint

[18] S. Ct., 74To3506, February 10, 1975.
[19] Criminal Procedure, art. 420 (5).
[20] Seoul App. Ct., 2009ChaeNo19, April 30, 2010.
[21] Criminal Procedure, art. 325.
[22] Criminal Procedure, art. 326.

system (*Verfassungsbeschwerde*) was introduced in the 1987 Constitution, allowing individuals to lodge a petition with the constitutional tribunal when their basic rights were violated by the state.[23] Article 41 of the Constitutional Court Act stipulates: "When the constitutionality of a statute must be determined prior to reaching the judgment in a trial, the court (including the military court; hereinafter the same shall apply) before which the case is pending shall request, *sua sponte* or on motion by a party, a review of its constitutionality by the Constitutional Court." Article 68 of the Constitutional Court Act provides that, when an ordinary court fails to refer a constitutional question to the Constitutional Court, the party can petition the Constitutional Court directly, alleging his or her constitutional rights have been infringed by government action or omission. The article reads:

(1) A person whose constitutionally guaranteed basic rights have been infringed upon on account of an exercise of state power or a failure to exercise state power, except for the judgments of ordinary courts, may file a constitutional complaint with the Constitutional Court. Provided, in case relief processes are available under other statutes, no constitutional complaint may be filed unless all such processes have been exhausted. (2) When a motion made pursuant to article 41, section 1, for adjudication on the constitutionality of a statute has been rejected, the motioning party may file a constitutional complaint with the Constitutional Court. Upon filing, that party may not move the court at which the case is pending to adjudicate on the constitutionality of the statute on the same grounds.[24]

Under article 68 (2), therefore, a party whose motion for certification for constitutional review of a statute has been rejected by the court of the original jurisdiction still has recourse to obtain a judgment on the statute's constitutionality by the Constitutional Court. This means the ordinary court's decision poses no practical obstacle to the parties. The overwhelming majority of the Constitutional Court's caseload consists of constitutional complaints under this provision.[25] In Mr. O's case, the Appeals Court had rejected his request for constitutional review certification for lack of judicable controversy – that is, since the case had been dismissed there was no dispute or controversy left for judicial determination. Mr. O then filed a petition under article 68 (2).

[23] Constitution (1987), art. 111 (5).
[24] Constitutional Court Act, art. 68.
[25] Article 68 (2) was amended on April 5, 2011.

The gist of his appeal was that Emergency Decree No. 1 was unconstitutional, a nonlaw, and therefore there was no crime.

In Mr. O's case, the retroactive effect of overruling a constitutional decision emerged as a critical issue. Under the Constitutional Court Act issued in 1988, a statute or statutory provision that was declared unconstitutional lost its legal effect from the date of the decision, except for criminal statutes or statutory provisions for which their invalidity was retroactive.[26] Juristic opinions were divided. Of particular difficulty were laws which had been declared constitutional but were later found unconstitutional: should they be regarded as unconstitutional only from the time of that decision or from the time of their enactment? In 2002, a law that punished obtaining sex under the false promise of marriage was held constitutional. Subsequently, in 2009, the Constitutional Court found the same law unconstitutional and recognized the comprehensive retroactive effect of its unconstitutionality decision from the time of the law's enactment.[27]

In 2011, the Supreme Court acknowledged that recognizing the retroactive effect of an unconstitutionality decision all the way to the point of enactment might not always serve justice; for example, a law, once constitutional, could become unconstitutional not due to its defect but due to changes in society.[28] Yet, the Court, following the language of the Constitutional Court Act, ruled that a criminal law provision declared unconstitutional should be treated as invalid from its enactment. The Court added that it was a question that needed to be resolved through legislation. This decision triggered much debate over the question of reasonable reliance on the prior state of the law.[29] Eventually, in 2014, the legislature revised the Constitutional Court Act. Under the newly established article 47 (3), the effect of a decision declaring a criminal statute or statutory provision unconstitutional would be retroactive; however, a statute or statutory provision that had previously been found constitutional would lose its effect retroactively from the day following the date of that decision.[30] The famous adultery law jurisprudence was a case in

[26] Constitutional Court Act (1988), art. 47 (2).

[27] Const. Ct., 2008HŏnKa58 and 2009HŏnPa191 (consol.), November 26, 2009.

[28] S. Ct., 2010To5605, April 14, 2011.

[29] See *Pŏmnyul Sinmun*, April 22, 2011.

[30] Constitutional Court Act (2014), art. 47 (3) (amended May 20, 2014). The retroactivity of constitutional decisions poses serious jurisprudential issues.

point. In 2008, the Constitutional Court failed to strike down the adultery law, but seven years later, in 2015, it declared the law unconstitutional.[31] Newspapers reported that there were thousands of people who had been convicted of adultery between 2008 and 2015; they were now entitled to retrial and compensation from the state as a result of the Court's overruling of its earlier decision.

For Mr. O in 2010, if Emergency Decree No. 1 were declared unconstitutional, the retroactive effect of that decision would deny the decree's existence and he would be entitled to a not-guilty verdict.[32] Nullification of this and other emergency decrees would then have an impact on the overall legitimacy of Yusin rule. The legal and political implications at stake were high. Under the Constitutional Court Act, no appeal is allowed against the court's rejection of the request to certify for constitutional review.[33] As seen above, the party, once a constitutional petition has been lodged, cannot ask the ordinary court again to hear the same constitutionality question.[34] The Supreme Court decided to review the emergency decree, however, despite the fact that Mr. O had already filed a constitutional complaint.

In December 2010, the Supreme Court declared Emergency Decree No. 1 unconstitutional and handed down a not-guilty verdict. The Court acknowledged that, in principle, appeal of a court judgment of dismissal of the charges would not be permitted, but it noted that appeal ought to be allowed in this case to determine whether the defendant deserved an acquittal on the merits.[35] The lower court

See Paul Bender, "The Retroactive Effect of an Overruling Constitutional Decision: Mapp v. Ohio," *University of Pennsylvania Law Review* 110 (1962), 650–683.

31 Const. Ct., 2009HŏnPa17, February 26, 2015.

32 A judgment of not guilty must be entered if the law was found invalid because of its unconstitutionality. S. Ct., 91To2825, May 8, 1992. A practical difference between a not-guilty verdict and a judgment of dismissal concerned restitution: a not-guilty verdict in retrial constitutes grounds for criminal restitution; a dismissal judgment does not. Art. 28 of the Constitution; art. 13 of Criminal Restitution Act; art. 325 of Criminal Procedure.

33 Constitutional Court Act, art. 41 (4).

34 Const. Ct., 96HŏnMa172 & 173 (consol.), December 24, 1997. Constitutional Court Act, art. 68 (2).

35 The Supreme Court cited S. Ct., 64To57, April 7, 1964; and S. Ct., 2004To3532, September 24, 2004.

erred, the justices found, when it failed to determine whether Emergency Decree No. 1 was constitutional. When the law upon which the original judgment of conviction had been grounded was subsequently abolished, the court, in retrial, must render a not-guilty verdict if that law was unconstitutional and therefore invalid *ab initio*.[36] Mr. O was not guilty because Emergency Decree No. 1 was unconstitutional "from the beginning." The case required acquittal, according to the Supreme Court, because the facts against him accrued when there was no law to make his actions criminal. The Court overturned all previous decisions in the 1970s that had been rendered on the basis of Emergency Decree No. 1.[37]

The Supreme Court Decision (2010)

The Supreme Court first had to deal with the provision in the 1972 Constitution that placed the emergency decrees beyond judicial reach. It did so by treating the language of Article 53 (4) – no judicial review for emergency measures – as mere procedural constraints of judicial review power. The Court wrote: "Article 53 (4) excluded judicial review but it merely imposed procedural limits on judicial review; one cannot say that the Article guaranteed the constitutionality or legitimacy of the emergency decree." In retrial, the court must apply procedural laws in force at the time of the new trial, while it must apply substantive laws in force at the time of the criminal acts.[38] The laws that were presently in force did not impose any procedural limitation on judicial review. Therefore, reasoned the Court, Article 53 (4), of a procedural nature, should be disregarded. It concluded: "Any citizen can challenge the constitutionality of the emergency decree without being bound by such procedural restraints set forth by the Yusin Constitution."[39] The Article was inapplicable, furthermore, because it was incompatible with the general standard of constitutional normativity and also conflicted with other provisions in the same Constitution that set forth the basic

36 "Even if the laws that governed the original adjudication were repealed before the time of the retrial, if those laws were unconstitutional from the outset, the judgment of acquittal must be entered." S. Ct., 2010To5986.

37 The Court specifically declared that the Inhyŏktang judgment (S. Ct., 74To3323) was overturned.

38 S. Ct., 96To477, June 14, 1996.

39 S. Ct., 2010To5986, December 16, 2010.

requirements of justice. Recall that the Supreme Court in 1975, and in the following years, refrained from making a positive declaration of the constitutionality of the emergency decrees and instead affirmed the legality of the constitutional limitations that prohibited the review of those decrees. But the Supreme Court in 2010 diverged from such a stance; it declared that Emergency Decree No. 1 was not constitutional because it "infringed upon the citizens' fundamental rights guaranteed by the Constitution by excessively restricting their freedoms and rights beyond the allowed limits."

An important part of the Court's reasoning was that Emergency Decree No. 1 was invoked groundlessly. It was issued, wrote the Court, when there was no urgent national crisis requiring the president's exercise of emergency powers: "The domestic political and social situations at the time of the issuance of the emergency measure did not constitute a situation warranting the exercise of emergency powers." This finding was a direct refutation of the Yusin regime's assertion that the urgent measures were necessary to protect vital national interests. Korean courts had traditionally left the determination of emergency to the president. Now the Supreme Court in 2010 departed from that position. Since there was no situation requiring emergency orders as allowed in Article 53, wrote the justices, the imposition of the decree was illegal. They added "the head of state cannot alone determine the state of national emergency." With this, the justices seemed to enter a political thicket that their predecessors had preferred to avoid.

The Court allowed that a state action of a highly political nature could be regarded as part of sovereign act and that the court of law could abstain voluntarily from the exercise of judicial review. Nevertheless, "recognition of such a concept must be done with extreme prudence so that excessive restraint on judicial review would not result in the evasion or abandonment by the court of law of its duties to protect basic rights and implement the principle of the rule of law."[40] The justices in 2010 concluded that their predecessors in the 1970s should not have refrained from judicial review because "the basic principle of the constitutional state under the rule of law requires

[40] The Court cited S. Ct., 2003To7878, March 26, 2004 (whether the court should refrain from exercising its judicial review power for a state action is up to the court alone).

that any state action or operation be based on and exercised within the framework of the Constitution and law. Determination of constitutionality and legality is an essential function of the judiciary."[41]

The justices pointed out that the Constitution of 1987 granted the president the power to issue emergency orders but did not allow him or her to exclude them from constitutional review: "Article 76 of the current Constitution does not have a provision excluding from judicial review the exercise of the state's emergency power, such as the president's emergency order or emergency finance and economy order."[42] Thus, Article 76 should override Article 53 (4) of the Yusin Constitution, wrote the Court.

This specific analysis can be compared with the position of the Court in the Fifth Republic. In 1985, as seen in Chapter 7, the Supreme Court declared the invalidity of the emergency decree, but its reasoning was narrower.[43] The 1985 Court did not reject the precedents that the Court did not have the power to review the emergency measures, but it ruled that the Yusin Constitution, along with the emergency decrees, had no legal force because they were replaced by a new constitution. Determination of the continuing effect of the emergency decrees was different from a determination of their constitutionality.[44] This way it avoided the need for constitutional review. One recalls that the majority of the Court made a tentative move to consider the emergency decrees in light of the current constitution, inviting Justice Yi Hoe-Ch'ang's rebuke in his supplemental opinion. After that, the courts' position mostly stayed in line with Yi's argument that the decrees lost legal effect because the old constitution was abolished and not because the decrees were unconstitutional under the new constitution. In Mr. O's retrial, the lower courts relied on the same interpretation when they dismissed the charge of the emergency decree violation.[45] But this approach was now abandoned by the highest court.

41 S. Ct., 2010To5986.
42 Constitution (1987), Art. 76.
43 S. Ct., 74To3501, January 29, 1985.
44 Pak Chi-U, "Hyŏngbŏl chohang e kwanhan wihŏn kyŏlchŏng ŭi sogŭp hyo e taehan pip'anjŏk koch'al" [A Critical Examination on the Retroactivity of Unconstitutionality Decisions], *Segye hŏnpŏp yŏngu* 17 (2011), 427–428.
45 For instance, the judgment by the Seoul Central District Court [Seoul Cent. Dist. Ct.], 2002ChaeKoHap6 and 2003ChaeKoHap5, December 27, 2005.

Whether Article 53 (4) merely placed procedural limitations on judicial review has been debated by scholars. It has been pointed out that the obvious purpose of that Article was to forestall any dispute, from the start, over the constitutionality of the emergency decrees, an aim that exceeded the goal of merely insulating them from procedural challenges. In that regard, the retrial itself would be possible only on the premise that Article 53 (4) was not in operation. The Court's explanation that the procedural laws currently in force did not place limitations on judicial review seemed to be sidestepping the question why Article 53 (4) was inapplicable.[46]

A principal difficulty with the 2010 decision lay in that the Court's consideration of Emergency Decree No. 1 ignored the normative reality of the Yusin regime. Focusing on the obvious fact that the emergency decree encroached upon basic rights, the Court did not explain why a right, even one assumed to have a claim to natural justice, could not have been modified by a constitutional change. The Court rightly determined that Article 53 authorizing the issuance of emergency decrees was incompatible with the basic standards of justice, but it invoked a fundamental rights argument without engaging adequately in the threshold question of what precisely a law is or when a constitution becomes a constitution, other than stressing the natural law commitments of the constitution.[47]

All in all, it was a decision heavily skewed to the substantive realm of the law. The question of formal legality was sidelined in favor of the idea that legal interpretations were hinged to fundamental principles of justice. That the 1972 Constitution prohibited judicial review of the decrees was dismissed on the grounds that such a prohibition infringed on fundamental rights. Without explaining adequately why Article 53 (4) was inapplicable, the opinion seemed to skirt around the central issue. The Supreme Court overturned all previous decisions that held

[46] Yun Chin-Su, "Wihŏn in taet'ŏngnyŏng ŭi kingŭp choch'i palryŏng i pulpŏp hangwi rŭl kusŏng hanŭnji yŏbu: Taebŏpwŏn 2015. 3. 26. Sŏngo 2012Ta48824 p'angyŏl" [Whether the Issuance of the Presidential Emergency Decree Which Has Been Declared Unconstitutional Creates Tort Liability: The Supreme Court 2012Ta48824, March 26, 2015], *Minsa pŏphak* 81 (2017), 93–154 (see 127–141 in particular).

[47] See Gary Jeffrey Jacobsohn, "An Unconstitutional Constitution? A Comparative Perspective," *International Journal of Constitutional Law* 4 (2006), 460–487.

that Emergency Decree No. 1 was not subject to constitutional review.[48] By doing so, the justices implied that their predecessors in the 1970s should not have followed the constitutional language faithfully. They affirmed the ideas that a constitutional article could be declared void when it was in conflict with other articles in the same document that were grounded on superior norms and that natural law could serve as a limitation on the powers of government. This was a position that marked a significant deviation from Korea's jurisprudential tradition.

It was difficult to dissipate the impression that the court opinion of 2010 concerned not so much correcting what were viewed as erroneous decisions – wrong interpretations of the Constitution – as adapting to changed political circumstances. It showed that the Court was keenly mindful of the denunciation in society of the Yusin regime and its violation of human rights. In the wake of transitional justice, the courts were under significant pressure from the public to undo the wrongs of the past regimes. The decision of the Supreme Court to sweep aside all previous judgments involving the emergency decrees amounted to a veritable *mea culpa*, an effort in part to rehabilitate its reputation. By distancing itself from the courts of the Yusin period, the Court ended up assuming a more politicized stance. The Supreme Court may have been pushed further in this direction by the robust jurisprudence of the Constitutional Court.

The Constitutional Court Decision (2013)

As soon as the Supreme Court rendered its decision, legal circles speculated about what the Constitutional Court's reaction would be. The immediate question that fascinated scholars, apart from the constitutionality issue, was which court, the Supreme Court or the Constitutional Court, had jurisdiction over the case. A number of observers asked whether the Supreme Court overstepped its power when it conducted constitutional review of the emergency measure. Mr. O appealed his case to the Supreme Court and at the same time filed a constitutional petition with the Constitutional Court. As it turned out, both the Supreme Court and the Constitutional Court exercised jurisdiction and rendered separate decisions on basically the

48 S. Ct., 74To3492, January 28, 1975; S. Ct., 74To3498, January 28, 1975; S. Ct., 74To3323, April 8, 1975.

same issue. The question of which court had rightful jurisdiction depended on whether the emergency measures were "laws" or "executive decrees." The issue that had vexed jurists from the promulgation of the 1948 Constitution resurfaced as the crux of the matter.

The 1987 Constitution created a new constitution-adjudicatory body without modifying the existing judicial structure; it simply superimposed a new institution, in a chapter separate from that of the ordinary courts. Unlike the United States where its Supreme Court serves as the highest court of judicial power and also the final arbiter in constitutional and legal interpretation, in Korea the Constitutional Court has the power of constitutional review (and other enumerated functions), while the Supreme Court, the highest court in the judicial hierarchy, has the power to interpret the laws and apply them in concrete cases brought before it. It gives rise to a situation in which a specific construction of a constitutional provision does not always control how inferior legal norms are interpreted and implemented.

The 1987 Constitution maintains the traditional division of labor in judicial review. Article 107 provides:

1. When the constitutionality of a law is at issue in a trial, the court shall request a decision of the Constitutional Court, and shall judge in accordance with the decision thereof.
2. The Supreme Court shall have the power to make a final review of the constitutionality or legality of administrative decrees, regulations or actions, when their constitutionality or legality is at issue in a trial.
3. Administrative appeals may be conducted in proceedings prior to a judicial trial. The procedures for administrative appeals shall be determined by law, and shall be in conformity with the principles of judicial procedures.[49]

Under this Article, the Supreme Court has power to make a final review of the constitutionality of administrative decrees or regulations while the determination of the constitutionality of legislation is reserved to the Constitutional Court. Article 111 (1) of the Constitution reiterates that the Constitutional Court determines on "the constitutionality of a law upon the request of the courts." The binary constitutional review

[49] Under Article 107 (3), the judicial branch has the final jurisdiction over administrative appeals.

system has been in place since 1948, but after 1987 it became an arena of new, more focused frictions, thanks to the introduction of constitutional petition.

The constitutional complaint system has proven to be an effective mechanism for the Constitutional Court to exercise a degree of control over the Supreme Court. But the Constitution does not include the ordinary court judgments in the Constitutional Court's review powers, and the Constitutional Court Act expressly excludes them from the scope of state power and therefore from the subjects of constitutional petition.[50] This means under the current system the ordinary courts have little incentive to follow the Constitutional Court's interpretation of law which departs from their own accumulated interpretations of law. In practice, administrative actions are excluded from the constitutional complaint process, as they are subject to decisions by the ordinary courts in accordance with the prior exhaustion rule, a legal requirement that the would-be petitioner must exhaust all available relief processes before he or she files a constitutional complaint.[51] Almost all administrative actions concern the infringement of fundamental rights. Because court judgment does not fall under constitutional review, however, once an ordinary court takes in a case challenging administrative action, the party is blocked from filing a constitutional complaint. The Constitutional Court has tried to correct this situation by expanding exceptions to the prior exhaustion rule.[52] Supporters of the Supreme Court have argued that the broadened scope of constitutional complaint would amount to creating a quadripartite hearing system, in violation of the tripartite system provided in the Constitution.[53] In turn, partisans of the Constitutional Court have claimed that the Supreme Court's inflexible position has a detrimental effect on the protection of basic rights of citizens.

50 Constitution (1987), Art. 111 (1); Constitutional Court Act, art. 68 (1).

51 Constitutional Court Act, art. 68 (1).

52 Jongcheol Kim, "The Structure and Basic Principles of Constitutional Adjudication in the Republic of Korea," in Kuk Cho (ed.), *Litigation in Korea* (Cheltenham: Edward Elgar Publishing, 2010), 115–134. Arguments have been made that the Constitutional Court has the power to perform review of ordinances and regulations under Article 111 (1) and (5) of the Constitution and article 68 (1) of the Constitutional Court Act, whereas the Supreme Court performs review under a mandate of Article 107 (2) of the Constitution.

53 *Chosŏn Ilbo*, September 2, 2013. For a view that the Supreme Court has the ultimate power to interpret the laws, see Pak U-Tong, "Taebŏpwŏn p'angyŏl i ch'wiso toen sakŏn" [A Case That Voided the Judgment by the Supreme Court], *Pyŏnhosa sil anp'ak* (Seoul: Hanguk Sabŏp Chŏngch'aek Hakhoe, 2010), 403–415.

It was in the context of this long-brewing conflict between the two highest courts that the issue of the constitutional review of the emergency decrees came up. Did the Supreme Court in 2010 hijack the Constitutional Court's jurisdiction? According to the Supreme Court, Emergency Decree No. 1 was not a "law" so it was not subject to review by the Constitutional Court. The conventional view among scholars was that a law, in order to be reviewed by the Constitutional Court, must have passed the vote of the National Assembly or must have substance that would make it equivalent to the exercise of legislative power, for example requiring approval or consent by the National Assembly. None of these elements were found in Emergency Decree No. 1, argued the Supreme Court. It noted that Article 53 (3) of the Yusin Constitution merely required that the president notify the National Assembly without delay upon issuing an emergency measure; no prior consent or subsequent approval by the legislature was needed.[54] There was no record that the National Assembly ever discussed the emergency decrees, nor requested their repeal. The Supreme Court thus concluded that they contained no substance pertaining to the National Assembly's legislative power and that the right to review them belonged to the ordinary court.

The Constitutional Court disagreed. Even if the emergency decrees were issued by the president without legislative approval, it argued, their practical legal effect equaled and even exceeded that of statutes because they comprehensively, albeit temporarily, suspended the fundamental rights guaranteed in the Constitution. The Constitutional Court thus declared that their exceptional nature transcended the purview of the Supreme Court.[55] The result was a highly awkward situation in which the two highest courts each rendered a decision on the same issue independently and separately, and, in many aspects, redundantly.

[54] S. Ct., 2010To5986.

[55] Kim Sŏng-Su, "Kingŭp choch'i wihŏn simsakwŏn e taehan kwangyŏn: Taebŏpwŏn p'angyŏl (2010.12.16., sŏngo 2010To5986) e taehan p'yŏngka rŭl chungsim ŭro" [An Observation on the Power to Review the Emergency Decrees: Assessment of the Supreme Court Decision (December 16, 2010, 2010To5986)], *Kongpŏphak yŏngu* 12 (2011), 315–336 (arguing that the Supreme Court's claim of jurisdiction amounted to the negation of the citizens' right to be heard by the Constitutional Court).

Some scholars distinguished the two decisions by arguing that, whereas the Supreme Court's decision governed the case before the Court only, the declaration of unconstitutionality by the Constitutional Court had a controlling effect on all the cases adjudicated under the emergency decrees. Still, there was no mistaking that the public standoff of the two courts drew keen attention to the rivalry between them. Since the opening of the Constitutional Court in 1988, the question of hierarchy between the two – which court has the ultimate authority in the nation's judicial matters – has remained an unsettled issue. The ordinary court's distrust of a separate constitutional review body has a long history around the world. In Korea, the Supreme Court may have felt that its judgments in the 1970s should be revisited, and modified if necessary, by itself, not by an outside body. The flare-up of jurisdictional dispute over the emergency decrees had these complex backgrounds. Each court seemed determined not to be outdone. Some suspected that the Supreme Court rushed to render a decision in December 2010 in the hope of preempting the constitutional tribunal; it did not deter the latter from rendering its own decision in a little over two years.

At the Constitutional Court, Mr. O's petition was consolidated with other cases. In the past, the Court had refused to hear complaints of the parties who were convicted but later exonerated in retrial. When the laws that had controlled the original case were abolished, the Court rejected reviews as there were no justiciable controversies.[56] "Even where the law had been abolished in the past," however, if the case involved a situation in which "there was an infringement of rights by that law and the legal effect of such infringement continues," the rights to be exercised through constitutional complaints must be recognized, held the Court.[57] The Constitutional Court in 2013 thus approached Mr. O's case as follows. First, it noted that "the Supreme Court in this case rendered a not-guilty verdict for the charges of the violation of Emergency Decree No. 1." Under article 68 (2) of the Constitutional Court Act, "the party in a criminal case who is the petitioner of constitutional review cannot, upon receiving a not-guilty verdict that became final, request another trial and dispute the non-guilty verdict, because whether or not the law

[56] Const. Ct., 95HŏnPa3, December 28, 1995; Const. Ct., 2000HŏnPa38, February 22, 2001.

[57] Const. Ct., 89HŏnMa240, January 16, 1997. The law in question involved the National Security Legislative Council Act, in force from October 1980 to April 1981.

is constitutional changes neither the judgment nor the legal meaning of the content and effect of the trial." In the present case, however, the prerequisite justiciable controversies must be found. The Court wrote:

> The emergency decrees had legal effects equivalent to statutes under the Yusin Constitution, and the right to review their constitutionality resides essentially within the exclusive jurisdiction of the Constitutional Court. There is a need for a constitutional clarification of the emergency decrees. The Supreme Court's judgment on a case has no general binding force whereas a decision by the Constitutional Court finding a criminal law unconstitutional has general and continuing effect and can be the grounds for retrial of a guilty verdict. . . . Therefore, it is necessary to find exceptionally the prerequisite justiciability in this case concerning Emergency Decrees Nos. 1 and 2 and to recognize the need for adjudication, for the sake of the protection and preservation of the objective constitutional order and for the relief of the party's rights. Conducting actively a determination on whether they are constitutional is the raison d'être of the Constitutional Court and it fulfills the duties of this Court.[58]

Throughout its opinion, the Constitutional Court stressed that the situations surrounding the emergency decrees were "exceptional." The justices noted that Article 53 (4), "stipulating that 'the emergency decrees are not subject to judicial review,' fundamentally closed the door on the constitutional review of the emergency decrees" and that, in accordance with this provision, the Supreme Court under the Yusin system consistently dismissed requests for their constitutional review. Under this "normative obstacle," observed the Court, those who were punished by the decrees were deprived of the opportunity to dispute their constitutionality in a judicial proceeding. But "even the exercise of the state's emergency power grounded on high-level political decisions can become the subject of determination by the Constitution Court if it directly encroaches on the citizens' fundamental rights." Prohibition of judicial review was an aberration, a perversion in modern constitutionalism. Therefore, it was only reasonable, and imperative, to allow the defendants to challenge the decrees' constitutionality. The Court justified its decision to disregard Article 53 (4) by reasoning that the now-defunct Yusin Constitution had no bearing on the determination of the case before the Court. It emphatically wrote that "only the Constitution currently in force has normative force."[59] Recall that

[58] Const. Ct., 2010HŏnPa132.
[59] Ibid.

this was a position similar to that of the Supreme Court in 1985. While the 1985 Court did away with judging the constitutionality of the emergency decrees, however, the Constitutional Court in 2013 ruled that determining whether they were constitutional was necessary and, further, that it must be done in light of the constitution currently in force.

Constitutions: Old and New

The Constitutional Court's position that the normative standard for reviewing the emergency decrees was not the Yusin Constitution but the Constitution of 1987 deserves attention. It reverts to the problem of Article 53 (4) that prohibited the judicial review of the decrees. The Supreme Court in 2010 stated that Emergency Decree No. 1 was unconstitutional under both the Yusin Constitution and the 1987 Constitution, but its reasoning of excluding Article 53 (4) was far from clear or persuasive. The Constitutional Court took a narrower view by limiting the grounds of its ruling to the provisions of the 1987 Constitution. By this it avoided the problems in which the Supreme Court got bogged down. But its exclusion of Article 53 (4) by referring to the absence of a similar provision in the 1987 Constitution appeared just as inadequate. That left unresolved the question how the current constitution could be retroactively applied to serve as a standard for determining the constitutionality of a law that had been repealed well before the constitutional change.[60] How could the already abolished laws, issued under the old constitution, be evaluated under the "principles residing in the Constitution currently in force"? The Constitutional Court's proffered explanation was that, since the citizens decisively rejected Article 53 of the Yusin Constitution through the constitutional revision in 1987, attempting to determine the emergency decrees' constitutionality by resorting to the provisions of the Yusin Constitution would "not only negate the sovereign will of the citizens but also contradict the very historical nature of the constitution that purports to strengthen and expand fundamental

60 Yun Chin-Su, "Wihŏn in taet'ŏngnyŏng ŭi kingŭp choch'i," 133–134.

rights."[61] The justices also stated that Article 53 was merely a provision from which the issuance of the emergency decrees was derived; because the petitions before them in 2013 were limited to determining the constitutionality of the emergency decrees, they did not need to consider the Yusin Constitution.

As late as March 2010, in response to the challenges that Article 53 was invalid, the Constitutional Court maintained that constitutional petitions against individual provisions of the Constitution were not allowed. The Court has repeatedly ruled that the subjects of constitutional review are "laws," not constitutional articles.[62] By bypassing Article 53 of the Yusin Constitution and holding that the emergency decrees were unconstitutional as they ran counter to the provisions of the 1987 Constitution, the Court averted contradicting its earlier position and circumvented the prohibition of constitutional review in Article 53 (4).

Ironically, the Constitutional Court's position that the emergency decrees ought to be judged against the current constitution seemed reminiscent of that of the Supreme Court during the Yusin years, when the latter consistently said it could not validate the laws and precedents that were contrary to the constitution presently in force. The Supreme Court's decision in 1977 on the State Tort Claims Act, discussed in Chapter 5, is instructive. The 1977 Court said that the effect of the Act, which had been found unconstitutional by the Supreme Court in 1971 but subsequently incorporated into the Constitution in 1972, could not be denied in the case before the Court. This decision was much berated at that time because it looked as if the justices willingly abandoned the celebrated precedent of their predecessors. The Supreme Court's rejection in July 1975 of the constitutional challenge to the Requisition Act was of the same nature.[63] These were the examples that the judiciary's interpretation of the law was effectively dictated by modifications in the constitutional language that was

61 Ibid.

62 Const. Ct., 95HŏnPa3, December 28, 1995; Const. Ct., 94HŏnPa20, June 13, 1996; Const. Ct., 2000HŏnPa38, February 22, 2001; Const. Ct., 2010HŏnPa97, March 9, 2010.

63 S. Ct., 70Ta340 (*en banc*), July 8, 1975.

specifically intended to override contrary interpretations, including judicial precedents. The Supreme Court in 1977 was unable to render a decision in contravention of the existing constitution, even for the acts that had taken place before its promulgation. The rulings of 2013, and of 2010, seemed inadvertently to affirm the reasoning in those decisions in the 1970s.

The Constitutional Court held that the emergency decrees, viewed under the 1987 Constitution, were plainly unconstitutional. Emergency Decrees Nos. 1 and 2 "not only lacked the legitimacy of legislative purposes and the appropriateness of the means to achieve them but also violated the principle of legality." By prohibiting any criticism of the regime, the government violated the freedom of expression; by subjecting civilians to court martial and allowing arrest without judicial warrant, it deprived citizens of the right to trial by judge. Likewise, Emergency Decree No. 9 was in violation of the freedom of expression, the freedom of assembly, and the rights to vote and protest, and its arbitrary order to close down universities deprived students of their right to study.[64]

Questions remained, however. How could the emergency decrees be declared unconstitutional without considering the validity of the constitutional clause that authorized such measures? Did the Court's refusal to review the constitutionality of the emergency decrees under Article 53 not clash with its decision to review the decrees in the first place? These were not new questions. Was it not because of the same difficulties that the Supreme Court in 1985 and subsequent courts sidestepped constitutional review and instead relied on the fact that the decrees lost their legal force when the Yusin Constitution was replaced?

It is not hard to see the quandary of the Constitutional Court, forced to walk a tightrope in rejecting the applicability of Article 53 (4) to the present case. In fact, it is possible to look at the tortuous reasoning of the Court in a more positive light. Its opinion reflected an effort to reduce the uncertainty in the constitutional order that it deemed to have been created by the Supreme Court's sweeping decision in 2010. As the Constitutional Court correctly noted, the Supreme Court in 1975 did

64 Const. Ct., 2010HŏnPa132.

not declare that the emergency decrees were constitutional but simply stated that they were unreviewable. This was an important point which the Supreme Court in 2010 dealt with only in passing. The Constitutional Court in 2013 apparently took heed of the plight of the judges in the 1970s, working under a constitution that effectively tied their hands. It avoided saying that the Supreme Court in the 1970s was in error in declining to review the decrees.

Interestingly, a new set of decisions rendered subsequently by the Supreme Court seemed to show that it tried to moderate its earlier position. In March 2015, the Supreme Court ruled in a retrial regarding Emergency Decree No. 9 that "the president's exercise of emergency powers involved state acts of a highly political nature" and, as such, "the president owes citizens political accountability but no legal obligations."[65] The holding of the 2015 case was narrowly stated to the effect that the state's exercise of emergency powers, even if found unconstitutional subsequently, could not conclusively be seen as illegal activities incurring civil liability. Yet the Court's characterization of the president's issuance of Emergency Decree No. 9 as falling outside the sphere of tort liability appeared to limit the scope of its earlier decision of April 2013 that had declared the same decree illegal.[66] Whether an unconstitutional action of the state gives rise to tort liability continues to be debated by scholars. Yun Chin-Su has argued that such an action as the president's unlawful issuance of an emergency decree, as in this case, or the National Assembly's enactment of an invalid law constitutes tort when that action is "manifestly" unconstitutional.[67] One incidentally-relevant case can be mentioned here. In 2015, the Supreme Court held that those who received compensation under the Act for Restoring the Honor of Democratization Movement Participants and Providing Compensation were not eligible for indemnities against the state after they were vindicated in retrial. It ruled that the parties' agreement to compensation under the 2000 law amounted to a judicial compromise (also known as transaction) which had the same legal force as the final

65 S. Ct., 2012Ta48824, March 26, 2015. See also S. Ct., 2013Ta217962, October 27, 2014 (ruling that, even where the defendant was found not guilty in a retrial, the state was not automatically liable for reparations without proof of the state's illegal activities).
66 S. Ct., 2011Ch'ogi689, April 18, 2013.
67 Yun Chin-Su, "Wihŏn in taet'ŏngnyŏng ŭi kingŭp choch'i," 105–127.

judgment by the court, blocking claims of further compensation for damages.[68]

If the Supreme Court appeared backpedalling in those cases, subsequent decisions seemed to show that it was moving yet in the opposite direction.[69] Has court jurisprudence become more volatile? Was it possibly in reflection of changes in political climate?[70] These questions, and what has transpired during past few years in and around the courts, require separate discussion and are beyond the scope of this chapter. At least, however, one may be justified in concluding that the judiciary has become more politicized – of its own accord or not – than ever before. By holding that Article 53 of the Yusin Constitution was incompatible with the basic requirements of justice and needed to be set aside, both the Supreme Court and the Constitutional Court sent an unmistakable message: the authority and legitimacy of the legal apparatus of the Park government was open to question. The Courts treated Article 53 as an unconstitutional constitutional article.[71]

An Unconstitutional Constitution

The opinions of the Supreme Court and the Constitutional Court both resonated with legitimate expectations of corrective justice. The decisions were rendered on the basis of fundamental justice and constitutional ideals. They represented a reorientation of juristic thinking in Korea, a conspicuous leap from the country's tradition of legal

68 S. Ct. (*en banc*), 2012Ta204365, January 22, 2015. *Chosŏn Ilbo*, January 24, 2015.

69 Meierhenrich has observed of Germany: "[b]y trying to do justice to both facts and norms, the constitutional jurisprudence of postwar Germany took on a schizophrenic quality whenever it was concerned with cases arising from the law of the Third Reich." Meierhenrich, *The Remnants of the Rechtsstaat*, 8. The postdemocratization constitutional jurisprudence in Korea, trying to do justice to the "past history," has been frenetic.

70 Park Geun Hye (Pak Kŭn-Hye), the eldest daughter of Park Chung Hee, was sworn in as president in February 2013. In December 2016, she was impeached by the National Assembly and was forced out of presidency the following March upon conviction by the Constitutional Court. Const. Ct., 2016HŏnNa1, March 10, 2017. In 2018, Park was found guilty by the ordinary court of multiple charges, including the crime of peddling influence.

71 Roznai, "Unconstitutional Constitutional Amendments"; Jacobsohn, "An Unconstitutional Constitution?"; Gottfried Dietze, "Unconstitutional Constitutional Norms? Constitutional Development in Postwar Germany," *Virginia Law Review* 42 (1956), 1–22; R. George Wright, "Could a Constitutional Amendment Be Unconstitutional," *Loyola University of Chicago Law Journal* 22 (1990–1991), 741–764.

formalism and judicial restraint. The treatment of the emergency decrees illustrated the belief that the validity of legal norms should be judged by the consideration of the fundamental "constitutional order of liberal democracy" underlying the evolving language of the written constitutions. Limiting the authority of Article 53 (the product of *pouvoir constituant*) could not have derived from the court's own authority (an entity of *pouvoir constitué*); it had to come from substantive standards existing within the constitution.

Broadly considered, the two Courts' decisions seemed to be in line with the jurisprudential tendency worldwide to recognize implied substantive limitations on constitutional provisions. The Courts appeared to embrace the concept of unconstitutional constitutional amendments, an idea that has emerged as a "burning issue for modern constitutionalism" around the globe.[72] The notion of an unconstitutional constitution means a judge can declare a constitutional provision unconstitutional when it is deemed incompatible with the general principles of the constitution. Scholars have noted the increasing tendency of courts to assert their right to declare void constitutional amendments that violate the superior norms of the constitution or fundamental rights. It originated in postwar German jurisprudence that recognized the idea that certain constitutional norms – principles of the protection of human dignity and human rights based on natural law ideas – were superior to other constitutional norms. The Basic Law of the Federal Republic of Germany of 1949 designated the fundamental constitutional principles as "absolutely unmodifiable articles." These provisions (Articles 1–20) cannot be changed under any circumstances, even in accordance with the methods of amendment defined elsewhere in the Basic Law.[73] The Bavarian Constitutional Court wrote in 1950 that such constitutional principles were "of so elementary a nature and so much the expression of a law that precedes the Constitution, that the maker of the Constitution himself is bound by them. Other constitutional norms, which do not have this rank, can be void because they conflict with them."[74] This reasoning gave rise to the possibility of an invalidity of constitutional provisions.

72 Roznai, "Unconstitutional Constitutional Amendments," 719.

73 Grundgesetz für die Bundesrepublic Deutschland [Grundgesetz] [GG], May 23, 1949, BGBl. I. From this emerged the notion of the hierarchy in constitutional norms.

74 Bayerischen Verfassungsgericht [BayVerfG] [Bavarian Constitutional Court] April 4, 1950, 2 VerwGE no. 65, cited in Dietze, "Unconstitutional

Writing in 1956, Gottfried Dietze predicted that the development in Germany "may very well have a bearing upon the constitutional development of other nations."[75] His prognosis of transnational constitutional jurisprudence has proved prescient. The trend quickly spread to other countries that did not have historical experiences similar to Germany's tortured past under the Nazis. Even countries without explicit limitations in their constitutions prohibiting constitutional amendments came to recognize implicit limitations on constitutional amendment power through the working of certain supra-constitutional principles. The result was a claim by the courts of their right to strike down constitutional amendments.[76]

The idea that constitutional law does not escape judicial review has fascinated legal scholars, but it also raised concerns. First, there has been criticism that the ever-broadening scope of judicial review amounts to a usurpation of the powers of the constitution-maker. The expanding sphere of substantive limits imposed by the court may result in subjecting the prerogative of constitution-making to judicial review, which now far exceeds its original function of restricting the legislature. Second, the idea that constitutional amendments can be invalidated for substantive rather than procedural defects raised issues about the interpretive discretion of courts. The underlying notion of an unconstitutional constitution is that judicial review of the constitution can ensure basic requirements of justice. At a more specific level, it points to the idea that, by recognizing the existence of

Constitutional Norms?" 16. The Federal Constitutional Court cited this paragraph in 1951, and in 1953 it acknowledged the possibility of invalid constitutional norms. Roznai, "Unconstitutional Constitutional Amendments," 676.

75 Dietze, "Unconstitutional Constitutional Norms?" 9. See Riccardo Pilizzo, "Who Was Gottfried Dietze?" *Mises Daily* (blog), entry posted on August 11, 2006, http://mises.org/daily/2262/.

76 One of the most celebrated examples was the decision by the Supreme Court of India in 1973 in *Kesavananda Bharati* v. *The State of Kerala and Others* (1973) S.C.R. 1461. In the 1960s and 1970s, Prime Minister Indira Gandhi attempted to amend the Constitution and declare a state of emergency. The Indian Supreme Court invalidated a constitutional amendment initiated by her for violating the "basic structure" of the Constitution. It held that constitutional amendments could be voided in cases where they sought to alter the "essential features" of the Constitution. See Roznai, "Unconstitutional Constitutional Amendments," 690–693; Jacobsohn, "An Unconstitutional Constitution?" 473–476. The Court in this case asserted a broad jurisdiction over the Constitution's substantive core without a real textual mandate or standard. Ibid., 474.

limitations on the constitution, the judiciary can stop an autocratic regime's attempts to usurp power and violate human rights through constitutional amendments. But some scholars have asked whether the emphasis on natural law elements in the constitution will not render judicial review more arbitrary.

Commenting on the Federal Constitutional Court's decision of 1991 on expropriations in East Germany, Matthias Herdegen wrote: "The Court's reference to ill-defined concepts of fundamental justice as a yardstick even for the power to amend the constitution marks a thinly veiled renaissance of natural law, a rather striking phenomenon at the end of the 20th century."[77] It becomes more serious when there are no explicit limitations in the constitution to do so and there is "no substantive content amenable to objective verification."[78] Gary Jacobsohn has argued that the natural law argument has often been invoked by the court "as cover for its inability or unwillingness to engage the threshold question what precisely an amendment is, or, for that matter, the antecedent question of what a constitution is."[79] It does not explain "why a right, even one thought to have a natural endowment, cannot be modified."[80] More bluntly, "[w]hat if the people exercise their presumed constituent authority to destroy the Constitution in the name of change and progress?"[81] Could it still be a valid constitutional order, or should it be declared unconstitutional by the judiciary as a violation of the principles of natural justice and therefore void?

One can reasonably argue that constitution-amending power is subject to judicial control because it is a power granted to the legislature by a constitution. It is more difficult to claim the same for constitution-making power. The accepted function of the judiciary is to see that amendment takes place within the scope of the granted power and in observance of the requisite forms.[82] Justification for conjuring implicit substantive limits and rendering a constitutional law an unconstitutional constitutional law is that constitutional amendments must be confined to making changes that are absolutely necessary, not creating an essentially new document. Creating or replacing a constitution, as opposed to merely amending it,

[77] Herdegen, "Unjust Laws, Human Rights," 605.
[78] Ibid.
[79] Jacobsohn, "An Unconstitutional Constitution?" 469.
[80] Ibid., 470.
[81] Ibid., 464.
[82] Ibid., 466.

commonly takes place through a revolution or a coup, followed by the establishment of a constituent assembly.[83] A constitution normally includes provisions regulating the process of constitutional amendment, but no positive law sets forth how to create a constitution. In short, there exist few grounds or reliable standards upon which courts can intervene in constitution-making.

The recent Korean constitutional jurisprudence indicates that its development is not far removed from these general trends of constitutionalism around the world. The 2010 and 2013 decisions held that the emergency decrees were unconstitutional because the constitutional provision that mandated them was in conflict with other superior norms in the same document. But in reality comparing the relative force of individual constitutional provisions is far from easy. Further, it would be almost impossible to decide in the Korean case whether a specific article is the result of the exercise of the constitutional-making power or of the constitution-amending power.[84] It was because of these difficulties that the Courts did not go so far as declaring that Article 53 of the 1972 Constitution was invalid, suggesting instead that it was a product of a substantively unconstitutional constitutional amendment.

In a way, these decisions corroborated, paradoxically, the Schmittian claim that the people, the holder of *pouvoir constituant*, can disregard individual constitutional laws. Both the Supreme Court and the Constitutional Court asserted that the judiciary must be diligent so that it does not evade its duty to implement popular will. But the judicial affirmation of primordial popular will failed to explain why the exercise by the people of their constituent power in 1972 should not be given as serious attention as it deserved. In other words, could the people have agreed, for whatever reason, to place emergency decrees beyond judicial oversight? This proposition, seemingly outrageous, may nevertheless be more than a purely theoretical exercise. Korean constitutional history brings to the forefront both the limits and the potentials of judicial power. As long as one refrains from brushing aside the 1972 Constitution as an aberration, the Korean case appears to provide

83 Roznai, "Unconstitutional Constitutional Amendments," 682.

84 Yun Chin-Su, "Wihŏn in taet'ŏngnyŏng ŭi kingŭp choch'i," 137.

ample grounds for discussion, which would delight both supporters and detractors of Schmitt.

Constitutional Identity

Modern courts in many jurisdictions have ascertained a defined set of basic principles that supposedly form the country's constitution's identity and thus cannot be abrogated through the amendment procedure. If one attempts to change these principles through constitutional amendments, the court is expected to exercise judicial review and declare them void, as part of its duty to preserve the identity, or spirit, of the nation's foundations. What constitutes Korea's constitutional identity? Most scholars cite fundamental values and rights that undergird liberal democracy. Beyond these aspirational concepts, however, there is little consensus. Interestingly, perusal of the Supreme Court decisions in history seems to shed some light on this issue. One can refer to the cases discussed in the preceding chapters. In the ill-fated Inhyŏktang case in 1975, the Supreme Court indicated an attempt to change the Korean state into a communist regime or a monarchy would amount to changing the substance of the Constitution and therefore be void. This formula may have come from Schmitt, who wrote that "an amendment that transforms the state that rests on the power of the people into a monarchy, or vice versa, would be unconstitutional."[85] Or, it may be a reflection of Korea's dynastic history. In any event, the Supreme Court seemed to define the unamendable foundation as a liberal republican form of government in opposition to communism. The inference is that, as long as this core basis is preserved, the constituent power can change the constitution without undermining the nature and legitimacy of the nation. The Court did not find that the 1972 Constitution modified Korea's constitutional identity or changed its basic structure in a substantive realm. Even with the notorious emergency decrees and grievous authoritarian practices, free elections continued to take place, and property rights were protected. The foundation of the Constitution could not be seen as having been altered, according to the Court.

[85] Schmitt, *Constitutional Theory*, 151.

As Roznai has pointed out, "foundational structuralism" is not to be confused with natural law; it is rather the "'spirit' of legality that pervades the forms of constitutionalism to which societies commit themselves."[86] Jacobsohn has argued that the identity of the constitution "is defined by the intermingling of universal values with the nation's particularistic history, customs, values, and aspirations."[87] This means whether the making of a new constitution conformed to legality depends on historical circumstances, rather than on the intrinsic morality of the law alone. Loughlin has stated that "constitutional legality is not self-generating: the practice of legality rests on political conditions it cannot itself guarantee. . . . Consideration of the origins of constitutional ordering invariably brings the concept of constituent power into play."[88] Political circumstances that lead to the decision to amend the constitution are crucially relevant.

Such theoretical reasoning, of course, does not make light of procedural violations in amending the constitution. In Korea in 1972, the government under martial law summarily set aside the existing amendment procedures. Approved by referendum, the new Constitution forbade any legal challenge to the process that created it. Scholars have argued that the constitution-making process must rely on external rules or institutions in order to ensure the democratic deliberation and compromise needed for a successful constitutional order and to avoid the dangers of plebiscitary dictatorship.[89] In Korea, just about the only preexisting institution that could fit this bill was the judiciary, the depository of "constitutional" constitutional rules. But the Supreme Court in the 1970s determined that it would not intercede since the Yusin Constitution was approved through a valid plebiscite.[90] It posited that

86 Roznai, *Unconstitutional Constitutional Amendments*, 143.

87 Gary Jeffrey Jacobsohn, "Constitutional Identity," *Review of Politics* 68 (2006), 361; Gary Jeffrey Jacobsohn, *Constitutional Identity* (Cambridge: Harvard University Press, 2010).

88 Martin Loughlin, "The Concept of Constituent Power," *European Journal of Political Theory* 13 (2013), 6.

89 Parlett, "The Dangers of Constitution-Making," 237–238.

90 Korean judges would have heartily agreed with the dictum by Justice Hugo Black of the United States Supreme Court that the process of constitutional amendment "is 'political' in its entirety, from submission until an amendment becomes part of the Constitution, and is not subject to judicial guidance, control or interference at any point." *Coleman et al.* v. *Miller, Secretary of the Senate of the State of Kansas, et al.*, 307 U.S. 433, 459 (1939) (Hugo Black, J, concurring).

a constitution could vest, or deny, a court the authority of judicial review without destroying its identity.

A common observation in postdemocratization years has been that the Yusin Constitution was not constitutional because it lacked people's will. But the circularity of this view is not difficult to see: popular will is the element that makes a constitution constitutional, but one can prove the presence of popular will only when a constitution is recognized as the constitution. Frederick Schauer asked: "What makes a constitution constitutional?" "Nothing," he answered, "nor does or can anything make a constitution unconstitutional."[91] What is constitutional and what is not is a question that cannot be considered in separation from the historical and empirical contexts.

The judicial opinions concerning the emergency decrees in the 2010s constituted specific reactions by the two highest courts at a time when calls for redress of Korea's recent history were on the rise. The courts' attempts to do justice to the past wrongs were not dissociated from their own institutional self-interest. After democratization, the courts tried to reestablish their authority and credibility as a key force in the Korean constitutional order. Faced with mounting demands in society for judicial accountability, the Supreme Court set out to take a fresh review of its traditionally depoliticized and deferential position. The 2010 decision may be seen as a result of its desire for self-redemption by renouncing its own past. The ordinary courts used to take a substantially different view of the constitution from that of a constitutional tribunal. But now the Supreme Court heralded broad constitutional principles and distanced itself from a narrower conception of adjudication that was blamed for the past illiberal legal system.

The dismal reality of authoritarian rule has given rise to a plea for politically active courts. Yet there is a danger that such courts may become too eager to resolve, once and for all, serious political issues that continue to haunt the country. There is no guarantee that political judges will always support democracy and the rule of law. In this respect, one may be justified in arguing that the oath judges take to uphold the constitution and apply the law should serve as a baseline for their choices. Judicial duties do not change regardless of whether judges

[91] Frederick Schauer, "Amending the Presuppositions of a Constitution," in Sanford Levinson (ed.), *Responding to Imperfection: The Theory and Practice of Constitutional Amendment* (Princeton: Princeton University Press, 1995), 145.

serve under military dictatorship or progressive democracy. Judicial conservatism or aloofness can certainly have adverse effects in an authoritarian context, but overcompensation has its own risks. In hindsight, judicial apoliticism is almost always seen in terms of compromise, co-optation, or complicity. But it is worth noting that it becomes a threat to justice in an illiberal political context mainly when other factors have already perverted the legal and constitutional structure.

Constitutions and the Courts

The emergence of a new jurisprudential direction in Korea can be viewed in light of the rise of transnational constitutional jurisprudence focusing on fundamental rights. There are universal trends of the constitutionalization of laws, in which seemingly every legal issue becomes predicated on constitutional rights, and major social, cultural, and political debates are progressively realigned as constitutional issues to be decided by the court.[92] Litigants before ordinary courts have increasingly resorted to constitutional arguments, not only in criminal procedure but also in civil law disputes, and they have filed constitutional complaints in large numbers. In Korea, the Supreme Court and the Constitutional Court have both actively accepted opportunities to decide constitutional cases. Jurisdictional clashes have had the effect of pushing the courts further away from the country's judicial tradition.

Constitutional discussions during the last three decades have taken place within broadly framed parameters of justice and human rights. Here, the thorny issue of negotiating between mounting democratic aspirations and the judicial role comes to the front. In transitional justice, whether to recognize judicial decisions rendered under the former regime as *res judicata* poses an important question.[93] The 2010 and 2013 decisions were a specific answer to this question. But the danger in overturning existing decisions is real. Kim Tong-Kil (Kim Dong Gill), a former history professor, was one of the most famous and vociferous dissidents in the 1970s. He was convicted of violating emergency decrees in 1974 and served time in prison. A confirmed victim of the Yusin system, he nevertheless expressed his

92 It can be seen as part of the trends of the judicialization of politics or the politicization of justice. See John Ferejohn, "Judicializing Politics, Politicizing Law," *Law and Contemporary Problems* 65 (2002), 41–68.

93 Osiel, "Dialogue with Dictators," 486.

concerns about setting aside the lawful court judgments on the grounds that the decrees were unconstitutional *ab initio*. In his opinion, the recent decisions overturning past rulings have seriously threatened legal stability and jeopardized the authority of the judiciary.[94] Kim asked flatly: is it really necessary to hold retrials and declare people guilty or not guilty of those ludicrous decrees? What will happen "if we continue turning the judiciary upside down?"[95] Some had suggested invalidating the emergency decrees through legislative means, but a judicial solution was chosen instead.[96] Kim's concerns deserve attention. The decrees were a sort of national disciplinary apparatus concocted by President Park, which effectively muzzled the Korean people for over five years. Still, it may be fruitless to deny their normative validity at the time. Courts cannot be expected to conduct a retrial each time the regime changes.

In certain retrials, the courts seemed to rely on democratic persuasion rather than legal reasoning. It has not been uncommon for a presiding judge to acknowledge the regrettable past of the judiciary and apologize publicly on behalf of his or her predecessors for failing to protect the citizens from political repression. The need for redressing past wrongs and rehabilitating innocent victims cannot be overemphasized, but reopening cases should be more than an occasion for sitting judges to distance themselves from their predecessors and blame them for failing their duties. The judiciary's momentous and daunting task to safeguard democracy may end up obscured if a retrial courtroom simply becomes an arena in which one shifts the responsibility.

A former judge compared the fate of a judge who had served under authoritarian rule to that of a soldier who returned from the front. His troops had been defeated, although the war subsequently ended in victory. "If he is asked why he came back alive [instead of fighting to the bitter end and perishing on the battlefield], what else can he say, other than 'I am sorry'?"[97] This rhetorical question, a faintly disguised

94 Kim Tong-Kil, "Sabŏppu twijipki ka panbok toemyŏn" [If We Continue Turning the Judiciary Upside Down], Chayu ŭi p'asukkun [Freedom Watch], entry posted on July 8, 2013, www.kimdonggill.com/mb/mb.html?num=3931; Kim Tong-Kil, "Ije wasŏ kingŭp choch'i rŭl" [What Are We to Do with the Emergency Decrees Now], ibid., entry posted on December 18, 2010, www.kimdonggill.com/mb/mb.html?num=2258.

95 Kim Tong-Kil, "Sabŏppu twijipki ka panbok toemyŏn."

96 Hong Sŏng-U, *Inkwŏn pyŏllon han sidae*, 736–737.

97 Pak U-Tong, *P'ansa sil esŏ pŏpchŏng kkaji*, 103.

protest, captures the plight of the judges at the crossroads of the country's political transition. In the highly polarized discussion about the judiciary, then, one may be excused for sounding caution against a sharp turn to judicial activism as a response to the public's desire for righteousness and substantive legality. Legal rules create order and predictability. Law is a stabilizing force in society and, as such, can at times compromise its moral values. Blind adherence to established law and precedents is a serious threat to substantive justice. Yet redefining the law and judicial role in the past retrospectively using current standards and perception of justice could be a source of an even greater danger.

Korean judges more or less engaged in faithful interpretation of the constitutions. By upholding the less-than-ideal constitutional authority, the courts helped sustain the idea that the government – whether authoritarian or progressive, whether President Park's or someone else's – must remain beholden to the foundation of the nation's liberal constitutional order. After all, constitutionalism can be more potent than a constitution.

9 Conclusion

The judicial history of Korea unfolded in the crucible of constitutionalism. The nation's founding Constitution of 1948 solidly laid down the principles of pluralism of political parties, free elections, the separation of powers, and the protection of fundamental rights. Since then, attempts to manipulate the legal process for political interests were frequent and constitutional makeovers recurrent. The exigencies of national security and economic development gave rise to strong state power, leading to authoritarian rule in the 1970s that compromised human rights and political freedoms. Still, the constitutional identity of the country was preserved and serious deviations from its ideals were met each time with vigorous popular resistance. The continued presence of the realms of legality and the rule of law allowed Korea to advance in its quest for liberal democracy.

Throughout the political transitions covered in the preceding pages, the role of the courts was limited to maintaining basic constitutional and legal frameworks. Judges envisioned that their duty was to give effect to the will of the people as expressed in the Constitution. During authoritarian rule, the judiciary's desire to avoid head-on collisions with the political branches was to a large degree prompted by the need to protect the institutional independence of the courts. Judicial restraint came at a price. Judges were criticized for taking shelter behind the Constitution when it was something other than a democratic document and for shielding questionable laws. They were accused of retreating excessively from exercising independent judgment when innocent victims were subjected to punishment. Evidence shows that the reluctance of the Supreme Court to take up the allegations of torture in police custody fostered prosecutorial and police impunity. By declining to descend to the political sphere, the highest court failed to intervene more actively to stop state abuses and to send a clear message about the illegitimacy of egregious government acts. Eventually, however, it was on the foundation of the constitutional order that authoritarian rule was overcome in the late 1980s. If the courts had willingly ignored the laws they deemed unjust, the principle of legality that was so essential for Korea's democratization process might have been jeopardized. Refusing to implement laws on the grounds that they were repressive would have been morally correct, but it would have caused a constitutional breakdown. After all, a judge who is satisfied with every judgment he or she has to reach may not be an ideal judge.[1]

This book has suggested that the court of the Yusin system be assessed within its own constitutional and legal order. A judge takes an oath to decide in accordance with the constitution and the law. In Korea, both the degeneration of politics into authoritarian rule and the restoration of democratic rule took place largely without reference to the courts. It was not judicial collusion that fostered illiberal rule; nor was it judicial fiat that saved democracy. Through all this, the courts continued in their basic function of interpreting the law faithfully and consistently. This consideration allows one to set charges of judicial complicity with the political regime to one side, and focus directly on the record of the courts.

There is a certain truth in the observation that Korean people tend to think of their history in terms of ruptures and changes rather than continuity. The exigencies of corrective justice during the last several decades have tended to depict judicial history, and indeed the overall political development following the birth of the modern Korean state, from polarizing perspectives, dismissing the pre-1987 period in Korea altogether as one marked by illegality and injustice. Just as one cannot brush aside the entire Yusin Constitution and laws as a sort of mass delusion, however, one cannot accept the notion that the whole judicial system somehow operated in bad faith. Discussion of the proper role of the courts is inevitably tinged by political preferences. At the very least, the Korean saga affirms that impatience with legal solutions entails as much risk as overconfidence in them. As one scholar aptly put it, clinging to "a blind faith in the courts to save us" from the popular transgression in the constitutional sphere would be futile, if not accompanied by reliance "on the people to see" to it that an unjust constitution

[1] "A judge who likes every outcome he reaches is very likely a bad judge." Speech by Neil M. Gorsuch, given on January 31, 2017, at his nomination to the US Supreme Court, reported in *The New York Times*, January 31, 2017.

must not be legitimated by popular referendum.[2] Holding the people accountable for a flawed constitution is much trickier than holding judges responsible, but that is precisely the challenge for democracy. In this sense, the conflict between legality and justice, the burden of judges in the 1970s, has not eased much. How the courts fare in the postdemocratization era is a question as relevant as how they fared under authoritarian rule.

This book, with its focus on law rather than politics, has made limited attempts to assess the political opinions of the judges. In his memoirs, Justice Yi Hoe-Ch'ang reminisced that "the judges were opposed, except a very few, to the military regime and its control of the judiciary."[3] His appraisal of President Park Chung Hee was mixed. The president held a "firm conviction and vision for the country's development and future" and "changed the country like no other president of Korea," but his attempt "to push forward the Yusin system in his later years caused him to lose the people's trust." Yi's observation did not seem to be far removed from the general sentiments of his fellow judges. In fairness to the judges, they were not alone in believing in the 1970s that the threat from communist North Korea was real and that the need for economic growth was urgent. They detested the emergency decrees like everyone else but doubted their illegality. They may have viewed the authoritarian rule as a phase and sought solace in telling themselves that their duty in the meantime was to uphold the constitutional order.

Individual readers may agree or disagree with Yi's opinion. Here it is important not to overlook the tentativeness that underlies his observation, or even its internal contradiction. He wrote that judges, rather than going against the Yusin Constitution, "resisted in a passive manner, making it more difficult to obtain warrants and reducing and suspending sentences and staying execution, whenever possible. Even doing these things was not easy because of political pressure. It may sound like an excuse, but it was the reality." Yet, Yi went on to say: "But now, looking back, I also believe that a constitution that limits fundamental rights, encroaches upon human dignity, destroys the basic democratic order, and prohibits judicial intervention violates the natural law order. I wonder whether judges should have declared the

[2] Jacobsohn, "An Unconstitutional Constitution?" 486.
[3] Yi Hoe-Ch'ang, *Hoegorok*, vol. 1, 215.

Yusin Constitution and the emergency decrees unconstitutional."[4] This elderly jurist's candid acknowledgment of his own ambivalence is a testimony to the agony of the entire generation of Korean judges who served under what they regarded as unjust laws.

One of the most egregious aspects of the Yusin rule – and arguably the gravest mistake of President Park – was that it condemned as illegal any peaceful talk of revising the Constitution. By forcibly putting down the grassroots campaigns calling for the amendment of the 1972 Constitution, and punishing citizens for wanting to discuss it, he ended up seriously eroding the popular will. The country and its population were overwhelmingly anti-North and anticommunist but, by painting political dissidents as pro-North and leftist-leaning, the government alienated a large sector among the citizens and diminished its political effectiveness. Park's apparent inability to accommodate or consider popular demands for constitutional revision seemed to show that he was aware of the democratic deficit of the Yusin system. This explains, in part, his tense responses to even a hint of criticism of his policies. Park was obsessed with the law in his chosen path of authoritarianism, as he tried to compensate for his regime's lack of legitimacy with legality. In this respect, it is to the immense credit of his opponents that they steadfastly advocated and called for a return to Korea's constitutional foundation through peaceful changes.

The judicial history presented in this book shows that there is reason for cautious optimism. It is unlikely that South Korea will again see the rise of dictatorial power or a degeneration into military-controlled government. One has witnessed a positive shift within the courts, as the once-stifling judicial hierarchy has loosened and the traditional excessive respect for authority has waned. Judges are less disposed to a quick retreat into legal formalism. These are welcome changes, befitting the remarkable achievements of democracy. Challenges continue, however. When judges graft their political beliefs onto the law, they invite the administration's overreach that threatens the independence of the courts; when the courts take on powers beyond judicial functions, public confidence in them diminishes and judicial independence suffers. Politicized justice is a perilous premise, especially in a society sharply split along

[4] Ibid., 244–246.

ideological lines. The trials and tribulations of the country during the last century, including colonial subjugation and struggles against communism, made the Korean people politically engaged but divided both under authoritarian rule and in democracy. Through a candid and well-rounded understanding of the past, one can aspire to mend the chasm in Korea's politics and society and to preserve its liberal democratic constitutional order.

Montesquieu's dictum that judges are "only the mouth that pronounces the words of the law, inanimate beings who can moderate neither its force nor its rigor" resonates as much today as ever.[5] Thus continue the travails of judges in Korea. History is never a destiny; it is merely a framework one can build upon.

[5] Montesquieu, *L'esprit des lois*, book 11, ch. 6 (Paris: Lavigne, 1845), 111.

Bibliography

Alexy, Robert. *The Argument from Injustice: A Reply to Legal Positivism*. Oxford: Clarendon Press, 2002.

An, Tong-Il. *10.26 ŭn ajikto sara itta: An Tong-Il pyŏnhosa ka tŭllyŏ chunŭn 10.26 sakŏn, kŭ chinsil kwa kŏjit* [The October 26th Is Still Alive: The October 26th Incident Told by Attorney An Tong-Il, Its Truth and Lies]. Seoul: Raendŏm Hausŭ Chungang, 2005.

Armstrong, Charles K. "America's Korea, Korea's Vietnam." *Critical Asian Studies* 33, no. 4 (2001): 527–539.

Barros, Robert. *Constitutionalism and Dictatorship: Pinochet, the Junta, and the 1980 Constitution*. Cambridge: Cambridge University Press, 2002.

"Courts Out of Context: Authoritarian Sources of Judicial Failure in Chile (1973–1990) and Argentina (1976–1983)." In *Rule by Law: The Politics of Courts in Authoritarian Regimes*, edited by Tom Ginsburg and Tamir Moustafa, 156–179. Cambridge: Cambridge University Press, 2008.

"Dictatorship and the Rule of Law: Rules and Military Power in Pinochet's Chile." In *Democracy and the Rule of Law*, edited by José María Maravall and Adam Przeworski, 188–219. Cambridge: Cambridge University Press, 2003.

Bedner, Adriaan. "An Elementary Approach to the Rule of Law." *The Hague Journal on the Rule of Law* 2, no. 1 (2010): 48–74.

Beer, Lawrence Ward, ed. *Constitutional Systems in Late Twentieth Century Asia*. Seattle: University of Washington Press, 1992.

Bender, Paul. "The Retroactive Effect of an Overruling Constitutional Decision: Mapp v. Ohio." *University of Pennsylvania Law Review* 110 (1962): 650–683.

Berlin, Isaiah. "Two Concepts of Liberty." In *Four Essays on Liberty*, 118–172. London: Oxford University Press, 1969.

Bix, Brian H. "Radbruch's Formula and Conceptual Analysis." *American Journal of Jurisprudence* 56 (2011): 45–57.

Bourgon, Jérôme. "The Principle of Legality and Legal Rules in the Chinese Legal Tradition." In *China, Democracy, and Law*, edited by Mireille Delmas-Marty and Pierre-Etienne Will, 169–188. Leiden: Brill, 2011.

Bourgon, Jérôme, and Pierre-Emmanuel Roux. "The Chosŏn Law Codes in an East Asian Perspective." In *The Spirit of Korean Law: Korean Legal History in Context*, edited by Marie Seong-Hak Kim, 19–54. Leiden: Brill Nijhoff, 2016.

Brand-Ballard, Jeffrey. *Limits of Legality: The Ethics of Lawless Judging*. Oxford: Oxford University Press, 2010.

Caldwell, Peter C. *Popular Sovereignty and the Crisis of German Constitutional Law*. Durham, NC: Duke University Press, 1997.

Carmen, Rolando V. del. "Constitutionalism and the Supreme Court in a Changing Philippine Polity." *Asian Survey* 13 (1973): 1050–1061.

"Constitutionality and Judicial Politics." In *Marcos and Martial Law in the Philippines*, edited by David A. Rosenberg, 85–112. Ithaca, NY: Cornell University Press, 1979.

Carothers, Thomas. "The Rule of Law Revival." *Foreign Affairs* 77, no. 2 (1998): 95–106.

Carter, Jimmy. *A Full Life: Reflections at 90*. New York: Simon & Schuster, 2015.

Cha, Victor D. "Bridging the Gap: The Strategic Context of the 1965 Korea–Japan Normalization Treaty." *Korean Studies* 20 (1996): 123–160.

Chang, Paul. *Protest Dialectics: State Repression and South Korea's Democracy Movement, 1970–1979*. Stanford: Stanford University Press, 2015.

Chang, Yŏng-Su. "Kyubŏm t'ongje ŭi ponjil e pich'uŏ pon Taebŏpwŏn kwa Hŏnpŏp Chaep'anso ŭi yŏkhal" [The Role of the Supreme Court and the Constitutional Court Seen in Terms of Normative Control]. *Koryŏ pŏphak* 55 (2009): 39–71.

Chen, Albert H. Y. "Emergency Powers, Constitutionalism and Legal Transplants: The East Asian Experience." In *Emergency Powers in Asia: Exploring the Limits of Legality*, edited by Victor V. Ramraj and Arun K. Thiruvengadam, 56–88. Cambridge: Cambridge University Press, 2010.

Chinsil-Hwahae Rŭl Wihan Kwagŏsa Chŏngni Wiwŏnhoe. *Truth and Reconciliation: Activities of the Past Three Years*, edited by An Pyŏng-Uk. Seoul: Chinsil-Hwahae Rŭl Wihan Kwagŏsa Chŏngni Wiwŏnhoe, 2009.

2006 nyŏn habangi chosa pogosŏ [Report of the 2nd half of Year 2006]. Seoul: Chinsil-Hwahae Rŭl Wihan Kwagŏsa Chŏngni Wiwŏnhoe, 2007.

Chisholm, Neil. "The Faces of Judicial Independence: Democratic versus Bureaucratic Accountability in Judicial Selection, Training, and Promotion in South Korea and Taiwan." *American Journal of Comparative Law* 62 (2014): 893–949.

Cho, Kuk. "Transitional Justice in Korea: Legally Coping with Past Wrongs after Democratization." *Pacific Rim Law & Policy Journal* 16, no. 3 (2007): 579–661.

Ch'oe, Chong-Ko. *Hanguk ŭi pŏmnyulga* [Jurists of Korea]. Seoul: Seoul Taehakkyo Ch'ulp'anbu, 2007.

Hanguk ŭi pŏphakcha [Legal Scholars of Korea]. Seoul: Seoul Taehakkyo Ch'ulp'anbu, 1989.

Sado pŏpkwan Kim Hong-Sŏp: Han pŏmnyulga ŭi sasang kwa sinang [Kim Hong-Sŏp, a Judge Apostle: A Jurist's Thought and Faith]. Seoul: Yukpŏpsa, 1985.

Choi, Dai-Kwon. "Law and Social Change: The Korean Experience." PhD diss., University of California, Berkeley, 1976.

Chŏng, Chong-Sŏp. "Hanguk pŏpwŏn chedo ŭi pyŏnch'ŏn kwa kwaje" [The Evolution of the Korean Court System and Its Tasks]. *Hŏnpŏphak yŏngu* 4 (1998): 188–219.

Chŏng, Yag-Yong. Admonitions on Governing the People: Manual for All Administrators. Translated by Byonghyon Choi. Berkeley: University of California Press, 2010.

Ch'ŏnjugyo Inkwŏn Wiwŏnhoe, ed. *Sabŏp Sarin: 1975 nyŏn sawŏl ŭi haksal* [Judicial Murder: The Massacre of April 1975]. Seoul: Ch'ŏnjugyo Inkwŏn Wiwŏnhoe, 2001.

Chōsen Kōtō Hōin Hanketsuroku [Chosŏn Kodŭng Pŏpwŏn Reports]. Seoul: Kōtō Hōin Shokika, 1908–1943.

Cohen, Jerome Alan, and Edward J. Baker. "U.S. Foreign Policy and Human Rights in South Korea." In *Human Rights in Korea: Historical and Policy Perspectives*, edited by William Shaw, 172–219. Cambridge, MA: The East Asian Legal Studies Program of the Harvard Law School and the Council on East Asian Studies, Harvard University, 1991.

Coniglio, Robert. "Methods of Judicial Decision-Making and the Rule of Law: The Case of Apartheid South Africa." *Boston University International Law Journal* 30 (2012): 497–527.

"Country Reports on Human Rights Practices, Year 1977." Washington, DC: 95th Congress, 2nd session, February 3, 1978.

Cover, Robert M. *Justice Accused: Antislavery and the Judicial Process*. New Haven, CT: Yale University Press, 1975.

Cumings, Bruce. *Korea's Place in the Sun: A Modern History*. New York: W. W. Norton & Company, 1997.

Dewind, Adrian W., and John Woodhouse. "Persecution of Defence Lawyers in South Korea: Report of a Mission to South Korea in May 1979." New York: International Commission of Jurists, 1979.

Dickson, Julie. "Is Bad Law Still Law? Is Bad Law Really Law?" (October 6, 2008). *Oxford Legal Studies Research Paper*, no. 39/2008. SSRN: http://ssrn.com/abstract=1279599.

Dietze, Gottfried. "Unconstitutional Constitutional Norms? Constitutional Development in Postwar Germany." *Virginia Law Review* 42, no. 1 (1956): 1–22.

Dominguez, Jorge I. "The Perfect Dictatorship? Comparing Authoritarian Rule in South Korea and in Argentina, Brazil, Chile, and Mexico." In *The Park Chung Hee Era: The Transformation of South Korea*, edited by Byung-Kook Kim and Ezra F. Vogel, 573–602. Cambridge, MA: Harvard University Press, 2011.

Dworkin, Ronald. "Hard Cases." *Harvard Law Review* 88 (1975): 1057–1109.

Taking Rights Seriously. Cambridge, MA: Harvard University Press, 1977.

Dyzenhaus, David. *Hard Cases in Wicked Legal* Systems. *South African Law in the Perspective of Legal Philosophy*. 2nd ed. Oxford: Oxford University Press, 2010.

ed. *Law as Politics: Carl Schmitt's Critique of Liberalism*. Durham, NC: Duke University Press, 1998.

Legality and Legitimacy: Carl Schmitt, Hans Kelsen and Hermann Heller in Weimar. Oxford: Clarendon Press, 1997.

"Schmitt v. Dicey: Are States of Emergency Inside or Outside the Legal Order?" *Cardozo Law Review* 27, no. 5 (2006): 2005–2040.

"'With Benefit of Hindsight': Dilemmas of Legality in the Fact of Injustice." In *Lethe's Law: Justice, Law and Ethics in Reconciliation*, edited by Emilios Christodoulidis and Scott Veitch, 65–89. Oxford: Hart Publishing, 2001.

Edlin, Douglas E. *Judges and Unjust Laws: Common Law Constitutionalism and the Foundations of Judicial Review*. Ann Arbor: University of Michigan Press, 2008.

Ely, James W. Jr. "Review of Justice Accused: Antislavery and the Judicial Process by Robert M. Cover." *Washington University Law Quarterly* 1975, no. 1 (1975): 265–274.

Feinberg, Joel. "Natural Law: The Dilemmas of Judges Who Must Interpret Immoral Laws." In *Problems at the Roots of Law: Essays in Legal and Political Theory*, 3–36. Oxford: Oxford University Press, 2003.

Ferejohn, John. "Judicializing Politics, Politicizing Law." *Law and Contemporary Problems* 65 (2002): 41–68.

Ferejohn, John, and Pasquale Pasquino. "Constitutional Adjudications: Lessons from Europe." *Texas Law Review* 82 (2004): 1671–1704.

Ford, Christopher. "The Indigenization of Constitutionalism in the Japanese Experience." *Case Western Reserve Journal of International Law* 28, no. 1 (1996): 3–62.

Förster, Christian. "Review of Law and Custom in Korea: Comparative Legal History by Marie Seong-Hak Kim." *Journal of Japanese Law* 20, no. 40 (2015): 299–302.

Fraenkel, Ernst. *The Dual State: A Contribution to the Theory of Dictatorship*. Translated by E. A. Shils, Edith Loewenstein, and Klaus Knorr. Oxford: Oxford University Press, 2017, 1941.

Ernst Fraenkel Gesammelte Schriften. Bd 3, Neuaufbau der Demokratie in Deutschland und Korea. Edited by Gerhard Göhler. Baden-Baden: Nomos, 1999.

Friedrich, Carl J. *Constitutional Reason of State: The Survival of the Constitutional Order*. Providence, RI: Brown University Press, 1957.

Fuller, Lon L. *The Morality of Law*. 2nd rev. ed. New Haven, CT: Yale University Press, 1969.

"Positivism and Fidelity to Law: A Reply to Professor Hart." *Harvard Law Review* 71, no. 4 (1958): 630–672.

Garlicki, Lech. "Constitutional Courts versus Supreme Courts." *International Journal of Constitutional Law* 5, no. 1 (2007): 44–68.

Gatmaytan, Dante B. "Can Constitutionalism Constrain Constitutional Change?" *Northwestern Interdisciplinary Law Review* 3, no. 1 (2010): 22–38.

Geddes, Barbara. "What Do We Know about Democratization after Twenty Years?" *Annual Review of Political Science* 2 (1999): 115–144.

Ginsburg, Tom. "The Constitutional Court and the Judicialization of Korean Politics." In *New Courts in Asia*, edited by Andrew Harding and Penelope Nicholson, 145–157. New York: Routledge, 2009.

Judicial Review in New Democracies: Constitutional Courts in Asian Cases. Cambridge: Cambridge University Press, 2003.

"Korea and the Reform of the Northeast Asian Legal Complex of Korean Law." In *The Spirit of Korean Law: Korean Legal History in Context*, edited by Marie Seong-Hak Kim, 233–260. Leiden: Brill Nijhoff, 2016.

Ginsburg, Tom, and Tamir Moustafa, eds. *Rule by Law: The Politics of Courts in Authoritarian Regimes*. Cambridge: Cambridge University Press, 2008.

Ginsburg, Tom, and Alberto Simpser, eds. *Constitutions in Authoritarian Regimes*. New York: Cambridge University Press, 2014.

Glendon, Mary Ann. "Partial Justice." *Commentary*, August 1, 1994. https://www.commentarymagazine.com/article/partial-justice/.

Graver, Hans Petter. *Judges against Justice: On Judges When the Rule of Law Is under Attack*. Heidelberg: Springer, 2015.

"Judicial Independence under Authoritarian Rule: An Institutional Approach to the Legal Tradition of the West." *The Hague Journal on the Rule of Law* 10, no. 2 (2018): 317–339.

"Why Adolf Hitler Spared the Judges: Judicial Opposition Against the Nazi State." *German Law Journal* 19, no. 4 (2018): 845–877.

Greitens, Sheena Chestnut. *Dictators and Their Secret Police: Coercive Institutions and State Violence*. Cambridge: Cambridge University Press, 2016.

Guichard, Justine. *Regime Transition and the Judicial Politics of Enmity: Democratic Inclusion and Exclusion in South Korean Constitutional Justice*. New York: Palgrave Macmillan, 2016.

Hahm, Chaihark. "Beyond 'Law vs. Politics' in Constitutional Adjudication: Lessons from South Korea." *International Journal of Constitutional Law* 10, no. 1 (2012): 6–34.

Hahm, Chaihark, and Sung Ho Kim. "Challenge and Change in East Asia: Constitutionalism on Trial in South Korea." *Journal of Democracy* 16 (2005): 28–42.

Making We the People: Democratic Constitutional Founding in Postwar Japan and South Korea. Cambridge: Cambridge University Press, 2015.

"'Stranger in a Strange Land': Carl Schmitt's Politics of Exception in South Korea." In *The European Mind: Narrative and Identity*, edited by Henry Frendo, 405–411. Msida: Malta University Press, 2010.

"To Make 'We the People': Constitutional Founding in Postwar Japan and South Korea." *International Journal of Constitutional Law* 8, no. 4 (2010): 800–848.

Haldemann, Frank. "Gustav Radbruch vs. Hans Kelsen: A Debate on Nazi Law." *Ratio Juris* 18 (2005): 162–178.

Haley, John O. "Constitutional Adjudication in Japan: Context, Structures, and Values." *Washington University Law Review* 88 (2011): 1467–1491.

"Review of Judicial Independence: The Political Economy of Judging in Japan by Ramseyer and Rasmusen." *Journal of Japanese Studies* 30 (2004): 235–240.

The Spirit of Japanese Law. Athens, GA: University of Georgia Press, 1998.

Halliday, Terence C. "The Fight for Basic Legal Freedoms: Mobilization by the Legal Complex." In *Global Perspectives on the Rule of Law*, edited by James J. Heckman, Robert L. Nelson, and Lee Cabatingan, 210–240. New York: Routledge, 2010.

Halliday, Terence C., Lucien Karpik, and Malcolm M. Feeley, eds. "Introduction – The Legal Complex in Struggles for Political Liberalism." In *Fighting for Political Freedom: Comparative Studies of the Legal Complex and Political Liberalism*, 1–40. Oxford: Hart Publishing, 2007.

Hamilton, Alexander, and John Jay. *The Federalist Papers*. Edited by Clinton Lawrence Rossiter. New York: New American Library of World Literature, 1961.

Han, Hong-Ku. Han Hong-Ku kyosu ka ssŭnŭn sabŏppu—hoehan kwa oyok ŭi yŏksa [Judicial History Written by Professor Han Hong-Ku: The History Filled with Regrets and Shame]. *Hangyŏrye Sinmun*. May 19, 2009–June 18, 2010. http://m.hani.co.kr/arti/SERIES/214/title1.html.

Han, In-Sŏp, ed. *Chŏngŭi ŭi pŏp, yangsim ŭi pŏp, inkwŏn ŭi pŏp* [Law as Justice, Law as Conscience, Law as Human Rights]. Seoul: Pagyŏngsa, 2004.

"Hoehan kwa oyok ŭi kwagŏ rŭl paro chabŭryŏmyŏn: Sabŏppu ŭi kwagŏ ch'ŏngsan ŭl wihayŏ" [To Correct the Past Filled with Regrets and Shame: For the Cleansing of the Judiciary's Past]. *Seoul Taehakkyo pŏphak* 46, no. 4 (2005): 84–120.

"Hŏnpŏp kwa hyŏngsapŏp: kwŏllŏk chŏngch'i, chiptan kaltŭng kwa pŏp ŭi chibae" [The Constitution and Criminal Law: Politics of Power, Group Conflicts and Rule by Law]. *Seoul Taehakkyo pŏphak* 39, no. 4 (1999): 128–168.

"Kukka pŏngnyŏk e taehan pŏpchŏk ch'aegim mit p'ihae hoebok: 5.18 minjuhwa undong ŭi pŏpchŏk haegyŏl ŭl chungsim ŭro" [Legal Liability and the Recovery of Damages for State Violence: Legal Solutions for the 5.18 Democracy Movement]. *Seoul Taehakkyo pŏphak* 43 (2002): 187–237.

"Ryu Kŭn-Il ŭi sunan (1)" [Yu Kŭn-Il's Ordeal (1)]. *Minju sahoe rŭl wihan pyŏllon* 85 (2009): 84–93.

Han, Sŭng-Hŏn. *Chaep'an ŭro pon Hanguk hyŏndaesa*. Seoul: Ch'angbi, 2016.

Han Sŭng-Hŏn Pyŏnhosa Pyŏllon Sakŏn Sillok Kanhaeng Wiwŏnhoe, ed. *Han Sŭng-Hŏn pyŏnhosa pyŏllon sakŏn sillok* [The Truthful Record of the Defense Cases of Attorney Han Sŭng-Hŏn]. 7 vols. Seoul: Pŏmusa, 2006.

Hanguk Pŏpche Yŏnguhoe, ed. *Mi kunjŏng pŏmnyŏng ch'ongnam: Yŏngmunp'an*. [The Complete Collection of the Laws and Regulations of the U.S. Military Government: English Edition]. Seoul: Hanguk Pŏpche Yŏnguhoe, 1971.

Hanley, Paul. "Transitional Justice in South Korea: One Country's Restless Search for Truth and Reconciliation." *University of Pennsylvania East Asia Law Review* 9 (2014): 138–166.

Hart, Herbert Lionel Adolphus. *The Concept of Law*. 2nd ed. London: Oxford Clarendon Press, 1994.

"Positivism and the Separation of Law and Morals." *Harvard Law Review* 71, no. 4 (1958): 593–629.

Hauriou, André. *Droit constitutionnel et institutions politiques*. Paris: Montchrestien, 1983.

Helmke, Gretchen, and Frances Rosenbluth. "Regimes and the Rule of Law: Judicial Independence in Comparative Perspective." *Annual Review of Political Science* 12 (2009): 345–366.

Herdegen, Matthias J. "Unjust Laws, Human Rights, and the German Constitution: Germany's Recent Confrontation with the Past." *Columbia Journal of Transnational Law* 32, no. 3 (1995): 591–606.

Hernandez, Carolina G. "Constitutional Authoritarianism and the Prospects of Democracy in the Philippines." *Journal of International Affairs* 2 (1985): 243–258.

Hilbink, Lisa. "Agents of Anti-Politics: Courts in Pinochet's Chile." In *Rule by Law: The Politics of Courts in Authoritarian Regimes*, edited by Tom Ginsburg and Tamir Moustafa, 102–131. Cambridge: Cambridge University Press, 2008.

Judges Beyond Politics in Democracy and Dictatorship: Lessons from Chile. Cambridge: Cambridge University Press, 2007.

Hŏ, Il-T'ae. "Inhyŏktang Chaegŏnwi sakŏn kwa sapŏp sarin" [The Inhyŏktang Restoration Committee Case and Judicial Murder]. *Tonga pŏphak* 40 (2007): 105–125.

"Pŏp waegok haengwi wa sabŏp sarin ŭi pangji rŭl wihan ippŏp chŏngch'aek" [Legislative policy for the Prevention of the Distortion of Law and Judicial Murder]. *Hyŏngsa chŏngch'aek yŏngu* 18 (2007): 5–48.

Holmes, Stephen. "Lineages of the Rule of Law." In *Democracy and the Rule of Law*, edited by José María Maravall and Adam Przeworski, 19–61. Cambridge: Cambridge University Press, 2006.

Hong, Sŏng-U. *Inkwŏn pyŏllon han sidae: Hong Sŏng-U pyŏnhosa ŭi chŭngŏn* [An Era of Human Rights Defense: Testimony of Attorney Hong Song-U]. Edited by Han In-Sŏp. Seoul: Kyŏngin Munhwasa, 2011.

Hong, Sŏng-U, and Han In-Sŏp, eds. *Inkwŏn pyŏllon charyo chip (1970 nyŏn dae)* [Collection of Sources for Defense of Human Rights (The 1970s)]. 6 vols. Seoul: Kyŏngin Munhwasa, 2012.

Hŏnpŏp Chaep'anso. *Hŏnpŏp Chaep'anso 20 nyŏnsa*. Seoul: Hŏnpŏp Chaep'anso, 2008.

Hwang, In-Ch'ŏl. "Kang Sin-Ok sakŏn ŭi kyŏnggwa" [The Unfolding of the Kang Sin-Ok Case]. In *Chŏngŭi ŭi pŏp, yangsim ŭi pŏp, inkwŏn ŭi pŏp*, edited by Han In-Sŏp, 259–272. Seoul: Pagyŏngsa, 2004.

Jacobsohn, Gary Jeffrey. *Constitutional Identity*. Cambridge, MA: Harvard University Press, 2010.

"Constitutional Identity." *The Review of Politics* 68, no. 3 (2006): 361–397.

"An Unconstitutional Constitution? A Comparative Perspective." *International Journal of Constitutional Law* 4, no. 3 (2006): 460–487.

Jayasuriya, Kanishka. "The Exception Becomes the Norm: Law and Regimes of Exception in East Asia." *Asian-Pacific Law & Policy Journal* 2, no. 1 (2001): 108–124.

Kalhan, Anil. "'Gray Zone' Constitutionalism and the Dilemma of Judicial Independence in Pakistan." *Vanderbilt Journal of Transnational Law* 46, no. 1 (2013): 1–96.

Kang, Chŏng-In. *Hanguk hyŏndae chŏngch'i sasang kwa Park Chung Hee* [Contemporary Korean Political Thought and Park Chung Hee]. Seoul: Ak'anet, 2014.

Kang, Pyŏng-Yong. "Kukka paesang chedo e kwanhan yŏngu: Kukka paesangpŏp che 2 cho rŭl chungsim ŭro" [A Study on the State Liability Compensation System: Focusing on Article 2 of the State Tort Claims Act]. Master's thesis, Yonsei University, 2002.

Kapiszewski, Diana, Gordon Silverstein, and Robert A. Kagan. *Consequential Courts: Judicial Roles in Global Perspective*. Cambridge: Cambridge University Press, 2013.

Karlan, Pamela S. "Judicial Independences." *Georgetown Law Journal* 95, no. 4 (2007): 1041–1059.

"Two Concepts of Judicial Independence." *Southern California Law Review* 72, no. 2–3 (1999): 535–558.

Kelsen, Hans. *Introduction to the Problems of Legal Theory*. Translated by B. L. Paulson and S. L. Paulson. Oxford: Clarendon Press, 1992.

"Law, State and Justice in the Pure Theory of Law." *Yale Law Journal* 57, no. 3 (1948): 377–390.

Pure Theory of Law, 2nd ed. Translated by Max Knight. Berkeley: University of California Press, 1967.

Kennedy, Ellen. *Constitutional Failure: Carl Schmitt in Weimar*. Durham, NC: Duke University Press, 2004.

Kim, Byung-Kook, and Ezra F. Vogel, eds. *The Park Chung Hee Era: The Transformation of South Korea*. Cambridge, MA: Harvard University Press, 2011.

Kim, Ch'ang-Rok. "Odaka Tomoo ŭi pŏp sasang" [Odaka Tomō's Legal Thought]. *Pŏpsahak yŏngu* 46 (2012): 433–458.

Kim, Ch'ŏl-Su. "Chayu kwŏn chŏk kibon kwŏn e kwanhan p'allye ŭi kyŏnghyang" [Jurisprudential Tendency regarding the Right to Liberty as a Fundamental Right]. *Seoul Taehakkyo pŏphak* 11, no. 2 (1970): 82–139.

"Ch'ŏnggu kwŏn chŏk kibon kwŏn e kwanhan p'allye ŭi kyŏnghyang" [Jurisprudential Tendency regarding the Right to Make a Claim as a Fundamental Right]. *Seoul Taehakkyo pŏphak* 12, no. 2 (1972): 93–128.

Hanguk hŏnpŏp sa [Korean Constitutional History]. Seoul: Seoul Taehakkyo Ch'ulp'anbu, 1988.

"Hanguk ippŏp e taehan t'ongje" [Control of Legislation in Korea]. *Seoul Taehakkyo pŏphak* 25, no. 4 (1984): 125–155.

"Hŏnpŏp kwa Taebŏpwŏn ŭi kwangye: pigyopŏp jŏk kŏmt'o" [The Relationship between the Constitution and the Supreme Court: A Comparative Examination]. *Hŏnpŏp Nonch'ong* 19 (2008): 57–85.

"Hŏnpŏp chejŏng kwa ku pŏmnyŏng ŭi hyoryŏk: pyŏnho kwŏn kwa pŏpchŏng moyok" [Constitutional Enactment and the Legal Force of Old Laws and Regulations: The Rights of the Counsel and the Contempt of Court]. *Seoul Taehakkyo pŏphak* 29, no. 1 (1988): 164–192.

Hŏnpŏphak kaeron [An Introduction to the Study of the Constitution]. Seoul: Pŏmmunsa, 1973.

"Kingŭp choch'i kwŏn" [Emergency Decree Power]. Kosigye (October 1973): 12–23.

"Kingŭp choch'i kwŏn" [Emergency Decree Power]. Kosigye (January 1979): 54–70.

"Minjujŏk kibon chilsŏ" [Basic Democratic Order]. *Seoul Taehakkyo pŏphak* 20, no. 1 (1979): 99–113.

"T'ongch'i kujo e kwanhan hŏnpŏp p'allye ŭi kyŏnghyang" [Jurisprudential Tendency regarding the Constitution as a Governing Structure]. *Seoul Taehakkyo pŏphak* 14, no. 1 (1973): 95–123.

Wihŏn pŏmnyul simsa chedo ron [A Theory of the Constitutional Review System]. Seoul: Hagyŏnsa, 1983.

Kim, Ch'ŏl-Su, and Sang Don Lee. "The Influence of US Constitutional Law Doctrines in Korea." In *Constitutional Systems in Late Twentieth Century Asia*, edited by Lawrence Ward Beer, 303–330. Seattle: University of Washington Press, 1992.

Kim, Hyung-A, and Clark W. Sorensen, eds. *Reassessing the Park Chung Hee Era, 1961–1979: Development, Political Thought, Democracy, and Cultural Influence*. Seattle: Center for Korean Studies, University of Washington Press, 2011.

Kim, Jongcheol. "Courts in the Republic of Korea: Featuring a Built-in Authoritarian Legacy of Centralization and Bureaucratization." In *Asian Courts in Context*, edited by Jiunn-rong Yeh and Wen-Chen Chang, 112–142. Cambridge: Cambridge University Press, 2015.

"Hŏnpŏp Chaep'anso kusŏng pangbŏp ŭi kaehyŏngnon" [A Proposal for Reform of the Composition of the Constitutional Court]. *Hŏnpŏphak yŏngu* 11, no. 2 (2005): 9–48.

"Some Problems with the Korean Constitutional Adjudication System." *Journal of Korean Law* 1, no. 2 (2001): 17–36.

"The Structure and Basic Principles of Constitutional Adjudication in the Republic of Korea." In *Litigation in Korea*, edited by Kuk Cho, 115–134. Cheltenham: Edward Elgar Publishing, 2010.

Kim, Kang-Un. "Hanguk e issŏsŏ wihŏn pŏmnyul simsa ŭi silch'e: p'allye rŭl chungsim ŭro" [The Substance of Judicial Review in Korea: Focusing on Precedent]. *Pŏphak yŏngu* (Wŏngwang Taehakkyo College of Law) 12 (1992): 363–384.

Kim, Marie Seong-Hak. "Colonial Jurisprudence and the Construction of Customary Law in Korea." *American Journal of Comparative Law* 57, no. 1 (2009): 205–247.

"Constitutional Jurisprudence and the Rule of Law in Korea: Revisiting the Courts in Yusin Korea (1972–1980)." *The Hague Journal on the Rule of Law* 5, no. 2 (2013): 178–203.

"In the Name of Custom, Culture, and the Constitution: Korean Customary Law in Flux." *Texas International Law Journal* 48, no. 3 (2013): 357–391.

Law and Custom in Korea: Comparative Legal History. Cambridge: Cambridge University Press, 2012.

ed. *The Spirit of Korean Law: Korean Legal History in Context*. Leiden: Brill Nijhoff, 2016.

"Travails of Judges: Courts and Constitutional Authoritarianism in South Korea." *American Journal of Comparative Law* 63, no. 3 (2015): 601–654.

Kim, Nyŏng. "Yusin sidae Myŏngdong Sŏngdang esŏ ŭi minjuhwa undong" [Democracy Movements at Myŏngdong Cathedral during the Yusin Period]. *Kat'olik sahoe kwahak yŏngu* 10 (1999): 57–80.

Kim, Sŏng-Su. "Kingŭp choch'i wihŏn simsakwŏn e taehan kwangyŏn: Taebŏpwŏn p'angyŏl (2010.12.16., sŏngo 2010To5986) e taehan p'yŏngka rŭl chungsim ŭro" [An Observation on the Power to Review the Emergency Decrees: Assessment of the Supreme Court Decision (December 16, 2010, 2010To5986)]. *Kongpŏphak yŏngu* 12 (2011): 315–336.

Kim, Sŏn-T'aek. "Wihŏn chŏk hŏnpŏp kaejŏng e taehan wihŏn simsaron: Yusin hŏnpŏp ŭi kyŏngu" [Study on the Constitutional Review of Unconstitutional Constitutional Amendments: The Case of the Yusin Constitution]. *Kongpŏphak yŏngu* 12 (2011): 165–200.

Kim, Sŭng-Il. "3–1 tongnip undong chŏnhu Ssun Wŏn ŭi Hanguk insik yŏngu [A Study on Sun Yat-sen's Opinion of Korea Before and After the March First Independence Movement]." *Hanguk tongnip undongsa yŏngu* 37 (2010): 101–128.

Kim, To-Kyun. "Hanguk pŏp ch'egye esŏ chayŏnpŏp ron ŭi hyŏngsŏng kwa palchŏn" [The Formation and Development of Natural Law Theory in the Korean Legal System]. *Pŏp ch'ŏrak yŏngu* 11 (2008): 183–226.

Kim, Un-Yong. "Hanguk Hŏnpŏp Wiwŏnhoe ŭi sabŏp chŏk sŏngkyŏk" [The Judicial Nature of the Constitutional Committee of Korea]. *Pŏmnyul haengjŏng nonjip* 19 (1978): 19–45.

Kim, Yong-Jick. "The Security, Political, and Human Rights Conundrum, 1974–1979." In *The Park Chung Hee Era: The Transformation of South Korea*, edited by Byung-Kook Kim and Ezra F. Vogel, 457–482. Cambridge, MA: Harvard University Press, 2011.

Kim, Young C. "Politics of Emergency Powers: The Case of Korea." In *Coping with Crises: How Governments Deal with Emergencies*, edited by Shao-Chuan Leng, 122–179. Miller Center Series on Asian Political Leadership, vol. 2. Lanham, MD: University Press of America, 1990.

Kitamura, Ichiro. "The Judiciary in Contemporary Society: Japan." *Case Western Reserve Journal of International Law* 25, no. 2 (1993): 263–291.

Kommers, Donald P. *Constitutional Jurisprudence of the Federal Republic of Germany*. 2nd ed. Durham, NC: Duke University Press, 1997.

Kukka Chŏngbowŏn. *Kwagŏ wa taehwa, mirae ŭi sŏngch'al* [Dialogue with the Past, Reflection on the Future], vol. 4 (Judiciary). Seoul: Kukka Chŏngbowŏn, 2007.

Kŭm, Hyo-Chŏn. "Hanguk hŏnpŏp II: Kwŏnwi chuŭi hŏnpŏp ŭi sŏngnip kwa punggoe" [The Korean Constitution II: The Making of the Authoritarian Constitution and Its Demise]. *Kongpŏp yŏngu* 17 (1989): 91–111.

"Kŭndaehwa int'eligench'ia ron kwa chisigin ŭi pyŏnjŏl nonjaeng" [The Modernization Theory of the Intelligentsia and Controversy over the Intellectuals' Defection]. Chugan Tong-A, October 19, 2015.

Kwon, Youngjoon. "Korea: Bridging the Gap between Korean Substance and Western Form." In *Law and Legal Institutions of Asia: Traditions, Adaptations and Innovations*, edited by E. Ann Black and Gary F. Bell, 151–184. Cambridge: Cambridge University Press, 2011.

Law, David S., and Mila Versteeg. "Constitutional Variation among Strains of Authoritarianism." In *Constitutions in Authoritarian Regimes*, edited by Tom Ginsburg and Alberto Simpser, 165–195. Cambridge: Cambridge University Press, 2014.

Lee, Namhee. *The Making of Minjung: Democracy and the Politics of Representation in South Korea*. Ithaca, NY: Cornell University Press, 2009.

Lee, Young Jae. "Law, Politics, and Impeachment: The Impeachment of Roh Moo-hyun from a Comparative Constitutional Perspective." *American Journal of Comparative Law* 53 (2005): 403–432.

Leng, Shao-Chuan, ed. *Coping with Crises: How Governments Deal with Emergencies*. The Miller Center Series on Asian Political Leadership, vol. 2. Lanham, MD: University Press of America, 1990.

Lindseth, Peter L. "The Paradox of Parliamentary Supremacy: Delegation, Democracy, and Dictatorship in Germany and France, 1920s–1950s." *Yale Law Journal* 113 (2004): 1341–1415.

Loughlin, Martin. "The Concept of Constituent Power." *European Journal of Political Theory* 13, no. 2 (2013): 218–237.

"The Rule of Law in European Jurisprudence." Strasbourg: European Commission for Democracy through Law (Venice Commission), May 29, 2009. CDL-DEM(2009)006.

Sword and Scales: An Examination of the Relationship between Law and Politics. Oxford: Hart Publishing, 2000.

Lummis, Charles Douglas. "Korea: The Trial of a Revolutionary Prophet." *New York Review of Books*, April 28, 1977.

MacCormack, Geoffrey. *The Spirit of Traditional Chinese Law*. Athens, GA: University of Georgia Press, 1996.

Major Speeches by President Park Chung Hee. Seoul: Samhwa Publishing, 1973.

Matsuo, Keiichi. "Odaka hō tetsugaku no keisei" [The Formation of Odaka's Legal Philosophy]. *Kōbe hōgaku zasshi* 15, no. 1 (1965): 1–47.

McAuliffe, Padraig. "Transitional Justice and the Rule of Law: The Perfect Couple or Awkward Bedfellows?" *The Hague Journal on the Rule of Law* 2, no. 2 (2010): 127–154.

McCormick, John P. "The Dilemmas of Dictatorship: Carl Schmitt and Constitutional Emergency Powers." *Canadian Journal of Law & Jurisprudence* 10 (1997): 163–176.

Meierhenrich, Jens. *The Legacies of Law: Long-Run Consequences of Legal Development in South Africa, 1650–2000*. Cambridge: Cambridge University Press, 2008.

The Remnants of the Rechtsstaat: An Ethnography of Nazi Law. Oxford: Oxford University Press, 2018.

Merryman, John Henry, and Rogelio Pérez Perdomo. *The Civil Law Tradition: An Introduction to the Legal Systems of Europe and Latin America*. 3rd ed. Stanford: Stanford University Press, 2007.

Min, Pok-Ki. Na ŭi pŏpkwan sijŏl [My Times as a Judge]. *Pŏmnyul Sinmun*, August 17, 1981–May 10, 1982.

Moustafa, Tamir. "Law and Courts in Authoritarian Regimes." *Annual Review of Law and Social Science* 10 (2014): 281–299.

The Struggle for Constitutional Power: Law, Politics, and Economic Development in Egypt. Cambridge: Cambridge University Press, 2009.

Müller, Ingo. *Hitler's Justice: The Courts of the Third Reich*. Translated by Deborah Lucas Schneider. Cambridge, MA: Harvard University Press, 1992.

Mun, Chun-Yŏng. *Pŏpwŏn kwa kŏmch'al ŭi t'ansaeng: sabŏp ŭi yŏksa ro ingnŭn Taehanminguk* [The Birth of the Courts and the Prosecutor's Office: The Republic of Korea as Seen in the History of the Judiciary]. Seoul: Yŏksa Pip'yŏngsa, 2010.

Mun, Hyŏng-Rae. "Pŏp e naejae toen chŏngch'i wa p'ongnyŏk e kwanhan yŏngu. Yusin ch'eje hyŏngsŏng kwa Inhyŏktang Chaegŏnwi sagŏn ŭl chungsim ŭro" [A Study on Control and Violence Embedded in Law: Focusing on the Establishment of the Yusin System and the Inhyŏktang Chaegŏnwi Case]. Master's thesis, Sŏnggonghoe University, 2009.

Myŏng, Sun-Ku. "Ajikto sara innŭn pŏp, 'Chosŏn Minsaryŏng': Chosŏn Minsaryŏn ŭi sogŭpchŏk p'yeji rŭl chean handa" [The Law that Is Still Alive, "Chosŏn Minsaryŏng": Calling for the Retroactive Abolition of Chosŏn Minsaryŏng]. *Chŏsŭtisŭ* 103 (2008): 220–236.

Nam, Pok-Hyŏn. "Hŏnpŏp Chaep'anso wa Taebŏpwŏn ŭi kwanhal munche" [Problems of Jurisdictional Division between the Constitutional Court and the Supreme Court]. *Hanguk kongpŏp hakhoe* 32, no. 1 (2003): 133–206.

North, Douglass C. *Institutions, Institutional Change and Economic Performance*. Cambridge: Cambridge University Press, 1990.

Structure and Change in Economic History. New York: Norton, 1981.

Understanding the Process of Economic Change. Princeton: Princeton University Press, 2010.

North, Douglass C., and Barry R. Weingast. "Constitutions and Commitment: The Evolution of Institutions Governing Public Choice in Seventeenth-Century England." *Journal of Economic History* 49, no. 4 (1989): 803–832.

O, Se-Hyŏk. "Hanguk esŏ ŭi pŏmnyŏng haesŏk" [Interpretation of Laws and Regulations in Korea]. *Pŏp chŏrak yŏngu* 6, no. 2 (2003): 119–150.

Oberdorfer, Don, and Robert Carlin. *The Two Koreas: A Contemporary History*. 3rd ed. New York: Basic Books, 2014.

O'Connell, Rory. "Guardians of the Constitution: Unconstitutional Constitutional Norms." *Journal of Civil Liberties* 4 (1999): 46–73.

Ŏm, Min-Yŏng. "Ŏllon ch'ulp'an ŭi chayu wa haengjŏng chŏk chaeryang" [Freedom of the Press and Administrative Discretion]. *P'allye yŏngu* 1, no. 3 (1959): 464–494.

Osiel, Mark J. "Dialogue with Dictators: Judicial Resistance in Argentina and Brazil." *Law and Social Inquiry* 20, no. 2 (1995): 481–560.

Pak, Ch'an-Chu. "Wihŏn kyŏlchŏng kwa sogŭp hyo" [Unconstitutionality Decision and Retroactivity]. *Seoul pŏphak* 19 (2011): 1–47.

Pak, Chi-Hyang et al. *Haebang chŏnhusa ŭi chae insik* [Reconsidering the History before and after Liberation]. 2 vols. Seoul: Ch'aeksesang, 2006.

Pak, Chi-U. "Hyŏngbŏl chohang e kwanhan wihŏn kyŏlchŏng ŭi sogŭp hyo e taehan pip'anjŏk koch'al" [A Critical Examination on the Retroactivity of Unconstitutionality Decisions]. *Segye hŏnpŏp yŏngu* 17 (2011): 405–432.

Pak, Hong-Kyu. "Inhyŏktang chaegŏn tanch'e sakŏn kwa pŏp" [The Inhyoktang Restoration Group Case and Law]. In *Sabŏp Sarin: 1975 nyŏn sawŏl ŭi haksal*, edited by Ch'ŏnjugyo Inkwŏn Wiwŏnhoe, 235–236. Seoul: Ch'ŏnjugyo Inkwŏn Wiwŏnhoe, 2001.

Pak, U-Tong. *P'ansa sil esŏ pŏpchŏng kkaji* [From Judicial Chamber to Courtroom]. 2nd ed. Seoul: Hanguk Sabŏp Haengjŏng Hakhoe, 2000.

Pŏp ŭi sesang [The World of the Law]. Seoul: Chisik Sanŏpsa, 2006.

"Taebŏpwŏn chŏnwŏn habŭi ch'e chaep'an e issŏsŏ ŭi ŭigyŏn ŭi p'yosi" [Expression of Opinion in the Supreme Court *En Banc* Decisions]. In *Sasilsim kwa pŏmnyulsim*, 680–707. Seoul: Hanguk Sapŏp Haengjŏng Hakhoe, 1994.

"Tangsaja wa p'igoin ŭi irŭm ŭl kamch'un p'angyŏl" [Court Opinions in Which the Names of the Parties and the Defendants Are Omitted]. *Pŏmnyul Sinmun*, January 21, 2010.

"Taepŏpwŏn p'angyŏl i ch'wiso toen sakŏn" [A Case That Voided the Judgment by the Supreme Court]. In *Pyŏnhosa sil anp'ak*, 403–415. Seoul: Hanguk Sabŏp Chŏngch'aek Hakhoe, 2010.

Pak, Ŭn-Chŏng. "Hanguk pŏp ch'ŏrak ŭi pansŏng kwa kwaje" [Reflections and the Tasks of Korean Legal Philosophy]. *Pŏp kwa sahoe* 10 (1994): 189–223.

Pang, Sun-Wŏn. *Na ŭi kil, na ŭi sŏnt'aek, pŏpcho panbaengnyŏn* [My Way, My Choice, a Half-Century in the Judiciary]. Seoul: Hanguk Sabŏp Haengjŏng Hakhoe, 1994.

Pangalangan, Raul C. "Political Emergencies in the Philippines: Changing Labels and the Unchanging Need for Legitimacy." In *Emergency Powers in Asia: Exploring the Limits of Legality*, edited by Victor V. Ramraj and Arun K. Thiruvengadam, 412–435. Cambridge: Cambridge University Press, 2010.

"Human Rights Discourse in Post-Marcos Philippines." In *Human Rights in Asia*, edited by Thomas W. D. Davis and Brian Galligan, 56–69. Cheltenham: Edward Elgar Publishing, 2011.

"Park: Survival Is at Stake." *Time*, June 30, 1975.

Park Chung Hee Taet'ongnyŏng yŏnsŏlmun chip [Collection of Speeches by President Park Chung Hee]. Seoul: Taet'ongnyŏng Pisŏsil, 1973.

Park, Yong Chul. "Does It Matter Who Wrote It?: The Admissibility of Suspect Interrogation Record Written by Prosecutors in Korea." *Journal of Korean Law* 6, no. 2 (2007): 180–190.

Parlett, William. "The Dangers of Constitution-Making." *Brooklyn Journal of International Law* 38 (2012): 193–238.

Pereira, Anthony W. *Political (in)Justice: Authoritarianism and the Rule of Law in Brazil, Chile, and Argentina.* Pittsburgh: University of Pittsburgh Press, 2005.

Pŏmnyul Sinmunsa. *Pŏpcho 50 nyŏn yasa* [Unofficial History of the 50 Years of the Judiciary]. 2 vols. Seoul: Pŏmnyul Sinmunsa, 2002.

Pŏpwŏn Haengjŏngch'ŏ, *Hanguk pŏpkwansa* [History of Judges in Korea]. Seoul: Yukpŏpsa, 1981.

Pŏpwŏnsa [History of the Courts]. 2 vols. Seoul: Pŏpwŏn Haengjŏngch'ŏ, 1995.

Sabŏp yŏngam [Judiciary Yearbook]. Seoul: Pŏpwŏn Haengjŏngch'ŏ, 1975–2005.

Sosong ch'okchin tŭng e kwanhan tŭngnyepŏp sihaeng kyŏlgwa ŭi punsŏk [Analysis of the Results of the Implementation of the Act on Special Cases to Expedite Litigation and Related Matters]. Seoul: Pŏpwŏn Haengjŏngch'ŏ, 1987.

T'onggye yŏnbo [Statistics Yearbook]. Seoul: Pŏpwŏn Haengjŏngch'ŏ, 1964–1974.

Presidential Truth Commission on Suspicious Deaths of the Republic of Korea. *A Hard Journey to Justice: First Term Report by the Presidential Truth Commission on Suspicious Deaths of the Republic of Korea.* Seoul: Samin Books, 2004.

Pyŏn, Chŏng-Su. *Pŏpcho yŏjŏng* [Reminiscences of a Traveler in the Judiciary]. Seoul: Kwanak Sa, 1997.

Radbruch, Gustav. "Gesetzliches Unrecht und übergesetzliches Recht." *Süddeutsche Juristen-Zeitung* 1 (1946): 105–108.

"Legal Philosophy." In *The Legal Philosophy of Lask, Radbruch, and Dabin*, edited by Kurt Wilk, vol. 4. Cambridge, MA: Harvard University Press, 1950.

Radbruch, Gustav, and Erik Wolf. *Rechtsphilosophie.* Stuttgart: K. F. Koehler, 1950.

Rajah, Jothie. *Authoritarian Rule of Law: Legislation, Discourse, and Legitimacy in Singapore.* Cambridge: Cambridge University Press, 2012.

Ramraj, Victor V., and Arun K. Thiruvengadam, eds. *Emergency Powers in Asia: Exploring the Limits of Legality.* Cambridge: Cambridge University Press, 2010.

Ramseyer, J. Mark, and Eric B. Rasmusen. *Measuring Judicial Independence: The Political Economy of Judging in Japan*. Chicago: University of Chicago Press, 2003.

Raz, Joseph. "The Rule of Law and Its Virtue." In *The Authority of Law: Essays on Law and Morality*, 2nd ed., 210–229. Oxford: Oxford University Press, 2009.

Reimann, Mathias. "National Socialist Jurisprudence and Academic Continuity: A Comment on Professor Kaufmann's Article." *Cardozo Law Review* 9 (1988): 1657–1658.

Rommen, Heinrich. "Natural Law in Decisions of the Federal Supreme Court and of the Constitutional Courts in Germany." *Natural Law Forum* 4 (1959): 1–25.

Rossitor, Clinton. *Constitutional Dictatorship: Crisis Government in the Modern Democracies*. Princeton: Princeton University Press, 1948.

Roznai, Yaniv. *Unconstitutional Constitutional Amendments: The Limits of Amendment Powers*. Oxford: Oxford University Press, 2017.

"Unconstitutional Constitutional Amendments: The Migration and Success of a Constitutional Idea." *American Journal of Comparative Law* 61 (2013): 657–719.

Russell, Peter H., and David O'Brien, eds. *Judicial Independence in the Age of Democracy: Critical Perspectives from around the World*. Charlottesville, VA: University Press of Virginia, 2001.

Ryu, Youngju. *Writers of the Winter Republic: Literature and Resistance in Park Chung Hee's Korea*. Honolulu: University of Hawaii Press, 2015.

Sabŏpsa P'yŏnch'an Wiwŏnhoe. *Yŏksa sogŭi sabŏppu* [The Judiciary in History]. Seoul: Sabŏp Palchŏn Chaedan, 2009.

Sartori, Giovanni. "Constitutionalism: A Preliminary Discussion." *American Political Science Review* 56, no. 4 (1962): 853–864.

Schauer, Frederick. "Amending the Presuppositions of a Constitution." In *Responding to Imperfection: The Theory and Practice of Constitutional Amendment*, edited by Sanford Levinson, 145–162. Princeton: Princeton University Press, 1995.

Scheppele, Kim Lane. "Aspirational and Aversive Constitutionalism: The Case for Studying Cross-Constitutional Influence through Negative Models." *International Journal of Constitutional Law* 1, no. 2 (2003): 296–324.

"Law in a Time of Emergency: States of Exception and the Temptations of 9/11." *University of Pennsylvania Journal of Constitutional Law* 6, no. 5 (2004): 1001–1084.

Scheuerman, William E. *Carl Schmitt: The End of Law*. Lanham, MD: Rowman & Littlefield, 1999.

Schmitt, Carl. *Constitutional Theory*. Translated by Jeffrey Seitzer. Durham, NC: Duke University Press, 2008.

Legality and Legitimacy. Translated by Jeffrey Seitzer. Durham, NC: Duke University Press, 2004.

Political Theology: Four Chapters on the Concept of Sovereignty. Translated by George Schwab. Cambridge, MA: MIT Press, 1985.

Shaw, William R. "Introduction." In *Human Rights in Korea: Historical and Policy Perspectives*, edited by William R. Shaw, 1–22. Cambridge, MA: The East Asian Legal Studies Program of the Harvard Law School and The Council on East Asian Studies, Harvard University, 1991.

Legal Norms in a Confucian State. Berkeley: Institute of East Asian Studies, University of California Berkeley, Center for Korean Studies, 1981.

"Traditional Korean Law and Its Relation to China." In *Essays on China's Legal Tradition*, edited by Jerome A. Cohen, R. Randle Edwards, and Fu-mei Chang Chen, 302–326. Princeton: Princeton University Press, 1980.

Shin, Gi-Wook, and Kyung Moon Hwang. *Contentious Kwangju: The May 18 Uprising in Korea's Past and Present*. Lanham, MD: Rowman & Littlefield, 2003.

Silverstein, Gordon. "Singapore: The Exception That Proves Rules Matter." In *Rule by Law: The Politics of Courts in Authoritarian Regimes*, edited by Tom Ginsburg and Tamir Moustafa, 73–101. Cambridge: Cambridge University Press, 2008.

Sim, Hŏn-Sŏp. "Sŏk-U Hwang San-Tŏk paksa e issŏsŏ ŭi chayŏnpŏp ron kwa pŏp silchŭng juŭi" [Natural Law Theory and Positivist Legal Ideology of Dr. Hwang San-Tŏk]. *Seoul Taehakkyo pŏphak* 35 (1994): 72–80.

Sin, Tong-Un. "Hanguk kŏmch'al chedo ŭi hyŏnhwang kwa kaesŏn ch'aek" [The Current State and the Reform Measures of the Prosecution System in Korea]. *Seoul Taehakkyo pŏphak* 29, no. 2 (1988): 39–58.

P'allye paeksŏn hyŏngpŏp kakron 1 [One Hundred Selected Judicial Decisions in Criminal Law Provisions I]. Seoul: Kyŏngsewŏn, 1999.

Sŏ, Chung-Sŏk. "Ch'ŏnjugyo Chŏngŭi Kuhyŏn Chŏnguk Sajedan ŭi ch'ulbŏm paegyŏng kwa hwaltong" [The Background of the Rise and the Activities of the Catholic Priests Association for Justice]. *Sarim* (Sŏngdae sarim) 27 (2007): 223–248.

Sŏ, Hi-Sŏk. "Hanguk minpŏp e taehan Ilbon minpŏp ŭi yŏnghyang kwa hyanghu ŭi kwangye: pigyo pŏp ŭi yŏngu taesang ŭro sŏŭi Ilbon minpŏp ŭl wihayŏ" [The Influence of Japanese Civil Law on Korean Civil Law and the Future of Their Relationship: Japanese Civil Law as a Subject of Comparative Law]. *Minsa pŏphak* 52 (2010): 101–156.

Sohn, Hak-Kyu. *Authoritarianism and Opposition in South Korea*. London: Routledge, 1989.

Song, Kŏn-Ho et al. *Haebang chŏnhusa ŭi insik* [Understanding the History before and after Liberation]. 6 vols. Seoul: Hangilsa, 1979–1989.

Song, Sang-Hyŏn. "Taebŏpwŏn ŭi kinŭng kwa sosong ch'okchin dŭng e kwanhan t'ŭngnyepŏp sang ŭi munjechŏm" [Functions of the Supreme Court and Problems regarding the Act on Special Cases to Expedite Litigation and Related Matters]. *Sabŏp haengjŏng* 23, no. 2 (1982): 14–19, 65.

Stolleis, Michael. *The Law under the Swastika: Studies on Legal History in Nazi Germany*. Translated by Thomas Dunlap. Chicago: University of Chicago Press, 1998.

Taegŏmch'alch'ŏng. *Kŏmch'al yŏngam* [Prosecution Yearbook]. Seoul: Taegŏmch'alch'ŏng, 1986.

Tamanaha, Brian Z. "Good Casuistry and Bad Casuistry: Resolving the Dilemmas Faced by Catholic Judges." *University of St. Thomas Law Journal* 4, no. 2 (2006): 269–279.

On the Rule of Law: History, Politics, Theory. Cambridge: Cambridge University Press, 2004.

Tate, C. Neal, and Stacia L. Haynie. "Authoritarianism and the Functions of Courts: A Time Series Analysis of the Philippine Supreme Court, 1961–1987." *Law & Society Review* 27 (1993): 707–740.

Teitel, Ruti G. "Transitional Jurisprudence: The Role of Law in Political Transformation." *Yale Law Journal* 106, no. 7 (1997): 2009–2082.

Transitional Justice. Oxford: Oxford University Press, 2000.

Truth and Reconciliation Activities of the Past Three Years. Seoul: Truth and Reconciliation Commission, 2009.

Weber, Max. "Parliament and Government in a Reconstructed Germany (1917)." In *Max Weber: Economy and Society*, edited by Guenther Roth and Claus Wittich, vol. 2: 1451–1459. Berkeley: University of California Press, 1978.

West, James M., and Edward J. Baker. "The 1987 Constitutional Reforms in South Korea: Electoral Processes and Judicial Independence." In *Human Rights in Korea: Historical and Policy Perspectives*, edited by William Shaw, 222–252. Cambridge, MA: The East Asian Legal Studies Program of the Harvard Law School and the Council on East Asian Studies, Harvard University, 1991.

Wright, R. George. "Could a Constitutional Amendment Be Unconstitutional?" *Loyola University Chicago Law Journal* 22, no. 4 (1991): 741–764.

Yang, Kŏn. "Hanguk hŏnpŏp III: Che 4 konghwaguk mit che 5 konghwaguk hŏnpŏpsa ŭi kaekwan (1972–1988)" [The Constitutional Law of Korea III: A Survey of the Constitutional History of the Fourth and the Fifth Republics]. *Kongpŏp yŏngu* 17 (1989): 113–141.

Yang, Pyŏng-Ho. *Pŏpcho pan paengnyŏn e irŭn na ŭi sosin* [My Beliefs during a Half-Century in the Judicary]. Seoul: Kyŏngch'on Aein, 1995.

Yang, Sam-Sŭng. "Pŏpcho kaejoron: Pŏpcho samryun ŭi paramjikhan mosŭp kwa irŭl wihan pangan" [A Theory of Judicial Reform: The Ideal Image of the Three Wheels of the Judiciary and Measures for Its Achievement]. *Chŏsŭt'isŭ* 118 (2010): 5–56.

Yi, Ch'ang-Sŏk. "Ku pŏmnyŏng ŭi wihŏn simsakwŏn" [The Power to Review the Constitutionality of Old Laws and Regulations]. *Pŏpche wŏlbo* 2, no. 11 (November 1959): n.p.

Yi, Hoe-Ch'ang. "Sapŏp ŭi chŏkkŭk chuŭi: t'ŭkhi kibonkwŏn pojang kinŭng kwa kwallŏn hayŏ" [Judicial Activism: Focusing on Its Function of Protecting Fundamental Rights]. *Seoul Taehakkyo pŏphak* 28, no. 2 (1987): 147–161.

Yi Hoe-Ch'ang Hoegorok [Yi Hoe-Ch'ang Memoirs]. 2 vols. Seoul: Kimyŏngsa, 2017.

Yi, Hŏn-Hwan. "Chŏngch'i kwajŏng e issŏsŏ ŭi sabŏpkwŏn e taehan yŏngu: Hanguk hŏnjŏngsa rŭl chungsim ŭro" [A Study on Judicial Power in the Political Process: Focusing on Korean Constitutional History]. PhD diss., Seoul National University, 1996.

Yi, Kwang-Wŏn. "Wisuryŏng ŭi haesŏk kwa ippŏp panghyang" [Interpretation of Garrison Decrees and Legislative Directions]. *Pŏphak nonch'ong* 24, no. 1 (2011): 231–260.

Yi, Kyŏng-Ho. "Kunjŏng pŏmnyŏng ŭi wihŏn simsakwŏn ŭn pŏpwŏn e ittanŭn p'allye" [The Decision that the Power to Review the Military Government Laws and Regulations Resides with the Courts]. *Seoul Taehakkyo pŏphak* 1, no. 2 (1959): 441–455.

Yi, Sang-Ch'ŏl. "Kukka Paesangpŏp che 2 cho 1 hang tansŏ ŭi wihŏnsŏng" [The Unconstitutionality of Section 2 Proviso of the State Tort Claims Act]. *Anam pŏphak* 1 (1993): 259–280.

Yi, Si-Yun. *Sin minsa sosong pŏp* [New Civil Procedure]. Seoul: Pagyŏnsa, 2003.

Yi, Sŭng-Il. *Ch'ongdokpu pŏpche chŏngch'aek: Ilche ŭi singmin t'ongch'i wa Chosŏn Minsaryŏng* [A Study on the Legal Policy of the Chosŏn Government General: Colonial Rule by Imperial Japan and Chosŏn Minsaryŏng]. Seoul: Yŏksa Pip'yŏngsa, 2008.

Yi, Tŏk-In. "Sahyŏng p'yeji ŭi chŏngdangsŏng: Sabŏp sarin kwa op'an e ŭihan sahyŏng" [Justification for the Abolition of the Death Penalty: Judicial Murder and the Death Penalty Resulting from Wrongful Conviction]. *Chung-Ang pŏphak* 12 (2010): 111–140.

Yi, Yŏng-Rok. "Che 1 konghwaguk Hŏnpŏp Wiwŏnhoe chedo ŭi hyŏngsŏng" [The Formation of the Constitutional Committee System during the First Republic]. *Hŏnpŏphak yŏngu* 11, no. 2 (2005): 307–336.

Yoon, Dae-Kyu. "Constitutional Amendment in Korea." *Korean Journal of Comparative Law* 16 (1998): 1–13.

"Judicial Review in the Korean Political Context." *Korean Journal of Comparative Law* 17 (1989): 133–178.

Law and Political Authority in South Korea. Boulder and Seoul: Westview and Kyungnam University Press, 1990.

Youm, Kyu Ho. "Judicial Interpretation of Press Freedom in South Korea." *Boston College Third World Law Journal* 7 (1987): 133–159.

Yu, Chin-O. *Hŏnpŏp haeŭi* [Interpretive Exposition of the Constitution]. Seoul: Myŏngsedang, 1949.

Hŏnpŏp kich'o hoegorok [Reminiscences on the Making of Constitutional Law]. Seoul: Ilchogak, 1980.

Yu, Pyŏng-Chin. *Chaep'angwan ŭi komin: Yu Pyŏng-Chin pŏmnyul nonjip* [The Dilemmas of a Judge: A Collection of the Legal Writings of Yu Pyŏng-Chin]. Edited by Sin Tong-Un. Seoul: Pŏmmunsa, 2008.

Yun, Chin-Su. "Wihŏn in taet'ŏngnyŏng ŭi kingŭp choch'i palryŏng i pulpŏp hangwi rŭl kusŏng hanŭnji yŏbu: Taebŏpwŏn 2015. 3. 26. Sŏngo 2012Ta48824 p'angyŏl" [Whether the Issuance of the Presidential Emergency Decree Which Has Been Found Unconstitutional Creates Tort Liability: The Supreme Court 2012Ta48824, March 26, 2015]. *Minsa pŏphak* 81 (2017): 93–154.

Index

Lightning Source UK Ltd.
Milton Keynes UK
UKHW020655070321
379822UK00019B/660